KU-227-104

CUTTING-EDGE TECHNOLOGIES IN HIGHER
EDUCATION VOLUME 6G

INCREASING STUDENT ENGAGEMENT AND RETENTION IN E-LEARNING ENVIRONMENTS: WEB 2.0 AND BLENDED LEARNING TECHNOLOGIES

EDITED BY

CHARLES WANKEL
St. John's University, New York, USA

PATRICK BLESSINGER
St. John's University, New York, USA

IN COLLABORATION WITH

JURATE STANAITYTE
NEIL WASHINGTON

Created in partnership with the Higher Education
Teaching and Learning Association

http://hetl.org/

United Kingdom – North America – Japan
India – Malaysia – China

Emerald Group Publishing Limited
Howard House, Wagon Lane, Bingley BD16 1WA, UK

First edition 2013

Copyright © 2013 Emerald Group Publishing Limited

Reprints and permission service
Contact: permissions@emeraldinsight.com

No part of this book may be reproduced, stored in a retrieval system, transmitted in any
form or by any means electronic, mechanical, photocopying, recording or otherwise
without either the prior written permission of the publisher or a licence permitting
restricted copying issued in the UK by The Copyright Licensing Agency and in the USA
by The Copyright Clearance Center. Any opinions expressed in the chapters are those
of the authors. Whilst Emerald makes every effort to ensure the quality and accuracy of
its content, Emerald makes no representation implied or otherwise, as to the chapters'
suitability and application and disclaims any warranties, express or implied, to their use.

British Library Cataloguing in Publication Data
A catalogue record for this book is available from the British Library

ISBN: 978-1-78190-515-9
ISSN: 2044-9968 (Series)

ISOQAR certified
Management System,
awarded to Emerald
for adherence to
Environmental
standard
ISO 14001:2004.

Certificate Number 1985
ISO 14001

INVESTOR IN PEOPLE

284969

INCREASING STUDENT ENGAGEMENT AND RETENTION IN E-LEARNING ENVIRONMENTS: WEB 2.0 AND BLENDED LEARNING TECHNOLOGIES

CUTTING-EDGE TECHNOLOGIES IN HIGHER EDUCATION

Series Editor: Charles Wankel

Recent Volumes:

CONTENTS

v

UCB

284969

LIST OF CONTRIBUTORS

Catherine Althaus	University of Victoria, Canada
Marcia L. Ashbaugh	MLA Instructional Designers, USA
Tara S. Behrend	George Washington University, USA
Patrick Blessinger	St. John's University, Queens, NY, USA
Katerina Bohle Carbonell	Maastricht University, Netherlands
Amber Dailey-Hebert	Park University, USA
Andrew Doig	Southampton Solent University, UK
Martina A. Doolan	University of Hertfordshire, UK
Anthony Foley	Waterford Institute of Technology, Ireland
Maike Gerken	Maastricht University, Netherlands
Therese Grohnert	Maastricht University, Netherlands
Cathy Gunn	University of Auckland, New Zealand
Denis Harrington	Waterford Institute of Technology, Ireland
Steve Hogg	Southampton Solent University, UK
Mary T. Holden	Waterford Institute of Technology, Ireland
Peter Hubber	Deakin University, Australia
Jennifer Hussey	Waterford Institute of Technology, Ireland
Michael N. Karim	George Washington University, USA
Esther Loong	Deakin University, Australia
Patrick Lynch	Waterford Institute of Technology, Ireland
Kamna Malik	GlobalNxt University, Malaysia
Julia L. Parra	New Mexico State University, USA

Lynne Siemens	University of Victoria, Canada
Charlotte Stange	University of Victoria, Canada
David Starr-Glass	SUNY, Empire State College, USA
Charles Wankel	St. John's University, Queens, NY, USA

PART I
ADOPTION OF WEB 2.0 AND
BLENDED LEARNING
TECHNOLOGIES

NOVEL APPROACHES IN HIGHER EDUCATION: AN INTRODUCTION TO WEB 2.0 AND BLENDED LEARNING TECHNOLOGIES

Patrick Blessinger and Charles Wankel

INTRODUCTION

The chapters in this book focus on using an array of different Web 2.0 technologies and web-enabled learning platforms to create technology-rich learning environments. These types of social learning technologies can be used to build flexible and agile learning environments and foster collaborative learning activities for students. Whereas Web 1.0 is considered a content-centric paradigm, Web 2.0 is considered a social-centric paradigm. In other words, at the heart of Web 2.0 is social networking, social media, and a vast array of participatory applications and tools. This book examines the possibilities of Web 2.0 technologies in general and social technologies in particular, including blended (hybrid) learning technologies and applications. At least four factors have driven the rapid changes we have experienced in the way we teach and learn with these technologies: (1) these technologies are digital, making them highly versatile and integrative, (2) these technologies are globally ubiquitous, making them accessible to anyone and

Increasing Student Engagement and Retention in e-Learning Environments:
Web 2.0 and Blended Learning Technologies
Cutting-edge Technologies in Higher Education, Volume 6G, 3–16
Copyright © 2013 by Emerald Group Publishing Limited
All rights of reproduction in any form reserved
ISSN: 2044-9968/doi:10.1108/S2044-9968(2013)000006G003

anywhere there is an Internet connection, (3) these technologies are generally low cost or free, making them accessible to anyone with a computer or mobile device, and (4) the development of more sophisticated learning theories, greatly increasing our understanding of how to best apply these technologies in an academic setting.

Web 2.0 technologies can also be viewed as mediating technologies. Park (2011) noted that both personal and social activities are mediated by these types of communicative technologies which is supported by several learning theories including cultural-historical theory (Vygotsky, 1978), activity theory (Leontiev & Luria, 1968), and situated learning theory (Lave & Wenger, 1991). Web 2.0 technologies are especially useful because they overlap and integrate with many other technologies such as mobile technologies and blended learning technologies to create a more seamless and transparent experience for instructors and students. These technologies are also supported by several learning theories because they support the building of human relationships and global communities, not just the simple exchange of information. This implies that they also aid in both affective and social learning, not just cognitive learning, thus addressing all learning domains of students. These technologies can be used at any grade level and in any discipline. Regardless of the setting, the idea is to create better learning by making it more meaningful, more purposeful, and more authentic. To that end, these social technologies have the potential to create new possibilities for instructors to create more interesting and dynamic learning environments.

The dramatic effects of these global technologies are also transforming our notions of what it means to teach and learn in a postindustrialized, interconnected globalized world. Web 2.0-based technologies have become more established as teaching and learning tools at all levels across all disciplines as a means to more deeply engage students and foster more participatory learning activities. Many colleges and universities see the potential benefits of adopting Web 2.0-based technologies in the context of appropriate pedagogical practices and learning theories (Scardamalia, 2001). Thus, it is important to use these technologies in a purposeful manner based on sound design principles and relevant learning theories.

Web 2.0-based technologies have the potential to both enhance and transform the learning environment and make learning more interesting, more meaningful, and more authentic. All else being equal, implementing these tools can increase student motivation and academic achievement. Students today are often referred to as digital natives or the net generation and this matters to the extent that the technology they use is an inescapable and normal part of their lives (Tapscott, 2009). It is important to understand how most students live their lives, their level of technological sophistication, and what specific technologies they use and are comfortable using. For instance, the widespread use of mobile devices, smart phones, and tablets by students provides an opportunity for instructors to tailor learning activities that make use of these devices via social software applications (e.g., blogs, social networking, wikis, texting, Twitter, collaborative authoring). In this way, social learning applications can be used to trigger the mechanisms of learning in ways that are more natural and authentic to learners. As such, these tools can be viewed as one among a set of tools that are available to instructors to increase student participation.

However, the use of web-based applications alone or increased participation alone cannot guarantee more effective learning. These technologies must be used in a purposeful manner and within a framework of sound design principles and relevant theories. These technologies must also be in alignment with the content and pedagogical knowledge of the instructor as well as the course objectives. Web 2.0 applications focus on learner-centered activities where students are encouraged to participate in dialogue that is personally meaningful by providing them a medium to share their knowledge, experiences, and views. When aligned properly with appropriate learning outcomes, these technologies have the potential to cultivate deeper holistic learning. However, there is no one right way to use these technologies for all courses. Each instructor and course designer must determine how to use these technologies appropriate to the specifics of the course.

Web 2.0 and blended technologies are being used within a large set of teaching and learning tools, strategies, and theories to (1) increase student participation and collaboration through more authentic ways to use everyday technology for learning activities, (2) create a meaningful learning environment by creating students as self-directed, self-regulated active agents in their own knowledge construction, and (3) foster a sense of belonging and global connectedness by using technologies that enable global interconnectedness and collaborative knowledge creation (Woo & Reeves, 2007). The power of using these tools is in their ability to break down barriers (physical, geographical, political, economic, social, technological) and create more agile, inclusive, and democratic learning environments. Using Web 2.0 technologies expands our teaching capabilities and creates more flexible and dynamic learning situations.

However, as with any technology, novelty or technical sophistication alone cannot guarantee engagement of learners. These technologies should be used in a purposeful and integrated way and within an appropriate theoretical framework germane to the teaching and learning context (e.g., institutional mission, educational level, type of course, course objectives, learning outcomes). Thus, technical knowledge, pedagogical knowledge, and content knowledge must come together in a coherent and integrated way. Using valid, reliable pedagogical methods and learning theories and design principles is an important element in proper course design. It is also vital to be mindful of the appropriate epistemological, ontological, and phenomenological bases that are germane to applying these technologies.

ADOPTION PRINCIPLES

Two key principles emerge from the findings of the chapters in the adoption section of the book that help to frame the content of this specific set of technologies:

(1) Web 2.0-based social technologies can be viewed as global learning communities and participatory systems that help to interconnect learners with learning activities and subject matter content within a milieu of diverse cultural-historical dimensions and multiple perspectives, thereby fostering critical and collaborative thinking.
(2) Building globally social learning communities that extend beyond the boundaries of the physical classroom can help create a greater sense of belonging and group cohesiveness which enhances learning in the affective and social domains.

The growing use of these social technologies suggests the growing emphasis and importance on active learning, meaningful learning, situated learning, and integrative learning. The use of these social technologies also indicates that creating a sense of social presence and emotional involvement has the potential, if applied properly, to increase student happiness and academic motivation because it provides students with an authentic and concrete vehicle for social interaction and community building. As such, authentic learning comprises creating learning activities that are meaningful to how students live their lives. Contextual learning comprises the multifaceted nexus of situated interactions. Integrative learning consists of the ability to connect diverse and multidimensional concepts and meanings across different courses and varied life experiences. Developing these skills and abilities is of great importance in a postindustrial, globalized world. Conversely, it also follows that using these social technologies as a mediating system to reduce a student's sense of isolation has the potential to decrease student attrition. For instance, teleconferencing, texting, blogging, and synchronous and asynchronous learning platforms all can be used to increase social interaction.

The great usefulness of these technologies is that they can be tailored to work in any course and in any discipline, with the aim to create a greater social presence inside and outside the classroom. Social presence (both affectively and cognitively) can help foster a sense of community membership and emotional connection with others in the course and a greater sense of meaning about the relevance of the course to their lives (Shen & Khalifa, 2008). This, in turn, can help reduce barriers and help bring about a greater sense of inclusion. Thus, participation with these technologies should provide students an opportunity to feel more comfortable to engage with their classmates and their instructors. Even though these technologies offer many new possibilities, the challenge for instructors and course designers is to create a rich, dynamic social exchange that is grounded in meaningful dialogue and co-construction of new knowledge and based on sound design principles and relevant learning theories.

APPLICATION BENEFITS

As illustrated in the chapters in the application section, these types of Web 2.0 social learning environments support:

(1) flexible forms of learning via a vast array of integrated digital platforms,
(2) ubiquitous, global access to low cost web-based devices and applications,
(3) social learning that fosters collaborative and participatory learning,
(4) affective learning via meaningful and authentic learning activities, and
(5) self-directed and self-regulated learning by fostering a sense of belonging and a sense of community.

If integrated into courses in a purposeful and sound way, these web-based and blended communicative technologies have the potential to increase learner engagement by encouraging a more inclusive learning environment by fostering group cohesiveness and interconnectedness. Based on situated learning theory by Lave and Wenger (1991), learning is socially situated within a community of practice. Thus, these Web 2.0-based social tools help to foster these communities inside and outside of the classroom. In short, to increase learner engagement and academic achievement, learning activities

should be designed in such ways that create meaningful learning activities
via participatory, social relationship based contexts.

THEORETICAL FRAMING

The theoretical basis for using these tools in an academic setting derives
from social constructivist based theories (Vygotsky, 1978) more broadly
and situated learning theory (Lave & Wenger, 1991) more specifically.
Vygotsky's cultural-historical theory focused on how language, culture,
history, and social interactions impacted learning. Cognitive and social
constructivism is the process of constructing new knowledge and meaning
based on learners' contextualized, situated, and authentic experiences. Lave
and Wenger's theory holds that learning is situated within the specific
culture-based context of the learner. According to this theory, learning is
most effective when it is embedded within a specific activity and cultural
context that is *personally meaningful* to learners.

In addition, learning can occur unintentionally and unconsciously and
tangential to formal classroom learning. As such, other types of learning
such as informal learning, collateral learning, and tacit learning are also
important. Meaningful interpersonal communication and collaborative
activities are crucial to learning in these situated learning settings. A crucial
aspect of learning is participation in and development of learning communities where technology and other tools, signs, and symbols are used to
mediate and facilitate a process wherein both instructors and students play
an active role in learning and community development. Language, culture,
history, shared values, and personal values and beliefs are important
determinants in the development of learning. At a personal level, acquiring
new knowledge and making meaning of present situations is done within the
context of one's values and goals and one's prior knowledge and history.
Thus, constructivism and situated learning provide a plausible framework
for designing web-based social learning contexts that support learner
engagement.

With the framework of these theories, social technologies can present new
and stimulating possibilities for teaching and learning in more innovative
and participatory ways. One important element is creating meaningful
interactions. So, instructors and course designers should be cognizant to
create learning activities that enhance meaning making and foster personally
meaningful interaction including the sharing of different perspectives
and experiences and ideas. Through varied approaches and in the spirit of

cognitive and social constructivism and situated learning, the authors in this volume explain and provide examples of how to operationalize the use of Web 2.0 technologies and tools. To that end, the innovative use of these social technologies is limited mainly by the imagination and knowledge of instructors and course designers.

Thus, these theories inform us that learning is first constructed in a social, cultural, and historical context and then situated at a personal level (Eggen & Kauchak, 2006). These theories posit that students continually endeavor to make meaning of their lives through meaningful participation in their broader envirnoment and through meaingful interactions with their fellow students, instructors, and others. Web 2.0 technology, by definition, includes applicaton for participation, interactivity, and collaboration, so it follows that these theories can provide a plausible framework for appropriately integrating these technologies with discipline-specific content and pedagogy. Thus, the main challenge is not cost or access but how to most effectively implement the technology to increase engagement and academic achievement.

TECHNOLOGY

The Web 2.0 social learning based tools discussed in this book are especially useful as supporting tools that foster social learning and participatory communities. The term Web 2.0 was created in the late 1990s as a way to describe interactive and social applications on the web (DiNucci, 1999). The idea of a global social network with the web as its medium was originally advocated by bloggers, chat room enthusiasts, and those who envisioned the web as the backbone of a democratic global community where the power and responsibility was distributed among all users to not only create their own content but also to help create an architecture of collaboration and participation. So, in a social web, it is ultimately the users (students) who determine its future. The qualities that describe the social web – freedom of movement and self-determination, participation and contribution, openness and distribution of information, distributed locus of control – are similar to the qualities we find in a democratic system.

So, these tools can provide a relatively easy and flexible way to enhance the teaching and learning environment depending on the needs of the students, the course objectives, and the pedagogical preferences of the instructor. In this way, this technology supports the notion of meaningful and authentic learning as well as academic and pedagogical pluralism. As such, these tools should be viewed as another means by which instructors can break down barriers to learning and expand the classroom to the global community. Of course, these technologies also bring with them challenges such as privacy concerns and teacher–student boundary issues, but given the flexibility of these tools, all these issues can be addressed and should pose no greater concern than those found in traditional nonelectronic forms of group collaboration.

This book presents several studies about social technologies that demonstrate how these technologies are being used in a variety of educational courses as active learning and participatory learning tools. As such, social oriented technology mediated instruction has the potential to support instructors in creating higher quality of interaction and more meaningful learning activities for students. So, by integrating Web 2.0-based technologies into the classroom in a more conscious and purposeful manner, these technologies create the potential to support more democratic, more open, and more self-regulated forms of learning.

CHAPTER OVERVIEWS

In "Leadership from ID (Instructional Design) for Web 2.0 Adoption: Appropriate Use of Emerging Technologies in Online Courses," by Marcia L. Ashbaugh, the author focuses on the role of the instructional designer and the process of designing for Web 2.0 technologies (social sites) which aim to produce engaging (effective and memorable) learner experiences. The author emphasizes the role of engagement with 21st century learning activities and draws links between enhanced instructional design competencies and the context for relevant instructional strategies. The author calls for leadership from the instructional design field within the context of a shifting educational landscape and explains why Web 2.0 technologies are appropriate pedagogies for online course designs.

In "Controlling Engagement: The Effects of Learner Control on Engagement and Satisfaction," by Michael N. Karim and Tara S. Behrend, the authors examine the types of control learners may exercise over their training programs and how these controls affect engagement. The authors define learner control as a multidimensional construct and provide evidence that instructional control features over training content may decrease engagement while scheduling control features over the training's time and location may increase engagement. To support these claims, the authors draw from extant learner control and e-learning research as well as established psychological theories. Based in this evidence, the authors provide recommendations for developing learning programs that use control to maximize engagement. The chapter concludes by examining how the outlined framework may be used to understand emergent mobile learning technologies.

In "Increasing Learner Engagement of Learning Technologies and Science TPACK through Representational Challenges," by Peter Hubber and Esther Loong, the authors examine their attempt to embed ICT into a preservice teacher science curriculum course and to ascertain the level of ICT engagement and TPACK of preservice teachers undertaking the course. The study found that students engaged with ICT and enhanced their TPACK during the period of the course. Features of the ICT embeddedness that contributed to the findings include: (1) part of the formal assessment for the course required students to construct digital objects and provide a rationale for their use in the science classroom, (2) modeling of best teaching practice by the tutor within a wider pedagogy than a digital one where the wider pedagogy is one of representation construction, (3) authentic tasks were undertaken by the student in the sense that they had a direct relationship to similar tasks that might be employed in the classroom, and (4) multiple roles are expected of the preservice teachers in undertaking the tasks, and from the teacher in terms of exploring the benefits of the task for application to a science classroom. However, issues still remain in terms of time allocation, resource access, and lack of models in nonscience and practicum schools.

In "From Connectivity to Connected Learners: Transactional Distance and Social Presence," by David Starr-Glass, the author considers issues confronted in creating and facilitating distance learning environments in a time when a multitude of technological options are available. The author reviews the literature and contemporary understanding of transactional distance theory and social presence. The author argues that distance learning is best advanced when actively linked to, and supported by, theories of learning. Historically, distance learning theory has evolved to accommodate technological possibilities and in an era of expanding connectivity it may be time to reconsider the core process and dynamics of learning. Connectivity, as a ubiquitous potential, is differentiated from connectedness, which is understood in terms of cognitive relevance and social affinity. Web 2.0 possibilities present exciting and novel learning opportunities; the challenge for educational designers and instructors is to utilize these possibilities in ways that support and enhance engaged learning.

In "Promoting Learner Engagement and Academic Literacies Through Blended Course Design," by Cathy Gunn, the author situates cutting-edge e-learning practice in principles of learning psychology that have developed over the past hundred years. A raft of social networking, Internet, and multimedia technologies is rapidly becoming an integral part of university education, as well as the hub of social life for the current generation of learners. The author examines how the effects in both areas are transformational, but it is mainly the pedagogy that leads to learning and engagement. Three case studies span a range of pedagogical aims, including the use of basic online learning management and assessment tools to promote mastery learning in first year Science; online tutorials geared toward a major assignment to embed key academic literacies into Business courses; and the use of Web 2.0 tools to promote teamwork, independent research skills, and student-generated resources in the study of Pharmacy. The key to success in all these cases is good pedagogy enabled through technology. Some of the challenges of rolling out this type of learning innovation in university teaching practice are discussed.

In "Engaging Learners as Moderators in an Online Management Course," by Kamna Malik, the author examines how teachers have used a variety of tools and techniques to engage learners. One such way is to assign them higher levels of responsibility by way of positional shift of roles. In this chapter, the author suggests the application of positional shift by way of assigning online learners the role of moderator. Based on a comparative study of three modes of engaging students as moderators, the author establishes the effectiveness of inviting students as voluntary moderators for online asynchronous discussions, shares the method adopted and initial inhibitions of the students who volunteered as moderators, and discusses the impact of student moderation on individual experience, overall discussion quality, and long-term learning of students. The author also emphasizes the increased complexity of teacher's role when students act as moderators and recommends change management, flexibility, and hand holding while planning to adopt student moderation as a pedagogical tool for student engagement.

In "Engaging Entrepreneurs with a Blended Problem-Based Learning Degree Programme," by Patrick Lynch, Mary T. Holden, Anthony Foley, Denis Harrington and Jennifer Hussey, the authors detail a design journey that harmonizes blended learning with face-to-face problem-based learning to produce an innovative program that engaged a disconnected and sceptical cohort as to the benefit of formal education for delivering the needs of their industry. The intricacies of integrating the benefits of blended and problem-based learning elements into the program posed challenges for the design team and required considerable time resources to overcome. Central to success was the co-involvement of both the learner and the educator in the program design process and in essence ensured the "voice of the industry" was captured and incorporated in its implementation and delivery. This collaborative mind-set helped ensure the relevance of the program to meet industry needs. The authors explain how educators will obtain implementable guidelines that can be used to enhance the design and delivery of business degree programs for owners/managers of micro/small business enterprises.

In "Engaging Distance and Blended Learners Online," by Andrew Doig and Steve Hogg, the authors examine work carried out by Southampton Solent University (SSU) to meet the needs of a new constituency of learner, the professional learner – students who are usually in full time work, have progressed in their professional career, often have other commitments such as families, and are time constrained. The approach described has been to introduce more flexible access to learning, in particular through the increase in the University's provision of online distance and blended learning. SSU has implemented strategies to ensure high-quality provision, exploiting cross-disciplinary skills, creating collaborations between learning technologists and academic staff. A set of Solent Online Learning Standards were developed, along with a new instance of the institutional VLE, also called Solent Online Learning. A new Flexible Delivery Development and Support Team was created working within in a new model of collaboration with academic staff, a model to which academic champions have been added – those academics who have had past success in developing and running online courses. The authors conclude that the successes so far are attributable to responsiveness to the particular needs of this constituency of learner, as well as a good working relationship between the collaborating colleagues.

In "A Pedagogical Framework for Collaborative Learning in a Social Blended E-Learning Context," by Martina A. Doolan, the author details a pedagogical framework, the dialogic shamrock for collaborative learning through technology, which is drawn from learner centric, constructivist, and sociocultural perspectives. The principles of these perspectives are related to the concepts of online learning and collaborative technology including Web 2.0 in higher education. The dialogic shamrock and examples presented are intended to help educators across the educational sector understand the key concepts to encourage learners to work collaboratively supported by technology within a blended learning framework in a social learning context. The dialogic shamrock presented is not intended to be prescriptive but rather to act as a guide for educators who seek to use a blend of technology and class-based activities to engage learners in collaborative social learning contexts. The dialogic shamrock highlights that good curriculum design purposely builds the learner and involves learners in co-constructing and co-designing their learning; this can result in dynamic, active, and interactive student engagement, the development of skills, and co-constructed knowledge.

In "Developing Technology and Collaborative Group Work Skills: Supporting Student and Group Success in Online and Blended Courses," by Julia L. Parra, the author states that the use of collaborative group work is an important teaching and learning strategy for online and blended courses. However, the challenges of collaborative group work, such as the lack of online technology skills, time conflicts, differences in team member participation, and logistics of online and blended teamwork, often leave students dissatisfied by the process. To maximize the benefits and minimize the challenges, students should be supported in the development of skills with the use of relevant (often emerging or Web 2.0) online technologies and the development of skills related to online and blended collaborative group work. The "Phases and Scaffolds for Technology Use and Collaborative Group Work" course design process was developed to address this need and is shared along with an action research-based case study designed from an action research approach. The purpose of this study was to find out what students thought about the aforementioned course design process, as well as to find out which online tools were most beneficial for online collaborative group work. Based on the results of the survey, the "Phases and Scaffolds for Technology Use and Collaborative Group Work" course design process had a positive impact on student satisfaction, student learning, and student success and the most beneficial and valued online collaborative group work tools included Skype, Google Docs, and Adobe Connect.

In "Balancing Students' Privacy Concerns While Increasing Student Engagement in E-Learning Environments," by Lynne Siemens, Catherine Althaus, and Charlotte Stange, the authors state that despite the increased use of online learning environments, little is known about students' perception of privacy, confidentiality, and information security in the online learning environment and the potential implications for learning engagement. To explore this issue further, the authors conducted interviews with master-level students who take courses online at a Canadian university. They found that students are not generally consciously aware of privacy, confidentiality, and information security issues in regards to personal information within an online learning environment and do not tend to read the relevant university policies that may in fact provide guidance on methods to protect one's information. However, despite this apparent lack of awareness, students do take active steps to create a safe learning environment and expect that instructors will facilitate this by communicating expectations for sharing personal information and modeling appropriate behavior. Consequently, responding to student needs may be less about appropriate policies and more about communication and action to create engagement.

In "Problem-Based Learning in Hybrid, Blended, and Online Courses: Instructional and Change Management Implications for Supporting Learner Engagement," by Katerina Bohle Carbonell, Amber Dailey-Hebert, Maike Gerken, and Therese Grohnert, the authors state that problem-based learning (PBL) is an instructional format which emphasizes the role of the learner. Learning is understood to be an active process in which the learner, through collaboration with fellow students, constructs his or her knowledge. Traditionally, PBL instruction has included face-to-face discussions. Yet today, with the plentitude of tools which offer the opportunity for online collaboration, the need to revamp PBL becomes evident. The authors examine how a European university committed to PBL underwent a change process to reposition its offline PBL format in light of current technological advances and learner demands. To be able to experiment with various tools and hybrid formats, several enthusiastic faculty members were given the funds to create online and hybrid courses. Three different change processes, course formats, and course experiences are described resulting in a hybrid, blended, and online PBL course. Instructional and change management implications for the implementation of hybrid, blended, and online PBL courses are presented. Instructional implications deal with the needs of the learner, the role of the instructor, and the importance of sound technology integration in the course. Change management implications highlight the need to foster intra-institutional collaboration.

CONCLUSION

In this group of chapters, we have provided varied views and research on how to use technology-mediated social learning platforms in order to fully engage learners. Current research suggests that these enabling technologies have the potential to increase engagement and retention if implemented in the correct manner. Relative to the specific course and discipline, if the course is designed with sound pedagogical principles and grounded in relevant learning theories and content knowledge, the technologies presented in this book have the potential to encourage student participation and sense of belonging and community. Compared with more passive methods of teaching and learning (e.g., pure lecture, textbooks), technology-mediated social learning environments can enable greater levels of student participation.

Finally, regardless of the technology used, education should be viewed as a space where self-regulated and self-directed learning is nurtured and where collateral learning (e.g., attitudes and values) is also developed. In this sense, the classroom can serve as a safe social space where multiple forms of learning are cultivated. As such, instructors can use these technologies to reframe what it means to teach and learn in a postindustrial, globalized world. These technologies are not passing fads, but rather, they are opportunities to better engage students in ways that connect with them on their level. Please join us in exploring the novel use of these technologies as we continue to search for better means to engage and retain students.

REFERENCES

DiNucci, D. (1999). Fragmented future. *Print*, *53*(4), 32–35.

Eggen, P., & Kauchak, D. (2006). *Educational psychology: Windows on classrooms* (7th ed.). Upper Saddle River, NJ: Prentice Hall.

Lave, J., & Wenger, E. (1991). *Situated learning: Legitimate peripheral participation.* Cambridge: Cambridge University Press.

Leontiev, A. N., & Luria, A. R. (1968). The psychological ideas of L.S. Vygotsky. In B. B. Wolman (Ed.), *Historical roots of contemporary psychology* (pp. 338–367). New York, NY: Harper & Row.

Park, Y. (2011). A pedagogical framework for mobile learning: Categorizing educational applications of mobile technologies into four types. *International Review of Research in Open and Distance Learning*, *12*(2), 78–102.

Scardamalia, M. (2001). Big change questions "will educational institutions, within their present structures, be able to adapt sufficiently to meet the needs of the information age?" *Journal of Educational Change*, *2*(2), 165–176.

Shen, K. N., & Khalifa, M. (2008). Exploring multidimensional conceptualization of social presence in the context of online communities. *International Journal of Human-Computer Interaction*, *24*(7), 722–748.

Tapscott, D. (2009). *Grown up digital: How the net generation is changing your world.* New York, NY: McGraw-Hill.

Vygotsky, L. S. (1978). *Mind in society: The development of higher psychological processes.* Cambridge: Harvard University Press.

Woo, Y., & Reeves, T. C. (2007). Meaningful interaction in web-based learning: A social constructivist interpretation. *The Internet and Higher Education*, *10*(1), 15–25.

LEADERSHIP FROM ID (INSTRUCTIONAL DESIGN) FOR WEB 2.0 ADOPTION: APPROPRIATE USE OF EMERGING TECHNOLOGIES IN ONLINE COURSES

Marcia L. Ashbaugh

ABSTRACT

A social movement is sweeping the globe in the form of Internet delivered and open access sharing spaces. People are connecting in new ways while personalizing their daily experiences with shared websites called Web 2.0 technologies. This chapter looks into the implications of taking these technologies beyond social interactions into the learning experiences of students. With a literature review and case study analysis, the goal of this chapter is to gain a better understanding of what is needed to appropriate quality instructional strategies to the online university course room including social sites such as Facebook, Twitter, Second Life®, and wikis. Following a brief history and descriptions of the Web 2.0 sites and functions, the reader is introduced to the design expectations typical of

Increasing Student Engagement and Retention in e-Learning Environments:
Web 2.0 and Blended Learning Technologies
Cutting-edge Technologies in Higher Education, Volume 6G, 17–56
Copyright © 2013 by Emerald Group Publishing Limited
All rights of reproduction in any form reserved
ISSN: 2044-9968/doi:10.1108/S2044-9968(2013)000006G004

instructional designers (IDs) with definitions and standards from the field's literature. Support is offered from the business and educational literature for incorporating leadership into design practice through vision, strategy, and theory-based decisions. Definitions, benchmarks, and examples of instructional strategies and activities for learner engagement complete the theoretical framework for the chapter. Given the added complexities of advanced technologies, this chapter suggests evaluating social learning through an ID leadership perspective for a more informed recommendation of Web 2.0 online affordances. Following a case analysis of Second Life®, a 3-D virtual world used for learning activities, implications for ID practice are discussed, along with the various benefits and barriers of adopting Web 2.0 technologies. In the conclusion, suggestions are given for future research on the potential for integration of Web 2.0 affordances into online learning designs for rich, engaging learning experiences.

INTRODUCTION

Recent changes in higher education online learning strategies include design selections from a suite of social networking and sharing websites termed *Web 2.0* (O'Reilly, 2005) – virtual spaces that promote collaborative expression and media-sharing. Increased interest in the use of these technologies as new pedagogical affordances is in reaction to a proliferation in social Internet activities with dimensions characteristic of a *movement* – a movement that is gaining way into online higher education course rooms (Daniels, 2009). This shift in instructional approaches suggests course designers have responded to modern learners who expect more autonomy of learning, and more from an educational system that aligns its pedagogies with students' daily activities. For example, students frequently connect with "friends" to share thoughts and ideas on Facebook, a mega social website. Such exchange of ideas by a community is a form of learning through social interactions (Bruner, 1986); although, conceptualizing the numbers of participants in Facebook transcends a traditional understanding of community. Statistics show that, since it was released to the general public in 2007, Facebook has attracted nearly 950 million subscribers worldwide. More astounding, and more relevant to the younger demographic of college entrants, 45% of the one *billion* Internet profiles (web access identities) are under the age of 25 (Bennet, 2012).

To meet the educational needs of a rapidly growing *connected* population, the instructional designers (IDs) of web-based courses are tasked with evaluating new technologies for their potential learning value. Along with new technical considerations, questions that need addressing include the appropriateness of social sites for educational use (Cain & Fox, 2009): do they afford or hinder learning? For the ID, choosing appropriate pedagogies means prefacing design selections with more diligent and pragmatic research (Yanchar, South, Williams, Allen, & Wilson, 2010), particularly research on what has worked in new learning situations. Concerns have been raised by educators over core pedagogical issues such as engagement and quality of learning (Magolda & Platt, 2009). Nimon (2007) found that, without elements of engagement, Gen Y learners (also known as *millennials* and generally categorized as those born in the 1980s–1990s) will quickly abandon a new technology. The students' reactions in the Nimon study alerts IDs to make good decisions for the affordances and strategies selected to compose a course design. Faust (1977) posed an abiding question for instructional strategy selection, "how do we know which set of displays [strategies] is best in a given situation?" (p. 18). Echoing this concern for the present day, Magolda and Platt (2009) remarked that "knowing when it is appropriate to invoke a technology to enhance learning is much harder than knowing how to use it" (p. 11). Clearly, a challenge for educators and course designers is to avoid the type of fallout that results from imposing ineffective means on unsuspecting students through strategic missteps.

To meet the challenges of designing for appropriate pedagogies, seasoned designers have historically made selections for a learning event based on professional experience, with a certain *know-how* or intuition and judgment (Chi, Glaser, & Rees, 1982; Yanchar et al., 2010). However, the decision-making process is more complex when inundated by rapidly developing, fluid technologies (Jonassen, Davidson, Collins, Campbell, & Haag, 1995) with little known consequences to learners. From this perspective it is posited that a designer ought to possess a particular foresight for future innovations and societal trends (Ashbaugh, 2011; Reigeluth, Watson, Watson, Dutta, Zengguan, & Powell, 2008). On the other hand, a futures view can be problematic as the future is increasingly unpredictable. In addition, design decisions are compounded by research that is often contradictory in its assessment of effectiveness for new and proposed pedagogies (Clark, 2010; de Jong, 2010; Masterman, Jameson, & Walker, 2009). In other words, academic courses are created by designers who make difficult decisions (Dooley, Lindner, Telg, Irani, Moore, & Lundy, 2007) in a shifting educational environment with competing appraisals of new technologies and changing theories on pedagogies for engaged learning.

The core assumption in this chapter is that the complexity of new technologies (represented by Web 2.0 websites and applications) has created an ethos of education in need of better equipped IDs, in particular with leadership capacities – competencies, skills, characteristics, and mindsets (Ashbaugh, 2012a; Fullan, 2001; Kowch, 2009). In part, this need stems from a continued perception of lower quality in web-based courses (Allen & Seaman, 2012). Past suggestions for online course improvements included calls for leadership in recognition of its centrality to the practice of ID (Beaudoin, 2007; Kowch, 2009; Naidu, 2007; Sims & Koszalka, 2008). However, those demands assumed a range of competencies which Sims and Koszalka (2008) asserted IDs did not possess for properly designing the new technology-driven and supported learning environments. Sims and Koszalka recommended that design specifications more closely align with the conditions of the environment, and to accomplish this, they suggested the addition of a leadership skillset for IDs. Whereas, the multidimensional nature of education has been augmented by Web 2.0 technologies, the ID skills once identified for creating effective academic courses for modern learning (IBSTPI, 2000; Richey, Fields, & Foxon, 2001; Smith & Ragan, 1999) may lack in current relevancy. As a result, without a complete perspective of the ID's critical role in guiding the social learning movement, adoption of cutting-edge Web 2.0 affordances may be hindered.

From the rationale offered, it is the purpose of this chapter to introduce and support the notion that a new generation of emerging technologies demands a new generation of design practice standards for leading in the instructional strategy selections that will result in learner engagement. The notion resonates with a dated yet enduring notion that a movement will be more successful when guided by leadership competencies applicable to the cause (Lang & Lang, 1961). In the following sections the reader will be (a) familiarized with Web 2.0 and its potential for learning, (b) introduced to a fresh view of IDs in leading a modern education technology movement, (c) provided a case study of how a Web 2.0 affordance may be assessed for appropriate use in the online course room, and (d) led into a discussion on how IDs may overcome barriers to adoption through a leadership approach. To explore the opportunities online course designers and developers are offered with emerging technologies, the following section outlines a brief history of Web 2.0 technologies followed by descriptions of the most well-known and used applications.

AN INTRODUCTION TO WEB 2.0 FOR LEARNING

During the transition period between the 20th and the 21st centuries, digital social activities often included 1- and 2-way noneditable communications in the forms of playing web-based games, instant messaging, chatting in public or private virtual rooms, and cell phone texting. With more recent inventions education was alerted to the potential learning power of the Web 2.0 multi-way communication affordances, especially for online course enhancements. The socialization of the Internet began with an idea in the mid-1990s to provide access to everyone wishing to interact with and contribute to the world wide web, an idea that developed into the notion of *free and open* software (*free* to collaborate on and *open* to add input for improvements). From the design-by-collaboration Linux operating system, inspired by Linus Torvalds (Moody, 2002), it was a short reach to a user-empowered suite of participatory (social) applications and websites. The phenomenon, coined *Web 2.0* by O'Reilly (2005), introduced new ways for consumers to use and influence a world wide web of expanding information complete with new opportunities for learning. At the present, selected websites include social sharing and bookmarking (MySpace, Facebook, Twitter, Del.icio.us, Digg), video and photo sharing (YouTube, Flickr), blogs (personal online journals), collaborated projects (wikis), and multiuser virtual worlds (MUVEs, e.g., Second Life®), and mashups (combinations of applications resulting in a new one). While not yet fully developed for education, the freedom for open expressions through creative and collective contributions aligns with modern didactic goals for co-created knowledge (Jha, 2012).

A guiding theory for learning with Web 2.0 technologies is found in *social negotiation*, a theory proposed by Bruner (1986) who considered learning a "communal activity, a sharing of the culture" (p. 127). Along with 20th century situated cognitivists who believed learning occurs in certain settings (Brown, Collins, & Duguid, 1989; Cunningham, 1992; Vygotsky, 1978), most modern educators recognize the validity of learning collaboratively within one's community. In fact, inclusion of collaboration in learning designs exhibits an important 21st century designer competence (Richey et al., 2001) as well as sets a critical standard for online learning requirements (Ashbaugh, 2012a). More importantly, Web 2.0 technologies afford learning through negotiation of meaning from the shared beliefs, insights, and inventions of the group (Vygotsky, 1978; Wertsch, 1998). When viewed through this lens, Web 2.0 "gatherings" exhibit communal actions with implications for meaningful learning. The following section describes four of the most recognizable social technologies.

Facebook

The dialogue created on social sharing sites are multi-way, unedited discussions, and may be deleted or hidden by the reader, but not changed except by the owner. Sites such as Facebook (www.facebook.com) represent these *user-centered* technologies. Facebook is accessed by logging into a personal account and allows the owner to customize profiles and share personal information with "friends." Typically, users display icons of favorite music and entertainment preferences; online multiuser game "moves" and invitations to join in; vacation, travel, family, and friends' photos; and links to videos and other external sites of common interest. These sites allow the user to update personal "statuses" on work, school, and other activities, often using idiomatic expressions understood by only the readers. Together, the transparent conversations build a sense of community caring. Recently, businesses, newsgroups, and academicians have joined the "conversation" with a Facebook presence; albeit, their diverse purposes include marketing products and attracting readership.

The elements of engagement present in Facebook support the venue as a potential online learning affordance. A Lester and Perini (2010) study linked engagement through the use of social sites such as Facebook to at least five major predictors of online success: interaction, active learning, feedback, collaboration, and complex tasks. The study (Lester & Perini, 2010) results showed that students connected more readily with administrative services and student supports which created a sense of being cared for, often lacking in distance learning. Meaningful interactions took place between faculty and students through shared ideas, thoughts, pictures, and videos which resulted in formation of important community networks. Active learning was observed in frequent and immediate inquiry and feedback through instant messaging and chat functions, shared research notes from uploading and downloading capabilities, and collaborative assignments afforded by built-in collaboration applications. In addition, a degree of cognitive complexity was observed while participants performed the functions of social sites, such as textual "updates" to existing information. The observations support the notion that participation in community learning tasks leads to increased collective knowledge growth (Scardamalia & Bereiter, 1994). A newer study by Tu, Sujo-Montes, Yen, Chan, and Blocher (2012) indicated that "analysis, contextualization, and conceptualization" (p. 15) take place when an activity is shared by a group, and create learning points that culminate in "distributed cognition" (p. 15), or dispersed knowledge.

Wikis

Wikis are multiuser created and edited web pages that exemplify true open source spaces. The pages usually offer unlimited viewership unless privatized by the author, and foster collaborative use; thus, wikis are *group-centered*. Wikis may be conceived as data visualization spaces where individuals and groups are able to log on at any time, from anywhere, to create text, edit existing multimedia, or add links to external data such as simulations. Wikis usually have a common subject goal, may contain many pages, and are editable by anyone within the website's stated format and functions; at times, this will include setting up an access login. The most recognized example is Wikipedia™, a free online encyclopedia (http://en.wikipedia.org/wiki/Wikipedia) considered attractive as a low budget educational resource; however, the site is not recommended for academic use by most instructors due to its perceived unreliability. The premise academic critics stand on, that peer review and editing is prone to error, is contradicted by the notion that collective expertise is the foundation of the free and open sharing of ideas that builds knowledge (Scardamalia & Bereiter, 1994) – a notion that contributed to the extremely stable Linux operating system (Moody, 2002). In response to the critics and to ensure integrity, careful attention is given by Wikipedia editors to the inclusion of sources and cross references, with caveats added when poor or no referencing is present in a narrative.

In support of the value of user contributions to a wiki, a particularly meaningful application was demonstrated by students who collaboratively developed chapters on course topics, which were later compiled into a textbook for future learners to use or to revise (Tu et al., 2012). The activity demonstrated how interactivity on a wiki platform guided by a shared learning goal may produce a high-level academic outcome.

Second Life®

Second Life® (http://secondlife.com), which is either *uni- or multiuser* created and edited, is used for 3-D concept modeling within virtual environmental variables and populated with life-like animated personas, people, or concept representations, called avatars. The MUVE concept is usually activated for collaboration purposes, and yet its initial generation by one owner classifies it as *creator-centered*. While visually captivating, virtual worlds are not always found on the Web 2.0 product lists due to ethereal game-like appearances that evoke perceptions of dissimilarity to the real

world (Warburton, 2008). It may be argued, however, that the Second Life®
environment contains elements for potentially enriched learning in terms of
authentic task representations that involve collaboration and interactivity.
For example, a "community" is able to create music tracks, videos,
drawings, and photo collages from within the virtual world places or
territories (which have previously been constructed by members of the
virtual community). Collaboration is afforded by voice and text chat
features, blogs, and forums. For more presence, places are easily accessed
through built-in teleporting capabilities for leaping from one destination to
another. In addition, creativity is initiated, expressed, and shared widely,
inexpensively, and in ways not possible in a traditional venue – art gallery,
museum, recording studio, or classroom.

Building places, events, and people (in the form of avatars), whether
imaginary or authentic representations, is a way of creatively constructing
and sharing knowledge on unlimited topics. Dr. Brad Hokanson, professor
in the University of Minnesota Design Department, has utilized the virtual
environment to allow students to redesign computer labs and stated, "it's a
great environment to walk through and demonstrate space" (Landsberger,
2009, p. 24). Fig. 1 is an example of a design space created for educating in
architectural concepts, and portrays a visiting avatar (student). The visual
effects in the virtual classroom create a sense of immersion in the topic. A
case study is offered later in the chapter to provide a more precise view of

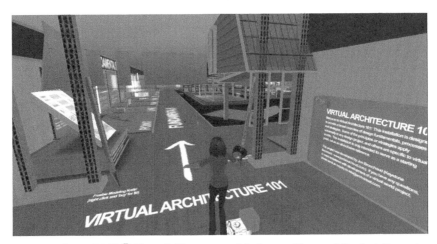

Fig. 1.   Second Life® Virtual Classroom with Avatar Form of Student Present.

this technology and how an ID may lead the way for specifying Second Life® as an engaging pedagogical strategy for online course curricula.

Sloodle

A most promising Web 2.0 development for educational use has recently come from innovators who created a *mashup* (a combination of two or more websites) for linking the open source Moodle LMS (Learning Management System) with Second Life® to create *Sloodle* (Simulated Linked Object Oriented Dynamic Learning Environment). The combining of two distinct sites to create a hybrid educational site has served to integrate the social learning concept directly into the online courseroom. A few of the features are listed below:

- Web-intercom. A chat room that brings Moodle chat room and Second Life® chats together.
- Registration booth. Identity management for Second Life® and Moodle. Link students' avatars to their Moodle user accounts.
- Quiz tool and 3D Drop Box. Assess in Second Life® – grade in Moodle. Set quizzes or 3D modeling [sic] tasks in an engaging 3D environment.
- Choice tool. Allow students to vote (and see results) in Second Life® as well as in Moodle.
- Multifunction SLOODLE Toolbar. Enhances the Second Life® user interface. Use a range of classroom gestures, quickly get a list of the Moodle user names of the avatars around, or write notes directly into to your Moodle blog from Second Life®.
- Presenter. Quickly author Second Life® presentations of slides and/or web pages on Moodle. Present in Second Life®. (Sloodle blog site: What Does Sloodle Do? https://www.sloodle.org/blog/?page_id=2)

In addition to the benefits of connecting with others and forming relationships from a distance, social sites foster interdependent knowledge building (Stahl, 2004), and intersubjectivity – "the product of knowledge construction resulting from the coordination of multiple perspectives among learners engaged in course room discourse" (Hall, 2010). These notions represent an online pedagogical approach of *learner-centeredness*, a concept that is not only based on *personal* control of one's path of learning but on individual contribution to the creation and perpetuity of what is being learned. To the extent of engagement in modern social technologies,

Sims and Stork (2007) posited that an effective course design will not prescriptively provide for learning rather will afford learners an opportunity to construct knowledge and meaning through an individualized, or personalized, perspective. An autonomous orientation situates the learner so that "she can create meaning through self-driven inquiry, experiential learning, and collaborative analysis" (Magolda & Platt, 2009, p. 13). This is important, as Winter, Cotton, Gavin, and Yorke (2012) suggested, no matter the technology, without meaning for the learner, electronic pedagogical agents will remain useless distractions. With this concern in mind, a call is put forth for the experts in learning designs (IDs) to lead the way in creating appropriate educational solutions with Web 2.0 affordances. IDs are tasked with responding to such a call from a unique professional skillset; although, designers in practice today may need to be retooled to consider modern technologies (Ashbaugh, 2012b).

DEFINITION AND SCOPE OF INSTRUCTIONAL DESIGN (ID)

The scope of competencies required of an ID is best understood from a definition of the field's central purpose: *instructional design* is "the process of deciding what methods of instruction are best for bringing about desired changes in student knowledge and skills for a specific course content and a specific student population" (Reigeluth, 1983, p. 7) and spans "tasks of management, implementation, and evaluation ... all in the service of designing and delivering good instruction" (Wilson, 2005, p. 238). At the core of their work, IDs are guided by the principles that seek learning (a) aims, *what* to achieve through learning goals and objectives; (b) ways, what *path* leads to learning goals through instructional strategies; and (c) means, *how* to achieve learning goals through substantive, motivational, and engaging learning activities. Campbell, Schwier, and Kenny (2009) characterized the practice of such principles as having a duty to the design and to the learner, a characteristic that is represented in appropriate and socially relevant design selections.

From a concise view, IDs operate from a comprehensive skillset under an overarching imperative to create structurally sound systems of learning with complex processes, to manage chaotic situations, to negotiate competing objectives, to predict success or failure, to test and revise, and to anticipate future consequences (Richey, Klein, & Tracey, 2011). From a macro view, an ID aligns the learning environment, instructional strategies and outcomes from expertise as an expected function of the profession (Richey et al., 2011). In specific, on a daily basis IDs envision, plan, and perform essential steps in the design process that include generating objectives and contriving instructional strategies to meet specific learning goals. This is followed by creating activities for the chosen affordances, or facilitators of learning. A Web 2.0 technology is an example of an affordance that is used to implement an activity and should correspond with the type of theoretical learning component specified, such as *interaction*. For example, the activity might ask for a group of students to learn the meaning of Pi and to display its value in a fractal diagram as portrayed in Fig. 2. Subsequently, a distinct assessment of learning outcomes usually completes the course design – term paper, test, class presentation; with Web 2.0, the outcome of an activity may in fact become the assessment.

In summary, the ID is both burdened and privileged with the opportunity to create environments and structures within which learners may play and experiment with ideas and concepts until fashioned into meaningful mental models. Given the extensive criteria for performance presented thus far in this chapter, IDs are uniquely positioned to lend expertise and leadership when confronted with new and sophisticated technologies, including the recent Web 2.0 technologies.

A LEADERSHIP APPROACH FOR WEB 2.0

When contextualized for the higher education curricula design process, leadership adds a dimension to established ID competencies generally restricted to work practices and skills. At the turn of the 21st century, numerous interpretations of practice stimulated the International Board of Standards for Training, Performance and Instruction (IBSTPI) organization to develop a comprehensive list of reasonable and essential competencies and standards for conducting the work of ID (IBSTPI, 2000). Unfortunately, although defining several managerial elements, the standards of practice fall short of specifying leadership capacities and characteristics. Likewise, the most recent version of standards of practice from the Association of Educational Communications and Technology (AECT) organization delineated just 1 out of 25 standards as a *leadership* (AECT, 2012) competency. In other words, the standards and descriptions for IDs to date fall short in explaining what leadership means for practice.

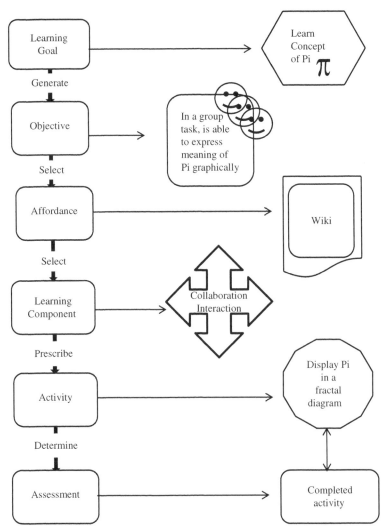

Fig. 2.   Process of Aligning an Instructional Strategy with an Activity.

With this in mind, a foundational construct for enhancing the limited ID concept has been developed from a selection of business and educational leadership resources. While the literature over the last century is inundated with diverse notions and theories on leadership (Zenger & Folkman, 2009), explicit characteristics are generally represented in the quality of key attributes, behaviors, and skills attributed to those perceived to be leaders (Dooley et al., 2007; Fullan & Scott, 2009; Katz, 1955; Sergiovanni & Corbally, 1984). Through this lens, the behavior and attitudes representative of an ID should be demonstrated by the following characteristics: having a vision and driving change as well as making strategic decisions for quality (effective and engaging) outcomes.

Leading with Vision for Change

Leadership denotes an ability to influence others toward excellence in work and personal practices (Howard & Wellins, 2008; Kouzes & Posner, 2007) and to sway others in a particular direction – to follow a vision. Leaders recognize innovation, forward-thinking, uniqueness, and "respond creatively to world conditions and the current state of their own society" (Greenleaf, 1977, p. 321). More recently, a Scott, Coates, and Anderson (2008) report described leadership as having a capacity to see the big picture and to "read and respond to a continuously and rapidly changing external environment" (p. 11). Staying "one step ahead" means foreseeing societal and technological fluctuations that have impact on education and learners. The environment referred to by Scott et al. (2008) depicts the current challenges of designing for a highly technical, rapidly changing student body swept up in a movement of digital social immersion.

A foundational aspect of vision is foreseeing and preparing for change. By focusing on the challenges of doing something new, IDs embrace change (Campbell et al., 2009). In a longitudinal study of IDs, Campbell et al. (2009) challenged the professional designers to ask of themselves, "Who am I, why am I practicing this way, and what effect does this have on others?" (p. 661). The results supported earlier findings that IDs believe they are moral change agents who lead in changing their culture, the institution, and society (Campbell, Schwier, & Kenny, 2005). Of significance to the focus of discussion in this chapter, Beabout and Carr-Chellman (2008) found that IDs consider themselves change agents with a duty to *lead* in educational and design innovations. Therefore, IDs are compelled to not resist change "because that's the way we've always done it"; instead, to be leaders who envision and embrace new ways for new technologies (Kowch, 2009).

The operationalization of change is not always easy as leaders are called on to face the conundrums of change by making difficult and critical

decisions (Sackney & Mergel, 2007). Campbell, et al. (2009) found that IDs'
perceptions on issues of practice included intentional decision-making, an
action regarded as maximizing capacities and capabilities (Kubicek, 2011)
of both processes and people. Of highest importance, course designers
make critical decisions that affect learners through the learning materials
they develop. Dooley et al. (2007) reported that, during the creation and
implementation of courses, critical decisions by IDs foreshadowed high
quality, effective, and relevant designs.

Finally, since leadership has been known to drive change through the
adoption of future-oriented inventions (Fullan, 2001; Fullan & Scott, 2009),
it is likely that the addition of leadership competencies and characteristics to
the ID toolbox will result in increased appropriate strategies in online
courses. In this way, an expanded perspective on the role of ID is consistent
with the designer's duty to guide and oversee the introduction of new
learning interventions like Web 2.0 venues, and to ensure pedagogical
relevance and effectiveness through strategic decisions.

Leading with Strategy

From a broad perspective, Zenger and Folkman (2009) studied the effectiveness of leaders from a cross section of organizations and identified a major
characteristic in operation: strategy, which was summarized as, "to translate
organizations [punctuation missing in original] vision and objectives into
challenging and meaningful goals for others" (p. 70). Similarly, Sergiovanni
(2003) approached educational leadership from an understanding of
strategy, a way of planning with a purpose for future expectations. Mean-
while, leaders in the field of ID have emphasized the competence of strategic leadership as critical for aligning practice with modern learning goals
and environments (Beaudoin, 2007; Kowch, 2009; Naidu, 2007; Reeves,
Herrington, & Oliver, 2004; Sims & Koszalka, 2008). When translated for
ID practice, a vision for adding a new affordance such as Web 2.0 to meet a
learning goal must be distilled into a strategic plan for design – otherwise
known as an instructional strategy (depicted in Fig. 2).

Thinking of design in this way was evident in the distinct themes of
leadership in practice that emerged from the Ashbaugh (2012a) study,
including the competency of creating context-relevant instructional strategies – a critical congruence that is necessary but not always present in online
courses (Bernard et al., 2009; Der-Thanq, Hung, & Wang, 2007; Naidu,
2007; Sims & Stork, 2007). For those not familiar with the terminology of

ID, an early definition of *instructional strategies* is yet relevant: "specific types of displays used in a given situation, their sequence, and the relationship among displays" (Faust, 1977, p. 18). Merrill (1999) offered an expanded definition,

> Instructional strategies include the presentation of the appropriate knowledge components, practice with or student activities involving these knowledge components, and learner guidance to facilitate the student's appropriate interaction with these knowledge components. (p. 400)

The appropriateness of an instructional strategy was addressed in a National Institute of Health (NIH) report (Cain & Fox, 2009) on the use of Web 2.0 for pharmaceutical training,

> Instead of beginning instructional planning with these tools [Web 2.0] in mind, the learning objectives and instructional strategies should guide the adoption process. An awareness of the different tools gives instructional designers and faculty members additional mechanisms from which to choose, but selecting an appropriate instructional strategy is more important. (Conclusion section, para. 1)

Consequently, as portrayed in Fig. 2, the goal of an instructional or pedagogical strategy is to match an activity with a theory-based approach for what type of knowledge is to be accessed and gained. From an antithetical position, a failure in the design to pass the test of appropriateness may render a strategic selection unadoptable.

To example the selection of a more appropriate and effective strategy, a scenario from a university biology program is played out for the reader. A traditional laboratory lesson in anatomy calls for examination of a human corpse for proper identification of the parts of the body. Students take turns looking at what the instructor chooses to present, memorize the parts of the body, and later demonstrate knowledge gained through testing. An alternative online version may present a video of the lab lesson followed by an uploaded multiple-choice test. Instead, the same lesson could add a significant engagement factor with a different prescription: interaction with a simulation during which the student guides a virtual three-dimensional camera over the corpse to peer directly at various parts and into hidden cavities. The learner has control over what part is viewed and in what order. The simulation allows the learner to hear the terminology while experiencing the functions of the parts. Arguably, this learning strategy is superior as it has been established that mastery of terminology is more likely as the parts of the body are understood in context (Holzinger, Kickmeier-Rush, Wassertheurer, & Hessinger, 2009). Ultimately, the learning goal – learn and name the parts of the body – has not changed; rather, the approach to presentation has. Consequently, engagement depends on not only what is being taught but also on how the learner will access, apply, and assimilate the information.

The previous example is an illustration of design leadership in practice in the decision to reject a traditional approach in lieu of a more appropriate and effective strategy for modern learning. Therefore, from a more complete set of competencies, an ID is equipped to make strategic decisions that will lead to quality course designs – an assumption more fully described and supported in the next section.

Leading for Quality

Quality of online learning has been defined as meeting research-based pedagogical standards that, when applied to a learning design, meets institutional goals and learner needs with effective outcomes (Quality Matters, 2006). When conceptualized as a learning goal, quality is an integral outcome of an academic course design (Ashbaugh, 2011). This conceptualization implies that quality of design is built on relevant and effective instructional affordances and from exemplary learning strategies. Various studies have revealed significant predictors of quality such as adaptation of pedagogies to the learning environment (Naidu, 2007), structural alignment of objectives and assessments with learning strategies and activities (Sims, 2012), as well as affordance of personalized learning (Sims & Stork, 2007). In addition, characteristics of relevant and effective instructional strategies display in the form of activities and assessments which include authentic or real-world tasks for problem-solving and transference (Jonassen, 1991, 2011); critical thinking challenges (Barab & Roth, 2006); and interaction and feedback with students, instructors, and content (Bernard et al., 2009; Dunlap, Sobel, & Sands, 2007; Gallien & Oomen-Early, 2008; Moore, 1989). Moreover, collaborative assignments and interactivity were found to be proven predictors of achievement (Bernard et al., 2009; Jonassen et al., 1995; Ostlund, 2008; Sims, 2003; Weaver, Spratt, & Nair, 2008) and have been linked to engagement, a predictor of quality (Ashbaugh, 2011).

Quality may be achieved in degrees or levels. In one extensive study (Bernard et al., 2009), the use of multiple learning techniques in a single online course resulted in increased engagement. Bernard et al. (2009)

described how, when an interaction treatment was included in the curricula, outcomes from a collaborative activity had a significant achievement effect ($g+ = .38$) over alternative treatments (see p. 1260, Table 8). The results were interpreted as increasing cognitive engagement and meaning-making, thereby suggesting an exponential increase in quality when more than one condition existed. A parallel may be drawn between the quality produced from a combination of appropriately selected instructional treatments and the effects of compound leadership competencies observed by Zenger and Folkman (2009). The survey-based study (Zenger & Folkman, 2009) on the effectiveness of nearly 25,000 leaders, as perceived by subordinates and peers, was designed to measure leadership on numerous characteristic data points. From an extensive analysis on the results, the researchers drew conclusions on what it takes to not just be a great leader but to be an *extraordinary* leader: when more than one leadership competency was observed in operation at the same time, those leaders were placed in the top 10% of the group. From this combinatorial competency viewpoint, it is conceivable that extraordinary online academic courses will result from both multiple theory-based design elements and a more complete set of ID competencies.

In the larger scheme of designing online academic courses, purposeful activation of the many dimensions of practice for the creation of engaging and quality learning events means having a leadership mindset. It is helpful to visualize the characterization of ID in this way as portrayed in Fig. 3.

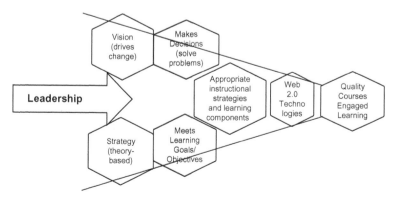

Fig. 3. A Leadership Model: Instructional Design for Web 2.0 Technologies.

DESIGNING FOR WEB 2.0 ENGAGEMENT (AND QUALITY)

The focus of the volume on Web 2.0 technologies this chapter finds itself in is *engagement* in online learning, without which learners may seek education from another source (Nimon, 2007). Engagement has been defined as "the amount of physical and psychological energy that the student devotes to the academic experience" (Astin, 1999[1984], p. 518); the degree to which students value their learning (McInnis, James, & Hartley, 2000); academic challenge, student–faculty interaction, and active and collaborative learning (Kuh, Kinzie, Schuh, & Whitt, 2010); and, "a collaborative learning process in which the instructor and learner are partners in building the knowledge base" (Conrad & Donaldson, 2011, p. vii). In addition to defining engagement for what it *is*, it is also helpful to suggest what it is *not* as in the following examples:

- capturing attention with an initial aesthetic response unaccompanied by sustained interest-building activities (Thompson et al., 2011);
- Internet surfing via web links with little time spent on course subject tasks (Hornik & Thornburg, 2010);
- surface knowledge of or casual use of social sites with little or no meaningful interaction, also known as *lurking*, although lurking can lead to contribution (Muller, 2012); and
- rule-following such as in video game protocols with no opportunity for critical thinking; and a "non-interactive mode that tends to focus on creating an online lecture" which may cause "learner isolation and high dropout rate". (Conrad & Donaldson, 2011, p. 4)

In contrast, Conrad and Donaldson (2011) reported that "engagement is synonymous with active learning, social cognition, constructivism, and problem-based learning" (p. 1) and involves increasing complexity, inserting the unexpected, and introducing new struggles for deep learning to occur (Parrish, 2009).

Designers of online courses, regardless of the affordances prescribed, seek to find those combinations of elements which will result in an engaging and deep learning experience. In other words, although learner engagement and high quality are both required goals and outcomes of a well-designed online course, they are not just happy e-accidents! To specify characteristics for quality and engagement in online course designs, Ashbaugh's (2012a) study group ranked essential instructional strategy

Table 1. Characteristics (Components) of a Quality Online
Course Design.

Characteristic or Learning Component	Definition	Example of Use in Web 2.0
Authentic tasks	Modeling knowledge of concept to solve a real-world problem; strategizing for solutions that have real-world relevance and utility, that provide varying levels of complexity with student control	Online civics course: Conduct a feasibility study on a proposed local water conservation project using a wiki with multiple graphs, graphics, and videos, and submit report to local town council via a website wiki link
Collaboration	Plan, organize, strategize, create in cooperation with others	Cultural issues for online Health course: Plan a multipurpose event in Facebook to bring awareness to the on-going problem of AIDS in the United States as well as raise funds for research
Interaction	Influential actions between two or more entities or persons as in student to student, student to instructor, and student to content	Online math course: Hold a courseroom discussion in Twitter on the implications of using the Pythagorean principle in the construction of a skate board ramp instructor is building; share personal examples of using the principle; solicit ideas from experts
Problem-solving	A process of finding optimal solutions to a given set of variables within a specific domain	Online geography course: Use online GPS mapping to locate a nearly inaccessible tribe and then design a system of transportation to fit the needs and *preferences* of the culture in Second Life®
Critical thinking	An approach to learning that asks questions of the obvious and dogmatic beliefs; higher-order thinking; elevated cognition	Online political science course: Engage in moderated debates through Skype calls on the topic of over-fishing and impact on the environment and small fishing businesses; after students argue opposing positions, explain in a blog how understanding has increased of the other's position

Table 1. (*Continued*)

Characteristic or Learning Component	Definition	Example of Use in Web 2.0
Feedback	Reinforcement of ideas, quality of work, progress in mastery of subject; scaffolding for increase learner control; timely response to learner inquiry, problems	Any course and technology: Qualitative responses to assignments, meaningful grading, personalized evaluations; training and assigning peer mentors; frequent online presence and interactions; instructor responses to email within 24 hours

Table 2.   NSSE Benchmarks for Engagement.

Benchmark	Example
Level of academic challenge	Higher-order thinking, integrative learning, reflective learning, analyzing, synthesizing, making judgments, applying to other or new situations
Active and collaborative learning	Multiple drafts of a paper, collaborative research projects, class presentations, tutored other students, service-learning projects (community)
Student–faculty interaction	Frequent instructor interactions; various types of instructor interactions; instructor feedback; grading turnaround time
Enriching educational experiences	Cultural training and interactions; co-curricular activities; practicum, internship, clinical assignment, other; community service, volunteer work; use of electronic media to complete assignments
Supportive campus environment	Institutional support with social, personal, academic life; quality relationship with students, faculty, admin

Note: Benchmarks cited from findings of the National Survey of Student Engagement (NSSE) 2008 Report.

components – authentic tasks, collaboration, interaction, problem-solving, critical thinking, and feedback. In addition to definitions, examples of each component are provided in Table 1 followed by predictors of engagement described in Tables 2 and 3. Together, the tables and their content, convey a comprehensive collection of the essential ingredients for

Table 3. Descriptions of Learner-Control Conditions for Engagement Components.

Component	Description	Conditions
Learner-centered	Design strategies will afford learners opportunity to construct knowledge and meaning through an individualized perspective	Based on prior knowledge, personal experience Students apply learning to personal context, situation Structured for all learning styles, not specified
Personal knowledge construction	Design structure will afford personalized learning, that knowledge acquired will be individualized by the learner	Student contextualizes within his/her culture (individual worldview offers unique perspective) Student controls how to advance his/her learning Student chooses preferred media for learning

Note: Adapted from Sims and Stork (2007).

gauging the appropriateness of an online affordance typified by Web 2.0 technologies. As presented in the previous section, inclusion of multiple components from the lists in one design signals a leadership approach for ensuring learner engagement.

The study (Ashbaugh, 2012a) additionally relied on five benchmarks of online course quality summarized by the National Survey of Student Engagement (NSSE) 2008 report that stimulated intellectual challenge through ready entrance into collaborative tasks, afforded deeper learning, and increased engagement with technologies (summarized in Table 2).

To extend the meaning of engagement, Table 3 describes the elements Sims and Stork (2007) posited as key components for engagement: a learner-centered design approach which leads to personal knowledge construction.

SECOND LIFE®: A CASE STUDY AND ANALYSIS FOR ONLINE LEARNING

It bears repeating that the enhanced mindset of leadership both tests and predicts the success or failure of proposed technologies, affordances, and strategies based on empirically generated data and personal research. The case (Hornik & Thornburg, 2010) researched and analyzed in the following section demonstrates how an ID interested in leading change will integrate critical analysis in his or her approach to the adoption of Web 2.0 technologies for online education. Nevertheless, in spite of best efforts to support learning objectives with appropriate instructional guides, the use of modern technologies can be ill-fitting and must be evaluated for adoption or abandonment. For example, in a case study of students in an online course with Web 2.0 inclusions, Cifuentes, Alvarez, and Edwards (2011) found a contrast between "surface learning and chaos" from Web 2.0 environments and "deep learning and self-regulation" (Cifuentes et al., 2011, Title, p. 1). Various levels of engagement with design features rested on a balance of cognitive load levels while interacting with multiple representations. The following study of one Web 2.0 technology considered for integration with a learning situation – Second Life® – highlights the importance of making intentional decisions and leading in current theories of how to effectively engage modern learners.

The Study: Second Life® for Really Engaging Accounting

One of the first empirical studies on the effects of engagement in a Second Life® educational setting was conducted by Hornik and Thornburg (2010) on a first-year university accounting course. In addition to other course activities, four assignments were completed in a Second Life® virtual classroom. Students ($n = 106$) answered a post-course survey to determine a relationship between engagement and performance. In addition, level of Internet expertise was measured on a Likert scale of Novice (lowest rating) to Proficient/Developer (highest rating). For a deeper meaning of survey answers, several demographic questions informed the results. The study looked at factors of engagement from a student perspective rather than an instructional one, providing an important lens through which to evaluate learning potential. The researchers (Hornik & Thornburg, 2010) pointed to unique learning challenges for introductory level accounting students in that the terms of accounting are so closely linked to the functions they describe that language and concept must be learned together. The difficulty in achieving good results from traditional pedagogies for teaching accounting in this way was noted in "low retention and high failure rates" (p. 361).

For an authentic experience the "classroom," located on a "plot" of ground called *Really Engaging Accounting*, was arranged in an open manner with areas for viewing lectures, spaces for study groups, and an instructor's office. Chapter lectures were selected by students in any order and in one of three viewing areas to accommodate multiple learners at once. Also available were brief pre-exam reviews, a calendar of due dates, and message boards. Of most importance was provision for interaction with the content, peers, and instructor during "in-world viewing" times. In this mode, interaction with the content took place as concepts assumed the form of avatars. Debits, T-accounts, and the accounting equation are examples of basic accounting concepts that carry their own meaning and functions within the language. The concepts came to life when the students interacted with the avatars using the built-in chat function for an immersive experience. For example, debits and credits would increase and decrease while "explaining" their impact on the accounting equation. In this way, students visualized an accounting process while receiving continual feedback from the accounting model (please see the study for yourself to enjoy a full description and snapshots of the interactions). More advanced concepts were presented in the form of an accounting game in which students would don a debit or credit avatar and "enter" an account model, upon which the accuracy of their placement would be reported back to them by the model.

The Results

In this case of affording a learning activity with Second Life®, several regression models were constructed to display the results of student perceptions of engagement, including one model that revealed a need for spatial presence (being immersed in the content) as a condition of learning. A general summary of the findings showed a positive relationship existed between engagement and better performance, which was demonstrated by improved learning outcomes across the spectrum of participants. However, lower performance on exams was evident in students reporting higher Internet skills; test scores and time on task measurements indicated the group spent less time on course material and more on perfecting computing skills. Another result showed that 15% of participants complained of adverse physical and psychological affects: dizziness, nausea, and eyestrain. That group scored lowest on performance, which was assumed by the researchers to be a result of illness-related lower time on task. In the overall study results, time on task increased with immersion in activity although the positive results were mediated by the adverse effects factor. In addition, a gender factor was noted: females with adverse reactions opted out more quickly than did males with negative reactions.

Analysis

The study results from using Second Life® as a learning platform displayed *collaboration* and *interaction* both with students and the content through mediated forms of avatars and animated objects. *Problem-solving* and *critical thinking* were encouraged during the assignments as questions were asked of the concept avatars, recorded on a virtual whiteboard, and discussed by the learner avatars until a correct display of the concept was confirmed by the concept avatars. Heightened interest in learning increased time on task as well as facilitated understanding of the content. In addition, *feedback* was available when a paging system alerted the students to the presence of the instructor in the connecting virtual office. Analysis of the Second Life® strategy determined that there was a clear alignment between course objectives, activities, and assessment of the outcomes through the learning that was evident in the performance of the tasks accurately and with *authenticity*. Further, the outcomes of engagement were clear in expressions of *learner control* and *satisfaction* recorded in the terminal course survey, except for those that experienced negative effects from the 3-D graphical interface.

A Comparison Study

In contrast to the Hornik and Thornburg (2010) results from an activity within Second Life®, another study (Gunter, 2011) found students uninterested in using the virtual space for learning. Gunter (2011) looked for associations between variables in various strategies for engagement utilized in the online component of a 4-year university mega-sized hybrid accounting class. The trend toward upsizing classes, particularly online courses, presents an instructional strategy problem of engagement and is the focus of current research for effective solutions. In the Gunter study streaming lectures, screen-captured lectures, a discussion tool, Twitter, and Second Life® were each measured for level of participation (attendance) and learning effectiveness. In terms of effectiveness, Second Life® showed no increase in engagement; rather, the majority surveyed considered it a hindrance to learning. This was not surprising considering attendance in the venue scored in the lower quartile; ostensibly, one must be present to experience engagement. Hornik and Thornburg (2010) found that "a necessary condition for engagement in these new virtual environments is the need for students to have a sense of actually being a part of and immersed in the created content" (p. 374). Additionally, disengagement was evident in that only 12% reported a teaching presence in the venue. Instructor presence has been strongly linked to student engagement (Garrison, Anderson, & Archer, 1999) and is expected of a lecture assignment.

Other factors for low engagement included the potential of redundancy. In addition to the virtual lecture, there were two other required lecture-based learning options (video-streamed and screen-captured presentations) which together may have over-loaded the students' tolerance to engage in yet another lecture. Second, although there was a measure of creativity exhibited in accessing and using the space, the minimal tasks of creating an avatar and finding their way to the virtual class could not be considered a fully authentic learning experience. Third, there was very little learner control, with choices related only to attendance and avatar control. Clearly, the sum of engaging learning predictors was minimal and explained the students' ratings of dissatisfaction with the technology. This case epitomizes the potential benefit of an ID's involvement and leadership in envisioning and designing an engaging pedagogical affordance from a place of expertise.

A Second Comparison

A design experience from the chapter author's own portfolio illustrates how an ID appropriately employed a Web 2.0 technology for an authentic task activity in Second Life®. At the time the course was created, several years before this writing, the decision to use the 3-D MUVE as an educational venue was not made lightly as the website appeared to be an extension of video gaming, and was not known for its learning value. Nevertheless, the idea gained favor after conducting research on the technology as well as personal experimentation with its functions. During the exploration process, Second Life® appeared to be a potential powerful learning tool. Ultimately, the level of learning it might deliver would be determined by the design's affordance for engagement culminating in learner growth and satisfaction.

For the activity, students in a history class were required to reconstruct an ancient civilization, including its geography, culture, daily activities, and military actions; and, to use the virtual world environment to create relevant objects, animations, and language. To conceptualize the socio-cultural aspects of the virtual world, the learners were required to generate avatars, acquire and develop property, and script actual events such as a major battle.

To achieve an accurate representation, the learners conducted research outside of Second Life® and, subsequently, applied the personally discovered facts to the civilization under construction. Forming small groups, students allocated tasks to facilitate completion by the assignment due date. Although individual assessment was based on each student's knowledge and contribution of facts to the site activity, a group grade was issued for authenticity of the people and culture, including a war with accurate outcomes.

As a result of the exercise, the learning objectives were achieved while engaging the students at multiple points. Moreover, the activity *became* the assessment eliminating a need for tests. Learning outcomes included decision-making, predictions of cause and effect (Bruner, 1957/1973), personal knowledge construction through research, strategizing as a group for intended outcomes, and management of team dynamics. In hindsight, the minimal barriers to the project included a significant time investment by the instructor to learn, implement, and manage the venue as well as to assist students not familiar with the technology. In addition, costs for the students to purchase "territory" proved to be a strain on student budgets.

The case study and examples given support the notion that richness of learning comes through the engagement predictors of self-regulation, learner control, personal knowledge construction, interaction, collaboration, accountability, peer learning, and instructor feedback. These learning components were evident in the Hornik and Thornburg (2010) study as well as in the author's example. Conversely, the use of an emerging technology in the Gunter (2011) study was neither quality-driven nor engaging, suggesting a failure in the course design. However, it is conceivable that the same course could be reenvisioned with a strategic design change by an ID with a leadership mindset. For a snapshot of the learning for engagement components and the barriers identified in the case study, please see Table 4.

IMPLICATIONS OF ID LEADERSHIP FOR WEB 2.0 ADOPTION

Implications from this discussion inform the ID field of the educational impact of Web 2.0, while they urge IDs to respond and to lead in appropriating engaging learning events. While the utility exists in Second Life® to offer content in the traditional online courseroom manner with PowerPoint slides, video lectures, and testing; leadership resists doing the traditional (Ashbaugh, 2012b; Naidu, 2003) and envisions a better solution while embracing change (Campbell et al., 2009) for quality and depth of

Table 4. Table of Learning Components for and Barriers to Engagement Second Life® Activity.

	Studies of Second Life® for Course Activity		
	Hornik and Thornburg (2010)	Gunter (2011)	Author example
Learning components for engagement			
Authentic task	Yes	No	Yes
Collaboration	Yes	No	No
Interaction	Yes	Unknown	Yes
Problem-solving	Yes	No	Yes
Critical thinking	Yes	Unknown	Yes
Feedback	Yes	Unknown	Yes
Learner-control	Yes	Minimal	Yes
Personal knowledge constr	Yes	No	Yes
Barriers to engagement			
	Distracted students	Lack of student interest	Student lack of familiarity with technology
	Physical/psychological effects: dizziness, nausea, headaches	Lack of teacher presence	Significant instructor time investment
	Opting out early from negative effects	Lack of learner control once in the venue	Cost of buying territory
		Redundancy of learning technique	
		Complexity level of task	

learning (Parrish, 2009). In this way, leadership extends the role of IDs toward guiding the adoption of Web 2.0 tools for online learning. However, there are multiple barriers to overcome when design practices are layered with leadership competencies and approaches.

Overcoming Barriers from the Case Study

Vision and Change Issues
The most glaring barriers to engagement in the Hornik and Thornburg (2010) study stemmed from a lack of provision by the course designer for the negative cognitive and psychological effects on students from a digital

screen, resulting in several who opted out of the study early. With a more visionary approach, it is expected a change in the initial design would have produced different results. Concern for a learner's well-being is centered in the ID's intentional decisions based on knowledge and with a moral obligation to envision both the positive and the negative outcomes of an instructional strategy (IBSTPI, 2010). For example, an experienced ID may have included instructions for students to minimize avatar movement or reduce the level of color contrast in the event of ill effects. With acknowledgment that best efforts often fail to predict the symptoms described in the study, it is the duty of an ID to review the most current literature, to look ahead for potential harmful outcomes, and to make exemplary decisions for a better design at the outset.

Strategy Issues
Although not a formal study, the author's example of prescribing Second Life® revealed barriers from using the site as a pedagogy in terms of functions and features. Students lacked familiarity with the technology and significant time was invested by the instructor during initial setup and design of the activity. Additionally, buying territory (server space) is not virtual but costs the users real dollars. More recently, institutions have found ways to buy up territory so that students need only to "borrow" the space for class projects. To prevent a barrier of access to his students, Brad Hokanson uses this method in his University of Wisconsin design courses to allow inexpensive creation of projects in Second Life® (Fraase, 2008). An ID could prescribe a solution within the design that would obligate the institution to make budgetary provision for the technology thereby ensuring a more appropriate and strategic use of the technology.

A learning barrier was found in Gunter's (2011) study in the form of an underutilization of Second Life®, suggesting poor quality in the underpinning instructional strategy. The instructor-designed course failed to engage the students in nearly every way resulting in low interest (attendance). Assumptions for the disengagement include a lack of applied learning theories that would gain and keep attention (Keller, 2010). Keller (2010) stressed that a lack of attention may be resolved by "developing motivational strategies that are directly related to the cause of the motivational problem" (p. 2). For example, antidotes for lack of attendance could be similar to those applied in a traditional classroom: engaging, tantalizing learning opportunities. Lester and Perini (2010) suggested faculty often attempt to integrate new technologies yet fail to include tasks for collaborative and active learning. In Gunter's (2011) study low complexity level task was observed – truly, mere attendance of a virtual lecture requires very little problem-solving or critical thinking.

Environmental Issues

Another misstep in Gunter's (2011) study appeared in the lack of user control once a student entered the venue from very few options to engage with the environment. In contrast, the Hornik and Thornburg (2010) design overcame the barrier by bringing the concepts to "life" and allowing the students to manipulate the learning adventure through vicarious interaction with the concepts. In the Gunter experiment, redundancy of activities was apparent in that the lectures were offered in three different ways: face-to-face, by video in the classroom or online, and in the Second Life® option. Learners were not offered interaction or feedback in any of the venues, which might have been tolerable for one lecture but possibly not for three. Additionally, there was a perceived lack of teacher presence in the virtual classroom reported widely to be a factor in low engagement.

To offer a caveat, presence was hindered by a lack of familiarity by students and faculty with the social sites. Intuitively, to prevent strategy failure, designers and designer/instructors would do well to become very familiar with the technology in order to provide a rich alternate universe for learning. Addressing the problem of inexperienced users and instructors, Rod Humble, CEO of Linden Labs (creator of Second Life®), recently implemented changes to make access and manipulations more user-friendly (Dutton, 2012). As an outcome of the upgrade, the company has seen a 40% increase in Second Life® users since early 2011. From an ID perspective, Lester and Perini (2010) offered an antidote to lack of instructor expertise: designers should provide instructor training within the context of the course.

In keeping with the focus of this chapter, ID involvement was implicated by Lester and Perini (2010) for ensuring appropriateness of Web 2.0 affordances for learning. This author agrees with the researchers and urges leadership from design professionals to overcome design issue barriers for both instructors and learners through visionary and strategic decisions.

Overcoming Other Barriers

Rapid Changes

It is important to consider the flexibility a designer must embrace for creating designs with pedagogies that will engage a modern learner who is *virtually* connected *virtually* all the time. On the one hand, the advances in technology grant an outlet for expression and reciprocity, as in the case of social networking venues; while on the other hand, the user is exposed to a barrage of alluring choices for accessing even more digital dalliances (Magolda & Platt, 2009). This is not to say a rich inventory of knowledge building and usefulness is not available through social networking; rather, the delivery format avails a potential learner to an endless periphery of non-learning selections, which burdens the ID to invent competing alternatives. Lester and Perini (2010) remarked that adoption of Web 2.0 technologies, with hopes of engagement, requires comprehending the shifting habits of student use and "adapting to the changes before they become superseded by future innovations" (p. 75). This is what compounds the dilemma of designing for emerging digital technologies and learning places that Siemens (2004) called "nebulous environments of shifting core elements" (Connectivism section).

In order to keep pace with the rapid changes of technology, IDs need to ask good questions. For example, will the design strategies be outdated, or abandoned, before the course is ready for implementation?

Competing Research

It has been established in this chapter that appropriately prescribed pedagogies are not just happy e-accidents, but are intentionally designed with best practices for learning and are grounded in current theories. However, the issues presented also reminded IDs of the complexity of interweaving instructional theories and learning theories, including those from cognitive science. For example, recent empirical studies continue to demonstrate the wisdom of integrating evidence of impact on cognition – through measurements of cognitive load levels, learning efficiency, cognitive flexibility, shared cognition, nonconscious learning, and limitations of cognitive processes (Cifuentes et al., 2011; Clark, 2010; de Jong, 2010; Holzinger et al., 2009). In one study of Web 2.0 for online courses, quality instruction of design was linked by Cifuentes et al. (2011) to a pedagogical ability to balance cognitive load through cognitive flexibility in the type and variety of tools used. This leads to the implication that an ID will overcome the potential failures of Web 2.0 affordances for creating quality online courses when he or she not only begins a project with theory-based decisions but also makes continual strategic decisions.

Poor Decisions

To advocate the adoption of new technologies for learning, IDs need to avoid making poor decisions. Theory-backed decisions persuade others of the ID's professionalism and judgment (Yanchar et al., 2010). Further, Ching and Hsu (2011) stated that "Web 2.0 practices will not simply 'happen' if there is no deliberate design of the learning and assessment to enable the practices" (p. 784). It is has been posited in this chapter that decisions by IDs have consequences for the quality of online pedagogies. Examples from recent studies contained many implications for IDs to reflect on and consider before selecting what may be appropriate in an online course; although, the feat poses a formidable scenario for what Hannafin, Hannafin, and Gabbitas (2009) considered an unpredictable environment.

Unpredictability brings an element of chaos from which a flurry of ideas and activity create new things on a whim that may look promising on the surface. However, a design leader will not get caught up with fads, but will examine the evidence for educational viability in specific situations and will choose strategies for engaging and satisfying experiences. Consequently, leading in a movement that will blend Web 2.0 technologies with learning, means that an ID will ensure that the prescribed technologies and methods are weighted for value to the intended learning event during the design process. Technologies will change, which means enduring principles of design must prevail to guarantee the alignment of potential pedagogies to evidence-based predictors of effective and engaging learning. Magolda and Platt (2009) offered advice to IDs on when to use strategies for learning, to resist jumping to use the latest discovery, and to spend time in reflection. The authors articulated an important consideration, "The hype of moving to a learning paradigm in which students define and control their own learning is just that – hype – without a commensurate pedagogical and philosophical change" (p. 15). In the same vein, Holzinger et al. (2009) stressed the criticality of interpolating "pedagogical and psychological expertise into the design and development of educational software" (p. 292) implying good ID decisions are good for the learners.

Privacy Issues
A reminder from Lester and Perini (2010) alerts the ID that some learners will be reluctant to integrate school-related interactions with places reserved for nonschool socialization. An ID is cautioned not to assume students will engage with an activity of social sharing, rather to integrate overt efforts to provide privacy, security, and non-recrimination for what is expressed. Course developers could include steps to add a layer of separation between personal and school conversations by integrating social networking into the LMS.

Finances and Value

Finally, whether for a large or small institution, a radical change in course structures will have an impact on program budgets. Through the lens of a cost/benefit study of Web 2.0 inclusions, Osimo (2008) suggested caution in adoption without a complete evaluation of the holistic value,

> One of the most common mistakes, typical of a hyped technology such as web 2.0 now, is considering that adding wiki, blogs and social networking features on a website is sufficient to achieve the goals of user involvement and contribution ... One of the great advantages of web 2.0 is that it lowers the cost of errors, as very little investment is needed to launch a collaboration. However, simply adopting the technologies, without embracing the value, will have little or negative impact. (p. 47)

In addition, it is important to analyze the volatility of a technology. For example, Facebook, Twitter, and Second Life® are all examples of for-profit entities with unknown futures. This was apparent when Facebook's recent IPO (initial public offering) fell flat (Laird, 2012). Moreover, a study showed one-third of users are spending less time on site (Murphy, 2012) while one analyst predicted Facebook's demise by 2020 (Pan, 2012). An ID decision to include a Web 2.0 affordance in an online course might then include a more sustainable option, such as a wiki. The complexity of issues for design practice is clear and yet, in the embryonic stages of Web 2.0, design possibilities only increase as IDs lead in the effort to overcome these and other barriers.

Future Research

Given the speed at which social technologies are advancing, the need for increased research in the area of social learning strategies is urgent. First, a voice of caution on the ethics of the alteration of contemporary society through group sharing seems worth entertaining for its significance to group work in Web 2.0 technologies. Jaron Lanier is a computer scientist and considered an early visionary of the web and its potential for changing the world. However, the book he has written (Lanier, 2010) amounts to a clarion call for supporters of social media and its value to the global citizenry. While an advocate of global collaboration and knowledge building, he voiced concerns about the effects of social media on the individuality and creativity it may in fact stifle. In concern was for a common social dynamic observed in the jockeying for position by a stronger participant in the group. The outcome of vying for dominance is seen when the weaker member in an effort to maintain equilibrium and acceptance by the group eventually acquiesces. Analogous to a physical community in search of commonality and goal-sharing, rather than building on ideas, the effect of power struggles can be compromise, relinquishment of original thoughts, groupthink, and bullying.

Echoing Lanier's (2010) apprehensions, we do not yet know at what level sharing is beneficial or when it is a barrier to human potential to fully grasp the physical and psychological effects of motion, vicarious experiences, or differentiation in personal and public spaces for a broad spectrum of learners. To limit distractions for learners when online, theories on cognitive, psychological, and physical impact of human–machine interactions need to be more fully evaluated. Action research by instructors of online courses with Web 2.0 learning activities needs to be undertaken on a wide scale to build data sets from which to draw accurate ethical conclusions.

In addition, more design research studies are needed on how enhanced leadership competencies for ID will bring about the changes critical to ensure learner engagement, in terms of what is lacking in skillsets for quality daily practices. Other studies may look at the graduate programs for ID candidates for voids in leadership training with conclusions that suggest ways of incorporating this critical perspective into the curricula. The beneficiaries of educational research, the learners, will be well-served as efforts to look into these and more concerns for Web 2.0 adoption increase.

CONCLUSION

After reflecting on the current ethos of education, it is the position of this author that leadership thinking is required for the kind of design decisions that will link instructional strategies to the type and level of engagement that will ensure depth of learning, especially with emerging Web 2.0 technologies for online education. An experienced researcher with a futures perspective on education articulated a goal of modern ID: "A well-designed learning experience, like an accurate map, does not detract from the learning journey nor does it necessarily dictate the final destination" (Salmon, 2009, p. 535). Consequently, an ID is capable of adding value to online course quality when she matches design decision with the realities of modern learners who are immersed in Web 2.0 websites and who demand more control over their learning journey. Through this lens, designers are urged to rethink the powerful influence they hold for driving a modern phenomenon and the pedagogical value of social knowledge construction. Adoption by the institution, instructor, and learner is the goal, therefore it is suggested that ID practice be reenvisioned and reconceptualized as a way of thinking and acting in social learning design practice.

REFERENCES

Allen, A. I., & Seaman, J. (2012). *Going the distance: Online education in the United States, 2011.* Sloan-C. Retrieved from http://www.onlinelearningsurvey.com/reports/going thedistance.pdf

Ashbaugh, M. L. (2011). Use of a modified QM rubric to validate qualitative research. Paper presented at the Quality Matters 2011 Conference, November 8, Baltimore, MD. Retrieved from http://www.DrMLAshbaugh.com

Ashbaugh, M. L. (2012a). *Online pedagogical quality questioned: Probing instructional designers' perceptions of leadership competencies critical to practice.* Doctoral dissertation, Capella University, Minneapolis, MN. Retrieved from http://gradworks.umi.com/3460621.pdf

Ashbaugh, M. L. (2012b). Conceptualizing instructional design processes through leadership competencies and modeling. Paper presented at the AECT July 2012 Research Symposium, Louisville, KY. (To be published by Springer in 2013).

Association of Educational Communications and Technology (AECT). (2012, July). Newly adopted AECT standards. *News Flash*!, pp. 9–12. Retrieved from http://aect.site-ym. com/resource/resmgr/Newsletters/Current.pdf

Astin, A. W. (1999[1984]). Student involvement: A developmental theory for higher education. *Journal of College Student Personnel, 40*(5), 518–529. Retrieved from http://psycnet.apa.org/psycinfo/1999-01418-006

Barab, S. A., & Roth, W. M. (2006). Curriculum-based ecosystems: Supporting knowing from an ecological perspective. *Educational Researcher, 35*(5), 3–13. doi:10.3102/0013189X035005003

Beabout, B., & Carr-Chellman, A. A. (2008). Change agentry. In J. M. Spector, M. D. Merrill, J. van Merriënboer & M. P. Driscoll (Eds.), *Handbook of research on educational communications and technology* (3rd ed., pp. 619–632). New York, NY: Erlbaum.

Beaudoin, M. F. (2007). Distance education leadership: An appraisal of research and practice. In M. G. Moore (Ed.), *Handbook of distance education* (2nd ed., pp. 391–402). Mahwah, NJ: Erlbaum.

Bennet, S. (2012). *The numbers just keep on getting bigger: Social media and the Internet 2011 [Statistics].* Retrieved from http://www.mediabistro.com/alltwitter/social-media-Internet-2011_b17881

Bernard, R. M., Abrami, P. C., Borokhovski, E., Wade, C. A., Tamin, R. M., Surkes, M. A., & Bethel, E. C. (2009). A meta-analysis of three types of interaction treatments in distance education. *Review of Educational Research, 79*(3), 1243–1289. doi:10.3102/0034654309333844

Brown, J. S., Collins, A., & Duguid, P. (1989). Situated cognition and the culture of learning. *Educational Researcher, 18*(1), 32–42. doi:10.3102/0013189X018001032

Bruner, J. S. (1957/1973). Going beyond the information given. In J. M. Anglin (Ed.), *Beyond the information given: Studies in the psychology of knowing* (pp. 218–238). New York, NY: Norton.

Bruner, J. S. (1986). *Actual minds, possible worlds*. Cambridge, MA: Harvard University Press.

Cain, J., & Fox, B. I. (2009). Web 2.0 and pharmacy education. *American Journal of Pharmaceutical Education, 73*(7), 120. Retrieved from http://www.ncbi.nlm.nih.gov/pmc/articles/PMC2779632/#B48

Campbell, K., Schwier, R., & Kenny, R. (2005). Agency of the instructional designer: Moral coherence and transformative social practice. *Australasian Journal of Educational Technology, 21*(2), 242–262.

Campbell, K., Schwier, R., & Kenny, R. (2009). The critical, relational practice of instructional design in higher education: an emerging model of change agency. *Educational Technology, Research & Development, 57*(5), 645–663. doi:10.1007/s11423-007-9061-6

Chi, M. T. H., Glaser, R., & Rees, E. (1982). Expertise in problem solving. In R. Sternberg (Ed.), *Advances in the psychology of human intelligence* (Vol. 1, pp. 7–76). Hillsdale, NJ: Erlbaum.

Ching, Y-H., & Hsu, Y-C. (2011). Design-grounded assessment: A framework and a case study of Web 2.0 practices in higher education. *Australasian Journal of Educational Technology, 27*(5), 781–797. Retrieved from http://www.ascilite.org.au/ajet/ajet27/ching.html

Cifuentes, L., Alvarez, O., & Edwards, J. C. (2011). Learning in web 2.0 environments: Surface learning and chaos or deep learning and self-regulation? *The Quarterly Review of Distance Education, 12*(1), 1–21. Retrieved from http://www.mendeley.com/research/learning-web-20-environments-surface-learning-chaos-deep-learning-selfregulation/

Clark, R. E. (2010). Cognitive and neuroscience research on learning and instruction: Recent insights about the impact of non-conscious knowledge on problem solving, higher order thinking skills and interactive cyber-learning environments. Paper presented at the 11th International Conference on Education Research (ICER), New Educational Paradigm for Learning and Instruction, Seoul, South Korea. Retrieved from http://www.aect.org/publications/whitepapers/2010/ICER3.pdf

Conrad, R-M., & Donaldson, A. (2011). *Engaging the online learner: Activities and resources for creative instruction*. San Francisco, CA: Jossey-Bass.

Cunningham, D. J. (1992). Beyond educational psychology: Steps toward an educational semiotic. *Educational Psychology Review, 4*(2), 165–194. Retrieved from http://www.springerlink.com/content/1040-726x/4/2/

Daniels, P. (2009). Course management systems and implications for practice. *International Journal of Emerging Technologies and Societies, 7*(2), 97–108. Retrieved from http://www.online-journals.org/i-jet

de Jong, T. (2010). Cognitive load theory, educational research, and instructional design: Some food for thought. *Instructional Science, 38*, 105–134.

Der-Thanq, C., Hung, D., & Wang, Y. (2007). Educational design as a quest for congruence: The need for alternative learning design tools. *British Journal of Educational Technology, 38*(5), 876–884. doi:10.1111/j.1467-8535.2006.00675.x

Dooley, K., Lindner, J., Telg, R., Irani, T., Moore, L., & Lundy, L. (2007). Roadmap to measuring distance education instructional design competency. *Quarterly Review of Distance Education, 8*(2), 151–159. Retrieved from http://www.infoagepub.com/index.php?id=89&i=4

Dunlap, J. C., Sobel, D., & Sands, D. I. (2007). Supporting students' cognitive processing in online courses: Designing for deep and meaningful student-to-content interactions. *TechTrends, 51*(4), 20–31. doi:10.1007/s11528-007-0052-6

Dutton, F. (2012, March 15). Pioneering MMO Second Life plots a comeback. *Eurogamer.net*. Retrieved from http://www.eurogamer.net/articles/2012-03-15-pioneering-mmo-second-life-plots-a-comeback

Faust, G. W. (1977). Selecting instructional strategies or once you've got an objective, what do you do with it? *Journal of Instructional Development, 1*(1), 18–22. Retrieved from http://www.aect.org/Publications/JID_Collection/A1_V1_N1/18_Faust.PDF

Fraase, M. (2008, Spring). *Creating with digital tools in the interactive media curriculum*. Retrieved from http://www.design.umn.edu/about/news/emerging/spring_2008/hokanson.html

Fullan, M. (2001). *Leading in a culture of change*. San Francisco, CA: Jossey-Bass.

Fullan, M., & Scott, G. (2009). *Turnaround leadership for higher education*. San Francisco, CA: Jossey-Bass.

Gallien, T., & Oomen-Early, J. (2008). Personalized versus collective instructor feedback in the online classroom: Does type of feedback affect student satisfaction, academic performance and perceived connectedness with the instructor? *International Journal on E-Learning, 7*(3), 463–476. Retrieved from http://www.editlib.org/p/23582

Garrison, D. R., Anderson, T., & Archer, W. (1999). Critical inquiry in a text-based environment: Computer conferencing in higher education. *Internet and Higher Education, 2*(2–3), 87–105. Retrieved from http://tccl.rit.albany.edu/knilt/images/9/90/Unit_1-a.pdf

Greenleaf, G. (1977). *Servant leadership: A journey into the nature of legitimate power and greatness/essays by Robert K. Greenleaf*. Mahwah, NJ: Paulist Press.

Gunter, G. (2011). Effective online tools for creating social presence in large online classes. Paper presented at the 2011 AECT International Convention, Jacksonville, FL.

Hall, B. (2010). Interaction is insufficient: Why we need intersubjectivity in course room discourse. *Journal of eLearning and Online Teaching, 12*(1). Retrieved from http://www.theelearninginstitute.org/journal_pdf/JeOT%20-%20Interaction%20is%20Insufficient%20-%20Why%20We%20Need%20Intersubjectivity%20in%20Course%20Room%20Discourse.pdf

Hannafin, M., Hannafin, K., & Gabbitas, B. (2009). Re-examining cognition during student-centered web-based learning. *Educational Technology, Research and Development, 57*(2), 767–785.

Holzinger, A., Kickmeier-Rush, M. D., Wassertheurer, S., & Hessinger, M. (2009). Learning performance with interactive simulations in medical education: Lessons learned from results of learning complex physiological models with the HAEMOdynamics SIMulator. *Computers and Education, 52*(2), 292–301. doi:10.1016/j.compedu.2008.08.008

Hornik, S., & Thornburg, S. (2010). Really engaging accounting: Second Life™ as a learning platform. *Issues in Accounting Education, 25*(3), 361–378. doi:10.2308/iace.2010.25.3.361

Howard, A., & Wellins, R. S. (2008). Global leadership forecast 2008–2009: Overcoming the shortfalls in developing leaders. Retrieved from http://www.ddiworld.com/pdf/global leadershipforecast2008-2009_globalreport_ddi.pdf

International Board of Standards for Training, Performance and Instruction (IBSTPI). (2000). Instructional design competencies report. *ibstpi*. Retrieved from http://www.ibstpi.org/downloads/InstructionalDesignCompetencies.pdf

International Board of Standards for Training, Performance and Instruction (IBSTPI). (2010). Code of ethical standards. *ibstpi*. Retrieved from http://www.ibstpi.org/Competencies/codesofethicalstandards.htm

Jha, A. K. (2012). Epistemological and pedagogical concerns of constructionism: Relating to the educational practices of creative education. *Creative Education, 3*(2), 171–178. doi:10.4236/ce.2012.32027

Jonassen, D. H. (1991). Objectivism versus constructivism: Do we need a new philosophical paradigm? *Journal of Educational Technology, Research and Development, 39*(3), 5–14. doi:10.1007/BF02296434

Jonassen, D. H. (2011). *Learning to solve problems: A handbook for designing problem-solving learning environments.* New York, NY: Routledge.

Jonassen, D. H., Davidson, M., Collins, M., Campbell, J., & Haag, B. B. (1995). Constructivism and computer-mediated communication in distance education. *American Journal of Education, 9*(2), 7–26. doi:10.1080/08923649509526885

Katz, R. (1955). Skills of an effective administrator. *Harvard Business Review, 33*(1), 33–42.

Keller, J. M. (2010). Challenges in learner motivation: A holistic, integrative model for research and design on learner motivation. In *The 11th international conference on education research new educational paradigm for learning and instruction* (pp. 1–18). Retrieved from http://www.aect.org/publications/whitepapers/2010/ICER4.pdf

Kouzes, J. M., & Posner, B. Z. (2007). *The leadership challenge* (4th ed.). San Francisco, CA: Wiley.

Kowch, E. (2009). New capabilities for cyber charter school leadership: An emerging imperative for integrating educational technology and educational leadership knowledge. *TechTrends, 53*(4), 41–48.

Kubicek, J. (2011). *Leadership is dead: How influence is reviving it.* New York, NY: Howard Books.

Kuh, G. D., Kinzie, J., Schuh, J. H., & Whitt, E. J. (2010). *Documenting effective educational practice (DEEP)* (pp. 10–17). *Student success in college: Creating conditions that matter.* San Francisco, CA: Jossey-Bass.

Laird, S. (2012, June 5). Facebook will disappear by 2020, says analyst. *Mashable.* Retrieved from http://mashable.com/2012/06/04/analyst-facebook-disappear/

Landsberger, J. (2009). Learning by design: An interview with Brad Hokanson. *TechTrends, 53*(2), 22–27. doi:10.1007/s11528-009-0263-0

Lang, K., & Lang, G. (1961). *Collective dynamics.* New York, NY: Crowell.

Lanier, J. (2010). *You are not a gadget: A manifesto.* New York, NY: Alfred A. Knopf (Random House).

Lester, J., & Perini, M. (2010). Potential of social networking sites for distance education student engagement. *New Directions for Community Colleges, 2010*(150), 67–77. doi:10.1002/cc.406

Magolda, P. M., & Platt, G. J. (2009). Untangling Web 2.0's influences on student learning. *About Campus, 14*(3), 10–16. doi:10.1002/abc.290

Masterman, E., Jameson, J., & Walker, S. (2009). Capturing teachers' experience of learning design through case studies. *Distance Education, 30*(2), 223–238. doi:10.1080/01587910903023207

McInnis, C., James, R., & Hartley, R. (2000). *Trends in the first year experience.* Canberra, Australia: DETYA Higher Education Division. Retrieved from http://hdl.voced.edu.au/10707/18781

Merrill, M. D. (1999). Instructional design based on knowledge objects. In C. M. Reigeluth (Ed.), *Instructional design theories and models: A new paradigm of instructional theory* (Vol. II, pp. 397–424). Mahwah, NJ: Erlbaum.

Moody, G. (2002). *Rebel code: Linux and the open source revolution.* New York, NY: Basic Books.

Moore, M. G. (1989). Editorial: Three types of interaction. *American Journal of Distance Education, 3*(2), 1–7. Retrieved from http://www.tandfonline.com/toc/hajd20/3/2

Muller, M. (2012). Lurking as personal trait or situational disposition? Lurking and contributing in enterprise social media. In *CSCW'12 proceedings of the ACM 2012 conference on computer supported cooperative work*, ACM, New York, NY (pp. 253–256). doi:10.1145/2145204.2145245

Murphy, S. (2012, June 6). Facebook engagement dips: 34% spend less time on site. *Mashable*. Retrieved from http://mashable.com/2012/06/05/facebook-engagement/

Naidu, S. (2003). Designing instruction for e-learning environments. In M. G. Moore & W. G. Anderson (Eds.), *Handbook of distance education* (pp. 349–365). Mahwah, NJ: Erlbaum.

Naidu, S. (2007). Instructional designs for optimal learning. In M. G. Moore (Ed.), *Handbook of distance education* (2nd ed., pp. 247–258). Mahwah, NJ: Erlbaum.

National Survey of Student Engagement (2008). *Promoting engagement for all students: The imperative to look within – 2008 results*. Indiana University Center for Postsecondary Research. Retrieved from http://nsse.iub.edu/NSSE_2008_Results

Nimon, S. (2007). Generation Y and higher education: The other Y2K. *Journal of Institutional Research*, *13*(1), 24–41. Retrieved from http://www.aair.org.au/2006Papers/Nimon.pdf

O'Reilly, T. (2005, September 30). What is Web 2.0? *The O'Reilly Network*. Retrieved from http://oreilly.com/web2/archive/what-is-web-20.html

Osimo, D. (2008). *Web 2.0 in government: Why and how?* JRC Scientific and Technical Reports. EUR – Scientific and Technical Research series. Retrieved from http://ftp.jrc.es/EURdoc/JRC45269.pdf

Ostlund, B. (2008). Prerequisites for interactive learning in distance education: Perspectives from Swedish students. *Australasian Journal of Educational Technology*, *24*(1), 42–56. Retrieved from http://www.ascilite.org.au/ajet

Pan, J. (2012, June 16). Facebook blames Nasdaq errors for its weak market debut. *Mashable*. Retrieved from http://mashable.com//2012/06/16/facebook-ipo-lawsuits/

Parrish, P. (2009). Aesthetic principles for instructional design. *Educational Technology Research & Development*, *57*(4), 511–528. doi:10.1007/s11423-007-9060-7

Quality Matters Project: Rubric for online and hybrid courses. (2006). Retrieved from http://www.qualitymatters.org/Rubric.htm

Reeves, T. C., Herrington, J., & Oliver, R. (2004). A development research agenda for online collaborative learning. *Educational Technology, Research & Development*, *52*(4), 53–65.

Reigeluth, C. M. (Ed.). (1983). *Instructional design theories and models: An overview of their current status*. New York, NY: Routledge.

Reigeluth, C. M., Watson, W. R., Watson, S. L., Dutta, P., Zengguan, C., & Powell, N. (2008). Roles for technology in the information-age paradigm of education: Learning management systems. *Educational Technology*, *48*(6), 32–40. Retrieved from http://cardinalscholar.bsu.edu/bitstream/123456789/194511/1/LMS.pdf

Richey, R. C., Fields, D. C., & Foxon, M. (2001). *Instructional design competencies: The standards* (3rd ed.). Syracuse, NY: Eric.

Richey, R. C., Klein, J. D., & Tracey, M. (2011). *The instructional design knowledge base: Theory, research, and practice*. New York, NY: Routledge.

Sackney, L., & Mergel, B. (2007). Contemporary learning theories, instructional design and leadership. In J. M. Burger, C. Webber & P. Klinck (Eds.), *Intelligent leadership* (Vol. 11, pp. 67–98). New York, NY: Springer. doi:10.1007/978-1-4020-6022-9_5

Salmon, G. (2009). The future for (second) life and learning. *British Journal of Educational Technology*, *40*(3), 526–538. doi:10.1111/j.1467-8535.2009.00967.x

Scardamalia, M., & Bereiter, C. (1994). Computer support for knowledge building communities. *Journal of the Learning Sciences, 3*(3), 265–283. doi:10.1207/s15327809jls0303_3

Scott, G., Coates, H., & Anderson, M. (2008). *Learning leaders in times of change: Academic leadership capabilities for Australian higher education.* University of Western Sydney and Australian Council for Educational Research. Retrieved from http://research.acer.edu.au/

Sergiovanni, T. (2003). A cognitive approach to leadership. In B. Davies & J. West-Burham (Eds.), *Handbook of educational leadership and management* (pp. 12–16). New York, NY: Pearson/Longman.

Sergiovanni, T., & Corbally, J. E. (1984). Leadership and excellence in schooling. *Educational Leadership, 41*(5), 4–13. Retrieved from http://www.sagepub.com/upm-data/11217_Serg__Article_1.pdf

Siemens, G. (2004, December 12). *Connectivism: A learning theory for the digital age.* Retrieved from http://www.elearnspace.org/Articles/connectivism.htm

Sims, R. C. (2003). Promises of interactivity: Aligning learner perceptions and expectations with strategies for flexible and online learning. *Distance Education, 24*(1), 87–101. doi:10.1080/01587910303050

Sims, R. C. (2012). Reappraising design practice. In D. Holt, S. Segrave & J. Cybulski (Eds.), *Professional education using e-simulations: Benefits of blended learning design* (pp. 25–40). Hershey, PA: Business Science Reference. doi:10.4018/978-1-61350-189-4

Sims, R. C., & Koszalka, T. A. (2008). Competencies for the new-age instructional designer. In J. M. Spector, M. D. Merrill, J. van Merriënboer & M. P. Driscoll (Eds.), *Handbook of research on educational communications and technology* (3rd ed.). New York, NY: Erlbaum.

Sims, R. C., & Stork, E. (2007). Design for contextual learning: Web-based environments that engage diverse learners. In J. Richardson & A. Ellis (Eds.), *Proceedings of AusWeb07,* Southern Cross University, Lismore, NSW. Retrieved from http://ausweb.scu.edu.au/aw07/papers/refereed/sims/index.html

Smith, P. L., & Ragan, T. J. (1999). *Instructional design* (2nd ed.). New York, NY: Wiley.

Stahl, G. (2004). Building collaborative knowing: Elements of a social theory of CSCL. In J.-W. Strijbos, P. Kirschner & R. Martens (Eds.), *What we know about CSCL: And implementing it in higher education* (pp. 53–86). Boston, MA: Kluwer Academic.

Thompson, D., Baranowski, T., Buday, R., Baranowski, J., Thompson, V., Jago, R., & Griffith, M. J. (2011). Serious video games for health how behavioral science guided the development of a serious video game. *Simulation Gaming, 41*(4), 587–606. doi:10.1177/1046878108328087

Tu, C-H., Sujo-Montes, L., Yen, C-J., Chan, J-Y., & Blocher, M. (2012). Personal learning environments and open network learning environments. *TechTrends, 56*(3), 13–19.

Vygotsky, L. S. (1978). *Mind in society: The development of higher psychological processes.* Cambridge: Harvard University Press.

Warburton, S. (2008). MUVEs and second lives: Exploring education in virtual worlds. In L. Gourlay & S. Saxby-Smith (Eds.), *Excellence in teaching conference 2008 annual proceedings*, Kings College Learning Institute, London (pp. 119–127).

Weaver, D., Spratt, C., & Nair, C. S. (2008). Academic and student use of a learning management system: Implications for quality. *Australasian Journal of Educational Technology, 24*(1), 30–41. Retrieved from http://scholar.googleusercontent.com/scholar?q=cache:NDr6AMKa_pIJ:scholar.google.com/&hl=en&as_sdt=0,6

Wertsch, J. V. (1998). *Mind as action*. New York, NY: Oxford University Press.

Wilson, B. G. (2005). Foundations for instructional design: Reclaiming the conversation. In J. M. Spector, C. Ohrazda, A. Van Schaack & D. A. Wiley (Eds.), *Innovations in instructional technology: Essays in honor of M. David Merrill* (pp. 237–252). Mahwah, NJ: Erlbaum.

Winter, J., Cotton, D., Gavin, J., & Yorke, J. D. (2012). Effective e-learning? Multi-tasking, distraction and boundary management by graduate students in an online environment. *ALT-J, 18*(1), 71–83. doi:10.1080/09687761003657598

Yanchar, S. C., South, J. B., Williams, D. D., Allen, S., & Wilson, B. G. (2010). Struggling with theory? A qualitative investigation of conceptual tool use in instructional design. *Educational Technology, Research & Development, 58*(1), 39–60. doi:10.1007/s11423-009-9129-6

Zenger, J., & Folkman, J. (2009). *The extraordinary leader: Turning good managers into great leaders* (2nd ed.). New York, NY: McGraw-Hill.

PART II
APPLICATION OF WEB 2.0 AND
BLENDED LEARNING
TECHNOLOGIES

CONTROLLING ENGAGEMENT: THE EFFECTS OF LEARNER CONTROL ON ENGAGEMENT AND SATISFACTION

Michael N. Karim and Tara S. Behrend

ABSTRACT

Learner control is a widely touted and popular element of e-learning, both in the educational and organizational training domains. In this chapter, we explore the concept of learner control, highlighting its multidimensional and psychological nature. We examine the theoretical basis for the effects of learner control on learning and engagement. Next, we provide the reader with empirically based recommendations for designing learner-controlled training. We conclude by discussing how learner control research may be adapted to accommodate a variety of instructional methods, such as textbooks, mobile learning, and Massive Open Online Courses (MOOCs).

Increasing Student Engagement and Retention in e-Learning Environments:
Web 2.0 and Blended Learning Technologies
Cutting-edge Technologies in Higher Education, Volume 6G, 59–82
Copyright © 2013 by Emerald Group Publishing Limited
All rights of reproduction in any form reserved
ISSN: 2044-9968/doi:10.1108/S2044-9968(2013)000006G005

INTRODUCTION

E-learning is often chosen to give learners flexibility and control over the content and schedule of training (Brown, 2001). For example, learners can choose to pause to take a break or rewind confusing topics; choose to train at three in the morning, or in five-minute increments in between meetings; and choose to learn in a quiet library, or in a bustling coffee shop. By allowing learners to adapt training to their needs, educators can create a learner-centered training program customized to each trainee.

Providing learners with control over the training program affects how they interact with and perceive the training content (Kraiger & Jerden, 2007). Motivated learners may use control to engage more deeply with the training content while unmotivated learners may use control to disengage completely (Brown, 2001). As such, evidence for a relationship between learner control and learning has been mixed, with some (e.g., DeRouin, Fritzsche, & Salas, 2005; Fisher, Wasserman, & Orvis, 2010) suggesting that control increases learning, and others (e.g., Aly, Elen, & Willems, 2005; Bell & Kozlowski, 2008) suggesting that control decreases or has no effect on learning.

When designing training, instructional decisions (such as learner control) should be based on an understanding of how control affects engagement. Psychological theories (e.g., self-determination theory, Ryan & Deci, 2000; the theory of planned behavior, Ajzen, 1991; and resource theories of attention, Kanfer & Ackerman, 1989) can provide a substantive framework to understand these effects. By basing decisions in research and theory, practitioners can ensure that training is maximally effective.

The current chapter seeks to provide a foundation for understanding how learner control influences engagement and learning processes and outcomes. This chapter will draw from practical examples and psychological theories to define learner control and examine how it affects learner engagement. We will present a model for how learners experience control. Finally, we will outline empirical evidence, recommendations, and applications of this model beyond computer-delivered learning.

AN OVERVIEW OF LEARNER CONTROL

Learner control research has drawn primarily from the perspective of instructional design. Learner control is often defined as the amount of objective control learners have over the pace, content, sequence, guidance, and design of training content (e.g., Kraiger & Jerden, 2007). Practitioners and researchers have been primarily concerned with how the set of these control features affects how much students learn from and enjoy training (e.g., Granger & Levine, 2010). To examine how learner control affects these outcomes, research has created a distinction between training that is learner controlled (allowing one or more learner control features) and training that is program controlled (not allowing any control features). Learner control research has thus focused on how learner-controlled training differs from program-controlled training.

Contrary to its common definition in literature, however, learner control should not be considered only as an instructional design element. That is, it is insufficient to simply classify training as learner controlled or not. Instead, learner control should be considered a multidimensional and psychological construct. By reframing it this way, we are able to answer psychological questions about control, such as: Who perceives control? What are the cognitive processes that underlie the effects of learner control and learning? And, why does control increase satisfaction and engagement? Control can exist in varying degrees along two dimensions (instructional and scheduling) and results in control perceptions that drive behavioral outcomes, including engagement (Orvis, Fisher, & Wasserman, 2009; Skinner, 1996). In the next section, we elaborate on both of these arguments.

The Multidimensional Nature of Learner Control

Learner control may be described by two dimensions: *instructional control* that allows learners to control the pace, content, sequence, guidance, and design of training content (Kraiger & Jerden, 2007) and *scheduling control* that allows learners to control the time and location that they complete training (outlined in Fig. 1; Karim, 2012; Welsh, Wanberg, Brown, & Simmering, 2003). There is no inherent relationship between instructional and scheduling controls; as suggested in Table 1, educators may create programs with a high degree of one and low degree of the other, high degrees of both, or low degrees of both. Because instructional and scheduling controls can function independently of each other, learner control should be conceptualized and operationalized as multidimensional.

Instructional Control
Researchers have proposed five major categories of instructional control: pace, sequence, content, advisory/guidance, and design (Granger & Levine,

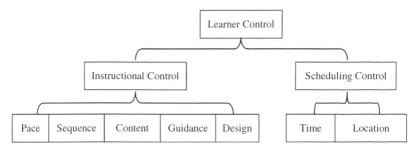

Fig. 1. Learner Control as a Multidimensional Construct. Reproduced from Karim (2012).

Table 1. Variations in Instructional and Scheduling Control.

	Instructional	
Scheduling	Low	High
Low	Program has a set time and location & Program has set control, sequence, content, and guidance	Program has a set time and location & Control over pace, content, sequence, and guidance
High	Complete program at a time and location of choice & Program has set control, sequence, content, and guidance	Complete program at time and location of choice & Control over pace, content, sequence, and guidance

2010; Kraiger & Jerden, 2007). These features are conceptually linked and allow learners to influence what information they learn and how this information is presented (Brown, 2001). Each form of instructional control is outlined below.

Pace Control. Programs with high degrees of pace control allow learners to pause, rewind, or skip material (Kraiger & Jerden, 2007). For example, video-based programs may include a navigational bar that allows learners to move back and forth through training content at their own discretion. Advanced learners in a Microsoft Excel training program might skim quickly through introductory material, such as entering and formatting data, to more advanced material, such as lookup functions and conditional formatting. Without spending time on material they have already mastered, these trainees are able to better concentrate on more challenging material. Pace control may be misused, however, by unmotivated trainees. By allowing learners to skip through training content, some may race through the training program to return to other tasks (Brown, 2001).

Sequence Control. Learners may be able to navigate freely through instructional content by using sequence control to choose the order of specific modules within the training (Kraiger & Jerden, 2007). For example, a new customer service representative might decide to start their training with strategies that relate directly to his or her own recent experiences with customers, such as "hostile customers," and then return to more unfamiliar topics, such as "phone system operations." By beginning with the information that is highly relevant to him or her, this trainee may become more engaged (Tennyson, Park, & Christensen, 1985). In order to create an effective training sequence, though, learners may need some prior familiarity with training content. Those who are less familiar with training content, however, may be less able to create an effective training sequence (Kruger & Dunning, 1999; Lawless & Brown, 1997). Often, learners are allowed to make decisions about the order of training content regardless of their ability to make informed decisions.

Content Control. Learners may be able to determine the information that is presented by using content control (Brown, 2001). Just-in-time learning programs such as the Khan Academy (Khanacademy.org) host free learning content (e.g., in the form of Youtube videos) on their websites and allow learners to select which videos they will watch (i.e., use content control). A new employee that needs to learn how to conduct an analysis of variance in an unfamiliar statistical program can search out that precise information exactly when they need it. This allows the employee to learn only the content he or she needs, without having to start with irrelevant information, such as the foundational assumptions and formulas of the analysis. In the other direction, a learner who prefers to see formulas when learning about statistical analyses might use content control to locate that information. Thus, learners may use content control to form an instructional program that is unique to them.

Advisory and Guidance Control. Advisory/guidance control refers to a learner's ability to determine what feedback is presented, and how. Often, educators will allow learners opportunities to practice their skills within the training program and get hands-on experience with training content (Kraiger & Jerden, 2007). Advisory/guidance control allows learners to customize how the feedback is presented in these exercises. A student who decided to challenge himself or herself by enrolling in an online calculus course may become frustrated and disengage if he or she receives repetitive negative feedback. Another student, however, may see this same feedback as motivating and set more challenging goals (Phillips & Gully, 1997). The way that feedback is provided to learners can have a great impact on their subsequent engagement. As such, advisory/guidance control allows a trainee to choose how feedback is presented in order to maximize engagement.

Design Control.   Learners may also be able to customize the aesthetic design of training content. For example, learners can choose the color scheme, whether the training includes subtitles, and even the narrator's voice. Students learning a foreign language can choose to have their narrator's voice be either male or female, if they have a preference for one or the other, or could choose how strong the narrator's accent is. When virtual coaches (or pedagogical agents; on-screen characters that deliver customized content to trainees) are used in e-learning, customizing the agent's appearance could be viewed as a form of design control. Past research has shown that allowing learners to customize an agent's race and gender results in increased post-training declarative knowledge (Behrend & Thompson, 2012). Although design control does not directly affect the content covered in training, it does affect how this information is presented and how learners interact with training content. This element of control can be beneficial for learners with visual impairments or those who are using specialized displays to view course material.

Scheduling Control
Scheduling control features are conceptually linked and allow learners more flexibility over the training environment. In practice, organizations often rely on time- and location-flexible training to reach geographically distributed learners (DeRouin et al., 2005; Welsh et al., 2003). For example, learning management systems (LMS; such as Blackboard®) allow educators to post lecture slides, full video and audio recordings, and other course content online. Students who are unable to attend lectures due to travel, illness, or physical distance are still able to access the course's content online at a time and location that is convenient to them. Learners, however, are required to know their ideal learning environments and must be motivated to complete the program within a timely manner. Those who are able to do

so may be more engaged with the program while those who are unable to or procrastinate may feel rushed to complete content within the acceptable window (Brown, 2001). By allowing learners flexibility over the training's time and location, scheduling control represents a distinct but related form of learner control.

Time Control. Learners with time control can choose when they will learn course content. For example, a learner who works part time may choose to watch course content during their lunch break or in the evening. Learners are still constrained by course deadlines (e.g., lecture one must be completed within two weeks), but are allowed to decide when within these deadlines they will complete training. Alternatively, highly synchronous programs are less time controlled as learners are required to complete the program at a set time. For example, a student enrolled in a distance-learning course that has live webcast lectures is required to attend the session at a set time so they can interact with other students and the professor. This student may not be able to fully clear his or her schedule and may have additional distractions, while a student that is allowed greater flexibility over timing is able to choose a time during which he or she is likely to have minimal distractions. By allowing learners to choose the specific time that they will learn, time control provides learners additional flexibility to fit learning into their schedules (Coates, James, & Baldwin, 2005). Learners who are able to fit the program into their schedule may be more engaged due to having fewer distractions while those who are not able to may be less engaged.

Location Control. Similarly, geographically dispersed learners can use location control determine where they will learn (Coates et al., 2005). Organizations that need to train and educate distance learners in a cost-effective manner often rely on this extra level of flexibility (DeRouin et al., 2005; Welsh et al., 2003). Instead of spending resources to travel and present information to dispersed learners, educators can save money and increase efficiency by hosting the same content online (Coates et al., 2005). By allowing learners to learn at a location of their choice, organizations can effectively reach trainees wherever they are in a cost-effective manner (DeRouin et al., 2005). This may also allow students who would have been unable to travel to attend in-person lectures to do so without leaving their home. Students who wish to take a course at Stanford University may be able to now do so online, thanks to Stanford's distance-learning initiatives. Stanford has supported innovative instructional methods, such as Massive Open Online Courses (or MOOCs, discussed in further detail later), that allow learners across the U.S. and across the world to receive education from renowned professors. As with other forms of control, learners must be able to make smart decisions about where they learn best. Learners who are able to successfully choose an environment that is conducive to their learning style may be more engaged than those who choose non-ideal learning environments (e.g., a bustling coffee shop).

The Subjective Nature of Learner Control

Learner control research stands to benefit from the addition of a psychological perspective. Instructional design perspectives are primarily concerned with the objective presence of control (i.e., whether or not learners may exercise control over training content). Psychological perspectives, however, consider individual differences and expectations that shape learners' subjective experience of control and how this subjective experience drives behavioral and attitudinal outcomes. A psychological perspective allows us to make hypotheses about from where learners' perceptions of control originate. For example, Skinner's (1996) work would suggest that the amount of control learners perceive may be a direct result of their expectations. Further, Ajzen's (1991) theory of planned behavior and Orvis and colleagues (2009) would suggest that learner perceptions of control may be more predictive of learning behaviors than objective control. Similarly, we would hypothesize that learners' expectations of control may be shaped by learners' prior e-learning experiences with control (Olson, Roese, & Zanna, 1996). Thus, the amount of control one learner perceives may differ from the amount another learner perceives, based on their expectations and prior e-learning experiences. When examining how control affects learning, an overall objective measure of the amount of control allows may be less related to a learner's behaviors than the amount of control that learner perceives.

Subjective control is a commonly studied psychological construct that can provide a substantive framework for learner control research. For example, in the theory of planned behavior, Ajzen (1991) suggests that behavioral outcomes are the direct result of behavioral intentions and perceived behavioral control. Research has largely supported Ajzen's (1991) theory by demonstrating that perceived behavioral control influences health-related behaviors (Godin & Kok, 1996; Schifter & Ajzen, 1985) and technology adoption (Pavlou & Fygenson, 2006). Subjective control has also been linked to increased satisfaction and motivation by Ryan and Deci's (2000) self-determination theory. Self-determination theory suggests that subjective control, as well as competence and relatedness, increases both satisfaction and motivation. Thus, research on subjective control can provide a baseline for understanding how learners use control, and how subjective control affects satisfaction and motivation.

Recent learner control research has begun to expand conceptual definitions and operationalizations of learner control to include subjective control (e.g., Kraiger & Jerden, 2007; Orvis et al., 2009). Little empirical work, however, has been conducted on subjective learner control. In order to better understand how subjective and objective learner control differs and how subjective learner control drives behaviors and outcomes, further research that examines subjective control is needed.

The Continuous Nature of Learner Control

Learner control should be conceptualized as a continuous, as opposed to categorical variable. Describing training by the *degree* of learner control (as opposed to the presence of it) allows for more meaningful comparisons across programs. Dichotomous distinctions between program-controlled training and learner-controlled training do not address gradients of objective or subjective control. For example, a training program with content and sequence control and a training program with only content control are both considered learner controlled. As is apparent, differences between these programs are not captured by the learner control/program control distinction. Alternatively, describing training by the degree of learner control would suggest that the first is more learner controlled than the second. Thus, learner control should not only be considered multi-dimensional and subjective but also continuous.

The Relationship Between Control and Engagement

Learner control has previously been described as a, "double-edged sword" (Scheiter & Gerjets, 2007, p. 289) that provides learners more freedom, "in becoming, or not, mindfully engaged" (Salomon, Perkins, & Globerson, 1991, p. 4). When learners are required to choose the content and sequence of their training material, learners who are unfamiliar with training content (Lawless & Brown, 1997) or who are unmotivated (Colquitt, LePine, & Noe, 2000) may be less able to do so and disengage (Ree, Carretta, & Teachout,

1995; Salas & Cannon-Bowers, 2001). It is also possible that the effort dedicated to making decisions about learning may take attention away from the material itself. This will depend on a number of factors, and as Scheiter and Gerjets (2007) suggest, the relationship is not easy to describe in a straightforward manner. In order to further examine the relationship between control and engagement, we must first define engagement.

Definition of Engagement

Two groups of researchers have defined engagement in different ways. One group has argued that learners' attitudes toward the training may be used as a proxy for engagement. The other group has taken a cognitive approach in examining engagement and has argued that the cognitive processes that underlie learning should be used as a proxy for engagement. We will briefly review each of these perspectives below in the context of learner control.

The Attitudinal Definition.   Attitudinal approaches to engagement argue that learner reactions to the training program are more indicative of engagement for e-learning programs than for face-to-face programs (e.g., Sitzmann, Brown, Casper, Ely, & Zimmerman, 2008). That is, learners who dislike the training program may use learner control features to skip through content and learners who enjoy the training may use these same features to further explore areas of interest (Sitzmann, Kraiger, Stewart, & Wisher, 2006). Subsequently, learner reactions to training have been shown to be predictive of engagement, learning, and intent to enroll in future courses (Brown, 2005; Long, DuBois, & Faley, 2008). Thus, some in the training literature have argued that engagement should be conceptualized as learners' reactions to training (e.g., Brown, 2005).

Attitudinal outcomes, however, may be less indicative of engagement when learners are able to control their program. Psychological theories, such as self-determination theory (Ryan & Deci, 2000), suggest that simply providing learners with control should increase their overall satisfaction with training. Overall, individuals enjoy feeling in control over their environment and their behaviors (Lang & Heckhausen, 2001). By providing learners with control, they may feel an increased sense of competence and ownership over their learning (Skinner, 1996). This increase in the amount of control learners perceive should result in more positive attitudinal reactions to training (Ryan & Deci, 2000). Learner control research has supported these theoretical hypotheses by overall suggesting that learner control increases satisfaction (e.g., Orvis et al., 2009). If engagement is conceptualized attitudinally as satisfaction, learner control should then always increase engagement. However, as suggested throughout this chapter, this is not always the case. Some learners will disengage from training content by skipping through important material (Brown, 2001). It is then possible that learner control features result in greater enjoyment and less engagement. Thus, while reactions to training are an important measure for predicting intent to enroll in future courses, they may not be an appropriate measure of engagement for learner-controlled programs.

The Cognitive Definition. A second group of learner control researchers have instead focused on the cognitive processes that underlie learning. This group can be split into two approaches: the self-regulatory approach and the attentional approach.

The Self-Regulatory Approach: Some have argued that a self-regulatory framework is appropriate for understanding learner engagement. Individual differences in self-regulatory ability and prior knowledge may determine a learner's engagement when they have control over their program (Baumeister, Vohs, & Tice, 2007; Kraiger & Jerden, 2007; Lawless & Brown, 1997; Scheiter & Gerjets, 2007). Self-regulatory ability refers to an individual's ability to use self-focused learning strategies, self-generated feedback, and independent motivational processes to guide information acquisition (Zimmerman, 1990). Those who are able to successfully monitor and adapt their behaviors are considered to have greater self-regulatory ability (Kozlowski, Toney, Mullins, Weissbein, Brown, & Bell, 2001). Thus, self-regulatory ability may have a direct effect on learners' success in highly learner-controlled programs and those who exhibit self-regulatory behaviors may become more engaged than those who do not (Lawless & Brown, 1997).

Individuals, however, are notoriously unable to judge their own ability and engage in the self-regulatory behaviors described above (Kruger & Dunning, 1999). For example, meta-cognitive perceptions may be affected by heuristics and biases (Schwarz, Bless, Strack, Klumpp, Rittenauer-Schatka, & Simons, 1991; Tversky & Kahneman, 1973). Learners are largely unaware of their own shortcomings and may overstate how much they already know (Kruger & Dunning, 1999) and their perceptions about the plasticity of intelligence may lead them disengage from training content (Miele, Finn, & Molden, 2011). Further, those who are able to engage in continuous self-regulation may be left with fewer cognitive resources to dedicate to training content (Kanfer & Ackerman, 1989). As such, training scholars have focused on how to shift the burden of self-regulation from trainees to the training program by designing training that can prompt self-regulation (e.g., Bell & Kozlowski, 2002; Bell & Kozlowski, 2008). Thus, though self-regulation may accurately predict how learners engage with training content, many learners are unable to engage in self-regulatory behaviors necessary to suppress urges and monitor their own behavior.

The Attentional Approach: Attentional approaches to defining engagement examine the mental processes that underlie learning. Recent learner control research (e.g., Brown, 2001; Karim, 2012; Orvis et al., 2009) has drawn from resource theories of attention, which are cognitive theories that argue that engagement should be conceptualized by learners' allocation of cognitive resources. Learners have a fixed number of cognitive resources that may be allocated to on-task, off-task, or self-regulatory behaviors (Fisher & Ford, 1998; Kanfer & Ackerman, 1989). Learners who are engaged with training content will focus on training materials while those who are disengaged will focus on off-task or self-regulatory behaviors. Importantly, proponents of resources theories of attention have argued that as attention to one of these three behaviors increases, attention to the other two necessarily decreases (Fisher & Ford, 1998; Kanfer & Ackerman, 1989). Those who focus heavily on off-task and self-regulatory behaviors will have fewer cognitive resources to allocate to training content (Fisher & Ford, 1998; Orvis et al., 2009). Thus, attentional focus serves as a proxy for engagement as it captures how learners are interacting with training content and the amount of cognitive resources they allocate to on-task behaviors.

Evidence for the Effects of Learner Control on Engagement
The relationship between learner control and engagement is highly debated in the research literature. Some have argued that learner control increases engagement by presenting learners with a series of decisions about their training (e.g., Orvis et al., 2009). Others, however, have argued that learner control decreases engagement and results in lower retention of information (e.g., Aly et al., 2005; Bell & Kozlowski, 2008). In their recent meta-analysis, Kraiger and Jerden (2007) demonstrated that overall, learner control may mildly benefit learning. This conflicting evidence has left practitioners unable to make empirically based decisions regarding how much control to provide learners.

One possible reason for discrepant evidence may be that learner control research has not fully covered the construct domain of control. Numerous studies have examined the effects of objective learner control on engagement, satisfaction, and learning (e.g., Brown, 2001; Orvis et al., 2009). However, as previously mentioned, objective measures of control may be only loosely related to behavioral and attitudinal outcomes (Orvis et al., 2009; Skinner, 1996). Further, this research has not fully differentiated between instructional and scheduling control and the two are often combined in analyses. Thus, the multidimensional, subjective, and continuous learner control framework laid out in this chapter may be used to further examine an expanded conceptualization of learner control.

Instructional Control. Instructional control may decrease engagement and learning. Learners with high levels of instructional control are required to customize how and what information is presented by determining the pace, sequence, content, guidance, and design of training content (Brown, 2001; Kraiger & Jerden, 2007). In order to use these controls, learners must thus shift their attention from training content (on-task attention) to navigational features (off-task attention) and self-focused behaviors (self-regulation). As suggested by resources theories of attention, learners who focus more intently on navigational features and self-regulatory behaviors are left with fewer cognitive resources to allocate to training content (Kanfer & Ackerman, 1989). Thus, providing learners with instructional control may result in them learning less as they shift their attention away from training content and onto off-task behaviors (navigational features) and self-regulation (self-focused behaviors).

Scheduling Control. Alternatively, allowing learners greater flexibility within their program may increase engagement and learning. Scholars within training (e.g., Noe, 2010) and education (e.g., Hanrahan, 1998) suggest that environmental factors, such as distractions, can negatively affect learning outcomes. Those who have flexibility over the training's time and location may be able to spend more time in training and work in a distraction-free environment (such as their home office). Further, the amount of time learners dedicate to training has been shown to be positively predictive of how much they learn (Brown, 2001; Frederick & Walberg, 1980). It should then follow that scheduling control may allow learners to choose a distraction free environment that increases engagement and learning.

Summary: Learner Control and Engagement
Numerous conceptualizations of engagement have been suggested. Engagement has been conceptualized in terms of training reactions (e.g., Orvis et al., 2009; Sitzmann et al., 2008), self-regulatory behaviors (e.g., Bell & Kozlowski, 2008), and attentional focus (Brown, 2001; Kanfer & Ackerman, 1989). We have argued that an attentional approach allows engagement to be conceptualized as learners' resource allocation and can account for discrepant evidence for a relationship between learner control and learning.

Drawing on psychological theories (e.g., Kanfer & Ackerman, 1989), we have provided a brief argument for why instructional control may decrease, and scheduling control may increase, learning.

A recent empirical test supports these assertions. In Karim (2012), we allowed 348 learners varying degrees of instructional and scheduling control over a Microsoft Excel training program that covered either the use of pivot tables or charts. The high instructional control trainings allowed learners to control the pace, content, and sequence of training content; the low instructional control trainings covered the same content but did not provide learners with these controls. Results indicated that the amount of instructional control learners perceived, as opposed to the amount they were provided with, increased off-task attention, and that off-task attention was negatively related to learning.

The high scheduling control programs allowed learners to choose when, within a one-week window of registering, they would complete the training; the low scheduling control program required learners to complete the training immediately upon registering. All learners, regardless of condition, were able determine where they learned (since the study was conducted online). Results indicated that perceived scheduling control was positively associated with learning and that this may be due to an increase in the amount of time dedicated to training.

Finally, results supported self-determination theory's suggestion that simply providing learners with control results in more positive reactions to training. The amount of instructional control and scheduling control learners perceived was associated with an increase in training reactions. Thus, the results of Karim (2012) suggest that learners enjoy both forms of control and support the overall argument that attitudinal approaches for engagement may be limited.

APPLICATIONS OF LEARNER CONTROL TO E-LEARNING

With an understanding of how learner control affects engagement, we will now discuss how learner control research can inform e-learning practice. In order to do this, we will provide examples of each type of learner-controlled program listed in Table 1. As indicated by this table, educators may provide learners with high or low levels of instructional and scheduling controls. Each cell of this table is detailed below.

High Instructional

High Scheduling

High instructional and high scheduling control training programs allow learners to customize training content while choosing when and where they complete the program. For example, learners may control the pace, content, and sequence of training content. Learners could choose which content they learn and how much time they spend within each module. Further, because this program is asynchronous and hosted online, learners would be able to complete the training at a time and location best suited to their needs and those who would like to take a break midway through are free to return to the program whenever they are ready.

As suggested by our above discussion on the effects of learner control on engagement, control over instructional elements of the training program may result in decreased engagement with the training content. Control over scheduling elements, however, may result in increased engagement as learners can dedicate more time to training and choose to take learn at a time and location that minimizes distractions. Thus, allowing learners to control both instructional and scheduling elements may result in trainees that are moderately engaged.

Low Scheduling

High instructional and low scheduling control training programs allow learners to control the presentation of training content while requiring them to complete the program at a set time and/or location. Though learners would have less control over when and where they will take training, the structure of training content remains unchanged and learners can still control instructional elements. The instructional elements in this training may decrease engagement by requiring learners to divert their attention to these features. Further, the lack of scheduling control may result in learners who are distracted by environmental factors and that dedicate less time to training content. Thus, allowing learners to control instructional, but not scheduling, elements would result in trainees that are less engaged with training content.

Low Instructional

High Scheduling

Learners in a low instructional and high scheduling control program are unable to determine the pace, content, sequence, guidance, and design of training content, but are allowed to learn whenever and wherever they like. If this content were hosted asynchronously online, learners would be able to choose when and where they completed training. As suggested by our above discussion, we would expect this program to have the most engaged learners out of the four examples. Learners in this training program are not distracted by instructional control features and are afforded the ability to take the program at a time that best suits their learning needs. Learners in this training program are thus able to dedicate cognitive resources to training content while minimizing external distractions.

Low Scheduling
Finally, learners who are not able to control either instructional or scheduling elements of training are likely to be moderately engaged with training content. Learners in this type of training would be required to complete the program at a set time and/or location and would not be able to control instructional elements of their program. Because learners cannot schedule this program around their needs, some may be distracted by external environmental factors and may spend less time learning training content. Thus, we would expect moderately engaged trainees within program that do not allow either instructional or scheduling control.

NONTRADITIONAL APPLICATIONS

The ideas presented in this chapter may be adapted to look both backward to examine more traditional programs and forward to examine new and emergent technologies. This section will highlight how learner control can be used to classify both extant and emergent learning platforms.

A Look Back

Our framework of learner control can be used to reexamine more traditional instructional methods, such as textbooks and classroom learning. Though textbooks have a suggested order and structure, learners are easily able to skip through content at their own pace, as well as read the book chapters in the order they prefer. Applying the framework described above, textbooks have a moderate to high degree of instructional control (in that they allow for pace, content, and sequence control). Furthermore, when learning from a textbook, students are often simply required to complete the readings within a week, at a time and location of their choice. Thus, textbooks allow for high degrees of both instructional and scheduling controls.

Similarly, learners may perceive instructional or scheduling control over a classroom environment. Students may ask the instructor to slow down or to revisit or skip certain instructional content. Similarly, they may be able to provide input regarding the lecture's time and location (although likely to a lesser degree than in an online environment). Not all instructors, however, will allow students to influence these areas and the amount of objective instructional and scheduling control should differ across instructors. Even in the absence of objective control over the classroom's content or schedule, some learners may subjectively feel that they are able to influence the content and schedule (Skinner, 1996). Thus, while classrooms may not always allow for objective instructional and scheduling controls, it is possible that learners perceive control over both of these. By examining learner control as a subjective experience, as opposed to an objective element of instructional design, learner control can be used to classify a variety of extant learning environments.

Looking Forward

Learner control research may also be adapted to examine new and emergent forms of e-learning. Below, we examine mobile learning and MOOCs as an extension of learner control.

Mobile Learning

With the recent growth in popularity and presence of mobile computing devices (including smart phones and tablets), e-learning is on the brink of a major change. Learners using these technologies may more easily fit learning into their schedules. Furthermore, this allows employees in remote or isolated locations to be trained. Organizations, such as the Army, are currently working on capitalizing on this technology to allow soldiers to download a training program on the go from isolated locations. Marketed in the form of mobile applications, these mobile learning programs allow for training content to be accessed on-demand with increased flexibility in delivery. Non-military organizations may also find benefits in mobile learning. Instead of requiring employees to come on-site or even go to a computer for training, employees may be able to access training on their train commute to work. This increased flexibility allows learners to get the necessary knowledge and skills presented in the training program at a time and location that is convenient for and adaptable to their needs.

As mobile platforms become more technologically capable, their functionality may begin to parallel those of computers and the two may begin to merge. New technologies, such as tablets and netbooks, already blur the line between mobile devices and computers. While training may be created to be mobile-specific (as with the Army example above), this does not necessarily need to be the case. For example, training may be accessed from either a computer or a mobile device's internet browser. As mobile browsers continue to develop, the need for content designed specifically for mobile devices may decrease.

Mobile learning platforms vary in how much instructional control they allow for, but inherently have a high degree of scheduling control. Instead of classifying programs by their delivery method (e.g., e-learning or mobile learning) it is more useful to classify them based on their characteristics (such as the degree and type of learner control provided). Mobile learning can be thus considered one extreme of scheduling control. Further research is needed on how a learner control framework may be applied to mobile learning.

Massively Open Online Courses

Massively Open Online Courses (MOOCs) allow large numbers of geographically distributed learners to enroll in university-sponsored courses, often free of charge (Mackness, Mak, & Williams, 2010). MOOCs are founded on the theory of connectivism, the notion that knowledge is distributed across individuals (Downes, 2007; Levy, 2011). Learners in MOOCs typically "attend" live lectures (or recordings) and use discussion forums, course wikis, and social media to connect with other students and further explore course content. As with learner-controlled programs, students who are highly motivated are able to explore content in greater depth than they would in classroom-based learning or training with lower degrees of control. Further, MOOCs do not require face-to-face interaction and allow learners to choose exactly where they will attend the virtual lecture and when, where, and how they interact with other trainees (Levy, 2011; Mackness et al., 2010).

In this sense, MOOCs can be considered an extension of learner control. Learners exercise content control by determining the content that they will explore outside of class and who they interact with. Further, because the course is hosted online, learners are able to exercise a degree of both time and location control over their course's schedule. Thus, learners in these programs may perceive themselves as more autonomous and in-control of their learning (Mackness et al., 2010). Mackness and colleagues' (2010) initial examination of learner expectations and perceptions within MOOCs is a critical first step toward an empirical examination of MOOCs. Building on their work, we believe that future MOOC research may be able to draw from a learner control framework to examine learners' perceptions of autonomy and how these perceptions affect their interactions with other students and course content.

RECOMMENDATIONS

While the content in this chapter may be taken to suggest that instructional control is always detrimental and that scheduling control is always beneficial, this is not necessarily the case. In fact, a growing body of literature suggests that learner-controlled training may be designed to prompt self-regulation and adapt to learners' needs and preferences to create an automatically customized program that suits learners' needs (Bell & Kozlowski, 2002). Thus, it is important to note that the above discussion regarding the effects of instructional and scheduling control on engagement (learners' attention focus and the amount of time that learners spend within the program) is geared toward the average learner (employee, student, or otherwise). That is, we have described how, overall, learners' perceptions of control over instructional and scheduling elements may lead them to interact with the training content. These effects do not account for an individual's prior knowledge, cognitive ability, or other individual differences. Thus, these recommendations are made broad enough to apply to the average learner (as opposed to making specific recommendations based on individual differences).

Further, we recognize that, though closely related, education and training do differ in a few areas (such as the length of the learning period). As possible, we have made the recommendations broad enough to apply to both education and training. Regardless, we recommend the reader consider their specific context and needs when developing a training program. With this in mind, we provide the following general recommendations:

- *Consider the training's purpose.* Learners like control. Consider the important outcome of training. If knowledge retention and learning are critical outcomes, then instructional control may not be beneficial. Furthermore, if it is critical that all learners be presented with the exact same content and deviation from this content is undesirable, low instructional control is better suited for this purpose. However, when using training and education as a reward or simply to increase morale, either (or both) forms of control will make learners enjoy the program more. Thus, educators should always consider the purpose of training when making instructional design decisions.

- *Consider your learners' needs and expectations.* While we have described overall effects of instructional and scheduling control, not all learners interact with training content in the same way. Consider your learners' needs and learning styles. Learner characteristics, such as their goal orientation, motivation, and self-regulatory ability may lead them to be more or less successful within instructionally-controlled training (Kraiger & Jerden, 2007). Further, learner expectations for the type and degree of control with which they should be provided may lead them to perceive and use control differently (Skinner, 1996). Considering learners' needs and expectations can help you design a program that is best suited for your learners.

- *Consider the institution's needs.* While we have suggested that scheduling control may increase engagement, satisfaction, and learning, scheduling control is not always practical. That is, there are times where scheduling control may not be feasible (e.g., if learners must complete the program at a set time). In these contexts, the situational press should override the benefits of scheduling control. It is thus critical to consider the institution's needs when designing training.

CONCLUSION

This chapter has briefly reviewed learner control literature and outlined an updated framework of learner control. Drawing on psychological theories, we discussed how subjective experiences of instructional and scheduling control can drive a learner's interactions with training content and subsequent engagement. After providing the results of a recent test of this framework, we outlined its applications beyond e-learning and provided the reader with recommendations for designing training.

This chapter has suggested that learner control is a multidimensional construct, that control is a subjective experience, and that the effects of control on engagement depend on the type of control allowed. Although customization of training content and delivery may lead to increased satisfaction with the training program, this control decreases engagement as learners shift their attention to off-task and self-regulatory behaviors. Alternatively, learners who have flexibility over the time and location that they learn may engage further with training by minimizing external distractions and dedicating more time to learning. Thus, we have argued that viewing learner control as a unitary element of instructional design is a limited approach that does not account for differences between dimensions of control and subjective experiences with control.

Finally, we have argued for a learner-centered approach to understanding learner control and designing training. Learning is inherently a psychological process that is unique to each individual. Practitioners designing training and researchers examining training should continue to take a learner-centered approach that understands how learner control may affect engagement and learning.

REFERENCES

Ajzen, I. (1991). The theory of planned behavior. *Organizational Behavior and Human Decision Processes, 50*, 179–211. doi:10.1016/0749-5978(91)90020-T

Aly, M. M., Elen, J. J., & Willems, G. G. (2005). Learner-control vs. program-control instructional multimedia: A comparison of two interactions when teaching principles of orthodontic appliances. *European Journal of Dental Education, 9*(4), 157–163. doi:10.1111/j.1600-0579.2005.00385.x

Baumeister, R. F., Vohs, K. D., & Tice, D. M. (2007). The strength model of self-control. *Current Directions in Psychological Science, 16*(6), 351–355. doi:10.1111/j.1467-8721.2007.00534.x

Behrend, T. S., & Thompson, L. F. (2012). Using agents in learner-controlled training: The effects of design control. *International Journal of Training and Development, 16*(4), 263–283. doi:10.1111/j.1468-2419.2012.00413.x

Bell, B. S., & Kozlowski, S. W. (2002). Adaptive guidance: Enhancing self-regulation, knowledge, and performance in technology-based training. *Personnel Psychology, 55*, 267–306. doi:10.1111/j.1744-6570.2002.tb00111.x

Bell, B. S., & Kozlowski, S. W. (2008). Active learning: Effects of core training design elements on self-regulatory processes, learning, and adaptability. *Journal of Applied Psychology, 93*(2), 296–316. doi:10.1037/0021-9010.93.2.296

Brown, K. G. (2001). Using computers to deliver training: Which employees learn and why? *Personnel Psychology, 54*, 271–296. doi:10.1111/j.1744-6570.2001.tb00093.x

Brown, K. G. (2005). An examination of the structure and nomological network of trainee reactions: A closer look at "smile sheets". *Journal of Applied Psychology, 90*(5), 991–1001. doi:10.1037/0021-9010.90.5.991

Coates, H., James, R., & Baldwin, G. (2005). A critical examination of the effects of learning management systems on university teaching and learning. *Tertiary Education and management, 11*(1), 19–36. doi:10.1080/13583883.2005.9967137

Colquitt, J. A., LePine, J. A., & Noe, R. A. (2000). Toward an integrative theory of training motivation: A meta-analytic path analysis of 20 years of research. *Journal of Applied Psychology*, *85*(5), 678–707. doi:10.1037/0021-9010.85.5.678

DeRouin, R. E., Fritzsche, B. A., & Salas, E. (2005). E-learning in organizations. *Journal of Management*, *37*(5), 249–265. doi:10.1177/0149206305279815

Downes, S. (2007). An introduction to connective knowledge. In T. Hug (Ed.), *Media, knowledge, & education – Exploring new spaces, relations, and dynamics in digital media ecologies*. Proceedings of the international conference, Innsbruck: Innsbruck University Press.

Fisher, S. L., & Ford, J. K. (1998). Differential effects of learner effort and goal orientation on two learning outcomes. *Personnel Psychology*, *51*(2), 397–420. doi:10.1111/j.1744-6570. 1998.tb00731.x

Fisher, S. L., Wasserman, M. E., & Orvis, K. A. (2010). Trainee reactions to learner control: An important link in the e-learning equation. *International Journal of Training and Development*, *14*(3), 198–208. doi:10.1111/j.1468-2419.2010.00352.x

Frederick, W. C., & Walberg, H. J. (1980). Learning as a function of time. *The Journal of Educational Research*, *73*(4), 183–194.

Godin, G., & Kok, G. (1996). The theory of planned behavior: A review of its applications to health-related behaviors. *American Journal of health Promotion*, *11*(2), 87–98. doi:10.4278/0890-1171-11.2.87

Granger, B. P., & Levine, E. L. (2010). The perplexing role of learner control in e-learning: Will learning and transfer benefit or suffer? *International Journal of Training and Development*, *14*(3), 180–197. doi:10.1111/j.1468-2419.2010.00351.x

Hanrahan, M. U. (1998). The effect of learning environment factors on students' motivation and learning. *International Journal of Science Education*, *20*(6), 737–753. doi:10.1080/ 0950069980200609

Kanfer, R., & Ackerman, P. L. (1989). Motivation and cognitive abilities: An integrative/ Aptitude-treatment interaction approach to skill acquisition. *Journal of Applied Psychology Monograph*, *74*(4), 657–690. doi:10.1037/0021-9010.74.4.657

Karim, M. N. (2012). *A multidimensional framework of learner control* (Master's Thesis). The George Washington University, Washington, DC.

Kozlowski, S. W., Toney, R. J., Mullins, M. E., Weissbein, D. A., Brown, K. G., & Bell, B. S. (2001). Developing adaptability: A theory for the design of integrated-embedded training systems. In E. Salas (Ed.), *Advances in human performance and cognitive engineering research* (Vol. 1, pp. 59–123). Bingley, UK: Emerald Group Publishing Limited.

Kraiger, K., & Jerden, E. (2007). A meta-analytic investigation of learner control: Old findings and new directions. In S. M. Fiore & E. Salas (Eds.), *Toward a science of distribu-ted learning* (pp. 65–90). Washington, DC: American Psychological Association. doi:10.1037/11582-004

Kruger, J., & Dunning, D. (1999). Unskilled and unaware of it: How difficulties in recognizing one's own incompetence lead to inflated self-assessment. *Journal of Personality and Social Psychology*, *77*(6), 1121–1134. doi:10.1037/0022-3514.77.6.1121

Lang, F. R., & Heckhausen, J. (2001). Perceived control over development and subjective well-being: Differential benefits across adulthood. *Journal of Personality and Social Psychology*, *81*(3), 509–523. doi:10.1037/0022-3514.81.3.509

Lawless, K. A., & Brown, S. W. (1997). Multimedia learning environments: Issues of learner control and navigation. *Instructional Science, 25*(2), 117–131. doi:10.1023/A: 1002919531780

Levy, D. (2011). *Lessons learned from participating in a connectivist massive online open course (MOOC)*. Paper presented at the Emerging Technologies for Online Learning Symposium, the Sloan Consortium, San Jose, CA.

Long, L. K., DuBois, C. Z., & Faley, R. H. (2008). Online training: The value of capturing trainee reactions. *Journal of Workplace Learning, 20*(1), 21–37. doi:10.1108/13665620810843629

Mackness, J., Mak, S., & Williams, R. (2010). The ideals and reality of participating in a MOOC. Paper presented at the Seventh International Conference on Networked Learning Conference, Aalborg, Denmark.

Miele, D. B., Finn, B., & Molden, D. C. (2011). Does easily learned mean easily remembered? It depends on your beliefs about intelligence. *Psychological Science, 22*(3), 320–324. doi:10.1177/0956797610397954

Noe, R. A. (2010). *Employee training and development* (5th ed.). Burr Ridge, IL: McGraw-Hill Irwin.

Olson, J. M., Roese, N. J., & Zanna, M. P. (1996). Expectancies. In E. T. Higgins & A. W. Kruglanski (Eds.), *Social psychology: Handbook of basic principles*. New York, NY: Guliford Press.

Orvis, K. A., Fisher, S. L., & Wasserman, M. E. (2009). Power to the people: Using learner control to improve trainee reactions and learning in web-based instructional environments. *Journal of Applied Psychology, 94*(4), 960–971. doi:10.1037/a0014977

Pavlou, P. A., & Fygenson, M. (2006). Understanding and predicting electronic commerce adoption: An extension of the theory of planned behavior. *MIS Quarterly, 30*(1), 115–143.

Phillips, J. M., & Gully, S. M. (1997). Role of goal orientation, ability, need for achievement, and locus of control in the self-efficacy and goal-setting process. *Journal of Applied Psychology, 82*(5), 792–802. doi:10.1037/0021-9010.82.5.792

Ree, M. J., Carretta, T. R., & Teachout, M. S. (1995). Role of ability and prior knowledge in complex training performance. *Journal of Applied Psychology, 80*(6), 721–730. doi:10.1037/0021-9010.80.6.721

Ryan, R. M., & Deci, E. L. (2000). Self-determational theory and the facilitation of intrinsic motivation, social development, and well-being. *American Psychologist, 55*(1), 68–78. doi:10.1037/0003-066X.55.1.68

Salas, E., & Cannon-Bowers, J. A. (2001). The science of training: A decade of progress. *Annual Review of Psychology, 52*, 471–499. doi:10.1146/annurev.psych.52.1.471

Salomon, G., Perkins, D. N., & Globerson, T. (1991). Partners in cognition: Extending human intelligence with intelligent technologies. *Educational Researcher, 20*(3), 2–9. doi:10.3102/0013189X020003002

Scheiter, K., & Gerjets, P. (2007). Learner control in hypermedia environments. *Educational Psychology Review, 19*, 285–307. doi:10.1007/s10648-007-9046-3

Schifter, D. E., & Ajzen, I. (1985). Intention, perceived control, and weight loss: An application of the theory of planned behavior. *Journal of Personality and Social Psychology, 49*(3), 843–851. doi:10.1037/0022-3514.49.3.843

Schwarz, N., Bless, H., Strack, F., Klumpp, G., Rittenauer-Schatka, H., & Simons, A. (1991). Ease of retrieval as information: Another look at the availability heuristic. *Journal of Personality and Social Psychology, 61*(2), 195–202. doi:10.1037/0022-3514.61.2.195

Sitzmann, T., Brown, K. G., Casper, W. J., Ely, K., & Zimmerman, R. D. (2008). A review and meta-analysis of the nomological network of trainee reactions. *Journal of Applied Psychology*, *93*(2), 280–295. doi:10.1037/0021-9010.93.2.280

Sitzmann, T., Kraiger, K., Stewart, D., & Wisher, R. (2006). The comparative effectiveness of web-based and classroom-based instruction: A meta-analysis. *Personnel Psychology*, *59*(3), 623–664. doi:10.1111/j.1744-6570.2006.00049.x

Skinner, E. A. (1996). A guide to constructs of control. *Journal of Personality and Social Psychology*, *71*(3), 549–570. doi:10.1037/0022-3514.71.3.549

Tennyson, R. D., Park, O., & Christensen, D. L. (1985). Adaptive control of learning time and content sequence in concept learning using computer-based instruction. *Journal of Educational Psychology*, *77*(4), 481–491. doi:10.1037/0022-0663.77.4.481

Tversky, A., & Kahneman, D. (1973). Availability: A heuristic for judging frequency and probability. *Cognitive Psychology*, *5*(2), 207–232. doi:10.1016/0010-0285(73)90033-9

Welsh, E. T., Wanberg, C. R., Brown, K. G., & Simmering, M. J. (2003). E-learning: Emerging uses, empirical results, and future directions. *International Journal of Training and Development*, *7*(4), 245–258. doi:10.1046/j.1360-3736.2003.00184.x

Zimmerman, B. J. (1990). Self-regulated learning and academic achievement: An overview. *Educational Psychologist*, *25*(1), 3–17. doi:10.1207/s15326985ep2501_2

INCREASING LEARNER ENGAGEMENT OF LEARNING TECHNOLOGIES AND SCIENCE TPACK THROUGH REPRESENTATIONAL CHALLENGES

Peter Hubber and Esther Loong

ABSTRACT

There have been calls to embed Information and Communication Technology (ICT) into pre-service teacher courses in preference to technology only courses as a means to provide graduate pre-service teachers with the necessary skills to integrate ICT into their teaching practice. This chapter describes a case study of a pre-service science education curriculum course that was designed to embed ICT into its curriculum, assessment and delivery. The tutor modelled best teaching practice in the use of learning technologies. The theoretical framework is Technological Pedagogical and Content Knowledge (TPACK) viewed through a representation construction approach. This approach involved the students

Increasing Student Engagement and Retention in e-Learning Environments:
Web 2.0 and Blended Learning Technologies
Cutting-edge Technologies in Higher Education, Volume 6G, 83–112
Copyright © 2013 by Emerald Group Publishing Limited
All rights of reproduction in any form reserved
ISSN: 2044-9968/doi:10.1108/S2044-9968(2013)000006G006

undertaking a series of representational challenges where they constructed and critiqued representations. The study found increased student engagement with learning technologies and an enhanced TPACK over the period of the course. Several factors that may have led to these findings are discussed.

INTRODUCTION

The integration of technology into schools and colleges has been seen as an essential step towards the improvement in teaching and learning in many countries. For this reason many governments have invested heavily in the building and maintenance of Information and Communication Technology (ICT) structures in schools (Pelgrum, 2001). For example, the Australian government has recently invested $2.5 billion into an initiative called the *Digital Education Revolution* (http://www.deewr.gov.au/Schooling/DigitalEducationRevolution/Pages/default.asp) with programs that aim at increasing ICT proficiencies in pre-service and practicing teachers and equipping Year 9–12 students with a laptop each. Investment by governments into school ICT structures has meant that many new educational technology tools are available to teachers.

ICT as a learning technology, facilitating mobility and connectivity, has now moved out of the computer room into the everyday practice of teaching and learning. However, whilst 'most teachers and students now benefit in some way from access to computers and digital resources, only a minority are reaping the full benefits of the information technology revolution' (COAG Productivity Working Group, 2008, p. 1). Integrating technology into instruction is still challenging for most teachers (Guzey & Roehrig, 2009). The level of ICT integration in classrooms remains low as teachers are using ICT to support, enhance and complement existing classroom practice rather than re-shaping subject content, goals and pedagogies (Prestridge, 2007). Well-integrated and effective classroom use of ICT is currently rare (Osborne & Hennessy, 2003).

Providing graduate teachers with the necessary skills to teach in classrooms of the 21st century has been the responsibility of pre-service teaching programs which involve the delivery of tertiary institution-based courses and practicum experiences in school settings. In terms of the development of pre-service teachers' competencies in ICT integration, there are still multiple gaps in curriculum design and delivery of teacher education courses (Lawless & Pellegrino, 2007; Tondeur, van Braak, & Valcke, 2007).

Whilst single technology courses are often provided in teacher education programs (Hsu & Sharma, 2006) such courses do not prepare teachers with the necessary skills involved in integrating ICT (Lawless & Pellegrino, 2007; Sanber, 2007). A recent study of pre-service teachers' perceptions of their ICT experiences in teacher preparation programs (DEEWR, 2009) found they expressed concerns at the lack of modelling by lecturers in embedding ICT into courses and insufficient assistance in how to embed ICT in classroom practices. The students also expressed concerns with the quality of support offered to them by practicum supervising teachers about teaching and learning with digital technologies.

Teachers need to understand the precise role of technology in teaching and learning (Mishra & Koehler, 2006) which provides a strong argument to embed ICT into teacher preparation courses and practicum experiences. Lawless and Pellegrino (2007) suggested that 'decisions about when to use technology, what technology to use, and for what purposes cannot be made in isolation of theories and research on learning, instruction, and assessment' (p. 581). There should be a focus on methods of teaching via technology within teacher preparation programs (Mishra & Koehler, 2006). Further, many of the activities of such programs should be set in a context of teaching and learning relevant to the participants. One method for accomplishing this with pre-service teachers is to have them use a variety of technological resources to explore problems and topics relevant to the levels at which they will teach (Hardy, 2010). Pre-service teachers are more likely to use technology when the technology is perceived to be useful, improves their performance and makes them more efficient (Teo, 2011). This view is consistent with the assertion made by Goodhue and Thompson (1995) that for a technology to have impact on individual performance it must be utilized and has a good task-technology fit. In other words, there is a match between the capabilities of the technology to the demands of the task.

In resolving the issue of lack of integration of ICT into classrooms, part of the Australian government's *Digital Education Revolution* has been funding for the Teaching Teachers for the Future (TTF) project. This project aims to 'drive change in Information and Communication Technology in Education (ICTE) proficiency of graduate teachers across Australia and enable pre-service teachers to achieve and demonstrate (upon graduation) competence in the effective and innovative use of ICTE to improve student learning' (ACDE, 2011, p.11). Key components of this project entailed the construction of a set of 'National Professional Standards for Graduate Teachers with ICT Elaborations' (AITSL, 2011) and the implementation of pre-service teaching courses designed to address these standards.

This chapter reports on a case study of a semester length course titled 'Resources in the Contemporary Science Curriculum' delivered to a mixed cohort of pre-service secondary science education teachers that was part of the TTF project. The course embedded learning technologies into its design not only to deliver the course curriculum but also to give the pre-service teachers insight into the manner in which they could embed learning technologies into their own teaching practice. The research questions that framed this case study were, 'Through participation in the course (a) what are the levels of pre-service teachers' engagement with ICT, and (b) what are the changes in pre-service students' understandings of the ways in which ICT can be embedded into the teaching and learning of science?'

THEORETICAL FRAMEWORK

In this case study, the theoretical framework is based on Mishra and Koehler's (2006) Technological Pedagogical Content Knowledge (TPACK) viewed through a representational construction teaching approach (Tytler & Hubber, 2011). TPACK is a framework for understanding the specialized, multi-faceted forms of knowledge required by teachers to integrate technology in their teaching. These forms of knowledge are content, pedagogy and technology knowledge (TK). For example, a teacher has the intention of introducing the particle model to explain various properties of matter to her Year 7 class. She will need to have the necessary content knowledge of the particle model and possess pedagogical knowledge of the ways in which Year 7 students effectively learn abstract concepts, for example, how to conduct a role-play to represent particle motion in a solid piece of matter. She may wish to elicit her students' prior views on the nature of matter using an online survey and so will require the technological knowledge to construct and administer the survey. Having an understanding of each of these knowledge domains is not sufficient for quality teaching. The teacher also requires a nuanced understanding of the complex interplays between these three key sources of knowledge (Mishra & Koehler, 2006). TPACK refers to the understanding that emerges from the interaction of content, pedagogy and TK. In the example given above, the teacher's TPACK informs her that the affordances of the instant feedback gained from the online survey will allow her to gain insights into the Year 7 students' prior understandings of the nature of matter. This information will be used in a formative way to plan a teaching sequence for a topic she knows will be difficult for the Year 7 students to learn because of its abstract content.

The representational perspective is based on a growing consensus that quality learning must involve richer and more sustained reasoning and engagement with the mediating tools of the discipline in ways that entail the acquisition of a subject-specific set of purpose-designed literacies (Lemke, 2004; Moje, 2007). Students use the multi-modal representational tools of science to generate, coordinate and critique evidence (Ford & Forman, 2006), involving models and model-based reasoning (Lehrer & Schauble, 2006). A recent Australian Research Council (ARC) funded project, Representations in Learning Science (RILS), successfully developed a theoretically sophisticated but practical, representation construction approach to teaching and learning that links student learning and engagement with the epistemic (knowledge production) practices of science (Prain, Tytler, Waldrip, & Hubber, 2010; Tytler & Hubber, 2011). This approach involves challenging students to generate and negotiate the representations (text, graphs, models, diagrams) that constitute the discursive practices of science, rather than focusing on the text-based, definitional versions of concepts. The representation construction approach is based on sequences of representational challenges which involve students constructing representations to actively explore and make claims about phenomena. It thus represents a more active view of knowledge than traditional structural approaches and encourages visual as well as the traditional text-based literacies. RILS has successfully demonstrated enhanced outcomes for students, in terms of sustained engagement with ideas, and quality learning, and for teachers' enhanced pedagogical knowledge and understanding of how knowledge in science is developed and communicated (Hubber, 2010a; Hubber, Tytler, & Haslam, 2010). This representation construction approach shows promise of resolving the tension between enquiry approaches to learning science and the need to introduce students to the conceptual canons of science (Klein & Kirkpatrick, 2010). It also shows promise in providing a wider pedagogical approach to embedding ICT into a teacher's classroom practice.

In successfully adopting a representation construction approach to the implementation of ICT, a teacher requires sophisticated levels of TPACK. In the words of Mishra and Koehler (2006) TPACK, 'requires an understanding of the representation of concepts using technologies; pedagogical techniques that use technologies; ... and how technology can help redress some of the problems that students face' (p. 1029). Pre-service teachers need to know that technologies have constrained and afforded a range of representations, analogies, examples, explanations and demonstrations that can help make subject matter more accessible to the learner and this understanding becomes part of a teacher's TPACK (Mishra & Koehler, 2006). Sutherland et al. (2004) cautioned that within a particular knowledge domain, such as science, it may be important for young people to be able to work with both digital and non-digital tools. Students should also be engaging in discussions about the relative merits of different tools, so that they can become resourceful learners. The students need to be made aware of the relative affordances of the ICT tools when using and communicating with such tools. This is part of a representation construction approach where students take into consideration the affordances and constraints of the representations they construct and critique.

There have been several attempts at enhancing the TPACK of pre-service teachers (Hardy, 2010; Haydn & Barton, 2007; Sanber, 2007; Shin et al., 2009). Hardy (2010) found practically oriented methods that meet a variety of teachers' technology needs which enhance pre-service teachers' TPACK. Similarly, Shin et al. (2009) found pre-service teachers gained a deeper and more complex understanding of TPACK in courses where they worked on a range of assignments that required them to learn and use technology in multiple pedagogical contexts. Sanber (2007) found an important factor in increasing pre-service teachers' TPACK was the level of ICT skills in the trainers, whilst Haydn and Barton (2007) indicated that it was the extent to which ICT was effectively modelled by the trainers. These researchers also indicated other factors such as the need for ICT activities to have a direct relationship with the pre-service teachers' subject areas. There was also a need for the provision of sufficient time for the teachers and their trainers to use and critique the multitude of ICT resources and devices for their efficacy in using them in the classroom. This is an important factor as computer self-efficacy, which is the users' beliefs about their ability to use a technology, has a direct effect on its utilization (Strong, Dishaw, & Bandy, 2006).

The representation construction approach provides an useful pedagogy with which to embed ICT into science classrooms and pre-service teacher training courses. In using ICT tools and devices, teachers require a certain level of technological knowledge. In addition, they require an understanding of the science content and appropriate pedagogy, informed by a representation construction approach, which underpins the TPACK framework.

METHODS

A mixed methods methodology was employed to answer the research questions. The data collection instruments included a pre- and post-course survey, field notes, focus group interview and students' artefacts, such as their digital portfolio of resources and their rationales for use in the science classroom.

The pre- and post-course survey was one developed by Schmidt et al. (2009) to ascertain pre-service teachers' knowledge of teaching and technology. It consisted of a series of statements related to each of the knowledge domains of the TPACK framework. The following are examples of statements found in the survey:

(a) I know how to solve my own technical problems (TK).
(b) I have sufficient knowledge about science (Content Knowledge).
(c) I know how to assess student performance in a classroom (Pedagogical Knowledge).
(d) I can select effective teaching approaches to guide student thinking and learning in science (Pedagogical Content Knowledge).
(e) I know about technologies that I can use for understanding and doing science (Technological Content Knowledge [TCK]).
(f) I can select technologies to use in my classroom that enhance what I teach, how I teach and what students learn (TPACK).

Respondents were to rate each statement on a 5-point Likert scale from *strongly disagree, disagree, neither agree or disagree, agree* to *strongly agree*. The respondents were also asked to describe a specific episode where each of their tutor, practicum supervisor and themselves demonstrated the use of ICT in their teaching practice.

The semester length course titled 'Resources in the Contemporary Science Curriculum' was delivered to a mixed cohort of pre-service secondary science teachers. The cohort of students consisted of 15 final year undergraduate double degree (bachelors of science and teaching) and 13 postgraduate master of teaching students. The course was delivered to 19 students in on-campus mode with a workshop format and delivered to 9 students in off-campus mode through a web-based online learning management system called *Blackboard* (http://www.blackboard.com/). The structure of each mode of the course is given below.

On-Campus Course Structure

The on-campus course was delivered as nine 3-hour workshop tutorials over the period of 12 weeks. During this period, the students undertook a 3-week practicum in a neighbouring secondary school. This practicum experience

was not embedded into the course as tasks undertaken by the student at the
school were solely determined by the student's supervising teacher. The
supervising teacher also provided the entire assessment of the student's
teaching performance at the school.

Each workshop involved exploring key elements of a particular theme (see
Table 1). This was done using a variety of pedagogical approaches that were
often enquiry and/or activity based. One of the prominent pedagogies was
the representation construction approach. As the title of the course implies,
the workshops involved exploring a range of resources that might contribute
to a contemporary science curriculum. Among the resources were ICT tools
that included Web 2.0 tools such as online surveys, *Prezi* (web-based
presentation http://prezi.com/), web quests, blogs and website building. The
resources were critiqued for their affordances for student learning of science
and many were presented to the students in a way that modelled their use in
practice. Importance was placed on the tutor as modelling the types of
pedagogical practices of an effective science teacher. For example, in the
first workshop the social bookmarking website, *Delicious* (www.delicious.
com), was presented to the students and the affordances of this resource for
student learning of science was discussed. The tutor created a *Delicious*
website for the course with full editing rights to all students with the purpose
of creating a shared repository of annotated online resources. Throughout
the semester both the tutor and students contributed to this site.

Apart from the many ICT resources in the form of tools and devices that
were embedded into the course, another resource was the use of experts
external to the university. Some of the workshops were run, in part, by
visiting experts, one of whom was a specialist in the Victorian Education
Departments' online system, called the *Ultranet* (http://www.education.
vic.gov.au/about/directions/ultranet/default.htm), which is used by teachers, parents and children in Victorian government schools. Other visiting
experts included early career practicing science teachers chosen for their
expertise in embedding ICT in their current practice. One of the workshops
was an excursion to the Melbourne Museum which had a pre-service teacher
program led by museum staff. The workshop program promoted current
learning theory and its application to museum experience, the deconstruc-
tion of exhibitions and practical activities for use in the classroom.

A feature of each workshop was the modelling of a representation
construction approach that began with the administration of a task in the
form of a representational challenge (refer to Table 1). The students were
required to complete the task within the time period of the workshop. These
challenges were modelled on similar tasks that might be administered to

Table 1. Workshop Outline of the On-Campus Course.

Workshop	Themes	Teaching Resources	Representational Challenges
1	Introduction National Professional Standards for Graduate Teachers – ICT Elaborations e^5 Instructional Model (DEECD, 2006) Laboratory safety and management	Social bookmaking website: Delicious (http://www.delicious.com) Website: AAAS Science Assessment (http://assessment.aaas.org/) Multimedia CD Rom: Animations – Particles in Motion (RSC/SEP, 2006)	Creating my webpage: wix.com (http://www.wix.com)
2	Representation construction pedagogy	Hubber (2010b)	Representing the concept of temperature Representing properties of matter Creating an animation: Ice-cream challenge (http://www.upd8.org.uk/activity/308/Instant-ice-cream.html)
3	Enquiry in the science classroom • The role of practical work • Nature of science Student presentations	Multimedia CD Rom: Inquiry-Based Teaching (Science by Doing, 2010) Website: Performance Assessment Links in Science (PALS) (http://pals.sri.com/) Multimedia CD Rom: Beyond Fair Testing (SEP, 2006)	Constructing molecules (Hollamby, 2007)
4	Assessment of student presentations	Website: Department of Education and Early Childhood Development (DEECD) Assessment Advice (http://www.education.vic.gov.au/studentlearning/assessment/preptoyear10/assessadvice/default.htm)	Construction of online survey: SurveyMonkey.com (http://www.surveymonkey.com)

Table 1. (Continued)

Workshop	Themes	Teaching Resources	Representational Challenges
5	Learning in informal settings: Excursion to Melbourne Museum	Website: Science Education Assessment Resources (SEAR) (http://cms.curriculum.edu.au/sear/) Guest Speaker: Early Career Science Teacher Melbourne Museum (http://museumvictoria.com.au/melbournemuseum/) Melbourne Museum Education Staff	600 million years in 60 seconds (Gaff, 2011)
6	Learning technologies	Web quest (Zunal Web Quest Maker http://zunal.com/) Guest Speaker: DEECD Ultranet Expert (http://www.education.vic.gov.au/about/directions/ultranet/whatis.htm)	Digital technology representational challenges • Pivot animation challenge • Digital microscope challenge
7	Argumentation	Guest Speaker: Early Career Teacher	Physics idol (http://www.upd8.org.uk/activity/144/Physics-idol.html)
8	Teaching a contemporary socio-scientific issue	STELR Project – Global Warming and Renewable Energies (http://stelr.org.au/)	Explaining an energy concept in your discipline Toy challenge
9	Topic planning	Website: Science Continuum (http://www.education.vic.gov.au/studentlearning/teachingresources/science/scicontinuum/default.htm)	ICT challenges: • White coffee problem • Adaptation challenge • Light reflection challenge • Hand motion challenge

secondary school science students. This placed the students in the role of the secondary science learner. Students often completed the challenges in groups of two to four students. Several of the challenges had an ICT component that required a certain level of technological knowledge. Therefore, apart from modelling representation construction pedagogy, these challenges were designed to enhance the students' technological knowledge. A significant component of the representation construction approach, which was modelled in the workshops, was the critique of the students' constructed representations. Following the completion of the challenge, each group presented their constructed representations to the class who then critiqued the representations as to whether they fitted the purposes of the challenge.

Following the critique of the students' constructed representations, there was usually a class discussion from a teachers' perspective as to the efficacy of the challenge for use in a secondary science classroom in terms of enhancing school students' conceptual understanding and/or skill development. The discussion included ways in which the challenge might be modified to support student learning of science at different year levels and science disciplines. The workshop activities where the students undertook the challenges and discussed their efficacy for implementation into science classrooms were seen as a means to enhance their TPACK and, in doing so, get greater insight into ways in which ICT can be embedded into a teacher's practice.

By undertaking the challenges and then discussing their efficacy for learning science in the classroom, the students switched roles from learner to teacher. Several of the students also took on the role as teacher providing advice and support to those students who lacked sufficient ICT skills in completing the challenges. A description of some of the ICT-based representational challenges is given in the following sections.

Creating My Webpage (Workshop 1)
This challenge required the construction and publication of a website which later would contain the electronic portfolio (see course assessment section below). A freeware webpage construction website (www.wix.com) was provided as a possible tool to complete this task.

Ice-Cream Challenge (Workshop 2)
This challenge was modified from a classroom activity from the *Science Upda8* website (http://www.upd8.org.uk/activity/308/Instant-ice-cream.html). It required the students to create an animation using *Microsoft PowerPoint* that provided a particle model explanation of the two physical change processes of mixing and freezing in making ice cream. The use of animation allowed for

model-based reasoning of dynamic processes which are involved when applying the particle model to explain macroscopic behaviour of matter.

Construction of Online Survey (Workshop 4)
This task challenged students to construct an online survey using the freeware option of the website resource *SurveyMonkey* (http://www.survey monkey.com). The purpose of the survey was to construct a diagnostic instrument designed to elicit children's prior learning on a particular science topic. Apart from considering the mechanics of constructing the survey the students needed to also consider the nature of the questions to be asked of children given the research literature, which suggested that they may hold misconceptions in the topic to be taught.

600 Million Years in 60 Seconds (Gaff, 2011) (Workshop 5)
This challenge was given as a group task whilst students were on an excursion (Table 1, workshop 5) at the Melbourne Museum. Each team member had a specific role – presenter, camera person or director. The challenge for the team was to create a 60-second video using flip camera technology, laptop, stopwatch and museum object (such as a fossil) to answer a mission question. The mission question was unique to each group, examples of which were, 'birds evolved from dinosaurs, how do we know?' and 'mega fauna roamed Australia, how do we know?' To answer the mission question, the group used the information presented in the *600 Million Years: Victoria Evolves* exhibition which brought the story of Victoria's evolution to life through animation, animatronics, models and multimedia interactives. This challenge was a new initiative by the museum to engage visiting school groups to the exhibitions (Gaff, 2011).

ICT Challenges (Workshop 9)
Students had the choice of undertaking one of four challenges: white coffee problem, adaptation challenge, light reflection challenge or hand motion challenge. After the completion of the challenge, students were to present their findings to the rest of the class. In the white coffee problem, students were challenged to use digital thermometers and other equipment to answer the question, 'if one has just poured a fresh brew of coffee and one can't drink for a few minutes should one add milk now or after two minutes?' For the adaptation challenge, students were challenged to collect evidence of adaptation in two animals and present their findings in a *Prezi* (http://prezi.com/) presentation. For the light reflection challenge, the students were to use digital light probes to determine which type of coloured paper other

than white reflects the most amount of light. For the hand motion challenge, the students were provided with a short video of a person walking and challenged to use motion analysis software to determine if a person's hand actually moves backwards when the person is moving in a forwards direction.

Off-Campus Course Structure

The same curriculum content was delivered to both off-campus and on-campus cohorts of students. For the off-campus students, the curriculum was delivered in each of the 12 weeks through a web-based online learning management system called *Blackboard*. The same ICT representational challenges were given to the off-campus students (except for the digital probe tasks). Students were often sent to a particular online resource to read, explore, investigate and then respond to a particular discussion thread. Assessment was the same as for on-campus students except for a hurdle assessment requiring a set number of quality submissions to the discussions associated with the weekly tasks. It is the author's university's policy that the same curriculum and assessment be applied to each course that is offered in on-campus and off-campus modes of delivery.

Course Assessment

The assessment for the course consisted of three tasks, details of which are given below. As stated previously, the same assessment was applied to both on-campus and off-campus delivery modes which was in line with university policy. The assessment tasks, with percentage weightings, were as follows:

(a) Teacher demonstration (25%): Students were to research and develop a teacher demonstration that could be used in the science classroom. Apart from a written report the on-campus students were required to provide an oral presentation that included the demonstration to the rest of the students. The off-campus students were required to provide a written report and an online presentation to fellow off-campus students.
(b) Electronic portfolio (40%): The students were to prepare an electronic portfolio of six teaching and learning resources that would be of benefit to them in their future professional practice as a secondary science teacher. There was a requirement that among the six resources two had to be specifically ICT based. The first one was a digital teaching resource

that would be used in the classroom. Two examples given were a web quest and online survey. A standard PowerPoint presentation was not allowed. The second one was a digital student work sample in response to a representational challenge given by the teacher. Apart from providing details about the challenge, the students were also required to complete the task as if they were the secondary science learner. Examples given were an animation and podcast.

For each resource, a rationale (including citations and references) was to be written outlining its features for its effective use in a science classroom in terms of improved learning outcomes for students. The overall challenge given to the students was for them to construct a website to be then used as a repository for their portfolio.

(c) Research report (30%): The students were to write a report that included a literature review on the theme 'learning science in settings other than the classroom' and construct a planning document that detailed an excursion that could be undertaken by students in a neighbouring school. The planning document was to include a rationale for conducting the excursion, details of the learning experiences to be handled by the students during the excursion as well as prior to and following the excursion and the protocols to follow at a school level to allow an excursion to be undertaken.

FINDINGS

The main findings in the data were increased engagement of ICT tools and devices and increased TPACK of the pre-service science teachers over the duration of the course. Table 2 provides pre- and post-course survey data related to students' ratings of statements within each of the TPACK framework knowledge domains. This data represents the pre-service teachers' perceptions of their own levels of teaching and TK. The data indicates increased levels in each of the knowledge domains, including TPACK, over the duration of the course. The data also indicates that at the beginning of the course the students' perceived levels of content and pedagogical knowledge were significantly higher than their TK and over the duration of the course most gains were found in those knowledge domains related to technology, namely, TK, TCK and TPACK.

Supportive evidence for the Table 2 data was found in data collected from the other instruments in this study. This data also provided evidence of

Table 2. Percentage of Respondents[a] Choosing Agree and/or Strongly Agree in the Pre- and Post-Unit Surveys.

Knowledge Domain	Pre-Test (%)	Post-Test (%)
Technology Knowledge (TK)	59.7	77.8
Content Knowledge (CK)	86.1	100
Pedagogical Knowledge (PK)	80.7	89.0
Pedagogical Content Knowledge (PCK)	83.3	91.7
Technological Content Knowledge (TCK)	58.3	83.3
Technological Content and Pedagogical Knowledge (TPACK)	63.3	79.2

[a]$n = 12$

increased engagement of ICT tools and devices and greater insights into the increased levels of technology and teaching knowledge perceived by the students. This is presented and discussed in the following sections.

Technological Knowledge (TK)

There was general agreement among the students in the focus group interview that through their participation in the course they had increased their engagement of ICT tools and devices. An outcome of this engagement was an increase in their TK.

One reason offered by the students was that the course gave them the opportunity to create something with the new technologies arising from the representational challenges given in the tutorials and the digital portfolio assessment task. When asked 'do you think your technology core skills have improved through participation in this unit (course)?' one student responded, 'Definitely. This unit actually is giving us a chance to create some things ... and actually we improve our knowledge as well'.

Another reason was suggested by a student who responded that improvement in TK for her was as a result of, 'being forced to use the software for assessment ... because we're actually forced to do it electronically or forced to do it that way for the assessment, then we do it'. There was a view that the assessment tasks placed the students out of their comfort zone in terms of adopting new technologies; this was not seen as a bad thing and is illustrated by the following comment,

But I think ... it puts people out of their comfort zone. So we sort of tend to go back to the things that we find comfortable like Word and PowerPoint and Publisher instead of

sort of venturing out into these other ones ... The assessment just forces you over that
resistance to use it ... It gets you over that barrier.

It was evident in the on-campus workshops that students readily engaged
in undertaking the representational challenges and, for many, their attempts
at the challenges meant learning new technological knowledge. These
challenges were often completed in small groups and support was provided
not only by the tutor but also other students. When presenting their constructed representations in response to the challenges it was often observed
that the students were pleased with their efforts, particularly if it involved
gaining new technological knowledge.

For the off-campus course, evidence of increased engagement with ICT
tools and TK was seen in the discussion threads within the *Blackboard*
learning management system that were constructed so that the students
could upload and discuss their responses to the ICT representational
challenges. The following discussion thread to the ice-cream animation
challenge indicated one student's posting and responses from another
student.

> This was a good challenge, I have not used PowerPoint like this before. This was very
> fiddly, but kinda fun and addictive. [This student attached his PowerPoint animation]
> [Student 1]
>
> That was great. How did you move all the particles- did you move each particle using the
> custom drawing? That is the kind of thing I wanted to get my particles to do but was
> unsure how to do it. Great Job! [Student 2]

Within the on-campus workshops, there was evidence of collaborative
support from the tutor and students to support those students in gaining the
necessary technological knowledge to complete the challenges. It was also
evident that the collective skill base of the whole group exceeded that of the
tutor. Course support for off-campus students was undertaken on a needs
basis where students would post a message outlining their problem. This
was often resolved by either the tutor or another student. Outside of the
workshop and online course environment, students resorted to publicly
produced video tutorial support or their peers. In the focus group interview
when asked, 'what information technology support the students had outside
of the university environment?', one student responded,

> Using the little web videos that they often provide for different things. Like particularly
> with software they'll have videos of tutorials for explaining this is how you do this.
> Whereas with the tools they think it was more a pick it up and play with it until we figure
> it out.

The following quotes were from students who used specific ICT resources or tools for the first time in the course. They indicate high levels of engagement and a sense of achievement in gaining a useful skill.

As you probably know my ICT knowledge is very limited. I was really impressed to see what a web quest is and I think it has huge benefits particularly for people like me who are just starting to get into web based learning ... I also think this is something that I could set up without too much trouble. [off-campus student]

It was the first time [in this course] I used a digital microscope that you plugged into your laptop. That's cool. [on-campus student]

Below is a link to an online quiz I designed on the topic of 'Mixtures' in Chemistry. While using SurveyMonkey, I particularly liked it, because it is easy to design a quiz/survey. [off-campus student]

I've made a Prezi today and actually found it pretty interesting and will probably make more for this assignment and in the future as well. [on-campus student]

We spent a whole afternoon in the library playing with Prezi and working it out. [on-campus student]

The major assessment task for the course, a digital portfolio, required the students to use their technological knowledge to construct a digital teaching resource and a student digital artefact in response to a representational challenge designed by the student. Whilst most of the students had not constructed a webpage before they all completed this challenge successfully producing well-designed web pages making it easier for the reader to access the embedded resources.

Apart from creating a website to contain their digital portfolios, the variation in the digital resources used by the students to construct the teaching resource can be found in Fig. 1 and for construction of the student artefact can be found in Fig. 2. Both Figs. 1 and 2 show evidence of students' abilities to construct digital resources using a variety of digital tools and devices.

The technological knowledge required for some tasks were seen as challenging and for other tasks easy to acquire. For example, in completing the digital portfolio one off-campus student remarked in an email, 'Have to say this was a monumental task for me so for you to be able to see anything will be a bonus!!'. Whilst the digital devices – data loggers and digital microscopes – were new to many of the students, they felt such devices were easy to use as evidenced by the following comment by a student in the focus group,

No, I haven't used them [digital devices] before, no USB video cameras and also motion detectors .... He [tutor] showed them to us and then I used it. They're all easy – just pop into your computer via USB. They're easy to use and they come with the software.

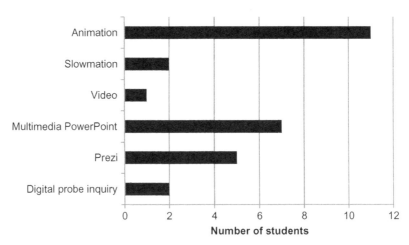

Fig. 1. Distribution of Digital Resources Used to Construct a Teaching Resource.

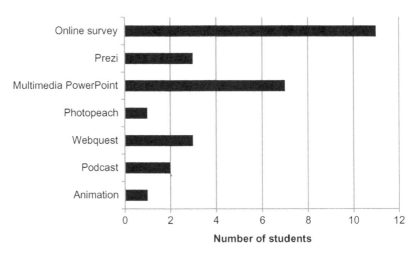

Fig. 2. Distribution of Digitial Resources Used to Construct a Student Artefact.

Content Knowledge (CK) and Pedagogical Knowledge (PK)

As indicated by Table 2, the students' perceived levels of CK and PK were
high at the beginning of the course. However, where the context of the

workshop activities was outside the specific expertise of the students they reported gains in CK. For example, when asked 'was this unit instrumental in improving your understanding of science?' One student responded, 'All the physics stuff. Because I don't have much of a basis in physics it did help sort of cement some of those concepts'.

Modelling best teaching practice informed by current findings from research by the tutor was seen by the students as beneficial in enhancing their PK.

> The way Peter [tutor] presented with some of his research done in a classroom ... I found that really useful to sort of help to both cement my understanding and help me to visualise what I should be teaching my students and how I should present stuff to them and that kind of thing.

Technological Pedagogical and Content Knowledge (TPACK)

The data showed evidence of gains in the students' TPACK where the students achieved a greater understanding of ways to embed ICT into the teaching and learning of science. Throughout the course, the tutor presented a view that technology should not be seen as an end in itself. Instead, it should be considered as the most appropriate representational tool for learning once the teacher has considered the specific learning outcomes for his/her students and an appropriate pedagogical approach to apply. This view was expressed by a student in the focus group interview,

> It wasn't so much a case of okay we need to teach them how to use this tool or we're going to use this for this reason. It was a case of 'this is the lesson that I'm teaching, what are the kids learning?' then matching an appropriate technology and pedagogy.

The emphasis on learning technologies was not seen as a panacea for effective teaching but the role played by the teacher. One student commented,

> It's something I've really found about the unit. I think that's what makes an effective teacher you can have all the tools in the world and still not be able to teach ... I don't think that it's just technology at the forefront. It's the teachers. It's what we're trying to aim to do in terms of students learning science.

In articulating the contribution ICT has for the science classroom one student made the point, 'It wasn't just technology for the sake of technology. It was how you could put this technology into your classroom, whether it's getting the students to utilize it or you're utilising it yourself and I think Peter (tutor) made that pretty clear'.

The role of the teacher in supporting ICT was mentioned by an off-campus student who made the following comment in relation to evaluating two flash animations that were given in one of the weekly tasks.

> After completing the flash animations on evolution I have found that there is learning to be accomplished through the use of animations but they need to be well guided and easy to follow ... Though ICT can encourage learning, activities that aren't clear can be ignored and rendered ineffective.

The students gained insights into the manner in which ICT could be embedded into the science classroom through modelling of best practice undertaken by the tutor. One student commented, 'Peter (tutor) was putting stuff in all the time. There was good modelling of the technology use'. In response to the survey question, 'describe a specific episode where a tutor/lecturer effectively demonstrated or modelled content, technologies and teaching approaches in a classroom lesson' several students made reference to the course in responding, 'Peter Hubber's class (all of them)'. Other comments included,

> Many examples from this tute class with the various resources which can be used for different fields of science.

> Everything we have done in this class from learning about new technologies to them being demonstrated in class, to modelling classroom science activities around the technologies.

The digital portfolio assessment task required the pre-service students to apply, and show, their TPACK as not only were they required to collect and construct digital resources but were also required to provide details as to how the resource might be specifically used in their own classroom as well as provide a rationale for its use. Fig. 3 shows the distribution of resource types among the students' digital portfolio each of which consisted of 6 resources. This figure shows that the majority of the resources were ICT based despite there being the requirement that only two of the resources be in this form. There was also a wide variety of resources. These findings reflect a high level of engagement with digital technologies several of which employed web 2.0 tools such as online surveys, *Prezi* (web-based presentation http://prezi.com/), web quests, blogs and website building.

The variety of resource type reflects the open-ended nature of the task in terms of allowing the students flexibility in the type of resource they could

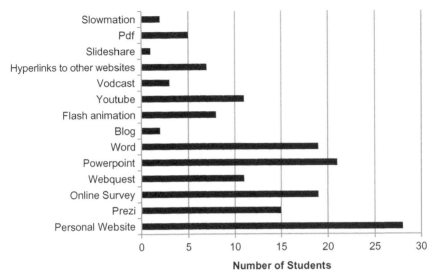

Fig. 3.   Distribution of Resources Used by Students in Their Digital Portfolios.

choose. This was seen as an important aspect of the assessment task as the decision to use a particular digital technology should not precede subject content and pedagogical decisions.

The students often showed evidence of TPACK in the rationales that accompanied each resource. An example is shown in Fig. 4 where the student created an online survey using the *SurveyMonkey* tool and provided a rationale for its use.

In the rationale reference was made to a connection with content knowledge expected of Year 12 biology students when she stated that 'Survey Monkey has been used to develop a series of questions for a year 12 Biology classroom, in preparation for their end of year exam'. She also stated that, 'Survey Monkey can also be used as a form of assessment tool … [which] can be accessed from both a home or school computer' and can be used, 'as a form of pre-testing to identify students prior knowledge and misconceptions of science concepts; knowledge which teachers can use to help plan their lessons on the unit, or the unit itself'. Reference was also made to pedagogical knowledge in terms of initially eliciting students' understanding of biology concepts and then using this information in class discussions, driven by students, to resolve issues of misunderstandings. The whole process was seen as a revision activity for students to prepare for their

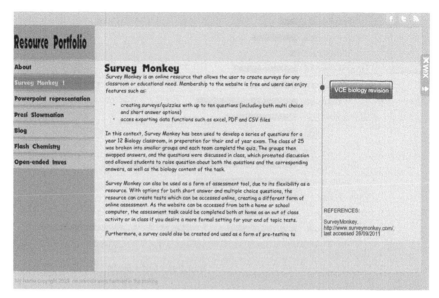

Fig. 4.   One Students' Digital Portfolio Website Front Page and One Resource Page.

final examination, which the pre-service teacher undertook as part of her practicum experience. She wrote,

> The class of 25 was broken into smaller groups and each team completed the quiz. The groups then swapped answers, and the questions were discussed in class, which promoted discussion and allowed students to raise question about the questions and the corresponding answers, as well as the biology content of the task.

Finally, reference was made to technological knowledge with the production of the online survey. The student highlighted the affordances of an online survey in terms of its accessibility in school or home and the formative assessment features in terms of providing the teacher about students' prior knowledge of a topic that could inform future teaching practices. The rationale illustrates the student's TPACK through the explicit links made to each of the three knowledge domains of content, pedagogy and technology.

Many of the students applied their TPACK gained in the course whilst on their practicum rounds. This was evident in the comments made in their digital portfolios, as in the case above, as well as in off-campus discussion and focus group discussion. Indicative comments are given below:

> I created my online survey on genetics which is what my current class of Year 10 students are completing. [off-campus student]

> I now use the Delicious website quite frequently. I'd never heard of it before I started the unit and I've used it several times in class situations … My supervising teacher thought it was a good idea to use it. [on-campus student]

Apart from the representational challenges the students showed evidence of their TPACK in other areas of the course. The students critiqued a range of online resources in terms of their efficacy of use in a science classroom. Several students used digital resources for their teacher demonstration, which was part of their formal assessment for the course. For example, a pair of students videotaped a dangerous experiment they had conducted and embedded the video into a multimedia *PowerPoint* presentation. One of the postgraduate students who had previous employment in the IT industry did not feel as if the course enhanced his technology core skills but gave him an 'awareness of other tools that are available that are quite straight forward to use' and better skills in determining the efficacy of an ICT resource's use in the classroom as 'there's an infinite amount of stuff on the Internet and you just don't know what's good and what's not for teaching'.

Issues Raised by Pre-Service Teachers

Issues raised by the students in undertaking this course related to time commitment necessary to learn a new technology, access to digital resources and a lack of good models of ICT practice in other courses and practicum schools. Each of these issues is discussed below.

Time Commitment
Whilst sufficient time was set aside in the workshop program for students to complete the representational challenges new technologies were often discussed or demonstrated without the students gaining class time to develop an expertise in their use. Students were then required to gain the technological knowledge outside of the class-time. In some cases the time taken to do this was an issue as illustrated by the following comment made by one of the students in the focus group interview.

> My first Prezi I did took me 6 hours and I only stuck with it because it was a requirement but after the first hour I got annoyed with it. I just wanted to give up. But as part of my assessment criteria was to do a prezi so I was just like "I've got to do it." But if it [the new technology] took me more than an hour to understand or to do something so simple, I just gave up on it because I don't have time and I know that it's going to be the same when I get out into a school. If it's going to take me too long – teachers don't have the time to do it.

This student's reference to teachers in schools being 'time poor' in learning new technologies is a valid one and supported by the literature (Bingimlas, 2009).

Access to Digital Resources
A significant issue for the students was accessibility to web-based resources. Whilst importance was placed by the course tutor to employ freeware software this was not always the case. Some of the restrictions on the freeware were limitations in capabilities (e.g. www.surveymonkey.com) or resources that only provided a limited 'free' trial period (e.g. www. inspiration.com). Comments made by students in relation to this issue are given below. The second quote refers to the *Ultranet* which is an online learning management system developed for the Victorian Department of Education and Early Childhood Development (DEECD) to provide extensive services to children, parents and teachers in government schools. The *Ultranet* gives teachers easy access to learning tools and resources; however, access is only possible to registered government teachers.

> The [Survey Monkey] resource provides an easy tool for teachers to create quizzes without much time needed for formatting. I found the website really useful except you can only create 10 questions for the basic package we sign up for, which as you can see by the structure of the quiz [I constructed] was unanticipated. [off-campus student]

> I found it quite irritating sometimes, a lot of the things that we're being introduced to, particularly the Ultranet that we don't have access to. So we're being taught about things that we can't actually use now or programs that we can have a 30 day trial to for free but if we have another assignment later on using the same program we can't go back and get it. [on-campus student]

The students did get some insight into the *Ultranet* through a presentation by a Victorian Education Department *Ultranet* expert during the week 6 workshop. Despite not getting personal access it was felt by one student that

> … it was good to know that it's there. It's frustrating that you can't use it and fiddle with it and work out how you'd use it but at least you know it's there.

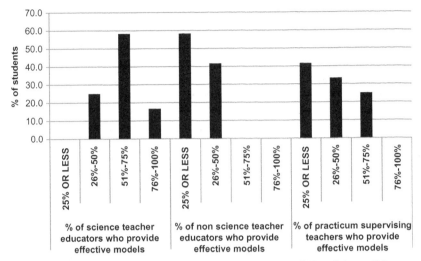

Fig. 5. Percentage of Effective Models Found in Science and Non-Science Educators and Practicum Supervising Teachers Perceived by the Pre-Service Teachers.

Insufficient Modelling of ICT Practice in Non-Science Courses and Practicum Schools

In the post-surveys the students were to indicate the percentage of science and non-science teacher educators and practicum supervising teachers who provided effective models of ICT practice. Fig. 5 indicates that whilst science teacher educators were seen as models of effective ICT practice this was not the case for non-science teacher educators. In terms of effective models seen by the students on the practicum experiences there were mixed results. Some students saw the majority of their teachers who were effective models whilst for other students such teachers were in the minority.

CONCLUSION

The course that formed the basis of the case study herein presented was a general science curriculum course as part of two pre-service secondary science teacher programs. This course was purposefully designed to embed learning technologies into its curriculum, assessment and delivery. A representational construction pedagogy that affords the integration of ICT into classroom practice was modelled by the tutor. A high level of engagement with Web 2.0 tools was evidenced by the number of students who chose to create web quests, prezis and other online tools as representations to teach science. There were also increased levels of TPACK achieved by the pre-service secondary science teachers. This was evident in the manner in which the students participated and succeeded in completing the representational challenges which were embedded in the weekly tasks as well as the major assessment task, the digital portfolio. Evidence was also provided by the student reflections of practicum experiences during which they incorporated learning technologies in their teaching. The increased levels of TPACK resulted from significant levels of student engagement with ICT in the course.

There are several possible drivers for the pre-service teachers' engagement with learning technologies and increased TPACK. One of these drivers is the nature of the representational challenges and the expectation that they be completed as part of the general course work as well as an assessment requirement. The challenges were authentic tasks which highlighted how learning technologies might be used in practice, that is, the school environment. The focus was not on the learning technology but on the outcomes of using the learning technology. An example of an outcome is the understanding of an abstract scientific theory, like the particle model. Another example is to fulfil a pedagogical aim to elicit students' views on a particular phenomenon or scientific issue. The challenges represented activities that were set in the context of teaching and learning of science relevant to the students which concur with the views expressed by Hardy (2010) and Mishra and Koehler (2006). Whilst the acquisition of technological knowledge was seen as challenging and time-consuming for some students it was considered as useful in terms of their improved future teaching practice. Teo (2011) saw these as reason why students might use the technology. This concurs with Goodhue and Thompson's (1995) idea of good task-technology fit.

Another possible driver for engagement with learning technologies and enhanced TPACK was the competence of a skilled educator modelling best practice in the ways in which ICT can be used in the science classroom. Fig. 5 shows that the students saw a lack of models in their non-science teacher training course and variation in different teachers' practices observed on practicum. By taking on the multiple roles of learner, pre-service teacher and teacher during the course the students directly experienced a representation construction approach (Tytler & Hubber, 2011), which involves the student construction and critique of representational forms. The representational forms do not necessary imply the products of a learning technology and so the students saw the use of technologies within a broader pedagogy. In other words, a learning technology needs to be seen as a tool for learning rather than the technology as an end in itself. There was evidence that several students were successfully using learning technologies in their practicum which they negotiated with their supervising teachers and so the student could appreciate what Teo (2011) described as the 'demands and stresses involved in integrating technology in a real school setting' (p. 95).

There were several issues that arose in the course that may point to areas for improvement. One issue for the students was the non-access to ICT system structures such as the Victorian government Schools' *Ultranet*. Teacher educators and pre-service teachers should be given access to the technologies they are likely to encounter in schools (Teo, 2011). Another issue for the course was the university requirement to provide the same curriculum and assessment to on-campus and off-campus students. Whilst the representational challenges were the same the manner in which they were undertaken was quite different in the two delivery modes. The issues faced by the off-campus students in online learning have not been discussed in this chapter but represent a fruitful research direction. Ma and Yuen (2011) point out that effectiveness of online learning is not guaranteed with learning technologies but may be enhanced through the facilitation of collaborative or group learning in a peer-support and exchange environment.

A final issue relates to embedding learning technologies into whole teacher training programs. This course was a core for the double degree program but not for the master of teaching program for the pre-service secondary science teacher programs and was not offered at all in any of the other secondary teaching programs. Therefore, the ICT experiences of pre-service teachers at this university can vary depending on the courses they undertake. Given that graduate standards for teaching involve ICT skills (AITSL, 2011), it becomes important for program leaders to ensure that all graduates have the necessary ICT knowledge base and confidence to integrate ICT into the curriculum and their teaching when they enter the teaching profession (Jamieson-Proctor, Finger, & Albion, 2010). Consistent with findings from Haydn and Barton (2007) a program approach to embedding ICT may resolve a time issue raised by students in this course in relation to gaining technological knowledge of new technologies. Pre-service teachers can develop their technological knowledge over many courses rather than a select few.

This study shows that where teacher training courses are designed in a manner that embeds learning technologies in the curriculum, assessment and delivery, increased engagement with learning technologies and enhanced TPACK among the pre-service teachers is possible.

REFERENCES

Australian Council of Deans in Education (ACDE). (2011). *Teaching teachers for the future*. Retrieved from http://www.acde.edu.au/pages/page30.asp

Australian Institute for Teaching and School Leadership (AITSL). (2011). National professional standards for teachers: ICT elaborations for graduate teacher standards. Retrieved from http://acce.edu.au/national-professional-standards-teachers-ict-elaborations-graduate-teachers

Bingimlas, K. A. (2009). Barriers to the successful integration of ICT in teaching and learning environments: A review of the literature. *Eurasia Journal of Mathematics, Science & Technology, 5*(3), 235–245.

COAG Productivity Agenda Working Group. (2008). *Success through partnership: Achieving a national vision for ICT in schools: Strategic plan to guide implementation of the digital education revolution initiative and related initiatives*. Retrieved from http://www.deewr. gov.au/Schooling/DigitalEducationRevolution/Documents/DERStrategicPlan.pdf

Department of Education and Early Childhood Development (DEECD). (2006). *The e5 Instructional Model*. Retrieved from http://www.education.vic.gov.au/proflearning/e5/

Department of Education, Employment and Workplace Relations (DEEWR). (2009). *Listening to students' and educators' voices*. Retrieved from http://www.deewr.gov.au

Ford, M., & Forman, E. A. (2006). Refining disciplinary learning in classroom contexts. *Review of Research in Education, 30*, 1–33.

Gaff, P. (2011). 600 million years in 60 seconds. *LabTalk, 55*(4), 4–6.

Goodhue, D. L., & Thompson, R. L. (1995). Task-technology fit and individual performance. *MIS Quarterly, 19*(2), 213–236.

Guzey, S., & Roehrig, G. (2009). Teaching science with technology: Case studies of science teachers' development of technology, pedagogy, and content knowledge. *Contemporary Issues in Technology and Teacher Education, 9*(1), 25–45.

Hardy, M. (2010). Enhancing pre-service mathematics teachers' TPCK. *Journal of Computers in Mathematics and Science Teaching, 29*(1), 73–86.

Haydn, T. A., & Barton, R. (2007). Common needs and different agendas: How trainee teachers make progress in their ability to use ICT in subject teaching. Some lessons from the UK. *Computers & Education, 49*, 1018–1036.

Hollamby, P. (2007). *Chemistry jigsaws*. Waltham Cross, London: Teaching Resources Ltd.

Hsu, P-S., & Sharma, P. (2006). A systemic plan of technology integration. *Educational Technology & Society, 9*(4), 173–184.

Hubber, P. (2010a). Year 8 students' understanding of astronomy as a representational issue: Insights from a classroom video study. In D. Raine, L. Rogers & C. Hurkett (Eds.), *Physics community and cooperation: Selected contributions from the GIREP-EPEC & PHEC 2009 International Conference* (pp. 45–64). Leicester: Lulu, the Centre for Interdisciplinary Science, University of Leicester.

Hubber, P. (2010b). *Ideas about matter: Teaching ideas with a representational focus*. Burwood, Melbourne: Deakin University.

Hubber, P., Tytler, R., & Haslam, F. (2010). Teaching and learning about force with a representational focus: Pedagogy and teacher change. *Research in Science Education, 40*(1), 5–28.

Jamieson-Proctor, R., Finger, G., & Albion, P. (2010). *Auditing the TPACK capabilities of final year teacher education students: Are they ready for the 21st century*. Paper presented at the Australian Council for Computers in Education (ACEC): digital diversity conference, Melbourne, Australia.

Klein, P., & Kirkpatrick, L. (2010). Multimodal literacies in science: Currency, coherence and focus. *Research in Science Education, 40*(1), 87–92.

Lawless, K., & Pellegrino, J. (2007). Professional development in integrating technology into teaching and learning: Knowns, unknowns, and ways to pursue better questions and answers. *Review of Educational Research, 77*(4), 575–614.

Lehrer, R., & Schauble, L. (2006). Cultivating model-based reasoning in science education. In K. Sawyer (Ed.), *Cambridge handbook of the learning sciences* (pp. 371–388). Cambridge: Cambridge University Press.

Lemke, J. (2004). The literacies of science. In E. W. Saul (Ed.), *Crossing borders in literacy and science instruction: Perspectives on theory and practice* (pp. 33–47). Newark, DE: International Reading Association and National Science Teachers Association.

Ma, W., & Yuen, A. (2011). E-learning system acceptance and usage pattern. In T. Teo (Ed.), *Technology acceptance in education: Research and issues* (pp. 201–216). Rotterdam: Sense Publications.

Mishra, P., & Koehler, M. J. (2006). Technological pedagogical content knowledge: A new framework for teacher knowledge. *Teachers College Record, 108*(6), 1017–1054.

Moje, E. (2007). Developing socially just subject-matter instruction: A review of the literature on disciplinary literacy learning. *Review of Research in Education, 31*, 1–44.

Osborne, J., & Hennessy, S. (2003). *Literature review in science education and the role of ICT: Promise, problems and future directions* (Report No. 6). Retrieved from http://hal.archives-ouvertes.fr/docs/00/19/04/41/PDF/osborne-j-2003-r6.pdf

Pelgrum, W. J. (2001). Obstacles to the integration of ICT in education: Results from a worldwide educational assessment. *Computers & Education, 37*, 163–178.

Prain, V., Tytler, R., Waldrip, B., & Hubber, P. (2010). *Pedagogical principles associated with an explicit representational perspective on learning in science.* Paper presented at the conference of the European Science Education Research Association (ESERA), Istanbul, Turkey.

Prestridge, S. (2007). Engaging with the transforming possibilities of ICT: A discussion paper. *Australian Educational Computing, 22*(2), 3–9.

Royal Society of Chemistry/Science Enhancement Programme (RSC/SEP). (2006). *Particles in Motion [CD Rom].* London: Gatsby Science Education Programme.

Sanber, S. (2007). *Teacher educators and the integration of ICT into education studies sequence: Threats and opportunities.* Paper presented at the International Study Association on Teachers and Teaching (ISATT) Conference University of Ghent, Brock University, Canada.

Schmidt, D., Baran, E., Thompson, A., Koehler, M. J., Shin, T., & Mishra, P. (2009). *Technological pedagogical content knowledge (TPACK): The development and validation of an assessment instrument for pre-service teachers.* Paper presented at the 2009 Annual Meeting of the American Educational Research Association. April 13–17, San Diego, California.

Science by Doing. (2010). *Inquiry-based Teaching [CD Rom].* Canberra: Australian Academy of Science.

Science Enhancement Programme (SEP). (2006). *Beyond Fair Testing [CD Rom].* London: Gatsby Science Education Programme.

Shin, T., Koehler, M., Mishra, P., Schmidt, D., Baran, E., & Thompson, A. (2009). Changing technological pedagogical content knowledge (TPACK) through course experiences. In I. Gibson et al. (Eds.), *Proceedings of Society for Information Technology & Teacher Education International Conference 2009* (pp. 4152–4159). Chesapeake, VA: Association for the Advancement of Computers in Education (AACE).

Strong, D. M., Dishaw, M. T., & Bandy, D. B. (2006). Extending task technology fit with computer self-efficacy. *SIGMIS Database*, *37*(2–3), 96–107.

Sutherland, R., Armstrong, V., Barnes, S., Brawn, R., Breeze, N., Gall, M., & John, P. (2004). Transforming teaching and learning: embedding ICT into everyday classroom practices. *Journal of Computer Assisted Learning*, *20*, 413–425.

Teo, T. (2011). Modeling technology acceptance among pre-service teachers. In T. Teo (Ed.), *Technology acceptance in education: Research and issues* (pp. 79–99). Rotterdam: Sense Publishers.

Tondeur, J., van Braak, J., & Valcke, M. (2007). Curricula and the use of ICT in education: Two worlds apart? *British Journal of Educational Technology*, *38*(6), 962–976.

Tytler, R., & Hubber, P. (2011). *A representation-intensive pedagogy for school science.* Paper presented as part of the symposium: Learning science through participation in its epistemic/symbolic language practices at the conference of the European Association of Research in Learning and Instruction (EARLI), Exeter, UK.

FROM CONNECTIVITY TO CONNECTED LEARNERS: TRANSACTIONAL DISTANCE AND SOCIAL PRESENCE

David Starr-Glass

ABSTRACT

Distance learning has proliferated significantly in the last 20 years. This chapter considers some of the issues and implications when teaching and learning moves from an in-person to a distance mode. It begins with a brief history of distance learning, considering both the technologies used and the dominant pedagogical approaches employed. This is followed by a survey of the impact of Michael Moore's theory of transactional distance, which considered the consequences of separating the learner from peers and instructor. Contemporary work on Moore's contribution includes transaction and participation, activity theory, and transactional presence. A second major aspect of distance learning has been the attempt to introduce social presence into learning environments. The history of social presence is explored, as are its levels and consequences for the learner. Contemporary aspects of social presence reviewed include communities of inquiry. While Web 2.0 has spectacularly resulted in connectivity, it

Increasing Student Engagement and Retention in e-Learning Environments:
Web 2.0 and Blended Learning Technologies
Cutting-edge Technologies in Higher Education, Volume 6G, 113–143
Copyright © 2013 by Emerald Group Publishing Limited
All rights of reproduction in any form reserved
ISSN: 2044-9968/doi:10.1108/S2044-9968(2013)000006G007

remains unclear as to whether this automatically resulted in more strongly connected learners. Connectivist approaches are considered and distinctions made between technological connectivity and pedagogical engagement. It is argued that the full and exciting potential of Web 2.0 in distance learning requires a commitment to the distanced learner, balancing learner autonomy and teacher presence, promoting meaningful social engagement, and meeting the specific needs of the distance learner.

INTRODUCTION

Distance learning, in which learners are physically separated from their instructors and peers, has a long history in both formal and informal education. Through much of its history distance learning has been regarded as a pragmatic compromise rather than as a legitimate paradigm. In the last 40 years, however, there has been a rapid increase in distance learning modalities in higher education and a growing sense that it provides not only increased flexibility but also unique learning opportunities.

In the fall of 2002, only about 1.6 million students enrolled in American colleges experienced online distance learning, representing 9.6% of the student population. In the fall of 2010, those enrolled in at least one online distance learning course had climbed dramatically to 6.1 million, or 31.3% of all students. In the same year, more than 67% of academic administrators at American public colleges considered online instruction to be at least as good as, or superior to, traditional in-person (face-to-face) teaching, and about the same percentage agreed that online education would play a significant part in the institution's strategic planning (Allen & Seaman, 2011). This optimism is felt not only for online instruction but also for blended courses that incorporate in-person and distance learning components. Blended courses have shown a significant growth rate in the last few years, even if that rate lags behind online modalities and even although there are indications that the growth curve may have peaked. The most complete survey data indicates that, in 2005, about 5.6% of all American colleges offered at least one blended course (Allen, Seaman, & Garrett, 2007).

The dramatic adoption of online learning and blended courses has only been possible because of exceptional advances in communication and connective technologies. New technologies provide the means of delivering distance learning, but more significantly they increasingly provide teaching and learning opportunities for more effective knowledge creation. From an institutional management and marketing perspective, distance learning technologies have been eagerly adopted to enter new student markets, to increase enrollment, and to provide colleges with competitive advantages (Elloumi, 2008; Stromquist, 2002). Communication and connective technologies have been significant in reducing instructional costs and in facilitating cooperation with other educational providers (Peters, 2000; Selwyn & Fitz, 2001). From a broader learning and social perspective, innovation in the technology of connecting learners has for the first time made it possible to establish global communities of knowledge (Maddux & Johnson, 2010; Rajasingham, 2009) and to prepare students for the networked world within which they will live and work (Zong, Wilson, & Quashiga, 2008).

The move from in-person to distance learning has been technology-inspired and sometimes technology-pushed; however, the shift cannot be accomplished by technology alone. It requires a significant reconsideration of two key aspects of the learning environment: the process through which learning takes place and the dynamics of instructor–learner interaction. Forty years ago, when distance learning began to flourish, in-person instruction in higher education was dominated by a model in which knowledge was considered to exist separately and independently from the learner. The learner's task was to acquire knowledge defined and presented by the instructor. The instructor's task was to indicate and explain relevant knowledge in ways that made acquisition possible. The instructor was centrally and actively present in the process; the learner was to an extent marginal and relatively passive. Distance learning radically changed these assumptions. Instructors could not be actively present and learners have to become responsible for the decisions about what they learned and how learning was to take place. Learners needed guidance in negotiating the change in dynamics, and support in understanding that "meaning is created or constituted in the relationship between the individual and the context" (Martin, Prosser, Trigwell, Ramsden, & Benjamin, 2000, p. 388).

Distance learning shifted the model from instructor-centered to learner-centered, with the understanding that knowledge was not passively acquired but personally constructed by learners, or co-constructed through collaboration with peers. The learner was highlighted as an autonomous individual, but the learner was also repositioned in relation to other distance learning participants. There was a growing appreciation that learning was a social activity, in which experience and new understanding could be tested and confirmed through others. When the educational experience was distanced, there was the danger that the learner would be isolated and separated from its social dimension. Distance learning faced the challenge of creating environments in which learners could sense social connectedness, recognize learning as a social activity, and explore new roles through which learner–instructor and learner–learner could interact.

Advances in communication technology provided extraordinary opportunities for distance learning. Increasingly, computer-aided communication platforms allowed learners to connect with one another. In a Web 2.0 era, global connectivity has provided the means of bringing physically separated people together in virtual environments. The evolution of distance learning indicates that learning takes place when the technological potential of connectivity is harnessed to the social and cognitive needs of the learner. As connectivity makes way for learner connectedness, the subject matter, the instructor, and fellow learners become more accessible and a dynamic process of knowledge creation can begin.

This chapter highlights this move from connectivity to connectedness by considering two bodies of research that have proved particularly insightful: transactional distance and social presence. Michael Moore's theory of transactional distance explores the consequences of distancing learners from their instructor. It provides a comprehensive framework for considering distance learning, a framework that is open enough to accommodate new parts but robust enough to provide practical solutions. Ongoing research shows that Moore's insights remain pertinent in designing distance learning environments for a Web 2.0 world. Theories of social and cognitive presence provide a second way of understanding the challenges and opportunities of distance learning. The contribution of social presence and cognitive presence research has been particularly useful in enhancing and enriching distance learning environments. Before considering transactional distance and social presence, however, it will be helpful to look at the evolution of distance learning.

A SHORT HISTORY OF DISTANCE LEARNING

Distance learning did not begin with a particular theory of teaching and learning; instead, it was grounded in a pragmatic consideration of increased access and inclusion. In the UK, for example, a growing demand for worker participation in higher education was met by Isaac Pitman, the originator of shorthand, who launched a series of correspondence courses in the 1840s (Schulte, 2011). By the mid-1850s, the University of London created a revolutionary program that allowed external students, studying independently via distance learning, to earn degrees that were academically identical to those earned on campus. A key issue in this move was to provide an opportunity for women, who at that time were unable to matriculate, or graduate from other English universities.

Distance education could be used to overcome social and cultural barriers and bring about wider inclusion. In other situations, the promise of distance education was in reaching students who were physically distanced from educational centers. In Australia, for example, territorial distance and widely dispersed student populations restricted learner mobility, making it impossible to attend a central campus. Distance education, initially through a correspondence model, allowed the remote learner to actively participate in higher education.

Adoption of distance learning came about in different places for different reasons. Once instituted, the evolutionary trajectory that it followed is remarkably similar. The evolution has been primarily driven by the availability of technology and media, rather than by educational considerations. While technological opportunity has been the driver, increasing interest has grown in the educational consequences for the learning process: a reconsideration of the social context of learning; theories of teaching and learning; and, learner autonomy (Schulte, 2011). This pattern can be summarized by drawing together two complimentary reviews of the technological opportunities (Taylor, 1995, 2001) and the pedagogical considerations that dominated and guided successive generations of distance learning (Anderson & Dron, 2011).

- *First Generation: The correspondence model (1840–1960).* In its early days, distance learning utilized the media and communication options available, relying on print and the developing postal services, with students receiving learning materials and responding via mail. There was no clear change in teaching or learning approaches to accommodate the adoption of a distance learning modality.
- *Second Generation: The multimedia model (1960–1980).* This era continued to use print and postal services but supplemented these with the latest audio (radio) and visual (television) technologies. Increasingly, advances in cognitive-behavioralist pedagogy were used in distance learning. These approaches focused on the individual, regarding knowledge as something independent from the learner but capable of being transmitted. The instructor's role, similar to that in traditional in-person teaching, was one of transmission: "the sage on stage." No social dimension was recognized and these delivery modes had a marked absence of what would now be recognized as social presence or teaching presence.

- *Third Generation: The telelearning model (1980–1995)*. Previous media and communication channels continued to be employed; however, advances in computer technology and telecommunications systems (such as email, electronic bulletin boards, and computer-mediated communication) made it increasingly possible for learning systems to operate synchronously, with learners responding in real time. Social-constructivist learning, in which the creation and validation of new understanding is socially mediated (Jonassen, 1991), began to be favored. Social interaction, which is central to the social-constructivist model, was provided by creating social presence and sustaining teaching presence. The instructor assumed the role of guide and helper.
- *Fourth Generation. The flexible model (1995–2005)*. Growing technological advances permitted improved learner access, synchronous and asynchronous possibilities, and real-time collaboration. An expanding information age sensitized learners to different ways of accessing information, creating social connections, and using technology to fulfill their goals. Social-constructivist remained the dominant pedagogical approach and there was growing interest in social presence and online communities of enquiry.
- *Fifth Generation: The intelligent flexible learning model (2005–present)*. Taylor (2001) understood this to be the current stage in evolution of distance learning systems. It is derived from Fourth Generation technologies integrated and enhanced by the Internet and Web 2.0. Learners are viewed as knowledgeable, self-assured, and capable of accessing informational networks to explore, confirm, and augment learning. Learners live in a world of digital connections and are familiar with social media and virtual possibilities. Some suggest that there is a move toward connectivist pedagogies, emphasizing social presence, and the creation of social capital through maintaining and accessing networked links with others. Teaching presence is viewed as enabling and empowering, with instructors themselves engaged in a process of continuous learning: "fellow voyagers."

Several points are significant. First, dates indicated are approximate and contestable. Distance learning generations have not displaced one another abruptly, but have gradually merged and coexisted. Second, new perspectives in technology have led and defined generational change. The growth curve for technology has consistently outpaced that of learning and instructional theory. Third, as a consequence, theoretical considerations of distance learning have retained a great deal of fluidity. They have remained open to new possibilities and have pragmatically reconsidered the past in a search for new ways to deal with the present.

TRANSACTIONAL DISTANCE: CONSEQUENCES OF SEPARATING LEARNER AND TEACHER

Michael Moore's original work (1972, 1973) focused on the consequences of separating learner and teacher, rather than on the nature of the separation or the means of subsequent connection. As such, it offers a useful window into the changed dynamics of distance learning, even although it was written 40 years ago. Moore was dealing with Second Generation distance learning, when distance learning was becoming more common. At such a time, it was inevitable that distance learning would be directly compared with traditional in-person instruction (what Moore refers to as "contiguous learning"). The dominant instructional approach was cognitive-behavioralist, where the learner was understood as the object of knowledge transfer or acquisition. Moore (1973, p. 31) was explicit "in challenging the behaviourists' hegemony" by considering the educational experience from the learner's perspective. Teachers, in so far as they were considered at all, had an implied role in initiating appropriate teaching activities to assist the learner.

Transaction distance is experienced by learners in contexts where they are separated from the instructor. Three elements are involved in recognizing and reducing transactional distance: structure, dialogue, and learner autonomy.

Structure, which Moore (1997) defined as:

> The ways in which the teaching programme is structured so that it can be delivered through various communication media. Programmes are structured in different ways to take into account the need to produce, copy, deliver, and control these mediated messages. Structure expresses rigidity or flexibility of the programme's educational objectives, teaching strategies, and evaluation methods. (p. 26)

Structure is a property of the learning environment. Although initially established by the instructor, structure must be understood and negotiated by the learner. Moore (1972, 1973) argued that while some degree of structure was required, a rigidly structured environment limited both meaningful communication and the learner's ability to make meaningful choices about how and what to learn. A perceived structural rigidity increased the learner's sense of transactional distance. Structure applies to both the instructional design of the environment and the technology, or media, used to support it.

Dialogue, which Moore (1997) understood to be:

> An interaction or series of interactions having positive qualities that other interactions might not have. A dialogue is purposeful, constructive and valued by each party. Each party in a dialogue is a respectful and active listener; each is a contributor, and builds on the contributions of the other party or parties. (p. 23)

Dialogue is the meaningful communication between those participating in the learning environment. It is monitored and evaluated by the learner in terms of quantity and quality. Transactional distance recognized, to a limited extent, that the process of learning was situated socially; however, the main interest was in the individual benefits accruing to the learner, rather than to the community of learners. Dialogue confirms personal access and the availability of others. Dialogue is inhibited by high structure. Low levels of dialogue add to the learner's perception that a high (unsatisfactory) level of transactional distance exists.

Learner autonomy, Moore (1997) defined this as follows:

> Many students used teaching materials and teaching programmes to achieve goals of their own, in their own way, under their own control. The term 'learner autonomy' was chosen to describe this process ... [it is] the extent to which, in the teaching/learning relationship, it is the learner rather than the teacher who determines the goals, the learning experiences, and the evaluation decisions of the learning programme. (p. 31)

In traditional in-person instruction, it is usually the instructor who controls the process through course content, teaching approach, and means of evaluation. Moore suggested that when the instructor was distanced, the learner had to assume a greater role in restructuring the learning experience. Increasing autonomy would provide the learner with a sense of control and reduce a sense of distance. Learner autonomy includes making decisions about what should be learned, redefining the learning process, reevaluating the anticipated outcomes, and reformulating evaluation. It includes conscious efforts to reduce course structure and/or to increase dialogue. Autonomy requires active learner involvement, which in turn is moderated by the significance that the learner attributes to the educational experience and by his/her capacity or ability (Moore, 2006).

Moore's theory of transactional distance was the first comprehensive consideration that addressed distance learning. For learners, Moore's contribution was to recognize their centrality in the educational process and to understand that they would have to adopt higher levels of autonomy than in traditional learning situations. The questions, which he did not answer, were whether learners would recognize this responsibility and have the capacity to respond to the challenge. For instructors, Moore's work raised three questions that anticipate learner concerns. How could instructors design courses with lower or more flexible structures? How could they design and facilitate distance learning environments to increase the level of meaningful exchange? How could they signal and support the need for learner autonomy?

Transactional distance theory provides a useful framework for understanding the distance learning experience, and empirical research has confirmed this utility in constructing effective learning environments. Bischoff (1993) attempted to measure perceived transactional distance in distance and in face-to-face learners, finding higher levels in the former. Reviewing qualitative data for online and in-person learning, Moore and Kearsley (1996) confirmed that instructors could reduce the perception of transactional distance by either increasing learner dialogue or reducing course structure. Saba and Shearer (1994) demonstrated that decreasing dialogue in distance learning environments resulted in an increase in perceived transactional distance. Their work, and that of others (Cookson & Chang, 1995; McIsaac & Blocher, 1998), showed specifically that a decrease in instructor–learner exchange caused learners to perceive greater transactional distance, which diminished the effectiveness of their learning.

Transactional distance should not be confused with spatial distance. Giossos, Koutsouba, Lionarakis, and Skavantzos (2009) affirmed that the "distance" intended was to be understood in terms of a distance in understanding, rather than in terms of physical separation. They argued that transactional distance was not an independent variable, but rather the consequence of action (teaching activities and strategies) mediated through preexisting mechanisms within the learning system (structure, dialogue, and autonomy). Transactional distance can still persist despite technological advances that have increased the possibility of easier and richer communication. Chen and Willits (1998), using pathway analysis, found no relationship between perceived transactional distance and prior online distance learning experience. They established, however, a weak negative correlation between transactional distance and the learner's computer skills, including familiarity with noneducational online media. Higher prior exposure to these media was associated with lower perceptions of transactional distance.

Transactional distance theory is not without its critics. Gorsky and Caspi (2005) have attacked its logic, the variables it employs, and considered it a theory that "when operationalized, is transformed into what may be construed as a tautology" (p. 4). This criticism notwithstanding, the consensus is that Moore's work is pertinent for advancing theory and research in distance learning. For example, Jung (2001) contended that Moore's theory "provides a useful conceptual framework for defining and understanding distance education in general and as a source of research hypothesis more specifically" (p. 527). To this Randy Garrison (2000), reviewing the theoretical challenges for distance education in the 21st century, added: "Moore's work remains one of the most appealing and well known theories of distance education" (p. 9). Research supports the contention that the theory is useful in understanding the challenges of the novice online learner (Stein, Wanstreet, & Calvin, 2009; Stein, Wanstreet, Calvin, Overtoom, & Wheaton, 2005) and in providing guidelines for more effective instructor action in distance learning contexts (Lemak, Shin, Reed, & Montgomery, 2005).

Transactional distance theory highlighted the consequences of distance learning and focused on the individual learner's response to it. The theory placed emphasis on the centrality of the learner in the educational process, but was descriptive rather than prescriptive. It responded to the relative novelty of distance learning, making the direct comparison with traditional in-person instruction, and was circumscribed by the educational climate of its time. Garrison (2000) has noted that while early distance education recognized and attempted to deal with transactional distance, these efforts were "made to fit the Procrustean bed created by the industrial and structural assumptions of the era" (p. 13). During the last 40 years, Moore's work has been reassessed with a growing emphasis on more effective facilitation of distance learning and distance teaching.

Transaction and Participation

For the distance learner, the degree of transactional distance becomes manifest through the perceived quantity and quality of dialogue in the system. It is dialogue – the exchange of meaningful information – that characterizes transactions. Transactions, in Moore's theory are dyadic: learner–instructor, learner–learner, and learner–content. To these, Chen (2001) added learner–interface transactions. Wallace (2003), in her extensive review of the online educational literature, used transactions as a proxy for participation – participation is the observable result of a transaction having occurred. She confirmed that, across a wide range of distance learning experiences, learners value the opportunity to engage in exchanges with instructor and peers. However, whereas transactional distance theory views exchanges as confirming access and availability, Wallace (2003) noted that "interaction that moves into cognitively complex engagement with ideas is not common, for reasons that are not clearly explained by research" (p. 247). The quantity and quality of exchanges between participants reduces individual perceptions of transactional distance; however, participation is also a precursor for a developing sense of involvement in a common learning enterprise and engagement in community.

Activity Theory and Thinking Outside the Box

The theory of transactional distance emerged at a time when technological possibilities were limited and social engagement of learners was not prioritized. Kang and Gyorke (2008) reassessed the theory, looking at context rather than the internal dynamics of the model. They proposed "thinking outside the box," situating transactional distance from the broader perspective of activity theory (Engeström, 1999). Activity theory links human activity, subjects, objects, rules, and community with the cultural and historical dimensions in which they are embedded. Using activity theory, they argued that the theory could be better understood in terms of the "interconnected human activities in the context of distance-education ... cultural–historical aspects of a particular online distance education system" (Kang & Gyorke, 2008, p. 212). This kind of reexamination positions the theory more clearly within the matrix of present-day communication options, and suggests a broader appreciation of the cultural aspects of the technologies employed and the activity of learning in higher education.

Park (2011) pursued this approach, looking at the social learning possibilities presented by mobile technologies, and argued that "individualized and socialized activities are *mediated* by communication technology, which is one kind of cultural-historical artifact in activity theory" (p. 89, emphasis in original). She reviewed the literature for mobile technology applications in considered four learning contexts: high transactional distance with learners receiving either individualized or socialized learning experiences; low transactional distance with either individualized or socialized learning. Mobile technology, it was suggested, could support each of these four learning and teaching approaches and could facilitate "seamless movement and switch" between low and high transactional distance, between personalized and socialized learning experiences.

An examination of Moore's theory has also been recently undertaken by Garry Falloon (2011) in a Web-based virtual learning environment. He considered the external and internal structure of the environment, evaluated the quality of dialogue, and measured learner autonomy. His study showed the complex manner in which the elements of transactional distance theory operate. Falloon's (2011) work suggested that transactional distance theory provided a useful conceptual lens through which to view distance learning. However, the move toward synchronicity – in which learners can respond instantaneously in real time – in Web-based online distance learning raises new questions about the nature of structure, dialogue, and learner autonomy for both educational designer and instructor. A key issue is learner preference and personal, or cultural, reluctance to be forced to make spontaneous responses.

Transactional Distance Versus Transactional Presence

Moore (2006) emphasized the interplay between learner and instructor in face-to-face learning situations. Spatial distance disrupts this dynamic, reducing the possibility of meaningful transactions. While the consequences of physical separate were foremost, little attention was given to how this transactional distance might be reduced. Munro (1998) stressed that "education involves a relationship, not just a transmission of information" (p. 39), and suggested that the instructors should be proactive in accentuating their presence in the distance learning environment.

Shin (2002) acknowledged that a relational aspect is critical for bridging perceived distance, and considered this best accomplished by creating a strong transactional presence. Transactional presence is a positive reaction to transactional distance theory and signifies the extent to which "distance students perceive the availability of, and connectedness with, teachers, peer students, and institution" (Shin, 2002, p. 132). Transaction presence differs from social presence, which will be discussed later, in that it only considers *availability* and *access*. Social presence, on the other hand, looks at social interaction, collaboration, and community building. Transactional presence, initiated by distance learning designers and instructors, attempts to compensate for the sense of distance experienced by learners. Transactional presence can be increased by the instructor's projection of self and by clear demonstrations of being accessible and available.

Shin (2002, p. 133), putting forward the construct, argued that transactional presence might reduce learner isolation, contribute to stronger learner-teacher and learner-learner relationships, and produce a deeper sense of connectedness for distance learners. Subsequently, she (Shin 2003) found that while higher measures of transactional presence did not correlate strongly with learner interaction, they did predict success in distance learning environments. In the Web 2.0 world, instructors have many opportunities to display access and availability through their learning environments using synchronous online systems (chat rooms, Elluminate, Skype, etc.), electronic text communication systems (SMS, email, and mobile technology), and through social media (Twitter, Facebook, etc.).

Transactional distance theory provided the first comprehensive way of understanding the consequences of physically separating learner and teacher. It described reactions, but did not prescribe proactive solutions. It was put forward within the context of the technological options available to distance learning in the early 1970s. It also aligned itself with the learner as an individual possessing the ability to control and personalize the learning experience. The learner might be better connected to instructor, peers, and content, but connectedness was understood primarily as access and availability rather than social interaction. The implications for a deeper social role though connectedness became clearer with the formulation of social presence.

SOCIAL AND COGNITIVE PRESENCE: MEDIATED REPRESENTATIONS OF THE OTHER

Social presence was first recognized by communication engineers Short, Williams, and Christie (1976), who were concerned about the immediacy and social representation of those engaged in electronic communication. Their work drew extensively from the existing literature of symbolic interactionism, social construction, and immediacy (Mehrabian, 1967; Wiener & Mehrabian, 1968). Short et al. (1976) defined social presence as "the degree of salience of the other person in a mediated interaction and the consequent salience of the interpersonal relationship" (p. 65). Social presence, initially viewed as a quality of the technology employed, allowed participants to recognize that they were communicating with other authentic persons. A sense of social presence permitted those communicating to realize that, although distanced, they had been brought together in a manner that supported social interaction. For social interaction and an interpersonal relationship to develop, we need to detect the presence of another empathetic person, recognize the immediacy of that person, and respond to social signals and cues.

Future investigation into social presence had a strong appeal for communication engineers and distance learning educators. Subsequent research focused on the "awareness of and the representation of the other, the medium's capacity for social interaction, and specifically the presence or absence of verbal or nonverbal cues in mediated communication" (Biocca, Harms, & Burgoon, 2003, p. 460). For educators, attempts to improve and utilize social presence grew in the Third and Fourth Generation of distance learning (starting approximately in 1980), when learning theorists were increasingly looking at social-constructivist approaches to learning. Charlotte Gunawardena stands out as one of the pioneer investigators of social presence. Her landmark paper (Gunawardena, 1995) extensively reviewed its history and considered the role that social presence played in learner interaction and learner collaboration in computer mediated environments.

Social presence had originally been described as a property of the communication system. Many, however, began to consider that social presence was essentially a "compendium of impressions regarding warmth, sensitivity, sociability, familiarity, and privacy" (Rafaeli, 1988, p. 117), located *within* users of computer-mediated communication systems. Gunawardena (1995) adopted and promoted this perspective, seeing social presence as a shared impression of those participating in the system: the degree to which each considered the other to be a real person capable of engaging in social exchange. Gunawardena (1995) found a strong positive correlation between learner-perceived social presence and learner satisfaction, a finding repeated in her later work (Gunawardena & Zittle, 1997) and subsequently confirmed by Cobb (2009), who revalidated the original Gunawardena and Zittle scale for measuring social presence.

Interest in social presence expanded rapidly because of three factors. First, in this generation of distance learning there was an acceleration of advances in computer-mediated communication that provided revolutionary new ways of linking distance learners in real time. Teleconferencing, Skype, and synchronous learning platforms provided mechanisms for mediated social contact and interaction. Second, educators generally were beginning to recognize that the learning process was socially situated (Wenger, 1998) and that knowledge was a social constructed (Harasim, 2002). With an increased interest in social-constructivist learning approach (Jonassen, 1991) distance learning designers and instructors began to reconstruct their learning environments accentuating social presence and richer social learning experiences.

A sense of social presence in distance learning environments increases learner satisfaction, but it also provides participants with the possibility for social interaction, exchange, and a tentative sense of community. Social presence allows the learner to appreciate that she is not simply interacting with *representations* of others, but that embodied in those representations are real and socially responsive others. As Robert Starratt (2004) put it: "we cannot be present to the other if the other is not present to us" (p. 87). Increasing awareness of social connection and mutuality has multiple outcomes. It can increase learner motivation (Aragon, 2003) and reduce performance anxiety (Lee & Chan, 2007). The disposition to act socially through mutual response has been positively correlated with social presence and the quantity of learner interaction (Tu & McIsaac, 2002). The quality of learner-exchanges changes often becomes richer and more nuanced as perceived social presence increases (Swan, 2001; Swan & Shih, 2005). At the programmatic level, higher social presence has been shown to reduce a sense of learner isolation (Annand, 2011), to decrease attrition in distance learning courses, and to promote higher student retention rates (DiRamio & Wolverton, 2006).

A third factor associated with increased interest in social presence was more subtle: social capital. In an increasingly connected world, social capital theory understands that there is value for actors within networks that bind similar people and that provide bridges to diverse groups (Dekker & Uslaner, 2001). Learners increasingly came to understand that the learning environments in which they engaged provided places to learn, but *additionally* provided the opportunity to use these connections to increase their social capital. Networks formed in distance learning provided present and future social resources, similar to those were becoming evident in popular social media communities such as Face Book and LinkedIn. There was the growing recognition that distance learning environments were similar to, not uniquely separated from, broader social Internet communities in which learners increasingly participated and which often characterize their nonacademic social worlds.

Social presence is a critical prerequisite for developing social capital. Torche and Valenzuela (2011), considering the sociology of communities of embodied actors, argued that social capital only results if participants sense copresence, recognize reciprocity, and possess social memory. When contact is with strangers, the predominant determinant of social capital is mutual trust. In virtual communities, whether educational or recreational, social presence makes participants appear less as strangers and more as community members. As learners recognize their inclusion in a community, they begin to appreciate the possibility of mutuality and reciprocity. As community members recognize this, there is the potential for creating and accessing new social capital, useful in enhancing present learning and in future dealings.

Enhanced social capital parallels the development of nascent community of learning in distance learning situations. For these communities to develop, albeit tentative and bounded, social presence must be present. Communities of learning open up educational opportunities for instructor and learner, opportunities that can lead to learning experiences perceived as richer and more enjoyable, whether in purely online courses (Shin, 2002; Wise, Chang, Duffy, & Del Valle, 2004) or in blended learning situations, where social presence can be cultivated in both in-person and virtual components of the course (Rovai, 2002; Rovai & Jordan, 2004).

Different Levels and Responses to Social Presence

Social presence is not simply present or absent in distance learning environment: learners perceive it in different levels. Biocca et al. (2003) proposed three levels. *(1) Copresence*, in which individuals sense that they are not alone in the virtual environment. They recognize the existence of others and believe that the others are also aware of them. *(2) Psychological involvement*, in which there is a cognitive and emotional response. Individuals focus attention, empathize, and respond to the feeling of others recognized as present. They believe that the others are aware of their intentions, motivations, and thoughts. This predisposes those in the virtual system to consider social exchange and interaction. *(3) Behavioral engagement*, in which individuals believe their actions are interdependent, related, and connected to others who are sensed to be present. There is enough social presence for them to respond to others, believing that the others will both recognize and reciprocate this responsiveness.

Shen and Khalifa (2008), after conducting a comprehensive review of the existing literature (including Biocca, Harms, & Gregg, 2001; IJsselsteijn, de Ridder, Freeman, & Avons, 2000), proposed a multidimensional conceptualization of social presence. They looked at the motivational pathways leading to community building in nonimmersive online experiences, and suggested that social presence could be inferred from the properties of interaction. They identified three demonstrations of social presence in distance learning environments (Shen & Khalifa, 2008, p. 729). *(1) Awareness* comes into existence when social actors believe that other social actors exist and are capable of reacting. *(2) Affective social presence* results when social actors sense an emotional connection with others using the virtual system. *(3) Cognitive social presence* occurs when the user of the system is able to "construct and confirm meaning about his or her relationship with the others and the social space" (p. 730).

Social presence is considered to be a multivariate construct, existing at different levels within a distance learning environment. As participants in the system experience different levels of social presence they react differently, moving from simply acknowledging the presence of others to an active interest in cognitively and affectively engaging with them. Engagement may be expressed in various ways: increased interaction, enhanced understanding, and the development of psychological attachment between participants. From a design and instructional perspective, the first challenge is to create higher levels of social presence in online learning systems. The second challenge is to utilize growing social responsiveness to promote more effective learning outcomes with greater levels of learner satisfaction.

Social Presence and the Community of Inquiry Model

The ability to recognize the authenticity of other social actors in computer-mediated environments results in a general sense of presence. Garrison, Anderson, and Archer (2000), after analyzing computer conference call transcripts, suggested that three different presences are involved in distance communities of inquiry. *(1) Social presence*, as described previously, is a critical requirement for the emergence of other perceptions of presence and "an important antecedent to collaboration and critical discourse because it facilitates achieving cognitive objectives by instigating, sustaining, and supporting critical thinking in a community of learners" (Akyol, Garrison, & Ozden, 2009, p. 67). *(2) Teaching presence* can manifest itself to other participants through the recognition that another person (the instructor) has consciously designed the learning environment, has selected appropriate of learning activities, and is skillful mediating the online discussion and interaction. *(3) Cognitive presence* becomes apparent to participants as they exchange and utilize communication in their attempts to construct new meaning. They may become aware that engagement within the learning environment encourages and supports higher orders of thinking: analyzing, synthesizing, and innovating. The learner may sense that the learning environment actively encourages an integrated understanding of the subject matter.

Social presence, in the community of inquiry model, works in conjunction with teacher presence and cognitive presence. It is theoretically unclear whether social presence is a separate variable, or whether it is a moderator, or modified, of teacher presence and cognitive presence (Garrison, Anderson, & Archer, 2010). Empirical research has found that the community of inquiry framework, which recognizes all three presences and tries to sustain them, seems to enhance perceived learning and satisfaction with the delivery-medium in distance learning environments (Arbaugh, 2008). Shea and Bidjerano (2008) have suggested that social presence and teacher presence work in conjunction to bring about cognitive presence, which participants recognize as the crucial and defining attribute of distance communities of inquiry. Their later research (Shea & Bidjerano, 2010) found weak relationships between both social presence and teaching presence in predicting cognitive presence outcomes, suggesting that an additional construct – learner presence – may be involved. Learner presence seems to be the dimension through which learners appreciate their self-efficacy and their sense of ongoing success in the learning environment.

CONNECTEDNESS, CONNECTIVITY, AND CONNECTIVIST APPROACHES

While pragmatism and expediency are valuable assets for distance learning practitioners, in the long-run learners are probably better served by theory-based innovation. Theory-driven innovation compels us "to see the big picture and makes it possible for us to view our practice and our research from a broader perspective than envisioned from the murky trenches of our practice" (Anderson, 2008, p. 45). Seeing the bigger picture, and the link between experienced gained in different contexts, becomes particularly important when there are so many different technological options available.

Transactional distance theory has provided this bigger picture – an inclusive appreciation of the dynamics involved when educational moves from traditional in-person teaching to distance learning. It highlights the psychological and social distance that the separated learner experiences in terms of dialogue quality and course structure. It centers educational dynamics on learner, rather than instructor, and predicts that the learner will reduce distance by assuming a greater degree of autonomy, making decisions about educational content, learning outcomes, and evaluation methods. The unit of analysis is the individual, rather than the collective, and the learner's response to distance is to seek greater access to course content and confirm the availability of the instructor.

Likewise, social presence theory has also generated a big picture of learning dynamics, centering on learning as a social process. Increased social presence provides a pathway for participation and collaboration, just as it allows the learner access to psychological empathy and community bonding. While social presence centers on the individual learner, the unit of analysis is often the developing communities of learning within the system. Social presence theory compliments transactional distance theory; indeed, the former can be seen as embedded within a transactional framework. Transactional distance underscores the general dynamics of distance learning; social presence describes how distance perceptions can be reduced by moderating structure and enhancing the quality of exchanges. Social presence goes further by suggesting that not only can learner isolation be reduced, but that the learner can be integrated into a mutually supportive community of learning. Taken together, transactional distance and social presence provide goals for distance learning designers and instructors. Empirical research has shown that both theories are reliable and valid with good predictive powers, even although neither theory can be viewed as comprehensive.

Transactional distance and social presence were responses to shifts brought about by technological advances. Terry Anderson (2009), considering technological or pedagogical determinism in distance learning, advanced a dance metaphor in which technology created the music, while pedagogy defined the steps. Music and dance ultimately come together seamlessly; however, a review of the evolution of distance learning indicates that the technological music comes before the pedagogical choreography. Educational theorists did not present perspectives and then tried to find appropriate technologies that would accommodate them. Instead, they looked at the consequences of advancing technology and tried to understand what opportunities and possibilities were provided by them. A critical issue in the Fifth Generation of distance learning is the extent to which pedagogical choreography is synchronized with the technological beat.

Connectivist Approaches

It has been argued (Anderson & Dron, 2011) that learning theory has shifted in the Fifth Generation from a social-constructivist emphasis to a connectivist perspective. Connectivist approaches center on a global understanding of learner, including their noneducational environment, and ask how the pervasive and ubiquitous technologies of connectivity and social media might further the learning process (Siemens, 2005a). George Siemens (2005b) argued that in a world of exponential knowledge growth, the critical learner competency is accessing knowledge as it forms. Learning is no longer internal and individualistic, but rather external and socially accessible. He considered that learning, defined as actionable knowledge (Siemens, 2005b) should no longer be considered a personal attribute but rather as something existing in external databases, organizations, and networks. Siemens (2005b) noted that the connections that we can make are more important than our current state of knowledge, the ability to learn what is needed tomorrow more important that what we know today, and that "the pipe is more important than the content of the pipe" (second last paragraph).

The learner confronts new information, continuously generated and technologically accessible, and requires a high degree of selectivity and discrimination. The learner is seen as part of information and communication networks that connects her to others, particularly organizations and learning institutions. The learner's personal knowledge flows into the network and is augmented, or modified, by others. Information and knowledge is then reaccessed by the learner through the network to provide new learning (Siemens, 2005b). Connectivist approaches stress social capital, which accumulates in a network as users share experience, add new knowledge, and access the accumulating knowledge-value in the system. Knowledge-value is increased for the learner by including "current and past learners and those with knowledge relevant to the learning goals" (Anderson & Dron, 2011, p. 88). The connectivist perspective focuses on interconnected learners, responsible for defining and generating learning content in the system. The instructor's role is that of a fellow-voyager, no longer defining content or outcomes but collaborating with learners as a critically informed helper, not a privileged authority (Guthrie, 2010).

Web 2.0, and the explosion in technologies to facilitate personal connections, presents exciting opportunities for distance learners and their instructors. There is little doubt that the connectivist approach provides an insightful *description* of the changed environment and new possibilities. These possibilities have energized and inspired both distance learning designers and instructors. Enhanced connectivity has often been enthusiastically adopted to enrich and democratize learning environments. What is still unclear is whether connectivist approaches only describe technological possibilities or provide pedagogical alternatives.

Competency in dealing with exponentially increased information is not the same as learning how to analyze, synthesize, and create new meaning. If learning is defined as actionable knowledge, it is unclear how the learner develops the skill of deciding what constitutes appropriate action and testing that decision. If knowledge is externalized and socially accessible, what motivation is there for the learner to reshape information in creative and innovative ways rather than simply access and reproduce it? Connectivism undoubtedly inspires and will shape future distance learning practice; however, many would contend that, "it does not seem that connectivism's contributions warrant it being treated as a separate learning theory" (Kop & Hill, 2008, p. 11). They would also look with interest toward empirical research and qualitative studies that demonstrate the validity of connectivist approaches (Bell, 2011).

Connectivity and Connectedness

A distinction between connectivity and connectedness has been made earlier; however, it might be useful to restate this. The possibility for effective distance learning grew dramatically because of technological connectivity. Increasingly, those who participated in distance learning belonged to personal and social networks and were accustomed to connectivity. Learning can become yet another network within which people wish to be included. But connectivity is only a technological potential that allows connections to be made. It permits connections, but it neither predicts the strengths of people-connections nor guarantees quality of the resulting social exchanges.

The two major distance learning theories considered looked at connected learners and predicted that there will be a lack of satisfaction and effective learning *unless* participants can improve the perceived quality and utility of their being connected. Connectivity is certainly a prerequisite for connectedness, but it does not ensure that learners will sense connectedness or find educational value in being connected. Connectedness is a psychological and social awareness that others are sharing empathetically in the learning process, contributing toward it, and engaged collectively in creating new knowledge. The connected learner is not only socially engaged in the process of learning but is also critically connected with subject matter being studied.

How might we approach the connectivist landscape of today's Web 2.0 world with a view to engaging and connecting distance learners?

Accepting the Discontinuity Between In-Person and Distance Learning
The exciting opportunities presented by online distance learning environments can be embraced only if the discontinuity with traditional instruction

is accepted. Distance learning not a change in delivery modality, but rather an educational paradigm shift. As such, it demands a reconsideration of the dynamics of both teaching and learning (Desai, Hart, & Richards, 2008; Morris, 2009). In the past, while embracing new technologies, theorists and practitioners have often tried to replicate in-person learning experiences for distance learners, offering them "an experience as much like that of traditional, face-to-face instruction as possible" (Schlosser & Anderson, 1994, p. 14). This seems paradoxical because in-person instruction cannot be replicated at a distance and face-to-face discussion can only be reproduced in a reduced form (Peters, 2000).

The challenge for the practitioner is to seek possibilities for increased connectedness and collaboration that were unimaginable in traditional instruction. That search should be tempered by a consideration of how new possibilities might be employed within a developing theoretical framework, and not appear quixotic or serendipitous. The challenge for the researcher is to measure and validate the learning effectiveness of distance learning contexts that innovatively employ the connective technologies of Web 2.0.

Balancing Learner Autonomy and Teacher Presence
When online distance learning environments are perceived as rigidly structured and poor in meaningful dialogue, the learner is forced to assert growing autonomy. With increasing access to a Web 2.0 world of infor-mation, the learner needs to assume autonomy in critically evaluating what is found. Information available through Web 2.0 varies markedly in quality and in its potential value for knowledge construction. Knowledge, in these "complex-adaptive domains" is accumulated and organically revised in ways not originally contemplated, in contrast to the "predictable domains" that are organized and propagated by instructors and educational insti-tutions (Williams, Karousou, & Mackness, 2011). Learners need the capacity to differentiate between the values of complex-adaptive and predictable information domains, and the ability to reconstruct information in ways that are reliable, valid, and innovative.

The critical issue with learner autonomy is the capacity of the learner. In online learning situations, novice learners may not have sufficient experience to critically engage with what they wish to learn. Teacher presence is essential in creating learning structures and exchanges that allow the learner to more effectively engage with subject matter and with others. For the practitioner, a balance has to be maintained between teacher presence and learner presence; between expressed authority and recognized autonomy. The instructor, whether as caring guide or as informed voyager, should be at least as engaged in the learning enterprise as other participants. More evidence-based research is also required to understand how learners evaluate, confirm, and personally reconstruct knowledge in our complex contemporary learning environments. A clearer understanding of the ways in which learners accept and demonstrate autonomy in the learning experience is essential.

Encouraging Meaningfulness in Social Exchange
Ravenscroft (2011) noted the advent of increased connectivity possibilities in distance learning required "new design metaphors for future learning that place the person, their social behaviour, and their community at the centre of the design process ... fundamentally we must remember that we will still be, mostly, people socially interacting with other people" (p. 155). The exciting range of connective technologies in a Web 2.0 world can be used to facilitate access and availability (Redecker, Ala-Mutka, & Bacig, 2009). Mobile technologies permit ongoing and instantaneous connections between distance learning participants (Traxler, 2007); however, the degree to which these technologies facilitate meaningful social exchange within the learning process remains unclear.

Increasingly, students have sophisticated appreciations of social media and yet it is still far from clear how learners incorporate this experience into the social exchanges and dialogues in learning environments. For the practitioner, the challenge is to translate the potential of connectivity into the richness of social exchange and meaningful dialogue in their learning environments in ways that stimulate learners, increase motivation, and facilitate learning outcomes. For the researcher, a better understanding is needed of the kinds of personal and social transactions that contribute to the self-construction, or co-construction, of knowledge in the learning space. We also need to have a better understanding of the similarities and differences that learners perceive in social networks and learning networks, and of the norms and outcomes that they associate with each.

Not Marginalizing Learners by a One-Fits-All Distance Learning Design
The Web 2.0 world provides novel and effective ways of connecting learners; however, there is always the danger that these technologies have unintended results. Instructional designers and online practitioners often assume that "the learner is a lot more like himself or herself than they in reality are [and] seriously underestimate how important the differences in context are" (Rogers, Graham, & Mayes, 2007, p. 212). The Web 2.0 world sometimes regards itself as culturally neutral; however, this is not the case. While some

have argued for cultural convergence, national cultural difference in degrees of power-difference, masculinity-femininity, and individuality-collectivism are often evident in online learning.

As online learning expands it is more likely to encounter learner diversity, where different cultural values and assumptions can lead to different perceptions of learner success, integration, and participation (Ku & Lohr, 2003; Liu, Liu, Lee, & Magjuka, 2010). For example, while there is a tendency to move to synchronous platforms, some individuals and many cultural groups prefer the ability to formulate and reconsider responses asynchronously because this reduces the risk of making premature judgments, or "feeling silly," in front of peers (Falloon, 2011). The challenge for the practitioner is to design learning environments that recognize cultural difference and to facilitate them in ways that encourage positive inclusion and productive diversity (Yang, Olesova, & Richardson, 2010).

The challenge for the researcher, in a time when distance environments bring together learners from different continents and countries, is to more fully explore cultural difference and the extent to which it enhances or limits learning outcomes. We need to know more about the cultural determinants associated with constructs such as learner autonomy, social presence, and collaboration. We also need to know how such knowledge could be used to construct more satisfying and effective learning environments for different learner populations.

CONCLUSION

Distance learning has evolved in a remarkable and confident manner. In its early history, many – learners, instructors, and institutions – regarded it as essentially a pragmatic compromise for problems of student remoteness and educational access. Its development, however, shows the emergence of an exciting and legitimate shift in a learning paradigm, in which critical issues of dynamics and process were reformulated. Distance learning remains a vibrant option in developed countries and particularly significant approach in developing countries, where expanding educational programs are hampered by physical distance, poor infrastructure, and a lack of democratization. As a paradigm shift, distance learning forces a reconsideration of the fundamental processes through which new understanding is created, and a reassessment of the dynamics involved. These reconsiderations have taken place against a background of staggering advance in communication technologies that have dramatically improved access to learning environments and enriched their educational potentials.

Exponential availability and sophistication of technology have provided online practitioners with countless possibilities to further effective learning. Most instructional designers and online instructors would endorse the sentiments of Irlbeck, Kays, Jones, and Sims (2006) who noted that distance learning practices have become "complex, flexible, dynamic, and organic" (p. 183). Complexity and organic dynamism is a hallmark of the Web 2.0 era of connectivity, and opens up exciting new vistas onto the purposeful process of enhancing active learning. New initiatives are currently linking high-reputation American and European universities into a network that will provide massively open online courses (MOOCs), available without prior educational requirements to interested learners. Undoubtedly, such environments provide complex and dynamic opportunities for learning to take place, but these initiatives raise questions about the way in which learning occurs, how it is measured, and how learning accomplishment will be recognized institutionally. To be productive, these possibilities have to permit learners to connect with subject matter and with co-learners. To be effective, the enterprise of distance learning has to be harnessed to an illuminating theory of action. The engaged learner, involved and attached to the processes of creating new understanding, will most likely not emerge incidentally. Rather, the engaged learner will result from designing and facilitating learning environments underpinned by theories that shape the experience and involve the learner personally with learning.

Transactional distance theory and social presence theory both suggest *why* and *how* available Web 2.0 options should be used; however, these theories provide only a partial framework – a bigger picture undoubtedly, but not the complete picture. More quantitative and qualitative research, centered on evidence-based measures of learning success, remains a critical component in advancing theory and in initiating effective learning experiences. A flexible, organic, and reflective approach is required in online practice to explore learner satisfaction. Such an approach is also required to investigate optimal learning outcomes and the ways in which knowledge creation might be furthered. In higher education, teaching and learning has been significantly recast and vitalized through the active promotion of a scholarship of teaching and learning (SoTL), in which practitioners actively considered what they do and what they accomplish (Shulman, 2011). Distance learning is a particularly fertile area for SoTL. It allows frontline practitioners to demonstrate professional judgment for their selection and implementation of pedagogical strategies, to measure the value that these bring to the distance learning process, and to share their findings with the broader community of practice.

We should carefully reconsidered old theories, and develop new ones, because they will provide us with Saba (2005) "a dynamic system that ... would also allow for learner creativity, which by definition can be potentially anticipated but not predicted and programmed in advance" (p. 264). The dance between technological richness and educational intent continues. The promise – undoubtedly one that will be realized in the next generation of distance learning – is that new technology and new theory, united, will lead to ever-more exciting and increasingly coordinated choreographies in distance learning.

REFERENCES

Akyol, Z., Garrison, D. R., & Ozden, M. Y. (2009). Online and blended communities of inquiry: Exploring the developmental and perceptional differences. *International Review of Research in Open and Distance Learning, 10*(6), 65–83.

Allen, I. E., & Seaman, J. (2011). *Going the distance: Online education in the United States, 2011.* Babson Park, MA: Babson Survey Research Group/Sloan-Consortium.

Allen, I. E., Seaman, J., & Garrett, R. (2007). *Blending in: The extent and promise of blended education in the United States.* Needham, MA: Sloan-Sloan Consortium.

Anderson, T. (2008). Towards a theory of online learning. In T. Anderson (Ed.), *The theory and practice of online learning* (2nd ed., Chap. 2). Edmonton, Canada: Athabasca University Press.

Anderson, T. (2009). *The dance of technology and pedagogy in self-paced distance education.* Paper presented at the 17th ICDE World Congress, Maastricht, the Netherlands.

Anderson, T., & Dron, J. (2011). Three generations of distance education pedagogy. *International Review of Research in Open and Distance Learning, 12*(3), 80–97.

Annand, D. (2011). Social presence within the community of inquiry framework. *International Review of Research in Open and Distance Learning, 12*(5), 40–56.

Aragon, S. R. (2003). Creating social presence in online environments. *New Directions for Adult and Continuing Education, 100*, 57–68.

Arbaugh, J. B. (2008). Does the community of inquiry framework predict outcomes in online MBA courses? *International Review of Research in Open and Distant Learning, 9*(2), 1–21.

Bell, F. (2011). Connectivism: Its place in theory-informed research and innovation in technology-enabled learning. *International Review of Research in Open and Distance Learning, 12*(3), 98–118.

Biocca, F., Harms, C., & Burgoon, J. K. (2003). Towards a more robust theory and measure of social presence: Review and suggested criteria. *Presence: Teleoperators & Virtual Environments, 12*(5), 456–480.

Biocca, F., Harms, C., & Gregg, J. (2001). *The networked minds measure of social presence: Pilot test of the factor structure and concurrent validity.* Paper presented at Presence conference, May 21–23, Philadelphia, PA.

Bischoff, W. R. (1993). *Transactional distance, interactive television, and electronic mail communication in graduate public health and nursing courses: Implications for professional education.* Unpublished Ph.D. dissertation. The University of Hawaii, Honolulu.

Chen, Y.-J. (2001). Dimensions of transactional distance in the World Wide Web learning environment: A factor analysis. *British Journal of Educational Technology, 32*(4), 459–471.

Chen, Y.-J., & Willits, F. K. (1998). A path analysis of the concepts of Moore's theory of transactional distance in videoconferencing learning environments. *Journal of Distance Education, 13*(2), 51–65.

Cobb, S. C. (2009). Social presence and online learning: A current view from a research perspective. *Journal of Interactive Online Learning, 8*(3), 241–254.

Cookson, P., & Chang, Y. (1995). The multidimensional audioconferencing classification system (MACS). *American Journal of Distance Education, 9*(3), 18–35.

Dekker, P., & Uslaner, E. M. (2001). Introduction. In E. M. Uslanger (Ed.), *Social capital and participation in everyday life* (pp. 1–8). London: Routledge.

Desai, M. S., Hart, J., & Richards, T. C. (2008). E-learning: Paradigm shift in education. *Education, 129*(2), 327–334.

DiRamio, D., & Wolverton, M. (2006). Integrating learning communities and distance education: Possibility or pipedream? *Innovative Higher Education, 31*(2), 99–113.

Elloumi, F. (2008). Value chain analysis: A strategic approach to online learning. In T. Anderson (Ed.), *The theory and practice of online learning* (2nd ed.), Edmonton, AB: Athabasca University Press.

Engeström, Y. (1999). Activity theory and transformation. In Y. Engeström, R. Miettinen & R. Punamaki (Eds.), *Perspectives on activity theory* (pp. 19–38). Cambridge: Cambridge University Press.

Falloon, G. (2011). Making the connection: Moore's theory of transactional distance and its relevance to the use of a virtual classroom in postgraduate online teacher education. *Journal of Research on Technology in Education, 43*(3), 187–209.

Garrison, D. R., Anderson, T., & Archer, W. (2000). Critical inquiry in a text-based environment: Computer conferencing in higher education. *Internet and Higher Education, 2*(2-3), 87–105.

Garrison, D. R., Anderson, T., & Archer, W. (2010). The first decade of the community of inquiry framework: A retrospective. *Internet and Higher Education, 13*(1-2), 5–9.

Garrison, R. (2000). Theoretical challenges for distant education in the 21st century: A shift from structural to transactional issues. *International Review of Research in Open and Distant Learning, 1*(1), 1–17.

Giossos, Y., Koutsouba, M., Lionarakis, A., & Skavantzos, K. (2009). Reconsidering Moore's transactional distance theory. *European Journal of Open, Distance and E-Learning,* II (2009/2, article 6) Available at http://www.eurodl.org/?p=archives&year=2009&halfyear=2&article=374.

Gorsky, P., & Caspi, A. (2005). A critical analysis of transactional distance theory. *Quarterly Review of Distance Education, 6*(1), 1–11.

Gunawardena, C. N. (1995). Social presence theory and implications for interaction and collaborative learning in computer conferences. *International Journal of Educational Telecommunications, 1*(2-3), 147–166.

Gunawardena, C. N., & Zittle, F. J. (1997). Social presence as a predictor of satisfaction with a computer-mediated conferencing environment. *American Journal of Distance Education, 11*(3), 8–26.

Guthrie, C. (2010). Towards greater learner control: Web supported project-based learning. *Journal of Information Systems Education, 21*(1), 121–130.

Harasim, L. (2002). What makes online learning communities successful? The role of collaborative learning in social and intellectual development. In C. Vrasidas & G. V. Glass (Eds.), *Distance education and distributed learning* (pp. 181–200). Greenwich, CT: Information Age Publishing.

IJsselsteijn, W. A., de Ridder, H., Freeman, J., & Avons, S. E. (2000). *Presence: Concept, determinants and measurement.* Paper presented at the proceedings of the SPIE: Human vision and electronic imaging V, San Jose, CA, January 24, 2000.

Irlbeck, S., Kays, E., Jones, D., & Sims, R. (2006). The Phoenix rising: Emergent models of instructional; design. *Distance Education, 27*(2), 171–185.

Jonassen, D. (1991). Evaluating constructivistic learning. *Educational Technology, 31*(10), 28–33.

Jung, I. (2001). Building a theoretical framework of web-based instruction in the context of distance education. *British Journal of Educational Technology, 32*(5), 525–534.

Kang, H., & Gyorke, A. S. (2008). Rethinking distance learning activities: A comparison of transactional distance theory and activity theory. *Open Learning, 23*(3), 203–214.

Kop, R., & Hill, A. (2008). Connectivism: Learning theory of the future or vestige of the past? *International Review of Research in Open and Distance Learning, 9*(3), 1–13.

Ku, H., & Lohr, L. L. (2003). A case study of Chinese students' attitude toward their first online learning experience. *Education Technology Research and Development, 51*(3), 94–102.

Lee, M. J. W., & Chan, A. (2007). Reducing the effects of isolation and promoting inclusivity for distance learners through podcasting. *Turkish Online Journal of Distance Education, 8*(1), 85–104.

Lemak, D. J., Shin, S. J., Reed, R., & Montgomery, J. C. (2005). Technology, transactional distance, and instructor effectiveness: An empirical investigation. *Academy of Management Learning & Education, 4*(2), 150–159.

Liu, X., Liu, S., Lee, S-H., & Magjuka, R. L. (2010). Cultural differences in online learning: International student perceptions. *Journal of Educational Technology & Society, 13*(3), 177–188.

Maddux, C. D., & Johnson, D. L. (2010). Global trends and issues in information technology in education. *Computers in the School, 27*(3/4), 145–154.

Martin, E., Prosser, M., Trigwell, K., Ramsden, P., & Benjamin, J. (2000). What university teachers teach and how they teach it. *Instructional Science, 28*(5/6), 387–412.

McIsaac, M. S., & Blocher, J. M. (1998). How research in distance education can affect practice. *Educational Media International, 35*(1), 43–47.

Mehrabian, A. (1967). Attitudes inferred from non-immediacy of verbal communication. *Journal of Verbal Learning and Verbal Behavior, 6*, 294–295.

Moore, M. G. (1972). Learner autonomy: The second dimension of independent learning. *Convergence, 5*(2), 76–88.

Moore, M. G. (1973). Towards a theory of independent learning and teaching. *Journal of Higher Education, 44*(9), 661–679.

Moore, M. G. (1997). Theory of transactional distance. In D. Keegan (Ed.), *Theoretical principles of distance education* (pp. 22–38). London: Routledge.

Moore, M. G. (2006). *Theory and theorists.* European Distance and E-Learning Network. Paper presented at the Barcelona Research Workshop, Castelldefels, Spain, October 27, 2006.

Moore, M. G., & Kearsley, G. (1996). *Distance education: A systems view.* New York, NY: Wadsworth.

Morris, D. (2009). Learning design approaches to curriculum redesign: A case study. *International Journal of Learning, 16*(9), 589–596.

Munro, J. S. (1998). *Presence at a distance: The educator-learner relationship in distance learning. ACSDE Research Monograph*. University Park: American Center for the Study of Distance Education, Pennsylvania State University.

Park, Y. (2011). A pedagogical framework for mobile learning: Categorizing educational applications of mobile technologies into four types. *International Review of Research in Open and Distance Learning, 12*(2), 78–102.

Peters, O. (2000). The transformation of the university into an institution of independent learning. In T. Evans & D. Nation (Eds.), *Changing university teaching: Reflections on creating educational technologies* (pp. 10–23). London: Kogan Page.

Rafaeli, S. (1988). Interactivity: From new media to communication. In R. P. Hawkins, J. M. Weimann & S. Pingree (Eds.), *Advancing communication science: Merging mass and interpersonal process* (pp. 110–134). Newbury Park, CA: Sage.

Rajasingham, L. (2009). Breaking boundaries: Quality e-learning for global knowledge society. *International Journal of Emerging Technologies in Learning, 4*(1), 58–65.

Ravenscroft, A. (2011). Dialogue and connectivism: A new approach to understanding and promoting dialogue-rich networked learning. *International Review of Research in Open and Distance Learning, 12*(3), 139–160.

Redecker, C., Ala-Mutka, K., & Bacig, M. (2009). *Learning 2.0: The impact of Web 2.0 innovations on educational and training in Europe*. European Commission, Joint Research Centre Institute for Prospective Technological Studies (EUR 24103 EN). Luxembourg: Office for Official Publications of the European Communities.

Rogers, P. C., Graham, C. R., & Mayes, C. T. (2007). Cultural competence and instructional design: Exploration research into the delivery of online instruction cross-culturally. *Education Tech Research Development, 55*, 197–217.

Rovai, A. (2002). Building sense of community at a distance. *International Review of Research in Open and Distance Learning, 3*(1), article 6. Available at http://www.irrodl.org/index.php/irrodl/article/view/79/153

Rovai, A. P., & Jordan, H. M. (2004). Blended learning and sense of community: A comparative analysis with traditional and fully online graduate courses. *International Review of Research in Open and Distance Learning, 5*(2), 1–13.

Saba, F. (2005). Critical issues in distance education: A report from the United States. *Distance Education, 26*(2), 255–272.

Saba, F., & Shearer, R. L. (1994). Verifying the key theoretical concepts in a dynamic model of distance education. *American Journal of Distance Education, 8*(1), 36–59.

Schlosser, C. A., & Anderson, M. L. (1994). *Distance education: A review of the literature*. Washington, DC: AECT Publication Sales. ERIC (382159).

Schulte, M. (2011). The foundations of technology distance education: A review of the literature to 2001. *Journal of Continuing Higher Education, 59*(1), 34–44.

Selwyn, N., & Fitz, J. (2001). The politics of connectivity: The role of big business in UK education technology policy. *Political Studies Journal, 29*(4), 551–570.

Shea, P., & Bidjerano, T. (2008). Measures of quality in online education: An investigation of the community of inquiry model and the net generation. *Journal of Educational Computing Research, 39*(4), 339–361.

Shea, P., & Bidjerano, T. (2010). Learning presence: Towards a theory of self-efficacy, self-regulation, and the development of a communities of inquiry in online and blended learning environments. *Computers & Education, 55*(4), 1721–1731.

Shen, K. N., & Khalifa, M. (2008). Exploring multidimensional conceptualization of social presence in the context of online communities. *International Journal of Human-Computer Interaction, 24*(7), 722–748.

Shin, N. (2002). Beyond interaction: The relational construct of transactional presence. *Open Learning, 17*(2), 121–137.

Shin, N. (2003). Transactional presence as a critical predictor of success in distance learning. *Distance Education, 24*(1), 69–86.

Short, J., Williams, E., & Christie, B. (1976). *The social psychology of communication.* New York, NY: John Wiley.

Shulman, L. S. (2011). The scholarship of teaching and learning: A personal account and reflection. *International Journal for the Scholarship of Teaching and Learning, 5*(1), 1–7.

Siemens, G. (2005a). Connectivism: Learning as network-creation. *ElearnSpace* (August 10, 2005). Available at http://www.elearnspace.org/Articles/networks.htm.

Siemens, G. (2005b). Connectivism: A learning theory for a digital age. *International Journal of Instructional Technology and Distance Learning, 2*(1), 3–10.

Starratt, R. J. (2004). *Ethical leadership.* San Francisco, CA: Jossey-Bass.

Stein, D. S., Wanstreet, C. E., & Calvin, J. (2009). How a novice adult online learner experiences transactional distance. *Quarterly Review of Distance Education, 10*(3), 305–311.

Stein, D. S., Wanstreet, C. E., Calvin, J., Overtoom, C., & Wheaton, J. E. (2005). Bridging the transactional distance gap in online learning environments. *American Journal of Distance Education, 19*(2), 105–118.

Stromquist, N. P. (2002). *Education in a globalized world: The connectivity of economic power.* Lanham, MD: Rowman and Littlefield.

Swan, K. (2001). Virtual interactivity: Design factors affecting student satisfaction and perceived learning outcomes in asynchronous online courses. *Distant Education, 22*(2), 306–331.

Swan, K., & Shih, L. F. (2005). On the nature and development of social presence in online course discussions. *Journal of Asynchronous Learning Networks, 9*(3), 115–136.

Taylor, J. C. (1995). Distance education technologies: The fourth generation. *Australian Journal of Educational Technology, 11*(2), 1–7.

Taylor, J. C. (2001). Fifth generation distance education. *Higher Education Series, Report 40.* Canberra: Australian Department of Education, Training and Youth Affairs.

Torche, F., & Valenzuela, E. (2011). Trust and reciprocity: A theoretical distinction of the sources of social capital. *European Journal of Social Theory, 14*(2), 181–198.

Traxler, J. (2007). Defining, discussing and evaluating mobile learning: the moving finger writes and having writ.... *International Review on Research in Open and Distance, 8*(2), 1–16.

Tu, C.-H., & McIsaac, M. (2002). The relationship of social presence and interaction in online classes. *The American Journal of Distance Education, 16*(3), 131–150.

Wallace, R. M. (2003). Online learning in higher education: A review of research on interactions among teachers and students. *Education, Communication & Information, 3*(2), 241–281.

Wenger, E. (1998). *Communities of practice: Learning, meaning, and identity.* Cambridge: Cambridge University Press.

Wiener, M., & Mehrabian, A. (1968). *Language within language: Immediacy, a channel in verbal communication.* New York, NY: Appleton Century Crofts.

Williams, R., Karousou, R., & Mackness, J. (2011). Emergent learning and learning ecologies in Web 2.0. *International Review of Research in Open and Distance Learning, 12*(3), 39–59.

Wise, A., Chang, J., Duffy, T., & Del Valle, R. (2004). The effects of teacher social presence on student satisfaction, engagement, and learning. *Journal of Educational Computing Research, 31*(3), 247–271.

Yang, D., Olesova, L., & Richardson, J. C. (2010). Impact of cultural differences on students' participation, communication, and learning in an online environment. *Journal of Educational Computing Research, 43*(2), 165–182.

Zong, G., Wilson, A. H., & Quashiga, Y. (2008). Global education. In L. S. Levstik & C. A. Tyson (Eds.), *Handbook of research in social studies education* (pp. 197–218). New York, NY: Routledge.

PROMOTING LEARNER ENGAGEMENT AND ACADEMIC LITERACIES THROUGH BLENDED COURSE DESIGN

Cathy Gunn

ABSTRACT

Leading edge practice in university teaching uses the affordances of technology to engage students in development of essential literacies for 21st-century learning. Learning designs are aligned with core principles of learning psychology, both general and specific to the discipline. Technology offers unique opportunities for every learner to acquire key literacies along with discipline knowledge and without increasing faculty workloads. This chapter presents a literature review tracking development of learning theories and design principles, and then describes their application in three blended learning cases from the author's institution.

INTRODUCTION

Universities around the world publish intellectual profiles that all their graduates will attain. Transferable skills such as critical and relational

Increasing Student Engagement and Retention in e-Learning Environments:
Web 2.0 and Blended Learning Technologies
Cutting-edge Technologies in Higher Education, Volume 6G, 145–174
Copyright © 2013 by Emerald Group Publishing Limited
All rights of reproduction in any form reserved
ISSN: 2044-9968/doi:10.1108/S2044-9968(2013)000006G008

thinking, reflective writing, reasoned analysis, problem solving and information literacy are common inclusions. 'Academic literacies' (Gunn, Hearne, &
Sibthorpe, 2011) is the general term used in this chapter to describe these
broadly applicable intellectual capabilities that are a core aim of university
education along with the acquisition of disciplinary knowledge.

A trend of increasing scale and diversity in university classes gathered pace
at the end of the 20th century. Faculty have to manage rising student
numbers, cultural diversity and variety in educational backgrounds, often
without access to additional funding or teaching resources. Another trend
sees a large proportion of today's learners arrive at university fluent in the
use of technologies that their teachers are not familiar with, and with
educational potential that promises to be transformational, but is yet to be
fully explored. Although the pervasiveness of the 'digitally literate' student is
contested in some quarters (e.g. Kennedy et al., 2007), it may be the first time
in history that what Prensky (2001) famously described as 'digital immigrant'
teachers are having to learn what their 'digital native' students already know
in order to engage them effectively. In this context, it is no small challenge
for faculty to ensure that each individual learner acquires the academic
literacies needed to work effectively with discipline-specific knowledge at
university, and in professional practice contexts after graduation.

This chapter focuses on the increasing use of e-learning tools and blended
learning designs to foster the development of core academic literacies in
course and curriculum design. A growing body of evidence shows that these
tools and designs present unique opportunities to maintain educational
standards in the face of increasing enrolments and student diversity. Some
of this evidence comes in the form of published cases that demonstrate how
standards of learner performance and engagement can be raised across large
cohorts of students without increasing faculty workloads on an ongoing
basis (e.g. de la Harpe & Radloffe, 2006; Gunn et al., 2011). Learning design
principles specific to the current raft of technologies remain emergent at this
stage. However, the underlying psychology is well established, and an
overview of literature is included to track key historic developments. More
recent research endorses the continuing relevance of core principles, and
shows high potential for learning gains when they underpin the use of
various technologies (e.g. Narayan & Baglow, 2010; Oblinger & Oblinger,
2005; Smailes, 2003; Weigel, 2002).

Three cases drawn from the author's practice context illustrate how
blended course designs used principles of learning psychology and the
affordances of various technologies to achieve a positive impact on learner
performance. The author had some involvement in each case for learning

design, development support, mentoring and evaluation. The chapter focuses more on the acquisition of academic literacies than discipline-specific knowledge.

THE CONCEPT OF ACADEMIC LITERACIES

The challenge for students 'learning how to learn' at university has been a focus for research since at least the 1980s (e.g. Martin & Ramsden, 1987). It was acknowledged then that skills for learning, described in this chapter as academic literacies, are key to student engagement and academic success. Two approaches to the development of these literacies involved either embedded or supplementary activities. Impact evaluations found the embedded approach to be more consistently effective (e.g. Chanock, 2003; Hattie, Biggs, & Purdie, 1996). Aligning the features of embedded skills designs with principles of learning psychology reveals fairly obvious reasons why this would be the case, as will be discussed later in the chapter.

At the time of this early research, the use of technology in education was an emergent trend, and the terms e-learning and 'blended learning' had yet to enter the discourse. The list of essential literacies has expanded since then, with the addition of ICT, information and digital literacy. However, research has also found that many university teachers expect students to arrive fully equipped, and do not take responsibility for imparting these skills (Gunn et al., 2011).

The ability to embed the development of academic literacies in blended course designs has proved to be an unanticipated benefit from the affordances of technology. Evidence suggests that this can be achieved regardless of scale and diversity in classes, or faculty experience in pedagogy and learning design. While the concept may sound deceptively simple, it typically involves an uncommon degree of collaboration across roles, as well as deep understanding of the principles of learning psychology described in the following sections.

THE VARIABLE RELATIONSHIP OF LEARNING PSYCHOLOGY AND LEARNING DESIGN

Like other cause and effect relationships in educational settings, the interaction of learning psychology and the practice of learning design has never been easy to predict. Tomlinson (2008, p. 507) noted that more than a century of investigation had failed to produce satisfactory understanding of the contribution of modern psychology to pedagogical practice. It is also more than a century since pioneer of educational psychology William James observed that:

> Psychology is a science and teaching is an art; and sciences never generate arts directly out of themselves. An intermediary mind must make the application by using its originality. (James,1899, p. 7)

The keywords 'science', 'art' and 'originality' reflect the case argued by many scholars who do not believe in a 'science' of instruction, as human behaviour is influenced by too many variable factors for reliable cause and effect relationships to be identified. According to the *Handbook of Educational Psychology* (Berliner & Calfee, 1996, p. 726), the complexities of the relationship between teaching and learning have been poorly researched and consequently, are poorly understood. So the search for a 'science of instruction' with or without the added complexities of new technology may add to the knowledge base, but is unlikely to lead to any definitive outcomes. Further research is needed to guide practice in the rapidly advancing domains of educational technology and blended learning. Many exciting innovations have emerged in recent years, and while the relationship remains complex, some long-established principles of psychology can inform learning designs where technology is an integral part of the art form. The early sections of this chapter outline the development of these principles as background to the later ones, which illustrate their application to innovative learning designs. A discussion of the current state-of-the art and critical success factors is offered in conclusion.

The Evolution of Learning Psychology

Regardless of whether or not technology is used, learning design is a form of pedagogical practice that is informed by relevant principles of learning psychology. Tomlinson (2008, p. 507) endorsed the concept of teaching as an art rather than a science, noting the core role of psychology as providing 'well-grounded indication of the nature of learning processes and the teaching functions that support them, rather than to generate particular ways of teaching.'

The principles of psychology now being applied to e-learning have a much longer history than the technologies being used in their application. One late

19th-century theorist has already been cited. In *Talks to Teachers on Psychology*, William James (1899) pointed to the importance of designing instruction to activate learner engagement at a time the context, beliefs and theories of learning were significantly different to what they are today. The role of engagement is pivotal, as many generations of scholars have acknowledged with the effort to activate it in learners. A brief historical sketch tracks the development of learning design for engagement, which began with understanding of the purpose and process of learning.

John Dewey wrote on the aims, methods and experience of education throughout the first half of the 20th century. In *Democracy and Education*, he outlined the aim 'to transmit the resources and achievements of a complex society' and 'provide individuals with a continued capacity for growth ... through the reconstruction of social habits and institutions stimulated by equitably distributed interests' (Dewey, 1916). In a later work, *Education and Experience*, he stated that experience involves the activation of two principles, that is, continuity and interaction. Continuity relates to the unique experiences of every individual, while interaction is the situational influence on that experience. Teachers should apply these principles to steer learners in the direction of desirable outcomes (Dewey, 1938). This work focused more on understanding how learning occurred than how learners might be encouraged to engage.

Skinner (1954) contributed research on a behavioural approach to learning in *The Science of Learning and the Art of Teaching* (1954) and *The Technology of Teaching* (1968). Skinner's model for learning design involved behavioural objectives broken down into small instructional tasks, self-pacing and active learner response to frequent questions with immediate feedback. The resulting forms of instruction lent themselves well to the early use of computers in education. Skinner's *Teaching Machine* provided the personal instruction and reinforcement he considered so important. However, the alignment of learner response with particular forms of feedback was a level of sophistication yet to be achieved.

Bloom's taxonomy of educational objectives (1956, 1964) defined the nature of the cognitive and affective domains in learning as a guide to curriculum and activity design. The taxonomy remains popular as a structure that progresses from the cognitive elements of recall and comprehensions of facts, procedural patterns and concepts to the ability to apply, analyze, synthesize and evaluate various forms of information. Higher-level skills in the affective domain involve selective attention, generation of appropriate responses, assigning value, organizing and internalizing knowledge. Contemporary researcher Jerome Bruner (1961,

1964) wrote about the techniques and technologies that help learners to represent complex environments and integrate different sources of information to solve particular problems. David Ausubel (1968) outlined the relationship between theoretical and practical elements of educational psychology that teachers need to understand and apply. His research on cognitive structure and readiness, intellectual abilities and individual differences also remains relevant today. This work defined various forms of learning support, including advance organizers as a device to initiate conceptual frameworks and 'scaffolding' for structured development of the frameworks to mature understanding. There was some focus on learner engagement, although understanding learning as a process remained the priority.

Throughout the next two decades, researchers such as Gagne (1970), Glaser (1976), Reigeluth (1983) and Entwistle (1985) focused on the connections between psychological theories and learning design. This gave rise to false optimism in some quarters that a 'science of instruction' would eventually be defined. During this period, the seminal work of Marton and Saljo (1976a, 1976b) introduced the concepts of deep and surface learning. They found important differences between surface approaches where students aim to recall disconnected facts and repeat the information given, and deep learning where the aim is to engage with the 'bigger picture' and in personal construction of knowledge. Learning and assessment design were identified as key influences on the adoption of these approaches, and thus on learner engagement. Picking up on this line of enquiry, Keller (1983, 1987) and Schiefele (1991) theorized and brought the complex issue of learner motivation to the forefront. Keller's (1987) ARCS model (attention, relevance, confidence, satisfaction) guided motivational aspects of learning design by focusing on ways to capture learner attention, demonstrate the relevance of activities and content, promote confidence in growing ability, and satisfaction through corrective and/or supportive feedback. This research added understanding of ways to activate and support the learning processes that earlier work had sought to define.

Concurrent developments from around 1970 onwards explored the potential of computers in education (e.g. UNCAL, 1976), reflecting the progression from behaviourist to constructivist and social constructivist theories of learning. Understanding of the mechanisms of learning in different situations and for different groups and individuals spawned a plethora of innovative learning designs, for example, interaction with simulations (Laurillard, 1978), cognitive apprenticeship (Collins, Brown, & Newman, 1989), situated (Seely-Brown, Collins, & Duguid, 1989) and problem-based learning (Grabinger, Dunlap, & Duffield, 1997). Combined with the raft of e-learning tools available in the late 20th and early 21st centuries, these designs are proving transformational. A growing body of literature addresses cognitive, affective and social aspects of the use of ICT, digital media, Web 2.0 and social networks for learning (e.g. Beetham & Sharpe, 2007; Haythornthwaite & Andrews, 2011; McLoughlin & Lee, 2010; Weigel, 2002). The challenge remains, however, of bringing these innovations into mainstream use and making them more sustainable in the process. At present they remain at the margins, perceived as a threat to established teaching practice and organizational norms (Callan & Bowman, 2010; Gunn, 2010).

Learning environments, theories and design practice have all developed considerably over the period outlined above. The historical sketch was presented as a reminder that the core theories and principles used by the current generation of learning designers have evolved over many years. Rather than superseding previous work, later developments added depth and breadth to the body of knowledge on teaching and learner engagement. Learners must be motivated to engage, and guided and supported in the development of cognitive and affective processes relevant to a body of disciplinary knowledge regardless of the preferred theoretical or learning design approach. Learning is driven by appropriate activities with assessment and feedback mechanisms reflecting progress towards objectives. It is a popular misconception that early theories of behaviourism and mastery learning have no place in today's university courses. They remain critical in some contexts, for example, entry-level science, maths and language learning. The most dramatic changes are in the relationships of teachers, learners and content; the raft of tools and methods available to support the art of teaching; and the contexts in which that art is now being practised.

The Role of Teaching

While it is logical that course and curriculum design should draw on the principles of learning psychology outlined above, Tomlinson (2008) noted two types of barriers that must be addressed for this to proceed. Barriers to implementation arise because many teachers and learning designers are unfamiliar with such principles, particularly those appointed on the basis of research expertise. Even some with teaching qualifications have developed their art through front-line experience, and are unable to identify the principles they apply to design. The aim to 'realize the teaching voice' in communicable form is a topic of current research (Donald, Blake, Girault, Datt, & Ramsay, 2009). So the underlying 'science' that should inform the 'art' of teaching may be absent or unexpressed in learning design conversations. If core principles are unknown or unexpressed, it is hard to know if or how they might contribute to learning designs.

Barriers of interpretation are reflected in the myriad opinions on how principles of learning psychology interact with learning design. A shift from discussing 'instructional design' (e.g. Merrill, Drake, Lacy, & Pratt, 1996) to 'learning design' (e.g. Sims, 2006) reflects the focus on learning (student centric) rather than instruction (teacher centric) as a key realm of influence. This shift from 'what the teacher does' to 'what the learner does' doesn't mean teaching is any less important, but acknowledges it as one part of a 'learning equation' that can influence, but not determine, what the outcome will be. In today's diverse classrooms, both virtual and physical, the focus has to shift from teacher to learner centric. Faculty and learning designers must focus on how to facilitate learning, as well as how to teach effectively using a mix of direct (transmission) and indirect (activation) strategies. This reflects emergent theories and beliefs about learning combined with the demands of current circumstances. Tomlinson's (2008, p. 510) idea of interaction between two complementary sides is a useful way to consider the teaching and learning relationship. In technology-rich environments, 'at the scene' monitoring may be a function of the learning design rather than personal presence.

The Affordances of Technology

With technology-supported learning designs, it is common for the key teaching functions of influencing and monitoring to be embedded in interactive resources. In such cases, strategies to engage learners and stimulate learning processes use presentation, interaction design, meaningful structure, performance monitoring and system-generated feedback. Motivational and cognitive elements can foster student engagement in activities such as enquiry, analysis and knowledge construction. The blended learning cases described later in this chapter show how the teaching role can be embedded in e-learning resources as well as being present in physical classrooms. The two aspects of the role are integrated in a seamless way, and geared towards particular groups of learners, the tasks in hand and the learning objectives in focus.

A wide range of technology tools are now in common use in educational settings, including the ubiquitous learning management system (e.g. Blackboard and Moodle), social networks and social media, e-books, online assessment systems, the Internet, virtual worlds, simulations, games, multimedia tutorials and interactive resources. The choice of tool depends on many factors, and support for applying the principles of learning psychology outlined above should be a main determining factor.

FOSTERING LEARNER ENGAGEMENT – THEN AND NOW

William James believed that learner engagement (though he used a different term to describe it) was the single most important success factor for an educational system. In the book *Talks to Teachers*, he discussed the concept of *sustained voluntary attention,* and proposed that an education system that activates this process learners is an ideal to aspire to (James, 1899, p. 101).

Much has been written since then on how activities should be designed to engage learners (e.g. Quinn, 1997; Radloff, 2011), with the popular approaches of active and authentic learning as key areas of focus. The contemporary theory of constructivism acknowledges the individual nature of knowledge and experiential basis of its construction. Collis and Moonen's (2006) concept of 'the contributing student' that has learners generating resources and taking responsibility to define learning processes is another important development. Whether learning designs are based on mastery or constructivism, digital media, the Internet and Web 2.0 technologies open up new ways to articulate the full range of theory-based approaches.

However, it is clear from the literature that James' ambition for an education system that can sustain learner attention is still a work in progress more than 100 years on. An observer of any institute of higher learning in 2012 would be likely to encounter as many examples of passive or moderately engaged students in large lecture halls as situations where creative, engaging and authentic learning environments are in use. Hung, Tan and Koh (2006) noted that educators all over the world are familiar with the concept of engaging pedagogies, but concur with Tomlinson (2008) who believed that many lack explicit knowledge of the psychology behind them. In the current context, this limited understanding extends to

Internet tools and other emergent technologies for either social or educational use. This is one key reason why teaching practice is slow to change, yet when a shift does occur, it is often transformative and heavily in favour of the new engaging pedagogies that are facilitated through technology. The key to success is actually simple, and hinges on the use of a theoretical framework, with attention to motivation and learner engagement, to ground design and guide technology choice. These simple principles should be non-negotiable, but are all too often overlooked.

Authenticity and Engagement

Hung et al. (2006) also made a connection between engaged learners and authentic experience. While their work focused on disciplinary content, the same principle applies to the acquisition of academic literacies. The concept of authenticity has obvious relevance in this context, as working with authentic material, for example, scientific data or business cases, is an ideal situation for learners to develop these capabilities along with disciplinary knowledge. Learning through real-world scenarios reflects the way these skills are applied for study, and later on, for professional practice. For example, one of the case studies below describes how business students engaged in activities designed to develop their information literacy skills to search for, process and present company information for completion of a major assignment (Gunn et al., 2011; Tooman & Sibthorpe, 2012). The idea is to create learning environments that mirror professional practice contexts so new content and associated literacy skills make obvious sense and allow knowledge to be constructed in meaningful ways. The appropriate technology tools model their use in learning and professional practice contexts.

Motivation

Motivation has been studied for many years as a necessary condition for learning. Keller (1983, 1987) defined the ARCS model with attention, relevance, confidence and satisfaction as the broad components of learner motivation. Schiefele (1991) and Schunk (1991) added interest to the list. The concepts of attention, interest and relevance are self-explanatory. Students must perceive the relevance of activities and content to their current course of study and to longer-term career goals and life interests.

Authentic tasks with obvious relevance to both study and life experience have proved to be an effective way to stimulate interest and sustain attention. They also offer opportunities to fit learning tasks with established cognitive frameworks and experiences. Confidence and satisfaction relate directly to the learning design concept of scaffolding. Datt and Aspden (2011) describe scaffolding as a conceptual framework for learning support that enables students to perform better than they would in the absence of any type of support. Like scaffolding on a building project, it can be removed in stages as the structure (or learner) develops to the extent it is no longer necessary (Steinberg, 1989). The role of motivation in learning goes much deeper than this brief summary, which outlines the concept as a reference point for the case studies presented below.

Integration

Integration of academic literacies into activities required to complete a course of study is an often-missed opportunity in learning design and assessment. While the rationale for integration may seem obvious, it is more common to find these literacies as the focus of supplementary support services. One reason is where university teachers are disciplined experts and accomplished researchers but not qualified in educational theory or instructional design. More general and transferable aspects of learning are assumed to pre-exist, or regarded as someone else's responsibility. In practice, they are left to chance or voluntary access to support services despite their presence in university graduate profiles (de la Harpe & Radloffe, 2006; Gunn et al., 2011).

This author believes that these essential literacies should be an integral part of courses and mapped across entire curricula. Academic literacies relevant to each discipline should be acknowledged as core learning objectives. To implement this proposal, faculty may need to acquire additional skills in learning design, or to access expertise through specialist course design teams. The practice of teaching academic literacies out of context is less effective, as it leaves faculty who lack essential knowledge and skills in sole charge of course development and teaching. The affordances of technology offer unprecedented opportunities to integrate academic literacies into subject-based courses without unreasonable increases in faculty workloads. The teamwork typically involved in blended course design initiatives is an open opportunity to bring all requisite skills into the mix.

IMPERATIVES FOR CHANGE

By the end of the 20th century, many factors had combined to drive significant change to formal education systems, that is, a greater percentage of national populations entering higher education; increased competition from private sector organizations; international student mobility; availability of mature educational technology systems; open, distance and e-learning environments; and evolving theories of learning. Some predictions about the impact of technology in education had proved more reliable than others. Many failed through the lack of understanding of core principles of learning psychology and learning design (Zemsky & Massy, 2004). While many aspects of university education have changed in recent decades, and various technologies have emerged as core tools for teaching and learning, the challenge to engage learners in development of essential academic literacies remains a work in progress.

CASE STUDIES OF EMBEDDED ACADEMIC LITERACIES

Three examples of blended course design are described to illustrate how applied knowledge of learning psychology and the affordances of technology have been used to foster learner engagement and development of academic literacies. The author of this chapter played a role in learning design, course development and/or evaluation in all cases, which took place at her institution, the University of Auckland. Each case demonstrates how changing circumstances fuelled the demand for new and effective learning design approaches. As class size and student diversity increased, new methods of teaching and strategies to engage learners became a necessity rather than a choice. Mature technology systems and collaborative learning design approaches facilitated the purposeful integration of core literacies with disciplinary content in ways that were previously impossible. Technologies that have become ubiquitous in recent years allowed innovative strategies to be developed and embedded, and new levels of learner engagement achieved. Authentic and meaningful activities incorporating the use of supportive technology tools helped learners to monitor and plan their own work regardless of the scale of operations. The cases suggest that embedding core literacies in courses is an essential way of learning how to learn in the 21st century, which is only feasible with the use of technology.

Case 1: Promoting Mastery in First Year Science

This case features a seven-year iterative process that resulted in transformation of first-year biology courses through blended learning. A summary of key points is provided here, with full details of the development and evaluation reported in Gunn and Harper (2007). Course teachers faced a number of common challenges in the 1990s. Student numbers and diversity were growing rapidly. General first-year courses serviced a number of major subjects including sciences and medicine. Student performance and prior knowledge of the subject varied widely, and teaching spaces were designed for a lecture/transmission model. The quality of student learning was compromised by the inability of a predominantly teacher centred model to accommodate individual differences in learners. Despite the considerable challenges, any attempt at teaching innovation tended to be driven by isolated individuals with limited resources. A culture of dependency resulted from the transmission model of teaching, and was at odds with the graduate profiles published by the department and the university. The strongest pressure, and the obvious place to begin the transformation, was at entry level.

Early trials of a new online learning management system aimed to facilitate communication and administration of the course, so faculty could focus on the core business of teaching. The system also offered formative assessment and feedback opportunities that were set up to help students monitor and enhance their own rate of progress. Lectures, lab classes and tutorials continued as before, but with supplementary activities and encouragement for students to self-test and receive feedback so they could focus attention and seek help where necessary. The blended learning model was designed to cater to individual differences, as tasks could be approached from different angles and peers and teachers consulted at any point. More experienced students could use supplementary activities for reinforcement, while those with less experience could use them for remediation. Further aims were to foster transferable skill development and promote autonomy by being clear about expectations and building students' knowledge about learning processes.

Theoretical Grounding of the Course Design
The discipline of Science depends on a sound body of knowledge, so mastery of the basics is essential. With this in mind, the blended course design applied the following principles:

• Provided accessible e-learning tools and tasks, and actively encouraged students to use them;

- Used online tests with built in instruction and feedback as a catalyst to attain mastery;
- Used errors as an opportunity to address misconceptions and offer immediate remedial instruction;
- Built rewards into formative assessments to sustain motivation;
- Supported the accumulation of learning experience and a sense of personal achievement;
- Encouraged deep learning by going 'beyond the information given' in traditional course activities for those learners who were capable of extending themselves.

At the time of the initial development, the concept of an online system that brought together course management with learning activities and communication tools was itself an innovation. The capacity to manage large-scale operations while encouraging individual interaction and providing personalized feedback planted the first seeds of change. Dynamic visual resources were already available for Biology courses through an early adopter of multimedia technology, and it was a simple task to incorporate these into the online system.

Online activities were designed to integrate with lectures and lab classes where students carried out experimental investigations. For the first time students had 24/7 access to resources and activities online, instead of being limited to synchronous events dictated by the teaching program. For the growing number of students with family and work commitments, this was revolutionary. System log data revealed many studying outside normal class hours at their own convenience. This supported reinforcement of learning 'on demand' and facilitated progress to more complex concepts in subsequent lectures.

Small group workshops with voluntary attendance proved to be another popular option. Students were encouraged to email ahead with issues and questions, so faculty could monitor frequency and type of questions, correct misconceptions and address gaps in understanding. Class discussion boards were archived and made available for searching and revision purposes. Email quickly became a key channel for dissemination of important information, and both students and faculty welcomed the immediacy.

Asynchronous discussions facilitated dialogue among students and with the teaching team. Importantly, this many-to-many dialogue offered potential for sharing that is not available in face-to face environments where fewer speakers can engage. Initial concerns about activating discussion boards in large classes were addressed when students used these as an alternative to faculty office hours. Moderation was not required at the level anticipated because students posted highly effective and usually accurate comments on learning issues. Those giving explanations gained confidence in their own ability by responding to requests for information. Those making requests were encouraged when they received accessible explanations and support from their peers. Exposure to multiple perspectives was also useful for learning and allowed faculty to identify common misconceptions.

On-line quizzes offered formative assessment opportunities with immediate feedback, allowing students to reinforce learning in ways most likely to impact on long-term memory. Online assessment throughout a course of study has been shown to promote learner engagement (e.g. Gunn, 2006; O'Reilly, 2001; Smailes, 2003). In this case, it helped students to understand the levels of knowledge and standards of performance required. This lack of clarity had previously been addressed too late for students to lift their performance.

In addition to formative assessment quizzes and the later addition of a pre-lecture quiz to give a sense of what they knew and didn't know, students were encouraged to engage in pre-lecture reading on the main concepts, key terminology and learning objectives. This provided what Ausubel (1960, 1978) called an 'advance organizer', and made it easier for learners to engage deeply with the lecture as they had an existing mental framework for the new material. The impact of this on long-term memory was explained to encourage adoption.

The Seeds of Transformation
This initiative eventually transformed the course structure and outcomes through the application of an appropriate theoretical basis and principles of learning design using the affordances of current technologies. It was published in a collection of chapters in *Making the Transition to eLearning* (Bullen & Janes, 2007) with evidence of the impact on learning (Gunn & Harper, 2007). Along with mastery of content, learners gained sound experience of learning how to learn science and potentially other disciplines, of self-management strategies, communication and ICT skills Further enhancements of the course design have occurred since then, as technology has advanced, confidence in its educational potential among faculty has grown and their skills for use have advanced. Now, Web 2.0 tools offer live video links to scientists working in locations such as Antarctica. Sophisticated online assessment tools that come packaged with textbooks and other rich media resources support mastery of core concepts in the

discipline knowledge base. Despite the technological developments, the same theory and learning design principles that proved so effective in the initial transformation continue to drive later iterations, that is:

- Making expectations and the benefits of particular learning strategies clear to students;
- Providing strategies that help students to gauge what they know and what they don't know so they can focus their learning effort and 'discover' new knowledge;
- Promoting mastery of terminology and concepts so students can operationalize the basics in order to engage at a higher level;
- Scaffolding and supporting students with various levels of knowledge and study goals;
- Using formative assessment with rich corrective feedback as a catalyst for learning.

While faculty generally embraced the course design and appreciated its overall effectiveness, some questions remained about levels of understanding of the pedagogy behind it. Teaching was managed by a team, so innovation was no longer left to isolated individuals, but strong leadership by a highly qualified and experienced individual remained a critical success factor.

Case 2: Knowledge Development and Management in First Year Pharmacy

In describing the use of various technologies, including Web 2.0 tools in a learning design for first year university Pharmacy students, Datt and Aspden (2011) reminded us that the tools alone cannot teach or result in effective learning. However, their use in theoretically grounded study tasks can make unique contributions to effective learning designs. Like Hung et al. (2006), Datt and Aspden (2011) focused on authentic tasks, motivation, scaffolding and transferable skills development as key learning design elements within a clearly defined theoretical framework for their course.

Their broad objectives were to use technology tools to provide flexible access and encourage student engagement, while facilitating development of discipline knowledge and knowledge management skills in the first year course. The teaching role was to monitor, guide and manage learner engagement. Assessed activities included compilation and presentation of an e-poster to explain a topical health issue to non-academic community groups; a written summary of the work undertaken to create this arte-fact; and justification for a selection of what students considered to be authoritative web resources on the topic. The group work element of these assignments reflected professional practice in the discipline, and was a key feature. As this took place at a time when students were off campus or heavily engaged in other activities, flexibility to communicate online and contribute from any location was important.

The e-learning tools chosen to serve these purposes were the Internet as a rich source of information requiring use of search, evaluation and selection strategies; an assignment presented in the form of a Webquest (i.e. an authentic web-based task designed to elicit higher order thinking through guided enquiry); and Web 2.0 tools for communication. Specifically, they used a wiki for collaborative tasks and social bookmarking to create and discuss a student-generated resource collection. An interesting addition to the e-tools list was a locally developed, easy to use editor for interactive multimedia course websites. While this is more commonly used by faculty and learning design teams, the Pharmacy students used it to create e-posters, so they could be stored for later use as web resources.

Datt and Aspden (2011) described a sequence of activities that were (a) explicitly aligned with the broad objectives to promote knowledge acquisition, co-creation and representation and (b) grounded in the theoretical concepts of authentic tasks, learner motivation, scaffolding and skills development. They cited Bates (2010) to endorse the points that a specific purpose and rationale for using technology tools, and teacher support and guidance all remain essential. They also acknowledged that assumptions made by some authors (e.g. Oblinger & Oblinger, 2005; Prensky, 2001) about students' digital literacy and ability to use technical skills in educational settings may not be reliable in every context. Other researchers (e.g. Kennedy et al., 2007; Narayan & Baglow, 2010) reported finding the ability of learners to use e-learning tools and skills for educational purposes to be generally lacking, so caution is required.

Pedagogy 2.0
Datt and Aspden (2011) opted for a learning design approach reflecting the Pedagogy 2.0 concept described by McLoughlin and Lee (2010, p. 59). This promotes the 'cultivation of digital competencies in ways that allow learners to develop critical thinking, knowledge building and creative skills'. Thus, the development of academic literacies is embedded in the acquisition, creation and processing of discipline knowledge. In this case, students searched, retrieved, analyzed, evaluated, organized, created and shared information in guided and supported use of web resources in ways that were obviously relevant to the curriculum goals.

The academic literacies addressed by this learning design, and the principles of learning psychology it aligns with are motivation, authentic tasks, and scaffolded skills development. Learner engagement was an important goal, and reference back to William James' (1899) idea of sustained voluntary attention provides insight into the quality of this design. An authentic task was designed to connect with students' experience of community health education campaigns at some time in the past. It is reasonable to assume this would influence their approach to design, and strategies to communicate key information to a target audience. It is also likely that they would have experience using technology tools for either social or educational purposes. Adding newly acquired knowledge, and the challenge to seek out information and present it in the required format, would build on what learners already knew, a key element of learning psychology that links back to the work of pioneers such as those cited above.

Initial Results Are Promising
While it was too early to claim that the outcomes of a post-course evaluation demonstrated positive impact on most or all learners, initial feedback from the Pharmacy course was generally of that nature, and modifications to the course structure resulted. More specifically, the authors reported that presenting an authentic task in the form of a Webquest was a successful way to engage learners in development of digital literacy and knowledge management skills. It also gave them experience of team-work and leadership in line with the university's graduate profile. Oral presentations and peer feedback provided opportunities for learners to articulate what they had learned, and to evaluate and comment on the work of others. Although the wiki activity was considered frustrating in some respects, this appeared to hinge on different levels of contribution and self-confidence for group activity. While it did present a challenge, it required learners to use initiative, and reflected the reality of many group work situations they might encounter in professional life.

As is often the case, learners set up their own communication channels using Facebook and email. While this was generally to be encouraged, it did create a problem for course lecturers trying to monitor individual engagement in tasks. Activities will be revised in future, to provide better scaffolding for group tasks, for use of less familiar Web 2.0 tools and to clarify expectations around what learners must do to succeed.

While further evaluation is required, it is reasonable to conclude that the innovative learning design for the first year pharmacy course showed promise of aligning well with the Faculty's graduate profile in areas including ICT, knowledge management and teamwork. It is also fair to conclude that the design could not have been so effective without the embedded use of e-learning tools to articulate the core principles of learning psychology.

Case 3: Business Information Skills Online

This case focuses on the information literacy skills that feature on the graduate profile of most contemporary universities and are required for many professions. Gunn et al. (2011) provide a full report on this development.

A program of information literacy skills development had been in operation at the host university for many years. A shift to blended learning had begun with the provision of self-paced, interactive tutorials on the web. Some were offered as part of credit bearing courses, although use was not mandatory. The broad aim of the initiative described here was to engage students with core information literacy concepts and tools through tutorials that were linked to curriculum content. A further aim was to produce tutorials that could be easily reused, and customized for different courses and assignments. Increasing first year class sizes and decreasing opportunities for face-to-face instruction in business information literacy skills motivated the shift to blended learning.

Prior to the introduction of blended learning, librarians gave a lecture to students on selected courses, and informed them about supplementary instruction that was available on a voluntary basis. While this approach reached many students, neither the learning design nor the opportunity was considered ideal. Not all students attended the lecture, and despite the aim to include meaningful examples, learners did not necessarily see the relevance, or perceive the information skills to be as well embedded as they could be. From a learning design perspective, this 'one off', limited exposure, or 'off topic' instruction did not fully address key dimensions such as relevance, motivation, interest and feedback. A general trend towards blended learning in large first year courses presented an opportunity to promote information literacy along with other ICT skills that were becoming increasingly important in all disciplines. Librarians approached the University's Centre for Academic Development, a unit that provides teaching and e-learning development services to all faculties, with a request for assistance to develop a suite of interactive multimedia tutorials that would address all requirements.

The design of the tutorials was deceptively simple. Rich media elements provided a gateway to common sources of business information. Self-paced activities offered guidance, examples and constructive feedback to students, as they acquired and practiced the requisite skills to complete a major assignment. However, it was attention to detail in the principles of learning design that arguably made this initiative succeed when previous attempts had failed.

The broad aims were (a) to design the tutorials around content and manageable tasks that built up to the cognitive and affective skills required to complete a major assignment and (b) to embed the actual search tools, databases and information sources that learners and professionals would use into the online tutorials. The difference between presentation of information literacy concepts as the discrete topics of optional extra activities, and as integral skills for the course to be incrementally developed was expected to be considerable. Using real search tools and information sources would provide scaffolding for learners without previous experience, and with variable levels of ability to follow written instructions.

The root of the problem in this case was the above noted expectation that students would come equipped with the necessary skills, and that it was not faculty's responsibility to impart them. Perhaps it was reasonable to expect learners to know this kind of thing in the days when a small percentage of top achievers from high schools went on to university. In today's large, diverse and multi-cultural classrooms, no such assumption can be made. While it may seem incredibly basic to be teaching such literacies at university level, there is ample evidence that it is necessary. In this case, the evidence was the Librarians' experience, year after year, of large numbers of stressed out students seeking help at the last minute to interpret assessment questions, or to find and present the information required for their assignments.

Pedagogical Approach
The basic design of tutorials used simple web tools to present content, and online assessment to test knowledge and present corrective or positive feedback. Key design features were as follows:

- Logical order for presentation of content;
- Clear definition of terms with the ability to explore meaning;
- Guidance on how and when to use different sources and types of information:
- Explicit alignment with curriculum content;

- Staged progress towards overall goals with practice opportunities and quizzes to reinforce learning and provide constructive feedback at each step.

The award of marks for completion of these tutorials, and the explicit link to a major assignment were considered key success factors in fostering learner engagement. Although the percentage of marks awarded was small, the first run with the tutorials achieved 100% participation, which was significantly more than attendance at a Librarian's lecture or use of supplementary services had ever been.

Positive Results Lead to Wider Adoption
It was important to gaining faculty support that no compromise to overall standards or coverage of course content resulted from teaching information literacy skills along with the course content. In fact, Tooman and Sibthorpe (2012) reported that use of the tutorials significantly reduced teaching time and front-line contact hours for library staff while delivering high quality, subject focused academic literacy programs to large cohorts of students. The impact on faculty workload was minimal in terms of contact time, but significant in the sense that fewer students sought assistance or turned in poor quality assignments. Online assessment allowed elements of marking and grading to be automated, so one of the mundane aspects of managing large classes was positively impacted.

The Business Information Skills Online initiative suggested that carefully crafted online tutorials were an ideal way to impart this kind of academic literacy. The online materials were available to all students through a familiar learning management system environment. Access and reinforcement opportunities were unlimited, and feedback on performance was immediate and relevant. All learning styles, educational backgrounds and language abilities were catered for, as students had the flexibility to engage in any of a number of ways either individually or in self-selected groups. Variation in teaching style of different faculty members or librarians was no longer an issue. Learners also had unlimited opportunities to discuss course related matters with their peers, or to contact librarians, who were more likely to be available for the few who did need individual support.

From an institutional perspective, the collaborative development model involving faculty, librarians and academic support professionals avoided dependence on any individual and placed ownership with a team. This represented a more sustainable proposition than a lone enthusiast driving an innovation. The use of simple and widely available e-learning tools avoided any complications in the ICT area, and supported self-reliance as faculty and support staff were able to upskill in learning design and use of the common technology tools. In this, as well as the other two cases, the learning design approach supported enhancements based on feedback from learners. The prospect now being explored is for the core learning design concept of embedded academic literacy skills development to be applied in different subjects and years of study. The online resources are freely available, and are easy to reuse and repopulate for different subjects, raising efficiency in course development as well as academic literacies to a new level. It is simply a case of knowing which principles to apply (implementation) and how to apply them (interpretation) as noted above in Tomlinson (2008).

DISCUSSION

A common factor across the cases outlined above is that faculty or learning support staff had an educational problem to solve, and the technology available at the time was an integral part of a creative solution. In contexts that demand flexible access and study options, along with the ability to manage large classes and student diversity without compromising educational quality, technology may be the only practical solution. Although the technologies used in two of the cases (learning management systems and web based, multimedia tutorials) are not what would be considered 'leading edge' in 2012, they are tried and tested tools that met the demands of learning designers in effective and reliable ways.

The choices offered by the current raft of Web 2.0 and digital tools to articulate particular theoretical approaches and learning designs are demonstrated in this chapter. Where mastery learning is the appropriate goal as it is in the first year science case, a drill and practice approach provides excellent opportunities. It can be embellished with multimedia elements, live data feeds, rich feedback options and communication tools. These compliment the individual activities designed to help students enter the discourse of a discipline where complex terminology and concepts must be mastered for early success and then operationalized for study at higher levels. Many textbook publishers provide high quality, ready to use resources. Many are developed in collaboration with discipline experts, so design skills and lead times for individual faculty are minimized. Different learning styles are accommodated by the provision of a range of resources, activities and communication tools. Flexible access accommodates students with busy timetables and other commitments to manage. While the principles behind the learning design may not be particularly innovative, the way learners engage with study materials, the nature of those materials, and the forms of interaction with peers and teachers were transformed in positive ways through the use of quite basic technology tools. The impact on learner engagement, outcomes and retention rates has been considerable, as Gunn and Harper (2007) describe.

The Pharmacy case demonstrates that constructivist approaches can also be well served by technology. If students are not familiar with the use of Web 2.0 tools for education when they arrive at university, many of them will be fluent users for other purposes. The learning curve is thus not so steep as if they were using new tools as well as new concepts, knowledge management skills and forms of active and interactive learning. The 'contributing student' concept asks them to generate resources and define study pathways using Pedagogy 2.0 with the affordances of Web 2.0 technologies (Datt & Aspden, 2011).

The embedded academic literacies approach outlined in the Business Information Skills Online case demonstrates how the broadly applicable skills that feature in graduate profiles can be acquired in the context of subject-based courses without adding to the workloads of teachers or learners on an ongoing basis. While some upfront investment is required, this produces building blocks for further development in the way that open source resources do. Instead of offering extra-curricular support for development of these literacies, they are an integral part of courses, and acquired in the meaningful context of the discipline-based knowledge they will be applied to. The overwhelmingly positive results described by Tooman and Sibthorpe (2012) may lead faculty to wonder why a different approach was ever pursued, although the embedded approach has only really become an imperative with the decrease in teaching resources and concurrent increase in scale and diversity of many university courses.

Transformation Through Collaboration

It is worth noting that all three cases featured in this chapter, as well as others cited as references, describe development initiatives that involved collaboration between subject matter experts from faculties, learning design, technical development and other professionals such as librarians. Most universities provide some form of support for teaching and faculty development. Evidence points to this being a key factor in e-learning strategy implementation and teaching innovation (Gunn, 2010). This kind of collaboration brings together all the skills necessary to design and implement pedagogically driven e-learning initiatives, that is, technical, learning psychology, subject matter, learning design and media production expertise. It is rare for an individual to be skilled in all these areas, and reflects an emergent culture of collaboration that is supported by the same e-learning tools that are transforming the educational experience of the current generation of learners.

Cross-functional collaboration is an elegant solution to the problem of implementation identified in the early sections of this chapter. It helps to address any learning skills deficit among faculty, and facilitates the development of strategies to manage the scale and diversity that are increasingly found in contemporary university classes. It is part of a trend towards collective responsibility for learning design in a context of scale where the previously common situation of one individual responsible for teaching is no longer sustainable. The model of flexible teamwork and cross-functional relationships involved is unfamiliar to many who will have to participate. This adds a further challenge to progress of new technologies and innovative pedagogies. The cases described above demonstrate why it must be addressed.

In the business information literacy case, librarians identified a learning need through many years of front-line experience, and invited e-learning design and production experts to collaborate on the development. Together they met the challenge of persuading a faculty member to adopt a concept that was theoretically well grounded, but untested in context at that stage. This was both an initial risk and a critical success factor. The decision had already been made that online tutorials should be based on course content and incremental steps towards completion of a major assignment in order to meet authenticity and relevance criteria of good learning design. In the event, a lecturer with previous experience of working with teaching and learning development staff agreed to give it a try. It was an incentive that others would do the development work, so demands on his time were minimal and potential benefits high. The success of the initiative was acknowledged when only three students from a cohort of more 1,100 submitted inadequately prepared assignments, a result that was 'unheard of'. The outcome was equally satisfying for librarians who realized that embedding information literacy skills through online tutorials with links to authentic business information sources and analysis tools had 'taken information literacy skills to a new level, and reached more students than the previous workshop model allowed' (Gunn et al., 2011, p. 11).

Once initial trials demonstrated how well the concept worked in practice, it was an easier task to get others involved. The 'embedded literacies' approach has since been adopted across a new first year core curriculum in the business school as well as for different academic literacies in other faculties. While each implementation has unique aspects, a common factor is bringing different areas of expertise together to create something that is greater than the sum of the parts. This is particularly important as the field of new technology becomes increasingly specialized. It is also arguably the most effective form of faculty development for e-learning, as sustained engagement leads to transformation of practice. It is also an effective way to ensure development activities are relevant to faculty needs and address authenticity requirements. But that is the topic of a different conversation (Gunn & Donald, 2010).

An Evolving Psychology of e-Learning

The principles of learning psychology and learning design featured in this chapter could be explored at a much deeper level if space permitted. As Bennett and Oliver (2011) note, the predominance of practice-focused studies of e-learning and case-specific phenomena, does little to inform the broader practice of design for learning with technology. Studies of principles separate from practice are fewer now than 20 years ago, and the trend towards case-based research is reflected in learning technology journals. Gunn and Steel (2012) suggest it is a necessary stage of a journey to define the fundamental issues of credible methodologies, relevant focus, sound research design and meaningful presentation formats for e-learning research. A central ground where studies of principles are reported *and* can be applied to cases of practice would be a welcome development.

CONCLUSION

The focus of the first half of this chapter is on core concepts of learning psychology and learning design without explicit reference to the technologies and e-learning tools that are now widely used to implement them. The author believes that this reflects a reasonable balance between pedagogy and technology for contemporary university education.

There is little room to doubt that the affordances of new technology are having a transformational effect on learning design, processes and outcomes at university, as well as in other areas of formal and informal education. The 'gatekeepers of knowledge' are losing ground as simple technology tools allow anyone to generate and instantly share rich media resources. Innovators among those 'gatekeepers' are creating and sharing knowledge in ways that were previously impossible for both conceptual and practical reasons. While there are challenges to overcome, a growing body of knowledge in the broad field of e-learning and in the scholarship of teaching and learning in the disciplines reflects the transformation that is taking place. This body of knowledge has its roots in the work of learning psychologists conducted over the past hundred or so years. More recently, it has branched out into new areas to accommodate emergent technologies, faculty development approaches, theories of learning and learning design.

As always, universities are quick to engage with technology as innovators and early adopters explore the opportunities created by new systems and tools. They are however slow to reach critical mass as this involves shifts in policy, culture and practice that took a long time to become embedded in the first place. Some observers believe that education is on the brink of a revolution fuelled by social media and social networking tools that are changing the ways people communicate, and knowledge is created, managed and shared. While this may be true, the evidence presently before us suggests something less radical, but equally transformational as students become creators rather than consumers of pre-packaged knowledge, and learning involves engagement with peers, experts, simulations, virtual worlds or authentic experiences as well as traditional activities of reading, writing, listening and absorbing. The connections between an increasingly diverse range of educational organizations and learning are also becoming more variable.

The cases presented in this chapter gave a glimpse of what is possible, through explorations of a mid-1990s technology enabled solution to the practical problems of promoting mastery learning in the context of scale and diversity in first year courses; strategies to embed academic literacies in subject-based courses so all students acquire them; and student ability to generate resources using Web 2.0 tools within a course of study. While the positive impact of such initiatives on learner engagement is noted, the challenges of upscaling such innovations to institutional adoption are not trivial, particularly in universities where research takes priority over teaching.

The idea of faculty development as a sustained relationship between professionals, rather than a series of workshops or courses, is itself an innovation that has yet to enter the mainstream. The cross-functional relationships that bring discipline knowledge, learning design, technical development and academic support expertise together in course design teams are equally novel. Perhaps the hardest relationship to mediate is with IT services where standardization and security are priorities, while innovators need to push boundaries to experiment with new e-learning tools. Speculation about the impact of new technologies on education is a further complicating factor. Studies of e-learning being published now will help to shape future developments in teaching and learning. The knowledge base of learning research built up over the last 100 years needs the addition of evidence from studies where established principles have been interpreted and applied using the latest technology tools combined with the art of the current generation of creative teachers. It is only possible to wonder what educational technology researchers might be reflecting back on 100 years from now.

REFERENCES

Ausubel, D. E. (1960). The use of advance organizers in the learning and retention of verbal material. *Journal of Educational Psychology, 51*(5), 267–272.

Ausubel, D. P. (1968). *Educational psychology: A cognitive view*. New York, NY: Holt, Rinehart & Wilson.

Ausubel, D. E. (1978). In defense of advance organizers: A reply to the critics. *Review of Educational Research, 48*, 251–257.

Bates, T. (2010). Understanding Web 2.0 and its implications for elearning. In M. Lee & C. McLoughlin (Eds.), *Web 2.0-based eLearning: Applying social informatics for tertiary teaching* (pp. 21–42). Hershey, PA: IGI Global.

Beetham, H., & Sharpe, R. (Eds.). (2007). *Rethinking pedagogy for a digital age: Designing and delivering elearning*. Oxon: Routledge.

Bennett, S., & Oliver, M. (2011). Talking back to theory: The missed opportunities in learning technology research. *Research in Learning Technology, 19*(3), 179–189.

Berliner, D., & Calfee, R. (Eds.). (1996). *Handbook of educational psychology*. New York, NY: Macmillan Library Reference.

Bloom, B. S. (Ed.). (1956). *Taxonomy of educational objectives; Book 1, cognitive domain*. London: Longman Publishing.

Bloom, B. S., Krathwohl, D. R., & Masia, B. B. (1964). *Taxonomy of educational objectives: Book 2, affective domain*. London: Longman Publishing Group.

Bruner, J. S. (1961). The act of discovery. *Harvard Educational Review, 31*(1), 21–32.

Bruner, J. S. (1964). The course of cognitive growth. *American Psychologist, 19*(1), 1–15.

Bullen, M., & Janes, D. P. (2007). *Making the transition to E-learning: Strategies and issues*. Hershey, PA: Information Science Publications.

Callan, V., & Bowman, K. (2010). *Sustaining e-learning innovations: A review of the evidence and future directions.* Canberra: The Australian Flexible Learning Framework. Department of Education, Employment and Workplace Relations, Commonwealth of Australia.

Chanock, K. (2003). *Challenges of the graduate attribute movement.* Paper presented at the "In the future…" 6th [Biennial] National Conference. Proceedings of the language and academic skills in higher education conference, Flinders University, Adelaide.

Collins, A., Brown, J. S., & Newman, S. E. (1989). Cognitive apprenticeship: Teaching the crafts of reading, writing and mathematics. In L. B. Resnick (Ed.), *Knowing, learning & instruction: Essays in honour of Robert Glaser* (pp. 435–490). Hillsdale, NJ: Lawrence Erlbaum Associates.

Collis, B., & Moonen, J. (2006). The contributing student: Learners as co-developers of learning resources for reuse in web environments. In D. Hung & M. S. Khine (Eds.), *Engaged learning with emerging technologies* (pp. 49–67). Dordrecht, the Netherlands: Springer Science and Business Media.

Datt, A., & Aspden, T. (2011). *Leveraging technology for engaging learning design.* In G. Williams, P. Statham, N. Brown & B. Cleland (Eds.), Changing demands, changing directions, Ascilite Conference, Hobart. Retrieved from http://www.ascilite.org.au/conferences/hobart11/procs/Datt-full.pdf

de la Harpe, B., & Radloffe, A. (2006). Lessons learned from three projects to design learning environments that support 'generic' skill development. *Journal of Learning Design, 1*(2), 21–34.

Dewey, J. (1916). *Democracy and education:* MacMillan. Retrieved from http://www.ilt.columbia.edu/publications/dewey.html

Dewey, J. (1938). *Experience and education.* New York, NY: Macmillan.

Donald, C., Blake, A., Girault, I., Datt, A., & Ramsay, E. (2009). Approaches to learning design: Past the head and the hands to the HEART of the matter. *Distance Education, 30*(2), 179–199.

Entwistle, N. J. (1985). Contributions of psychology to learning and teaching. In N. J. Entwistle (Ed.), *New directions in educational psychology: Learning and teaching.* London: Falmer.

Gagne, R. M. (1970). *The conditions of learning.* London: Holt, Reinhart & Winston.

Glaser, R. (1976). Components of a psychology of instruction: Towards a science of design. *Review of Educational Research, 46*(1), 1–24.

Grabinger, S., Dunlap, J., & Duffield, J. (1997). Rich environments for active learning in action: Problem based learning. *Association for Learning Technology Journal, 5*(2), 5–17.

Gunn, C. (2006). Engaging learners through continuous online assessment. In D. Hung & M. S. Khine (Eds.), *Engaged learning with emerging technologies* (pp. 255–273). Dordrecht, the Netherlands: Springer Science and Business Media.

Gunn, C. (2010). Sustainability factors for elearning initiatives. *ALT-J Research in Learning Technology, 18*(2), 89–103.

Gunn, C., & Donald, C. (2010). Tracking the invisible: An elearning group's approach to evaluation. In L. Stefani (Ed.), *The effectiveness of academic development* (pp. 133–142). New York, NY: Routledge.

Gunn, C., & Harper, A. (2007). Using elearning to transform large class teaching. In M. Bullen & D. Janes (Eds.), *Making the transition to elearning: Issues and strategies* (pp. 139–156). Hershey, PA: Information Science Publishing.

Gunn, C., Hearne, S., & Sibthorpe, J. (2011). Right from the start: A rationale for embedding academic literacies into university courses and curriculum. *Journal of University Teaching and Learning Practice, 8*(1).

Gunn, C., & Steel, C. (2012). Linking theory to practice in learning technology research. *Research in Learning Technology, 20*(2). Retrieved from http://www.researchinlearning technology.net/index.php/rlt/article/view/16148

Hattie, J., Biggs, J., & Purdie, N. (1996). Effects of learning skills interventions on student learning: A meta-analysis. *Review of Educational Research, 66*(2), 99–136.

Haythornthwaite, C., & Andrews, R. (2011). *eLearning theory and practice*. London: Sage.

Hung, D., Tan, S. C., & Koh, T. S. (2006). Engaged learning: Making learning an authentic experience. In D. Hung & M. S. Khine (Eds.), *Engaged learning with emerging technologies* (pp. 29–48). Dordrecht, the Netherlands: Springer Science and Business Media.

James, W. (1899). *Talks to teachers on psychology, and to students on some of life's ideals.* Cambridge, MA: Harvard University Press.

Keller, J. (1983). Motivational design of instruction. In C. M. Reigeluth (Ed.), *Instructional design theories and models*. New York, NY: Lawrence Erlbaum Associates.

Keller, J. (1987). Strategies for stimulating the motivation to learn. *Performance and Instruction, 26*(8), 1–7.

Kennedy, G., Dalgarno, B., Gray, K., Judd, T., Waycott, J., Bennett, S., Maton, K., Krause, K.-L., Bishop, A., Chang, R., & Chrchward, A. (2007). *The net generation are not big users of Web 2.0 technologies.* Paper presented at the Ascilite 2007 ICT: Providing choices for learners and learning, Nanyang Technological University, Singapore.

Laurillard, D. M. (1978). *A study of the relationship between some of the cognitive and contextual factors in student learning.* Unpublished Ph.D. Thesis, University of Surrey, UK.

Martin, E., & Ramsden, P. (1987). Learning skill or skill in learning. In J. E. Richardson, M. W. Eysenck & D. Warren Piper (Eds.), *Student learning: Research in education and cognitive psychology* (pp. 155–167). Society for Research in Higher Education and The Open University Press, Milton Keynes.

Marton, F., & Saljo, R. (1976a). On qualitative differences in learning: Outcome and process. *British Journal of Educational Psychology, 46*(1), 4–11.

Marton, F., & Saljo, R. (1976b). On qualitative differences in learning: Outcome as a function of the learners' conception of the task. *British Journal of Educational Psychology, 46*(2), 115–127.

McLoughlin, C., & Lee, M. (2010). Pedagogy 2.0: Critical challenges and responses to Web 2.0 and social software in tertiary teaching. In M. Lee & C. McLoughlin (Eds.), *Web 2.0-based elearning: Applying social informatics for tertiary teaching* (pp. 43–69). Hershey, PA: IGI Global.

Merrill, D. M., Drake, L., Lacy, M. J., & Pratt, J. (1996). Reclaiming the discipline of instructional design. *IT Forum Discussion List*. Retrieved from http://itech1.coe.uga.edu/itforum/extra2/extra2.html

Narayan, V., & Baglow, L. (2010). *New beginnings: Facilitating effective learning through the use of Web 2.0 tools.* In C. Steel, M. Keppell, P. Gerbic & S. Housego (Eds.), Curriculum, technology & transformation for an unknown future. University of Queensland, Sydney.

Oblinger, D., & Oblinger, J. (2005). *Educating the net generation*, Retrieved from http://www.educause.edu/educatingthenetgen. Accessed on June 25, 2012.

O'Reilly, M. (2001). *Improving student learning via online assessment.* Paper presented at the Improving student learning using learning technology conference, Oxford Centre for Staff and Learning Development, UK.

Prensky, M. (2001). Digital natives, digital immigrants. *On the Horizon, 9*(5), 1–6.

Quinn, C. (1997). Engaging learning, *IT Forum Mailing List January 1997*. Retrieved from http://www.listserv.uga.edu/archives/itforum.html. Accessed on June 25, 2012.

Radloff, A. (2011). *Student engagement in New Zealand's universities*. Retrieved from http://akoaotearoa.ac.nz/ako-aotearoa/student-engagement

Reigeluth, C. M. (Ed.). (1983). *Instructional design theories and models: An overview of their current status*. Hillsdale, NJ: Lawrence Erlbaum Associates.

Schiefele, U. (1991). Interest, learning and motivation. *Educational Psychologist, 26*(3&4), 299–323.

Schunk, D. H. (1991). Self-efficacy and academic motivation. *Educational Psychologist, 26*(3–4), 207–231.

Seely-Brown, J., Collins, A., & Duguid, P. (1989). Situated cognition and the culture of learning. *Educational Researcher, 18*(1), 32–42.

Sims, R. (2006). Beyond instructional design: Making learning design a reality. *Journal of Learning Design, 1*(2), 1–7.

Skinner, B. F. (1954). The science of learning and the art of teaching. *Harvard Educational Review, 24*(2), 86–97.

Skinner, B. F. (1968). *The technology of teaching*. New York, NY: Appleton-Century-Crofts.

Smailes, J. (2003). *Strategies for engaging students in computer based assessment-Stage 1, taking stock*. Paper presented at the 7th CAA Conference, Loughborough University, UK.

Steinberg, E. (1989). Cognition and learner control: A literature review 1977-88. *Journal of Computer Based Instruction, 16*(4), 117–121.

Tomlinson, P. (2008). Psychological theory and pedagogical effectiveness: The learning promotion potential framework. *British Journal of Educational Psychology, 78*(4), 507–526.

Tooman, C., & Sibthorpe, J. (2012). A sustainable approach to teaching information literacy: Reaching the masses online. *Journal of Business and Finance Librarianship, 17*(1), 77–94.

UNCAL. (1976). *The educational potential of computer assisted learning: Qualitative evidence about student learning*. Norwich: University of East Anglia.

Weigel, V. B. (2002). *Deep learning for a digital age: Technology's untapped potential to enrich higher education*. San Francisco, CA: Jossey-Bass.

Zemsky, R., & Massy, W. (2004). *Thwarted innovation: What happened to e-Learning and why?* Final report of The Weatherstation Project. The Learning Alliance, University of Pennsylvania.

ENGAGING LEARNERS AS MODERATORS IN AN ONLINE MANAGEMENT COURSE

Kamna Malik

ABSTRACT

In an online executive education setting, online discussions are seen as a frequently used pedagogical tool that promotes higher level of learning and critical thinking. A teacher's role is seen more as a moderator or facilitator of learning than as a lecturer or preacher. This shift of roles enhances the online students' opportunities to critically think and reflect; and encourages co-creation of knowledge by way of peer discussions. It is imperative that students apply their critical thinking as well as soft skills to effectively participate and contribute towards making the discussion forum as self-regulated. However, in reality it needs explicit planning and effort on the part of the teacher to motivate them towards this positional shift. This chapter presents the motivation and techniques for improving student engagement by way of assigning them the role of moderator in a predominantly asynchronous online course for management graduates. A qualitative analysis of the observations made based on the application of three techniques of student moderation on student cohorts is shared and implications are discussed.

Increasing Student Engagement and Retention in e-Learning Environments:
Web 2.0 and Blended Learning Technologies
Cutting-edge Technologies in Higher Education, Volume 6G, 175–197
Copyright © 2013 by Emerald Group Publishing Limited
All rights of reproduction in any form reserved
ISSN: 2044-9968/doi:10.1108/S2044-9968(2013)000006G009

INTRODUCTION

If cutting-edge technologies alone could get the learners engaged, online education would not have faced the challenges it faces today. Engaging learners involves helping them transcend beyond being a captive audience to being an active listener, high-order thinker and co-creator of knowledge. Traditionally, teachers have used various activities and technologies as stimuli for learner engagement. Experiments, class discussions, team projects, outdoor excursions, industry visits and role-plays have been some of the common practices used to enable knowledge transfer and high-order learning as well as to break the monotony of lecture sessions. However, as the effect of any stimulus reduces with time following the inverted U-shaped pattern (Huitt, 2011; Yerkes & Dodson, 1908), the real challenge for a teacher is to creatively apply a mix of various stimuli so as to retain the attention of learners.

This challenge gets multi-fold as the education delivery turns technology oriented. For example, lack of interactivity, reported as a weakness of online education (Beard & Harper, 2002; Jackson & Helms, 2008), can be seen as an offshoot of overuse of unilateral technologies, causing monotony (Knill, 2007) and turning students into passive audience. In addition, many extrinsic factors such as technology constraints, academic background, personnel issues such as income, family and health and employment status also hinder the engagement of online students (Packham, Jones, Miller, & Brychan, 2004). Such extrinsic barriers are beyond the control of a teacher or the educational institute and are particularly applicable to working students, who in many cases are constrained by time and space too. As a result, the online students are at higher risk of missing on many of the abilities that are often cultivated naturally in real time, face-to-face teaching by way of instant challenges thrown open to students during the class hours.

This chapter aims to take one step forward in improving engagement and learning outcomes of the online executive (professionally qualified and working at managerial positions) students. Towards this aim, it suggests the use of student moderation as a technique for better engagement. It presents the motivation, techniques and experience of engaging learners in an online course by assigning them the role of moderators. A comparative analysis of various tools and techniques used for inviting students to volunteer as moderators is presented. Insights are drawn based on the literature as well as a qualitative study carried out in a pre-dominantly asynchronous, online course for management graduates. Observations are shared with respect to students' initiation and participation in three different forms of moderation including initiating and moderating a new topic through discussion board, moderating an assigned topic through discussion forums and initiating and moderating an approved topic through webinar (web-based seminar). Issues related to assigning students as moderators are also discussed.

STUDENT ENGAGEMENT AND LEARNING IN AN ONLINE SETTING

Engagement implies the degree of student involvement and the amount of time and effort spent on an activity (Davidson & Amenkhienan, 2011; Molinari & Huonker, 2010). Handelsman, Briggs, Sullivan, and Towler (2005) link engagement with two motivational goals, namely learning goals and performance goals. They suggest that students with learning goals are better engaged. While administratively, student engagement is linked to student retention, from a teacher's perspective, the purpose of student engagement is to increase the quality of learning. Teachers adopt various methods to engage students such as setting assignments, using classroom response systems, power point slides, case days, 5-minute essays, crystal clear/muddy waters and team huddle (Davidson & Amenkhienan, 2011). Case-based discussions, simulations and role-plays are also quite commonly used methods to actively involve students. Molinari and Huonker (2010) iterate that student engagement is a motivational issue and is related to critical abilities. This issue gets aggravated when the mode of education turns online.

Online education is gradually picking up (Allen & Seaman, 2011) as a mode of study. It is being adopted in many different variants of synchronous and asynchronous delivery. Asynchronous delivery is often managed through a learning management system (LMS), which is an integrated software package with a set of teaching and learning tools managed as a central resource linked with other functions such as finance and administration (Sabau, Munten, Bologa, Bologa, & Surcel, 2009). The mode and extent of online education can be chosen based on the subject and student needs, teacher's preferences and technology readiness, as well as an institute's centralized infrastructure, policy and pedagogy.

In online education, particularly at the higher level, online discussion boards are seen as a prime pedagogical tool that promotes higher level of learning and critical thinking skills (Ackerman, Gross, & Perner, 2003; Brookfield & Preskill, 1999; Sautter, 2007). Sautter (2007) infers that the opportunity (available through discussion boards) to question and exchange ideas in writing appears to hold particular promise in advancing higher order thinking skills. In addition to discussion boards, the commonly used tools and techniques for reaching out to students include audio/video-based lectures, CD/web-based content delivery, studio-based audio and video conferencing and webinars (Malik, 2010). She suggests blending of suitable synchronous and asynchronous technologies so as to balance the conflicting variables of time, space and interactivity that characterize online education.

The conflict of time and space flexibility with interactivity affects the overall quality of student engagement and learning. While synchronous model of online education favours live lecturing and instant response, it imposes higher demand on technology, cutting down the flexibility of space and striking off the flexibility of time. Contrary to this, an asynchronous model favours time and space flexibility enabling more time for thinking and reflection, but loses on impromptu expression. At higher level of executive education, where students are working executives, and self-paced study and discussions become more useful compared with monolithic lectures, it is desirable to use asynchronous model as the base and top it up with better ways of facilitating interaction and critical thinking. The challenge in this scenario is to engage those students who develop a tendency to misuse the flexibility and end up using online system simply as a means of making submissions for evaluation. It is the responsibility of teachers and the institutions to provide guidelines and counselling to help students utilize the online pedagogy.

The learning environment has a crucial role to play in such a scenario. It has been observed that the key reason for failure of e-learning initiatives is not the technology but the failure of educators and organizations in providing quality content and learning experience (Engelbrecht, 2003; Salmon, 2005). An online teacher should act primarily as a moderator or facilitator of student learning (Salmon, 2000, 2002) and this role is even more relevant than the teaching or lecturing role (Kim & Bonk, 2006).

Garrison, Anderson, and Archer (2000) suggest the need to create three 'presences' namely, cognitive presence, social presence and teaching presence, for deep and meaningful learning. Cognitive presence supports the development and growth of critical thinking and is achieved through five levels of mental activities, namely memorization, analysis, synthesis, making judgment and application. These are also prevalent in online learning environment (Robinson & Hullinger, 2008). Social presence provides comfort and a sense of belongingness to the group. Online discussion boards are the most commonly used pedagogical tool to enhance social presence through encouraging student–teacher and student–student inter-activity. Teaching presence is critical for enabling cognitive as well as social presence. It includes structure, mentoring and subject expertise to give high-order learning to students. Though the current tools of technology and integrated LMS make online social presence an engaging reality, the three presences, particularly the cognitive and teaching presence, to a great extent depend on the way a teacher manages them. One way to achieve this is to entrust online students with higher responsibilities in the class and create a proactive and collaborative environment for learning.

The following sections discuss the motivation, methodology and findings of a study conducted by way of assigning students the role of moderator as a higher level of responsibility. The next section presents the role of a moderator in general and remaining sections share the experience of assigning three different forms of moderator role to students in an asynchronous online management course at postgraduate level.

THE ROLE OF A MODERATOR

A moderator is the leader of a group meeting and presides over a meeting, forum, or debate. In electronics & computer science terminology, it means a person who monitors the conversations in an online chat room for bad language, inappropriate content, etc.

Literature suggests various roles of a moderator, which may be broadly grouped into three dimensions namely task based, time based and delegation based (see Fig. 1). Task-based roles explain the kind of tasks that a moderator does. Edwards (2002) suggests two roles of a moderator as a filter and a democratic intermediary. In a filter role, an automated or a human moderator may hold privileges to accept, reject and delete messages (Pagano, n.d.). This role may be applied before or after the submission of a discussion post (Delort, Arunasalam, & Paris, 2011).

While there is a widely available range of prevention and detection-based techniques to filter unwanted messages like spam, malicious or obscene content, which is often applied in public online discussion forums (Pagano, n.d.), the suitability of filter-based moderation is limited in educational discussion forums as they largely operate under closed and closely monitored network bound by a centralized LMS and the university rules. Instead, there is a significant need to have manual intervention of the moderator to play a democratic intermediary in an educational setup. This role is typically assumed by the teacher facilitating an online subject.

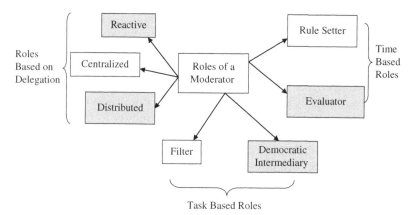

Fig. 1. Types of Roles of a Moderator. *Legend*: Shaded boxes indicate the roles adopted by student moderators in the pilot study. *Note*: The roles have been obtained through study of literature.

The nature of democratic moderation can be understood in line with the attributes identified by Salmon (2001), who suggests an e-moderator to

- be able to engage in reflective practice
- be democratic and open about their roles
- promote, encourage and enable such openness
- acknowledge personal experience
- avoid temptation to discount an experience or get into arguments
- comment suitably on sufficiency of data presented and argument around it
- exemplify ways of exploring and developing arguments

Time-based roles specify whether a particular task is carried out before or after the submission of a discussion post. A moderator may act before or after the discussion content is posted/shared. In an automated filter mode, most of the moderation activities happen post-submission. However, as human moderators, professors can choose to act as and when their intervention may be appropriate depending on the nature of discussion topic and participants. For fruitful discussions, professors can preset rules of the game and provide preliminary guidance to students explaining the pretext, necessary readings and expectations in the pre-submission mode. During post-submission stage, the moderation can get much more extensive in such guided forums with professor moderator acting as an evaluator of posted discussions to generate new threads/sub-threads of a

Table 1. Format for Alternate Modes Adopted for Student Moderation.

	Mode 1	Mode 2	Mode 3
Topic proposed by	Student	Teacher	Student
Topic approved by	Teacher	–	Teacher
Mode of discussion	Asynchronous	Asynchronous	Synchronous (webinar format)
Discussion moderator	Student proposer of the topic	Volunteer student	Student proposer of the topic
Knowledge creation	Co-created by students and faculty	Co-created by students and faculty	Major content by student proposer; supplemented by group
Grade associated with discussions	No	Yes	No
Grade associated with moderation	No	No	Yes
Size of cohort under study	32	12	45

discussion, provide instant and regular feedback to students and also grade their performance.

Moderation may also be carried out in centralized, reactive or distributive manner (Delortet al., 2011). As depicted in Fig. 1, these types of moderation suggest how the role of moderation can be delegated among the students and the teacher. In subject related and graded discussion forums, the moderation to a great extent is centralized around the teacher. However, depending on the teacher, learner and institutional pedagogy, it is not uncommon (and is in fact quite desirable) that students also bring in new dimensions and thus implicitly moderate discussions, even if in a reactive manner. In an ideal scenario, when students collaborate in a pro-active manner, moderation can get equally distributed turning a discussion forum into self-regulated forum where students and teacher position themselves as co-learners; and students may even take the position of a peer expert.

While all students cannot be equally motivated and engaged, intrinsic and extrinsic actions can help improve their level of motivation for involvement (Huitt, 2011). Some examples of intrinsic actions suggested by Huitt (2011) are to provide a variety of activities and sensory stimulations, to explain or show why learning a particular content or skill is important; to allow students some opportunities to select learning goals and tasks and to create and/or maintain curiosity. Extrinsic actions include providing clear expectations and corrective feedback, provide awards and allow students to engage in social learning activities.

In online discussions, the engagement may also be viewed in terms of presence (amount of posts) and position (interaction relative to those in student role) (Dennen, 2007). Traditionally, teachers and students are expected to assume authoritative and learner positions respectively. Dennen notes that alternatively teachers may hold the position of a guide, peer and co-learner, whereas students may hold the position of a co-learner or peer expert. Students are unlikely to engage in instructor positioning that falls outside the standard definition of instructor role unless doing so has been modelled by the instructor him/herself. Thus, it is the responsibility of the person in teacher role to initiate class-based positional shifts.

CONTEXT OF THE STUDY

Traditionally, teachers have been introducing positional shifts in classrooms by way of assigning administrative roles such as class representative, team leadership roles during group assignments or during co-curricular activities. However, when it comes to online education, developing such leadership skills becomes limited owing to technological and personnel constraints. Thus, team assignments/projects are the only manifestation of evident leadership role that students can play. This limits the overall skills development of students, particularly in higher education where the student groups are usually much more heterogeneous and critical thinking evolves through peer learning, resulting in co-creation of knowledge.

To encourage online students to exercise critical thinking, a planned change in the student positions was introduced and their performance and feedback was analysed. The study was conducted in a pure online business school (b-school) offering graduate programs in management. Typical student profile of this school includes working executives with an average age of 35. Each subject runs over a period of 12 weeks. Students are enrolled into cohorts as per a pre-defined annual course schedule. Size of a cohort varies from 10 to 45. A professor is assigned to a cohort based on the annual teaching load plan. Teaching pedagogy is learner centric. Interactions and assessments are predominantly based on asynchronous discussions, team assignments, final project and end-term open exam.

The school adopts the following major techniques for student engagement and learning.

Self-Study Resources

The study resources are all online, web based and designed by blending of video, audio, text, hypertext and animation. These include exercises for self-practice and reflection at one's own pace.

Digital Bytes from teachers

Teachers usually supplement the standard self-study resources through additional inputs such as latest updates on the subject, an introduction to a difficult concept, a set of guidelines or summary of a discussion topic. As such content is usually contextual, teachers take the help of social media and other Web 2.0 tools to create and disseminate it quickly. For example, using vodcast for lecture or discussion briefs, twitter to make announcements and blogs to exchange subject-related thoughts and invite students also to contribute. Such usage is not mandatory by the rules of the school, but the faculty members are encouraged to use them wherever appropriate.

Online Discussion Boards

Online discussion boards form the basis of student–teacher–student interaction in this school. Being a tool for collaborative learning, it is at the heart of student engagement, learning and a sense of community (Doolan, 2006, 2007, 2008). It is accessed through the LMS and is asynchronous. Both formal and informal discussions take place on the discussion board. Formal discussions are moderated by a subject teacher in a largely democratic manner. Discussion topics are provided by the teacher, linked to the study plan and form a part of student assessment. The performance is graded every month, that is, after week four, eight and twelve. Monthly grading is aimed at providing continuous assessment and feedback to students.

Informal discussions are off-topic discussions aimed at making students comfortable with the course and the group. These are monitored by the subject teacher but the extent of intermediation is extremely limited. Teachers and students may use them creatively, for example, to have an ice-breaking session or to share the latest news or a subject-related issue. Students may also use them for seeking general guidance/interaction that falls outside the formal discussion topics.

Webinars

A webinar is an online seminar conducted using a real-time, synchronous web-based conferencing tool. Webinars are frequently used for lectures by field experts where students learn through listening and enquiry. Recently, their use has been extended to subject-related case analysis and project presentations as well.

The first two forms of student engagement and learning (self-study resources and digital bytes) are aimed at internalization of concepts by the students. Discussion board and webinar provide the students with an opportunity to interact and thus socialize. The time and space flexibility embedded in asynchronous discussion boards makes it a suitable tool for interaction among geographically dispersed executive students while also providing them reasonable time for critical thinking and self-reflection. Webinar, on the other hand, provides synchronicity which is much needed to develop the abilities for listening, impromptu speaking, presentation as well as reasoning, while also making the students conversant and tolerant with diverse styles of students coming from diverse origins, cultures, age groups and work experience.

The interaction among students (through both the means) is aimed at cultivating their mental as well as soft skills in a learning environment conducive for the growth of cognitive, teacher and social presence. As a consequence, their evaluation parameters include critical thinking, depth of reasoning, originality, relevance, presentation, punctuality, consistency and quality of peer interaction. The students are encouraged to develop these traits by way of standing instructions, periodic persuasion by the teacher as well as recognition/penalties by way of grades. Based on internal meetings and review at the institute, it is felt that though the most consistent high performers of the subject are found to remain punctual and actively involved, making quality discussion posts, many others are not able to anticipate the extent of critical thinking that they can and should exercise to reach higher levels of learning.

Based on these observations, it was planned to engage students by inviting them to assume the position of peer experts and act as discussion moderator for a limited period. Guidelines were provided to help students take charge of the new position effectively. In the changed position, a student was to act as a moderator for a defined period of time. For the purpose of this chapter, a student moderator is defined as *a student who presides over peer discussions and may apply one or more types of roles of a moderator* (as summarized in Fig. 1).

METHODOLOGY FOR THE STUDY

As shown in Table 1, three modes of moderation were adopted in three different cohorts of a subject with comparable student demographics and facilitated by one professor. The modes of moderation were selected based on the professor's experience with online classes over the past five years and a qualitative review of the activities that high-performing students exhibited/appreciated in his/her classes.

Separate cohorts were chosen for the study with a purpose to avoid higher stress for students who are working executives and may not have the time and energy to accommodate multiple new ways of discussions, and which could potentially impact the student performance. No explicit constraint was put on the start time or size of the cohort selected for the study. Cohorts were picked for the study as and when they were available for the professor's facilitation.

Mode 1 – Topic Proposal and Discussion Board-Based Moderation

In this mode, all the students enrolled in a subject cohort ($n = 32$) were invited to propose a topic of discussion related to the subject under discussion. The topics were non-gradable. There was no time defined for opening or closing of the discussion topic. A topic could open as soon as a student proposed a topic. The group was invited to participate in asynchronous discussion mode using text-based discussion boards. The teacher reserved the right to approve, disapprove or refine the proposed topic.

Mode 2 – Discussion Board-Based Moderation on a Pre-Defined Subject Topic

In this mode, the professor called upon the students of another cohort ($n = 12$) to volunteer as moderators for the discussion topics already defined as a part of the session plan. Discussion topics were a part of the formal assessment plan as per the centralized pedagogy of the institute. Therefore every student was expected to join the discussions in the regular way. The change was to assign additional moderator positions to students who volunteered to do so. There was no additional benefit or evaluation criteria kept for the volunteers.

The student moderators were invited through a public announcement made in the beginning of the course. The technique suggested for moderation was democratic rather than filter-based and students were provided with guidelines as illustrated in Table 2. In addition, the professor responded to the specific mails of student volunteers seeking interim feedback to become more effective in the remaining days.

The assignment of moderation was for one week per topic. Students could nominate themselves as volunteers via a post to the discussion topic. Final assignment was made by the teacher on the first come first serve basis. The professor sent a confirmation post in reply to a student nomination post, thereby affirming the acceptance as moderator to the student volunteer as well as the entire group.

Table 2.   Guidelines for Student Moderators in Mode 2.

Rules for Moderation:
- The person who replies to this thread first will be the moderator for this topic. Others may look through other discussion topics and be the first one to volunteer.
- Tentatively, each topic will last for 1 week.
- If the first volunteer has already volunteered for a topic, preference will be given to the next volunteer. I'll use time stamp of the post to decide on this.

Role of Student Moderator
As a moderator, your role is to steer the discussions towards new dimensions and enable higher level of group interactions. If there are any peer queries that you can handle, do so. Being a moderator, you will need to be a bit more punctual, regular, analytical, proactive and involving compared to a normal participant. So, being moderator helps you in higher learning.

Role of Faculty
Needless to say, I remain as the default moderator and will be overseeing the whole discussion and learning.

Guidelines for Moderation
- Start in time.
- Read relevant concept thoroughly and keep your own analysis of the discussion topic with you as this will help you generate more queries on DB.
- Watch out for any contradictions that students may state or aspects that they may have missed.
- Keep your posts brief and share your own complete answer a bit later.
- It would be good if you can also summarize the class discussions towards the end or probably as a part of your own complete answer.
- Handle direct queries of students, if any
- Give summary (and critical analysis) after the discussion is over or even in between if there is enough content.

Mode 3 – Webinar-Based Presentation and Moderation

Based on the earlier success of use of webinars for team assignments reported in Malik (2010), the format was extended for use by the student moderators in yet another cohort ($n = 45$). Each student was asked to select an advanced topic of one's choice but related to the subject and duly approved by the professor. While approving a topic, the professor considered the scope of coverage as well as the uniqueness of the topic being covered by the group as a whole.

Each student was asked to go deeper into one's chosen topic and then present the understanding in a typical webinar format. This way, they were expected to be more authoritative on their chosen topic in comparison with their peers; and worthy of steering the discussion. This mode is comparable with the usual class presentations by students for their assignment or project works. The only differentiator in this case was the emphasis laid by the professor on peer interactions, which was a reasonable expectation from a group of executive students.

Panelist rights were provided to the student moderator enabling control over the presentation and discussions. After the topic presentation for initial 10–15 minutes, the forum was left open for class discussions for the next 15–20 minutes. The teacher retained the host role so that, if needed, she could take control any time in between for technical, managerial or pedagogical reasons.

Free slots of the professor, spread over a span of eight days (including late evenings, early morning and week ends), were fixed for student presentations to ensure that students did not have to take an off from work to present or attend a webinar. The free slots were posted on a dedicated discussion as 'booking slots for students'. Each student was advised to post two alternate slots convenient to one's work schedule by a defined timeline. Students were also advised to suggest an additional slot that suited them, for consideration of the teacher. After receiving all student preferences, webinar slots were assigned to moderating students considering their time preferences while also ensuring productivity of the teacher's day. A practice session was arranged to make them comfortable with the web-based conferencing tool and etiquette.

At the end of the course, students were sent a mail by the professor acknowledging the volunteers who participated in the new mode of interaction and seeking further advice on ways to improve the group learning. Feedback was also extracted from the individual mails proactively sent by the students to ask a query related to student moderation or to convey special thanks to the teacher. A qualitative analysis of student feedback and discussion posts was done and observations were grouped into four common factors to draw individual and comparative analysis of the three modes of student moderation.

RESULTS

Student Involvement

Mode 1, where the students were invited to propose a topic and then lead the discussion, did not work well. Thirty-two students were enrolled in this cohort. However, only 1 of 32 (3%) students suggested a topic. The participation by the group was negligible as only two students in the group (6%) responded to the topic.

In mode 2, the topic was suggested by the faculty and students were asked to volunteer. In all, 12 students had enrolled for this subject and there were ten scheduled discussion topics spread over the term. Seven of twelve (58%) students volunteered as moderators. Thus, 7 of 10 (70%) discussion topics were moderated by students and remaining three topics were directly moderated by the professor. As the discussion posts were visible to the entire group, only one student applied for a topic and was by default assigned the moderation role for the chosen topic. This way, there was no room left for conflict.

Discussion posts for each topic were counted to analyse the impact of student moderation on student's performance. Five of seven discussion topics moderated by the students exhibited that maximum number of posts were made by the student moderating the topic. In one of seven topics, the number of posts made by the moderating student was more than the class average, though not the maximum. In the remaining one of seven topics, the moderator made posts less than the class average.

The individual activity of student moderators during the moderation period was compared with that in the non-moderation period. It was observed that 5 of 7 student moderators made the maximum number of posts during their period of moderation as compared to the period when they were not moderating a topic. Discussion posts made by the non-moderating students (average 3.42 posts per student) were invariably less than the class average (5.2) obtained for the entire term.

In mode 3, 45 students were enrolled. As planned, performance of the student moderator was linked to assessments, but participation of non-moderating students was not. Thus, every student in the cohort had to present and moderate the follow-up discussion.

In one webinar session, two or three topics were grouped together to ensure adequate participation within the presenting students and to ensure that each presenting student gets an opportunity to moderate a peer-discussion as well. Despite being not associated with grades, non-moderating students (students attending a presentation other than the student presenter/moderator) were found to be interested in joining the webinar sessions and were actively participating in discussions. On an average, 6 of 44 non-moderating students (14%) joined a webinar session and contributed to the discussions following a student presentation. Their decision to join a session was observed to be influenced by their interest in the topic as well as by their personal work schedule, time zone and other compulsions.

Student Feedback

For mode 1, no feedback was shared by the students leading to the conclusion that mode 1 is not an effective form of moderation. The reasons may be rooted in this mode not being linked to the grades. As no significant contribution and feedback was obtained from the students, no further analysis to this effect was possible.

For mode 2, six of seven volunteers replied to the mail and shared their personal experiences. One of seven students turned silent after initiating the topic due to unexpected work pressure from his office. Two students, who did not volunteer to be a moderator, also shared their feedback.

In mode 3, students voluntarily expressed (through audio or chat modes) their liking for the use of webinar as a mode for class discussions. The level of interaction in the class discussions was observed to be related to the quality of presentation. Further research is required to study and statistically analyse this relation.

Factors Linked to Student Moderation

Based on a qualitative analysis of student feedback and level of interactions, the responses have been classified into four key factors, namely student inhibitions, individual experience, improved discussion quality and long-term learning. Table 3 provides a comparative summary of these factors.

Table 3.   Comparative View of Modes of Student Moderation with
             Respect to Student Engagement.

Mode	Student Inhibitions	Individual Experience	Discussion Quality	Long-Term Learning
1	–	–	–	–
2	• Lack of experience in moderation • Risk of lower level of learning due to reduced involvement of the teacher • Personnel issues	• Pushed to think and work harder • Soft skills for polite moderation	• Non-moderating students also worked better to match up with the moderating peers • Overall level of discussions improved in terms of volume and quality	• Motivated to apply the moderation skills in normal course of discussions in upcoming subjects also
3	• New to webinar format • Time constraint	• Improved feeling of social presence	–	• Soft skill development • Improved community building

– indicates that the factor did not have any visible impact on student engagement.

Representative responses of the students are shared below to illustrate the pattern of student responses. Similar responses have been filtered out to avoid repetition and the most detailed responses covering many facets of feedback obtained have been included. No negative feedback was obtained for any of the three modes of moderation.

Student Inhibitions

Some students shared their inhibitions with respect to mode 2 and mode 3 of moderation. For mode 2, three inhibitions were identified. First inhibition was rooted in the students' lack of experience in moderation. This inhibition was observed when three of seven volunteer students wrote an individual mail to the professor seeking guidance before their turn for moderation. For each such query, the faculty response settled their query and anxiety, so this inhibition was deemed as manageable.

Second inhibition observed for mode 2 was about the students' concern that the teacher's presence may be reduced, negatively affecting the learning effectiveness. This inhibition was identified in response to the professor's acknowledgement mail sent for the entire group. However, this inhibition also seems to have been sorted out, as indicated by a student in his feedback mail (as follows) to the teacher:

> Regarding the moderation by class, initially I was apprehensive that we may not have the learning as compared to a situation where the moderation is done by the more knowledgeable professor.
>
> However, by the end of this class, I can see that involvement of class was much more. There were these identified moderators and more importantly, many students continued even in the rest of the DBs (discussion boards). When my turn to moderate came, I was more conscious about it, prepared for it and by the end of moderation, I felt to have learnt much more than before moderation. Also, I observed that the moderation was being monitored by you. You came in wherever class was getting wayward or the class missed certain major points. I thought this was very important.
>
> I feel this was one of the highlights of this class. [sic]

Some students themselves were uncertain of their schedule owing to various reasons, and refrained from making a commitment for moderation. It is understandable as this mode of moderation expected students to make a commitment for one full week. However, being executive students, they may have personnel issues beyond the control of the professor and the institute (Packham et al., 2004). As it was not a mandatory task, they were not persuaded further for moderation.

For mode 3, the inhibitions were more related to lack of familiarity with the webinar format as some students did not have prior experience with any web-based conferencing tool. As some students started posting queries to know more about the tool, a demo session was organized for the class a week before the presentations started. This ironed out the students' anxiety and improved their readiness for a synchronous real time interaction while sitting across time zones. Some students' availability did not fit into the free slots announced by the professor. Those students were allowed to fix alternate slots in discussion with the professor.

Individual Experience
In mode 1, there was no participation by the class at large. Thus, the experience remained neutral. In mode 2, each student moderator invariably expressed that being a moderator motivated them to put in more time and focused effort in studies and discussions, thereby enhancing their learning also. Student expressions indicative of their personal experience as a moderator are listed below.

It is for sure a good way to increase engagement from students. Take me for example; I learnt more in the DB that I moderated than other DBs. [sic]

I was 'pushed' to care more specific thoughts & broaden mind. [sic]

It gave a sense of facilitation and therefore a more serious reading for a topic. [sic]

It also gave a perspective of how to facilitate and moderate politely. [sic]

Moderator practice is a good practice in DB, it encourages the students & also responsibility of students in a particular topic. Moderator definitely studies the particular topic in depth & also effectively participating in DB and cross questioning of other students. It is useful for students to learn topic more effectively. [sic]

Mode 3 required students to be more planned, punctual and organized to be able to present their work and discuss it with the peers and the teacher in real time. As the usual mode of their interaction was asynchronous, this mode gave them a near face-to-face experience of a live brain storming session. Most of the participating students acknowledged the sense of togetherness they felt by being in the webinar session. Six of fourty-five students even acknowledged the usefulness of webinar in their standard student evaluation survey, even though it was not designed for any specific feedback about the newly introduced moderation practice.

Discussion Quality
For mode 2, the average number of posts made during the last five topics was higher (5.5) than the average (4.9) recorded for first five topics. A qualitative analysis of the discussion posts made also indicated an improved quality of posts that was gradually increasing with time. Student feedback affirmed this observation, as one of them exclaimed:

I also noticed that the quality of the contributions noticeably improved from weeks 1 – 4 to weeks 9 – 12 – which I guess is as a result of learning from the other students' postings. [sic]

Another student, who had been consistently active throughout the term remarked,

I don't think that being a moderator changed the way I looked at any of the postings. But I think that asking for volunteers to be facilitators encouraged other students to not only build on what others were saying more frequently but also to pose questions to further the discussion as if they were a facilitator too. [sic]

No impact of mode 3 was observed on the quality of regular discussions.

Long-Term Individual Learning

Feedback obtained for mode 2 gave high indications of the long-term benefits that students drew from the experience. Example student reactions that led to this observation are like:

> It created a similar sense of seriousness for others topics as well subsequently. [sic]
>
> I shall endeavor to continue the same in the rest of my course. [sic]

As the moderation experience prompted students to think critically and interact with others on a proactive basis, the students learnt to put on their thinking caps for deep learning and critical analysis of others' posts. Some of them were observed to be continuing with their practice of moderation even after their formal term for moderation got over. Even the students who did not volunteer as moderators started performing better. As the approach to moderation was democratic, it resulted in many more implicit moderators that made the discussions even more effective. The student reactions indicate that having been sensitized to the role of a moderator; they have actually internalized the art of discussions and can benefit from this learning in upcoming subjects too.

Through mode 3, the students are expected to enhance their soft skills and speed of reflection. As per the feedback obtained, students enjoyed webinar-based moderation and discussions and suggested it to be a more frequent way of interaction. However, there was no feedback received to indicate its linkage with long-term learning.

DISCUSSIONS

Based on the review of discussions and explicit feedback received from the students, mode 1 does not appear to influence student engagement. Modes 2 and 3 of student moderation are identified as having positive impact on engagement of geographically dispersed executive students in a predominantly asynchronous online course in management.

Mode 2 appears to be the most effective form of engaging students due to its perceived positive impact on student's individual experience, overall discussion quality as well as long-term individual learning, all leading to improved cognitive, social as well as teaching presence. In a cohort of 12 students, 7 (58%) students volunteered for moderation in this mode. The remaining students did not come forward for moderation. No specific reason for their choice was asked as it would have affected the essence of volunteering.

Eighty-six per cent of the moderating students (in mode 2) participated more (in quality as well as number) during the moderation week as compared to the weeks when they were not moderating. Seventy-one percent of the students contributed more than the class average during their moderation week. Another significant observation captured from mode 2 analysis shows an increased interactivity compared to other comparable small size cohorts where students are not engaged as moderators and class discussions often suffer due to less number of students.

The analysis indicates that mode 3 of moderation also increases the personal experience of students during the session, giving them a high feeling and increasing the social and teaching presence, as established by Doolan (2006, 2007, 2008). However, its impact on long-term learning and quality of class discussion could not be established as the recording of online discussions was not under scope of the planned methodology.

Effectiveness of webinars as a tool for interactivity has been established in Malik (2010) and can be associated with the results of mode 2 for deriving further combination of moderation and student engagement. For example, by assigning student moderator for a select gradable discussion topic executed in a webinar format.

This study did not involve identifying the comparative impact of gradable versus non-gradable activities on student participation. It is quite likely that mode 1 may work better if proposal of a topic by a student is associated with grades. Similarly, mode 3 may get more effective if participation in discussions is linked with grades.

Implementation Issues and Recommendations

There are many challenges associated with student moderation that need to be addressed while planning to invite and assign student moderators. First and foremost, the role of faculty gets trickier during student moderation as they need to remain a silent observer and decide when to be visible – neither too early, nor too late. If the student moderator does not take off well, faculty may need to intervene sooner. For effective student moderators, a concluding remark by the professor at the end of discussion week can help supplement and wrap-up the discussion. A constant watch is required to ensure that student cohort does not continue missing or misinterpreting a topic just because the student moderator is unable to pick it. All said and done, student moderators are also students. Neither they nor other students can be punished for partial understanding of the moderator.

Second, change management needs to be given due attention. Though introducing a surprise factor can boost student engagement, moderation demands additional time and commitment that the student may not have planned for. To help them work better, students deserve to be pre-informed about any new style of teaching and learning that they may not have experienced before. As the students are working executives, they need to be informed about the pedagogy and required time commitments at least before the class starts and better before they enrol for the class. A clear set of task guidelines and expectations should be communicated before hand to enable students work better as moderators.

Third, they need to have the flexibility of picking their topic as well as slot for moderation rather than random assignment pushed by the professor. Imposing a topic outside may result in the risk of a student being assigned a subject area in which he/she is conceptually weak or is professionally less engaged. An unwarranted call on additional time of student may also adversely affect his/her other work/life commitments thus adversely affecting engagement.

Fourth, a student moderator may need additional handholding before/ during the moderation period. Some student moderators may also need coaxing. Though appreciation is welcome over the common discussion board visible to all students, any suggestions to improve should be sent in an individualized manner, say over the email. Though transparent feedback is an acceptable culture, privacy plays a significant role in improving the student performance, particularly for students who have taken the courage to walk an extra mile.

CONCLUSION

Student engagement is an important measure of teaching effectiveness and learning outcomes. Traditionally, teachers have used different tools and techniques to engage students. One such technique is to assign students higher level of responsibility by way of positional shift of roles (Dennen, 2007).

This chapter presents a study that involved students as moderators with an aim to engage them better. Three modes of moderation were applied based on the qualitative experience of the professor. Each of the selected modes was applied on a separate cohort. Involvement and feedback of students were analysed using a qualitative review. Observations made have been classified into four factors – student inhibition, individual performance, discussion quality and long-term learning. Results clearly establish the usefulness of changing the student position as a moderator in an online asynchronous discussion forum for executive management education.

Further research work is recommended to empirically investigate the inter-relation of student engagement with the three modes of student moderation as well as with the four factors identified in this study.

REFERENCES

Ackerman, D. S., Gross, B. L., & Perner, L. E. (2003). Instructor, student, and employer perceptions on preparing marketing students for changing business landscapes. *Journal of Marketing Education, 25*(1), 46–56.

Allen, I. E., & Seaman, J. (2011). *Going the distance: Online education in the United States, 2011.* Wellesley, MA: Babson Survey Research Group. Retrieved from http://sloanconsortium. org/publications/survey/going_distance_2011

Beard, L. A., & Harper, C. (2002). Student perceptions of online versus on campus instruction. *Education, 122*(4), 658–663.

Brookfield, S. D., & Preskill, S. (1999). *Discussion as a way of teaching: Tools and techniques for democratic classrooms.* San Francisco, CA: Jossey-Bass.

Davidson, D., & Amenkhienan, F. (2011). Student engagement should be fundamental. *Franklin Business & Law Journal* (2), 39–50.

Delort, J. Y., Arunasalam, B., & Paris, C. (2011). Automatic moderation of online discussion sites. *International Journal of Electronic Commerce, 15*(3), 9–30.

Dennen, V. P. (2007). Presence and positioning as components of online instructor persona. *Journal of Research on Technology in Education, 40*(1), 95–108.

Doolan, M. A. (2006). Effective strategies for building a learning community online using Wiki. *Proceedings of the 1st annual blended learning conference 2006, University of Hertfordshire, Hatfield.*

Doolan, M. A. (2007). Collaborative working: Wiki and the creation of a sense of community. In *Proceedings of the 2nd international blended learning conference 2007,* 14 June, University of Hertfordshire, Hatfield, Hertfordshire (p.70).

Doolan, M. A. (2008). Bridging the gap: Adapting curriculum design and teaching practice to engage the net generation learner in an online learning community. In *Proceedings of the 3rd annual blended learning conference 2008,* 18–19 June, University of Hertfordshire, Hatfield.

Edwards, A. R. (2002). The moderator as an emerging democratic intermediary: The role of the moderator in Internet discussions about public issues. *Information Policy, 7*(1), 3–20.

Engelbrecht, E. (2003). A look at e-learning models: Investigating their value for developing an e-learning strategy. *Progressio, 25*(2), 38–47. Retrieved from http://uir.unisa.ac.za/ bitstream/handle/10500/4992/engelbrecht.pdf?sequence=1

Garrison, D. R., Anderson, T., & Archer, W. (2000). Critical thinking in text-based environment: Computer conferencing in higher education. *Internet and Higher Education, 2*(2), 87–105. doi: 10.1016/S1096-7516(00)00016-6

Handelsman, M. M., Briggs, W. L., Sullivan, N., & Towler, A. (2005). A measure of college student course engagement. *The Journal of Educational Research, 98*(3), 184–191.

Huitt, W. (2011). Motivation to learn: An overview. *Educational Psychology Interactive.* Valdosta, GA: Valdosta State University. Retrieved from http://www.edpsycinteractive. org/topics/motivation/motivate.html

Jackson, M. J., & Helms, M. M. (2008). Student perceptions of hybrid courses: Measuring and interpreting quality. *Journal of Education for Business, 84*(1), 7–13. Retrieved from Business Source Premier (AN 34772191)

Kim, K. J., & Bonk, C. J. (2006). The future of online teaching and learning in higher education: The survey says... *Educase Quarterly Magazine, 29*(4). Retrieved from http:// www.educause.edu/EDUCAUSE + Quarterly/EDUCAUSEQuarterlyMagazineVolum/ TheFutureofOnlineTeachingandLe/157426

Knill, O. (2007). Benefits and risks of media and technology in the classroom, pp. 1–5. Retrieved from http://abel.math.harvard.edu/~knill/pedagogy/benefits/paper.pdf

Malik, K. (2010). Blending synchronous and asynchronous interactivity in online education. In H. Song (Ed.), *Distance learning technology, current instruction, and the future of education: Applications of today, practices of tomorrow* (pp. 162–184). Hersehy, PA: IGI Global.

Molinari, J. M., & Huonker, J. W. (2010). Diagnosing student engagement in the business school classroom. *Journal of the Academy of Business Education, 11*, 1–13.

Packham, G., Jones, P., Miller, C., & Brychan, T. (2004). E-learning and retention: Key factors influencing student withdrawal. *Education & Training, 46*(6), 335–342.

Pagano, M.T. (n.d.). *Moderating online chat room*s. Retrieved from http://ai-depot.com/Essay/ Moderation.html

Robinson, C. C., & Hullinger, H. (2008). New benchmarks in higher education: Student engagement in online learning. *Journal of Education for Business, 84*(2). doi: 10.3200/ JOEB.84.2.101-109

Sabau, G., Munten, M., Bologa, A. R., Bologa, R., & Surcel, T. (2009). An evaluation framework for higher education ERP Systems. *WSEAS Transactions on Computers, 11*(8), 1790–1799.

Salmon, G. (2000). *E-moderating: The key to teaching and learning online.* Sterling, VA: Stylus Publishing.

Salmon, G. (2001, June). Masters or slaves to the technology? The role of the e-moderator in e-learning. *eLearn Magazine.* Retrieved from http://elearnmag.acm.org/featured.cfm?aid= 566946

Salmon, G. (2002). *E-tivities: The key to active online learning.* Sterling, VA: Stylus Publishing.

Salmon, G. (2005). Flying not flapping: A strategic framework for e-learning and pedagogical innovation in higher education institutions. *ALT-J, Research in Learning Technology, 13*(3), 201–218.

Sautter, P. (2007). Designing discussion activities to achieve desired learning outcomes: Choices using mode of delivery and structure. *Journal of Marketing Education, 29*(2), 122–131. doi: 10.1177/0273475307302014

Yerkes, R., & Dodson, J. (1908). The relation of strength of stimulus to rapidity of habit-formation. *Journal of Comparative Neurology and Psychology, 18*, 459–482.

ENGAGING ENTREPRENEURS WITH A BLENDED PROBLEM-BASED LEARNING DEGREE PROGRAMME

Patrick Lynch, Mary T. Holden, Anthony Foley, Denis Harrington and Jennifer Hussey

ABSTRACT

While larger tourism enterprises benefit from a graduate management intake and continuing executive development, the owner of the small tourism operation is limited in continuing education and professional development opportunities due to resource poverty, lack of appropriate and available tertiary tourism education. This chapter details the pedagogical and technological challenges faced by the education team at Waterford Institute of Technology (WIT) in developing and implementing an innovative blended learning degree, customised to meet the requirements of the entrepreneur for a sense of involvement, relevance and flexibility. Understanding how to harmonise blended learning with face-to-face PBL was the cornerstone of success in the design and implementation of the programme and the insights gained will provide

Increasing Student Engagement and Retention in e-Learning Environments:
Web 2.0 and Blended Learning Technologies
Cutting-edge Technologies in Higher Education, Volume 6G, 199–227
Copyright © 2013 by Emerald Group Publishing Limited
All rights of reproduction in any form reserved
ISSN: 2044-9968/doi:10.1108/S2044-9968(2013)000006G010

guidelines to educators who are responsible for the development of relevant and accessible business degree programmes for owner/managers of micro/small business enterprises.

INTRODUCTION

According to Fáilte Ireland, the Irish National Tourism Authority, tourism is now the largest, indigenous industry within the Irish economy, with approximately 18,000 tourism enterprises. The industry contributed over 4.5 billion euro in earnings to the Irish economy in 2010 (Fáilte Ireland, 2011). This totalled almost four per cent of gross national product (Tourism Ireland, 2011). In employment terms, almost 180,000 jobs are sustained by the industry (Fáilte Ireland, 2011). Moreover, these jobs are geographically dispersed, with over seventy per cent outside Dublin (ITIC, 2011). Economic recession from 2008 onwards created difficulties for the industry in terms of reduced market demand, the drying up of lines of credit and rising cost pressures (Fáilte Ireland, 2009). Despite these difficulties there has been evidence of recovery in the industry. There was a ten per cent increase in overseas visitors during the first nine months of 2011 (Tourism Ireland, 2011). Nonetheless the future presents both opportunities and challenges. The high levels of overseas visitor numbers position the industry as a future economic engine of economic recovery (Tourism Ireland, 2011). There is potential for the industry to re-position itself from one of supplying low value and undifferentiated offerings to becoming an innovative powerhouse generating higher value through links to eco-tourism, arts and national culture and the embracing of new markets such as tourism education. More focused and improved marketing can enable the development of relationships with growing sectors of the world tourism industry such as Asia, which are increasingly providing high numbers of visitors (Fáilte Ireland, 2011).

Amidst these opportunities are challenges. There are concerns that an industry predominately characterised by individual, small-to-medium-sized enterprises competing in an increasingly global international tourism marketplace does not have the capacity to benefit from the strong economic growth envisaged in international tourism in the years ahead. Indeed, Irish tourism businesses tend to have a low skill base and engage in little formal education (Braun & Hollick, 2006; Jameson, 2000), and these owner/managers are lacking in innovativeness and competencies in such areas as marketing, knowledge management, information technology, quality assurance, pricing policy, innovation and management (Fáilte Ireland, 2005). While the larger tourism businesses benefit from a graduate management intake and continuing executive development, the owner of the micro/small tourism operation is limited in professional development. Indeed, continuing business education for owner/managers of micro/small businesses is problematic. Major barriers, which are perceived to be global are, their resource poverty – most especially the inability to leave their business, the lack of appropriate and available tertiary tourism education and isolation due to location (cf. Billett, 2001; Braun & Hollick, 2006; Fáilte Ireland, 2005, 2007; Inui, Wheeler, & Lankford, 2006; Jameson, 2000; Kelliher & Henderson, 2006; Sargeant, 1996; Walker, Redmond, Webster, & Le Clus, 2007).

As a consequence, a key aspect of European and national response is the enhancement of the industry's professionalism through targeted education of the micro/small enterprise owner/manager, as it is seen as a vehicle for improving the innovativeness and the overall competitiveness of Ireland's tourism sector (Government of Ireland, 2007; Tourism Policy Review Group, 2003). However, despite this recognition that education is seen as a major driver to support and facilitate small tourism firms growth and to stimulate innovation (Fáilte Ireland, 2005; OECD, 2004; Tourism Policy Review, 2003; Tourism Renewal Group, 2009), tourism educators have been severely criticised for lack of responsiveness to industry needs (Baum, 2006), over-emphasis on vocational training in craft skills and failing to provide appropriate and available tertiary education (Fáilte Ireland, 2004, 2007; Inui et al., 2006). The consequence has been a low uptake of either informal or formal education/training by small business owner/managers; indeed, much of the educational activity that is undertaken by small firms is informal, in-house and short term (Devins, Gold, Johnson, & Holden, 2005; Fuller-Love, 2006; Lawless, Allan, & O'Dwyer, 2000; Storey, 2004). Moreover, the lack of a tailored, formal educational delivery to meet industry needs has resulted in an industry-wide scepticism as to the benefit of engaging in formal education. To overcome this challenge, the Lambert report (2003) advocates the role of improved proximity between providers of education and business. One mechanism through which it is postulated where this can be achieved is by the development of academic programmes which involves interaction between students and practitioners. This fulfils a key tenet of Innovation Ireland's (2010) aspiration to reinforce the entrepreneurial culture and make commercial innovators socially popular.

In light of the foregoing, Fáilte Ireland began a tendering process for the delivery of an education programme to overcome the industry-wide scepticism as to the benefit of engaging in formal education and to design an innovative and tailored programme that met industry needs. The authors' tertiary institute was successful in this process, resulting in the development of a new three-year bachelor of science (BSc) in small enterprise management specifically designed to meet the needs of micro/small tourism enterprises. This chapter discusses the journey of the course development team in designing what evolved to be a distinctive blended learning programme that truly engaged the industry.

The design journey began with an initial 'feedback' workshop with target participants and finished with a pilot study with target student involvement. These key target student interventions proved to be critical in informing the design of the programme, in particular the programme's teaching/learning methodology and its delivery. In response to the need expressed by the target audience for relevance and topicality, the course development team adopted a problem-based learning (PBL) teaching/learning methodology. PBL is an andragogical approach which facilitates student-driven learning in teams, based on business problem diagnosis and resolution. Further, in order to meet the needs of the targeted audience for flexibility as well as time and access problems, the team 'blended' online technologies into the programme. From the outset, this included engagement with external experts, faculty and Waterford Institute of Technology (WIT's) in-house e-learning department, as a result, the online contact tools emerged. These included the Google suite (in particular, Chat and Documents) and Adobe Connect (employed synchronously). Moodle was identified as the virtual learning environment. The process of faculty training and engagement with these methods and the integration of the tools into the blended PBL design of the programme are described. Following on from the initial target student engagement with the blended learning nature of the programme, the chapter will describe the student induction process and student experience with the technologies employed. The chapter concludes with the lessons learnt from designing the innovative BSc in small enterprise management highlighting the centrality of both the learner and educator co-designing a blended PBL programme.

THE DESIGN OF A BLENDED PROBLEM-BASED LEARNING PROGRAMME

From the outset, in order to overcome the industry-wide scepticism as to the benefit of engaging in formal education and to design an innovative and tailored degree programme that met industry needs, the Graduate Business School (www.wit.ie) was very cognisant of the need to enter a collaborative and an expeditious two-way dialogue with the relevant stakeholders (see Table 1). To facilitate close proximity between the course design team, the tourism businesses and the National Authority, the school housed the design of the programme within the applied research centre responsible for tourism (see RIKON, www.rikon.ie). This ensured a tight integration between practice, teaching and research in the design process. For instance, through the RIKON research centre, the school had significant prior interactions with Fáilte Ireland through funded research degrees and participating on their advisory boards at both regional and national levels and also contributing to executive programme delivery at the agency. In terms of practice, the RIKON research centre has conducted over 200 innovation projects with service business entrepreneurs and designed, developed and managed the Fáilte Ireland Tourism Learning Networks (TLN) programme in the south-east and south-west of Ireland, with over 440 tourism enterprises engaged with the team. In addition, from a teaching perspective, the school was keen to explore the design and implementation of a programme of this nature. The school had developed a strong tradition of innovative teaching through practice-led research and pioneering the development of a Level 6 National Certificate in Tourism Business Practice, which provided an appropriate educational qualification for 210 graduates to date (all drawn from the micro/small tourism segment).

The design methodology involved 12 stages and was longitudinal in nature (see Table 1):

1. *National Tourism Authority Design and Implementation Requirements*
2. *WIT's Teaching Philosophy, Approach and Mode of Delivery*
3. *Practitioner Educational Requirements*
4. *Programme Design*
5. *Module Design*
6. *Course Team Development in Blended PBL Learning*
7. *Designing a Blended PBL Module Delivery*
8. *Blended PBL Pilot Study and Feedback*
9. *Post-Pilot Interviews*
10. *Final Design Modifications*
11. *Induction to the Blended PBL Programme*
12. *Launch of the BSc: Semester 1 Update*

The next sections present descriptive details on each stage of development.

Table 1. Course Design Time Lines and Key Stakeholder Engagements in Blended PBL Degree Development.

Stakeholder	Date	Detail
Engagement with funding agency	*March 2009–May 2010*	Six consultation meetings with Fáilte Ireland. A representative from the agency attended the course review in May 2010.
Student engagement	*June 2009 February 2010 March 2010*	1. Focus group with target participants 2. One week pilot programme with a target student cohort, testing the technology and the PBL approach 3. Post-pilot interviews
Staff development	*March 2009–June 2011*	1. Multiple course development team planning meetings. 2. Presentation to course design team on problem-based learning by staff with experience in this area through the strategic innovation fund (SIF) learning innovation initiative. 3. FACILITATE (national PBL network) event on PBL attended by a number of the course team. 4. E-learning workshops at WIT attended by a number of the course team. 5. Week-long e-Learning Summer School at Dublin Institute of Technology attended by course team members 6. Customised two-day workshop on PBL for the course team delivered by external expert on PBL. 7. Customised workshop on blended learning and PBL presented by external expert 2 8. Workshops on blended PBL curriculum and module design presented by PBL expert on design team 9. Workshops on online tools for staff delivered by WIT e-Learning Support Unit
External review and programme validation	*May 2010*	1. Presentation of course evaluation document to validation committee
Student induction and support	*September 2011 – Ongoing*	1. Two-day workshops on PBL and online learning 2. Ongoing support from lecturers and e-learning support unit on the use of the Google suite of online learning tools, and Adobe Connect

Table 1. (*Continued*)

Stakeholder	Date	Detail
Programme launch	*September 2011*	1. Semester 1: students engaged in two modules: critical personal skills (CPS) and technology and operations (TOP). 2. Both modules utilised a blended PBL model. 3. Google Chat; Google Documents; Adobe Connect were utilised

Stage 1: National Tourism Authority Design and Implementation Requirements

From the earliest discussions between the course of design team and the National Tourism Authority, Fáilte Ireland; it was obvious that they had a clear set of requirements that would need to be met by the nascent degree. The first stipulation stressed by them was that the ultimate outcome of the programme would be that:

> Participants will have developed the generic, specialist and functional skills necessary to plan and execute an effective business strategy for their enterprises and local networks.

The second stipulation from the National Tourism Authority was that the degree should reflect the latest thinking on design and delivery. Indeed, a major component of the design methodology involved an intense literature review in connection with learning theory and blended learning, particularly best practice which was pertinent to adult, micro/small business learners. In developing a programme which would meet the needs of the targeted learners as well as the needs of the sector, it was essential that the course design team gather detailed and rich information concerning the degree's major dimensions: content, context, process and outcomes. In many respects, each of these four dimensions of the BSc represented a 'blank sheet' to the course design team.

Reflecting the national nature of the Fáilte Ireland tourism remit, the third proviso was for the programme to be truly national in its design, development and delivery. This meant that the design team had to address issues connected with distance and online education such as technology and its support, broadband availability, learner IT skills, reduction in student engagement, staff resourcing and commitment, staff expertise, and course design (McAlister, Rivera, & Hallan, 2001; Sherman & Beaty, 2007).

The fourth stipulation from the National Tourism Authority was that the degree should be highly flexible in its delivery in order to accommodate tourism owner/managers delivery needs such as access, time and place. This was a particularly pertinent issue in terms of businesses located in rural areas where infrastructure is poor. The fifth proviso was that the degree needed to be relevant and customised to the needs of the micro/small tourism enterprise promoter. Fáilte Ireland was conscious that there were many academic programmes which were accessible and relevant for Irish tourism practitioners in larger enterprises, particularly hotels. The undergraduate interested in general business and tourism programmes is similarly full of choice. However, there was a dearth of academic programmes which addressed the business development needs of the owner/manager of the micro/small tourism enterprise. Indeed, for Fáilte Ireland, the ultimate imperative for the BSc was to develop these micro/small entrepreneurs as tourism professionals who would be multi-skilled and flexible; allowing them to become involved in general operations as well as performing more executive functions, thereby reflecting the 'hands-on' nature of the industry. In this fashion, Fáilte Ireland believed that professionalising the industry would develop business graduates with the ability to address challenges and opportunities facing the Irish tourism industry as well as enhanced entrepreneurship and innovation.

Finally, Fáilte Ireland stipulated that the following themes be integrated into the design and delivery of the programme:

- *Market Engagement and Web Technology:* Enabling the participants to develop effective business models in a Web 2.0 environment where the Internet is driving tourist information, communication and reservations.
- *Tourism Business Processes:* Highlighting effective practice in service operations for tourism entrepreneurs.
- *Network Development:* Addressing the challenge for the industry in developing sustainable tourism networks.
- *Entrepreneurial Development:* It is critical that owner/managers of small tourism enterprises develop the functional capability and critical skills needed in a hypercompetitive environment.
- *Sales and Strategic Market Development:* Effective engagement with the market is essential for Irish tourism.
- *Tourism Competitiveness and Innovation:* Key challenges for Irish tourism lie in driving a competitive tourism destination and also in developing innovation in service design, delivery and communication. Fáilte Ireland has highlighted the importance of assisting the industry to

address these challenges as articulated in a number of Irish tourism policy studies.

- *Environmental and Energy Management:* In line with the emerging green economy which has implications for cost control and target marketing for tourism enterprises.

Stage 2: WIT's Teaching Philosophy, Approach and Mode of Delivery

Based on the school of business experience and knowledge of the educational needs of micro/small business tourism enterprises, as well as previous course design team knowledge and experience of the philosophy of andragogy and PBL as a teaching/learning methodology, the team decided to apply both to the new BSc programme. Andragogy is particularly relevant to the micro/small business context as it focuses on the application of knowledge to real life and perceives the participant as a central and active component in the learning equation (cf. Knowles, 1980); it builds on and extends student experiences as it is 'predicated on the belief that during the span of living, humans accumulate experience ... Students bring applicable knowledge and skills to the learning process. They seek to fill the gaps of knowledge in their experience base' (Forrest & Peterson, 2006, p. 118). Additionally, due to the team's prior experience, it was known that small business owner/managers learn best when they are able to utilise their own business as a learning site (cf. Ehrich & Billett, 2004) – a context that matches PBL's emphasis on real-life problem solving through engaging the learner's previous knowledge and experience in the learning process. PBL is founded on Dewey's (1938) belief that experience is a major source of learning as well as Kolb's (1984) theory of experiential learning; it also has an action learning approach which Cunningham (1999) identified as central to an andragogical philosophy. Modern management problems require that students have the ability to leverage both their experience (know how) and new knowledge (know what), thereby exemplifying and centralising the relationship between experience and theory. Indeed, as Kessels and Poell (2004, p. 148) noted in discussing the importance of learning through andragogy to today's firm: 'In a knowledge economy, in which improvement and innovation are required for long-term survival, standardization is not the goal but the extraordinary, the surprising, the artistic'. It was also perceived by the team, as well as Fáilte Ireland, that PBL would be conducive to achieving the high-level skills, knowledge and appropriate personal traits to grow and transform enterprises (cf. Burns & Chisholm, 2005; Duch, Groh, & Allen, 2001).

The PBL ethos of the programme meant that students on the BSc programme would be presented with cases based on real-life, 'messy' scenarios, that is, business problems that are ambiguous, multifaceted and complex. Mirroring real-life experiences of a tourism business, problems will involve more than one subject area of a discipline or be cross-disciplinary, for example, a problem can involve people management, business planning and innovation or the problem can have both a marketing and financial component, thereby requiring students to learn and apply concepts and principles from both disciplines; this type of problem may also involve input/mentoring from more than one lecturer. Problem solution involves students determining 'what they know about the problem', 'what they do not know' and 'what they need to know' and 'defining the problem themselves' (Forrest & Peterson, 2006). Inherent in this learning approach is the philosophy that the students themselves will take 'ownership' of the problem and, hence, their learning. They identify, find and study those concepts and principles which are relevant to solving the problem. During the learning process, lecturers discuss and guide learners to appropriate resources. Students may even ask the lecturer for a lecture on a particular topic. Within the group context, lecturers assist learners to identify what they do and do not know, and summarise and link information. The target outcome being a new form of tourism services provider who will be capable of a leadership role in driving innovation in his/her own business and who will have a key positive role-modelling function in the local tourism area.

A cornerstone of the BSc programme was the choice of a blended learning approach to delivery. Rather than the traditional classroom-based, teacher-centred approach, the blended learning mode of delivery combines the benefits of face-to-face interaction between student and instructor with the advantages of synchronous and asynchronous learning. The design team was of the belief that a substantial online learning proportion of course delivery would offer the participant the advantage of choice in time and pace of study and should have a positive impact on learner retention. Further, as the attrition rate of online courses is high (Park & Choi, 2009), the course design team wanted to ensure that this component of the programme would be optimally crafted. Indeed, the need for flexibility in formal education by tourism micro/small tourism enterprise owner/managers had been a key imperative for this programme, as articulated by Fáilte Ireland from the earliest stage of development; this component of the programme involved the availability of content as well as the facilitation by faculty of online discussion boards/chat rooms combined with face-to-face interaction with peers as well as lecturers. The team felt that the participants would gain valuable experience of working and learning in both environments and in a PBL multidisciplinary group. The group support offered by the blended approach was particularly pertinent in light of previous research which has highlighted the isolation suffered by many geographically dispersed micro/small tourism operators (Braun, 2002). The team believed that the peer-to-peer support would offer both relief from educational isolation that these owners/managers (particularly home-based ones) often experience and would reduce the potential risk of an introverted approach to business management. It was perceived by the team that the opportunity on the programme for interactivity, communication and relationship building with multiple participants in a blended learning environment would increase the students' diverse experiences, contribute to exploration learning and to the development of new knowledge (Fiol & Lyles, 1985; Moorman & Miner, 1998) and have a positive impact on learner retention.

Stage 3: Practitioner Educational Requirements

Another major objective during the designing of the programme was to obtain the viewpoints of the targeted practitioners on module content – both generic skills and discipline-specific knowledge. A round-table discussion, involving 19 practitioners, was facilitated by two members of the design team. The round-table lasted approximately two hours. The sample of practitioners that were recruited was chosen via convenience sampling. The participants were from the targeted cohort (past TLN participants and graduates of the Certificate in Tourism Business Practice); closely located to WIT (from the counties of: Waterford, Wexford, Kilkenny and Tipperary) (as this was a busy time of year, the course design team did not want to ask individuals who would have to add extensive travel time to the time-out from their business); perceived by the team to be the most likely interested in the BSc and represented a diverse set of tourism providers, from hospitality services and attractions to micro/small and medium-sized accommodation providers. In order to provide a starting point for the discussion, practitioners were first asked to write down three major issues/challenges or three major problems that each were currently facing in their business or felt they would be facing in the future. This was then followed by the authors asking one of the practitioners to identify an issue/challenge/problem. What followed was a free-flowing discussion among the practitioners in which many issues/challenges were identified. The analysis of this stage found that there was considerable agreement among the participants concerning their needs. The issues/challenges which were identified by the participants are detailed in Table 2.

It is interesting to note that in the round-table discussion, the participants themselves spoke about their issues/concerns under three main headings:

- The participants wanted to develop their own personal skills and management capability.
- They wanted to develop a greater organisational capability across their firms.
- Participants articulated a desire to strategically position their firms within local networks to enhance competitiveness.

Stage 4: Programme Design

The findings emanating from the practitioner session and discussions with the National Tourism Authority allowed the course design team to make informed decisions about the programme design. It was decided that the three-year duration of the proposed degree would build in an integrated fashion towards the ultimate outcome of the programme. As illustrated in Fig. 1, and based on the practitioner input, the design team decided that the first year should focus on the critical personal skills (CPS) and management capability of the individual. The second year would focus on developing organisational capabilities across all functional areas, while the final year would concentrate on developing and executing an effective positioning strategy at enterprise and local network. Each outcome for the three years of the programme builds towards the overall programme objective (see Fig. 1).

Table 2. The Issues/Challenges Identified by the Participants.

Time management	IT/Web/social media skills	Stakeholder management	Business planning
Project management	Supply chain management	Marketing	Verbal communication skills
Negotiation	Customer service	Environmental law/regulations	Innovation
Finance/Accounting	Conflict management	Change management	Keeping a positive outlook
Human resource	Business writing	Leadership	Strategic perspective

Year 1 Learning Outcome:
Demonstration of critical personal skills & management capability

Year 2 Learning Outcome:
Development of organisational capability across all functional areas

Year 3 Learning Outcome:
Ability to develop & execute an effective positioning strategy at enterprise & local network level

Overall Programme Outcome:
Participants will have developed the generic, specialist and functional skills necessary to plan and execute an effective business strategy for their enterprises and local networks.

Fig. 1.   Progression in Programme Outcomes.

Stage 5: Module Design

Three separate teams, representing each year's programme learning outcome, were established to take responsibility for developing modules. The design of the modules was informed by the engagement with the target participants in the previously detailed round-table discussion. In addition, it was each team's responsibility to ensure that the integration of module outcomes would build towards their particular year's programme learning outcome. Cross-team meetings ensured the integration of year outcomes for the overall programme objective. In this fashion, the course development team proposed a module outline that integrated the year outcomes, and the discipline-specific knowledge and generic skills.

Stage 6: Course Team Development in Blended PBL Learning

The educational value for the design team for engaging in a blended PBL programme was to maximise the strengths of both face-to-face and online environments. However, the utilisation of blended PBL represented a key challenge for the course design team as only a few members of the design team had substantial PBL experience. In addition, the BSc was the first programme in the business school to utilise blended learning and no design team member had previously utilised this approach. In fact, nationally, the programme was distinctive in that it was being based on a PBL design as well as using a blended delivery approach. To exacerbate the situation, the design team was very soon overwhelmed by the sheer number of blended learning tools available, and was limited by a lack of understanding of the potential and use of the various technologies. The design team was also conscious of the fact that interactive technologies do not guarantee meaningful interactions or the delivery of effective education. Therefore, it was particularly important to strengthen the competence of the team in blended PBL.

From a technology perspective, the involvement of the e-Learning Support Unit (ESU: http://elearning.wit.ie) at WIT was critical. The ESU team provided much needed support and advice to the design team in developing their knowledge and skills in blending information and communication technologies into the teaching, learning and assessment activities to support the blended PBL learning interactions. In addition, this unit provided training in using the WIT virtual learning environment, namely Moodle, and how to use e-learning tools and technologies, including Moodle, in particular teaching scenarios. The pedagogical development of the programme was greatly influenced from by a number of tailored interventions on PBL and the use of an online learning environment (OLE) delivered by external experts. Further, members of the design team attended a week-long Summer school on e-learning at an external higher level institution. Finally, a key impetus in the learning process for the staff team was the establishment of an informal peer mentoring system that provided support for lecturers who were having difficulties with some aspect of blended PBL.

Stage 7: Designing a Blended PBL Module Delivery

Module delivery was designed to be accessible and relevant for participants, and was guided by the underlying blended PBL approach to delivery. Challenges for the design team involved staff resourcing issues, finding the correct balance of 'contact' hours involving face-to-face versus asynchronous versus synchronous online communication, as well as the recognition of prior learning and the content and delivery of the induction. Fig. 2 illustrates the semester format of a typical blended PBL module. Student engagement with peers on the problem would take place between a number of face-to-face workshops interspersed throughout the semester. It was planned that the online component of the programme would be complemented with residential workshops to provide a forum for more extensive peer-to-peer learning through networking, socialising, and intra/inter-class presentations and discussions. The conventional lecturer face-to-face contact with students is

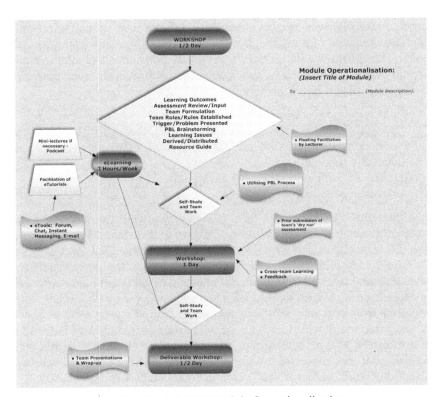

Fig. 2. Blended PBL Module Operationalisation.

36 hours over the semester. For the BSc programme, the blended delivery involved 12 hours physical contact, with the remaining 24 hours of contact time to be online. In addition, it was planned that the physical contact would be clustered over two days of workshops, in order to optimise convenience for the student cohort. It was also perceived by the design team that the blended PBL experience would be enhanced through using the online interactions to prepare the learners for in-class tutorials.

Stage 8: Blended PBL Pilot Study and Feedback

As identified in the literature, and based on the course design team's previous experience with the targeted cohort, the team wanted to ensure that the programme's blended PBL approach and delivery would meet micro/

small owner/manager needs; indeed, from beginning to end (and still continuing today), meeting the needs of the targeted learner was the central, guiding tenet for the course design team. In conjunction with Fáilte Ireland, a pilot study was crafted in order to gather information from potential participants of the BSc concerning:

(1) Their response to blended PBL,
(2) Perceived problems arising in connection with blended PBL,
(3) Particular challenges in connection with blended PBL and working in an online environment,
(4) Barriers to completing the assessment, and
(5) Any other issues/concerns arising.

Although the course design team made every attempt to make the pilot realistic, there were limitations to its 'reality'. For instance, the depth and breadth of resources that were reviewed for the assessment fell short of Level 7 (ordinary degree) standards, therefore, at that time, it was perceived by the team that results, in all likelihood, did not fully reveal latent issues/concerns in connection with study skills, time management, coping with level of work expected, teamwork, etc.; also, the assessment did not attract a grade, hence it was perceived that this had a negative impact on the level of individual and team efforts in completing the assignment. However, despite the foregoing, it was perceived by the authors that the blended PBL process accurately reflected that which occurs in an actual classroom context.

Eighteen graduates of the Certificate in Tourism Business Practice participated in the pilot programme. The format of the session held at WIT was

• Introduction to the programme, including update on progress to date.
• Overview of programme schedule and delivery plans.
• Introduction to the WIT e-learning support website and Moodle.
• Introduction to blended PBL.
• Division of learners into teams.
• Introduction to module and presentation of 'trigger'.
• Team roles allocated and team rules identified.
• Brainstorming session – identify learning issues.
• Presentation to teams of assessment to be completed; online resources were given to the learners by the facilitators.

The workshop unfolded as outlined above. Participants were divided into four groups; each group was facilitated by one of the members of the course design team. At the end of the workshop, each group was asked to produce a 'solution' to a trigger. The trigger in the pilot was drawn from remarks made at the round-table discussion concerning the number of 'hats' that the micro/small owner/manager had to wear in a day. As it turned out, the trigger addressed the discipline-specific content of one of the first modules that was delivered in the BSc programme, CPS. The trigger was presented as the assessment, which involved providing to the course design team a written report – no more than 250 words – which would be assessed. This document was to be uploaded to the pilot's Moodle site by each group one week later. The participants were also introduced in the pilot to the online forum function on Moodle. This was used by the students over this week to post comments and questions. Members of the course team engaged with the forum to address issues. All groups uploaded their assignment on time. In order to capture immediate feedback from the participants on the pilot study, a short, highly structured questionnaire was prepared; the feedback form's design was based on blended PBL feedback forms which had been previously utilised. All participants completed the feedback form after the session. Results are listed in Table 3 and reflect a high level of engagement which was observed during the pilot study. All mean scores are at the high end of the scale.

Based on extensive post-pilot discussions between the course design team and Fáilte Ireland, several major findings from this stage were determined:

- The practitioners quickly grasped the blended PBL process.
- The participants saw the blended PBL process and trigger as engaging and very relevant to them.
- The time that they would need to devote to their studies was a major concern (both in terms of time per week and the degree's three-year duration).

Stage 9: Post-Pilot Interviews

The interviews were scheduled for the week following completion of the team assignment, allowing the participants the time to reflect on their recent experience involving the pilot study; most specifically, the team was interested in gathering information on their experience of engaging in a blended PBL environment and in completing the assignment. Seventeen of the eighteen pilot participants were interviewed over eight days, with each interview lasting approximately 35 minutes; the semi-structured nature of the interviews allowed for follow-up questions and probing on pertinent

Table 3. Pilot-Study Participant Feedback Results.

Feedback Statements	Mean
My first impressions of the BSc degree programme were positive.	4.22
From what I have heard today, I believe the content of the BSc programme will suit my needs.	4.11
I found the subject content of the BSc programme was relevant to me and my business.	4.22
I believe the online forum provided (Moodle) will make it easier for me to communicate with others in my group.	4.35
I enjoyed the chance to discuss the problem posed amongst our team.	4.50
I understand the role each team member plays in problem-based learning.	4.39
The role of the facilitator in problem-based learning was made clear.	4.39
The problem presented to us as a trigger was of relevance to me.	4.33
I believe I have a fair understanding of what problem-based learning is all about.	4.28
I have a good idea of the steps involved in the process of problem-based learning.	4.11
I am interested in finding out about enrolling on the BSc degree programme.	4.39

$n = 18$
Scale: 1 = Strongly Disagree and 5 = Strongly Agree

issues raised by the participants. Key findings from the interviews are listed below:

• *Study time and semester timing:* All interviewees perceived that they did not have sufficient time in their schedule to devote to study; some concern was expressed concerning work/life balance. For example, one participant stated 'difficulty to set-out this time totally to myself ... added stress that this would bring'. Some participants indicated that semester scheduling would need to take into account that they take their holidays in September-October and that there is a national movement to extend the tourism season, stating: 'The problem is we take our break in September-October and there's probably quite a few others in the same boat'. and 'I'm organizing a festival in late September, so I won't be available until October, really'.
• *Length of degree:* Six participants indicated that the necessary three-year commitment was daunting.
• *Motivation:* Some participants found the pilot study to be motivating in regard to considering further education; one individual stated 'I am awake again' and another stated 'It has got me thinking again'.
• *Group work:* Some concern was expressed in connection with working with others to complete assignments such as an unequal burden of

work. Five participants indicated that they were accustomed to being self-sufficient and were concerned over having to rely on the skills and abilities of others. For example, one interviewee commented: 'What we had to do was a very small thing … but some of the others took forever to do it' while another participant stated: 'you always get studiers, then others not so into it'. However, others welcomed the added support from peers in completing assignments, stating: 'Gained a group with similar problems and needs' and 'People were willing to help each other' while others indicated that they were '… well used to running a meeting'.

- *Group mix:* Six of the participants indicated that groups should have a good mix of businesses/management roles.
- *Chairperson role:* Each of the four chairpersons drew attention to their role and the responsibilities that went with it – none of the other PBL roles (scribe, time-keeper and reader) were highlighted in the interviews.
- *Resource poverty:* This was in regard to manpower and financing the degree. As one participant stated: 'It's all down to me and my husband – everything' while others stated: 'With a young family, the cost is going to be a decider' and 'My workplace will not subsidise my training, or allow me time-off for it, so these six days [modules' residential workshops] would be my holidays'.
- *Distance learning:* The accessibility of participants from remote and highly inaccessible rural geographic regions and the need for face-to-face interactions in residential workshops was an issued raised by six interviewees.
- *Technology:* Several interviewees indicated concern in connection with using the forum function in Moodle, their IT skills, and their lack of broadband (however, only two indicated they didn't have broadband) while others indicated technology 'Will make it a whole lot easier' and 'Moodle side – a dream'.
- *Relevancy:* The BSc needs to be relevant for their business and for them personally; some indicated that they saw PBL as providing relevancy: 'Rather than having a lecture, everybody is involved in the problem … and rather than telling us the answer – our experience is brought into it', 'PBL is brilliant! … a workman's way of solving problems', and 'One really is getting to grips with the material – you are learning as you go along, going through the research'.
- *Academic self-confidence:* One individual felt reassured about having the ability to complete the degree after the pilot study whereas another individual indicated that it created a 'Tiny element of self-doubt in my mind'.

Stage 10: Final Design Modifications

The feedback from the pilot programme was valuable in prompting further modification of programme design, in particular to address participant concerns about: time commitment; some apprehension about the demands of a degree programme, and; the need to enhance skills in areas such as IT before entering the programme. For instance, a major concern of the targeted cohort appeared to be time to complete a degree; the recognition of prior learning was one means of addressing this concern.

Recognition of the participants' prior experience and competence aids in ensuring the programme helps individuals to learn rather than imposing prescribed solutions on them (see Deakins & Freel, 1998; Gomez, Lorente, & Cabrera, 2004). In essence, it is a means for recognising that learning occurs in many different contexts from work, social, community and life experience. However, the recognition of prior learning is a relatively new phenomenon in Ireland and because of its recency, the course design team had little knowledge of what RPL entailed; this then represented an area of research for the team and meetings with WIT's registrar's office in order to incorporate RPL into the BSc. The award of credits for RPL enabled the school of business to offer the three-year full-time programme in a part-time mode, thereby easing the learners' study burden and making formal education more accessible in terms of time for study and work–life balance.

The programme contact hours were also modified to provide an average of three contact hours per week, with two of these taking place online, through the Moodle interface (forums, chat rooms, wikis, etc.) (see Fig. 2). It was perceived that this would reduce the requirement for the participant to be away from the workplace and enhance the flexible nature of the programme. The team decided that all modules would be continuous assessment, which is consistent with a blended PBL ethos, and also removed a requirement for participants to come to WIT for end of term examinations in May, which is the beginning of the busy summer period for tourism operators.

Stage 11: Induction to the Blended PBL Programme

Due to the nature of a blended PBL programme, the course design team was very conscious of the importance of both staff and student induction.

Staff induction training: A series of induction workshops for lecturing staff, based on PBL and blended learning, took place in advance of the commencement of the degree programme. These included

- Workshop on blended PBL delivered by a national expert.
- Two blended PBL workshops, facilitated by one of the authors.
- IT lab session on Google Chat, Docs and Adobe Connect.

Student induction training: The two day induction programme for students took place on September 13th and 14th, 2011. This programme included workshops on teambuilding exercises for PBL activity, and IT lab sessions on the Institute's virtual learning environment (Moodle), Google Groups, and Google Documents. Following a teambuilding workshop using 'Serious Lego Play' on the first day of the induction, students were introduced to the blended PBL process, and a detailed handbook was distributed. The class was divided into groups, and roles and ground rules were defined in each group. At this stage, a trigger/problem was presented to the class. The students were then directed to go to the IT lab, where they used resources hosted on Moodle to identify the learning issues. The students were also shown in the lab how to use Google Chat to communicate within the groups, and group members contributed to a Google Document set up by each group. The purpose of this exercise was to integrate the training in the technologies with the PBL process. The e-Learning Coordinator at WIT also delivered a session on Moodle, and its features, at this workshop.

At the conclusion of the formal induction programme, an online survey was employed to assess participant evaluation of the programme. The response to the question 'How effective do you think the Induction programme has been in preparing you for Year 1 of the BSc?' yielded a mean response of 3.77 (based on a 5-point scale, where 1 = very ineffective and 5 = very effective, $n = 22$). The generally, positive response to the induction was moderated by specific concerns about components of the programme. There were complaints that the time allocated to the technologies and to Moodle was inadequate. This was addressed with additional Moodle support from the e-learning office at one of the first workshops. Induction in Adobe Connect took place at the first workshop also due to time restraints at induction.

Stage 12: Launch of the BSc: Year 1 Update

The programme which was launched in September has just completed its first year. In semester 1 of the programme, students engaged in two modules: critical personal skills (CPS) and technology and operations (TOP). Both modules, in line with the programme design, were based on a blended PBL model. Each module employed different technologies as part of the blended design. The CPS module utilised Google Chat and Google Documents. Each week at a predetermined time, the lecturer would engage separately with each group in the class, online, in a 30 minute chat session. The students developed their assessment through a Google Document, and used Google Chat to communicate between themselves. The TOP lecturer used Adobe Connect, again in 30 minute sessions with each group separately on a weekly basis. Adobe Connect was also used to deliver mini-lectures, which were recorded. In these sessions, the students used the chat facility in Adobe Connect to pose questions to the lecturer, who would respond in chat so that all the class could see the response. Again, this was recorded.

At the end of the semester, a feedback session focusing on the PBL and online aspects of the programme took place. Generally, the students considered that after some initial difficulty in adjusting to the different learning style, they enthusiastically engaged with the blended PBL dynamic. The support of the lecturers was seen as critical. However, it was considered that there should have been a greater emphasis on group role definition at the beginning of the academic year. As this was the first exposure that the students had to PBL (apart from a small number who had participated in the pilot programme), it did take time for students to become familiar with the group dynamic, and their role within that context. The students also expressed that they wanted to stay within the same groups in the second semester. The students commented that, while the online engagement with the lecturers and within the groups was beneficial, regular face-to-face contact between group members was essential. As the geographic spread of the class is quite wide, with students from the extreme north and extreme south of the country, location was a deciding factor in team formation. This, importantly, facilitated physical contact within the groups outside of the course schedule. As outlined earlier, the use of Google Chat and Google Docs was supplemented with an introduction to Adobe Connect by the TOP lecturer and the e-Learning Coordinator in the first workshop. There was also direct contact by telephone and email with each student by the e-Learning Support Office at WIT early in the semester. The purpose of this intervention was to ensure that each student was connected correctly for the technologies involved in the programme. Commentary from students at the feedback session was very much in favour of Adobe Connect rather than Google Chat. This response was due to a number of advantages which the students ascribed to Adobe Connect. These included: instant visual interaction with the lecturer; recording capability: the online sessions could be recorded and consulted later and the chat function in Adobe Connect allowed students to pose questions, with all the students seeing the lecturer's responses. This feedback has led to the adoption of Adobe Connect in both modules that are currently underway in semester 2.

In the second semester, in line with the feedback from semester 1, the lecturers of both modules (Management Competency and Financial Management) utilised Adobe Connect, to engage with students. This included delivering a conventional live lecture online, in one of the modules, and in the second module engaging with students on assessment work submitted, and on progress to date. The Connect sessions were held weekly (except the four weeks, when students attended on campus). Students continued to use Google Docs within their groups as a means of collaborating on project reports.

Student feedback on first year of programme: An online survey completed by students at the end of year 1, provided some interesting feedback on attitudes to the blended character of the programme (see Table 4). General reaction to first year was very positive, with the learning experience rated highly (mean = 4.36). Critically, the programme was seen to be effective in application to business (mean = 4.32). Most students were of the opinion that the online and offline components of the programme were well integrated (mean = 4.09 on of satisfaction). This was reassuring to the course design team, and appears to confirm that the correct decision was made in relation to the relative breakdown between online and offline student contact. However, the potential of online interaction as a motivator to work was less definite (mean = 3.95). This highlights the importance of physical interaction between faculty and students. This is also apparent when asked if there was too little online interaction between lecturers and students, with very little support for more online interaction (mean = 2.14).

Table 4. Year 1 Feedback.

Statement	Mean
Learning experience	4.36
Application to business	4.32
The online interaction ties in well with the workshops.	4.09
The online interaction is a motivator tow work.	3.95
I have had too little online interaction with my lecturer	2.14
The Adobe Connect interaction with the lecturer has been useful.	4.23
PBL has enhanced my learning effectiveness	4.27
(all measures on a 5-point scale)	

This would seem to indicate that a minimum level of physical interaction between the lecturer and the student is essential. In relation to the specific technologies used, a high level of satisfaction was apparent with Adobe Connect (mean = 4.23). Students found that the recording ability of Connect was very useful, as it facilitated revisiting the online session as many times as needed to recap on details. These positive perceptions are particularly interesting, as the BSc in Small Enterprise Management is not just a blended programme, but a blended PBL programme. This raised a number of challenges for the design team, as PBL is generally characterised by substantial face-to-face interaction, and the role of the lecturer as group mentor is critical. Because of the nature of this programme, much of this mentoring activity took place online. Interestingly, participants rated highly how PBL enhanced their learning efficacy (mean = 4.27). This indicates that online interaction between lecturer and group can be as effective, if not more effective, than offline. However, it must be complemented and anchored by a minimum level of blocked lecturer and participant interaction.

CONCLUSION AND LESSONS FOR BLENDED PBL DESIGN

In many respects, the authors feel that this chapter represents a 'one stop shop' for programme designers of blended PBL programmes for adult learners as the development process outlined in this chapter is based on the integration of varying streams of learning research as well as results from a long data gathering process involving major stakeholders. The development process highlights the centrality of both the learner and educator in the design of a blended PBL programme. However, the most important lesson emanating from the team's experience is the understanding that blended learning within the PBL context cannot be naively seen as a technology replacement for the class room based lecture. Indeed, it is far more complicated. The combination of PBL and online learning raised some particular challenges for students and lecturers. Students needed to become familiar with using online methods such as Google Chat to communicate with other members of their PBL teams. Google Docs was selected as a suitable method for collaborative work, as it allows contributors to add comments and material, and highlights the varying contributions. However, this is quite a different approach from the conventional PBL scenario, where the team is meeting physically to contribute and discuss progress. Students also needed to integrate this online work with Docs into the offline setting at their periodic face-to-face meetings. The PBL dimension also increased the workload for lecturers in the online setting. While in a non-PBL setting, the lecturer could have an Adobe Connect lecture online for the whole class; PBL requires individual contact with each group. This had the effect of increasing the amount of time that the lecturer was online each week, as he/she would have six separate online sessions rather than one.

Understanding how to harmonise blended learning with face-to-face PBL was the cornerstone of success in this design and implementation of the programme. Indeed, the positive feedback from the class, the lecturers and the National Authority indicates that there has been substantial success in doing this. Key lessons learnt from the team's experience of developing a blended PBL degree include the following:

1) Early and frequent engagement with the target student cohort was critical to achieve an optimum design. The initial round-table discussion and a subsequent pilot programme were essential for informing and confirming the appropriateness of the blended and PBL aspects of the programme.
2) Sustained interaction between members of the course design team was critical to ensure that a coherent structure and delivery model emerged. The team in this programme met for over 20 occasions during the development period for planning purposes.
3) Expert advice from external experts on PBL and blended learning was essential to inform the design of the programme.
4) Designing such a programme needed considerable time resources: The gestation period was almost two years, and this time was required to address the intricacies of the blended and PBL nature of the programme.
5) There was a need for internal competency: Involvement by members of the course design team in a national initiative on learning innovation provided the catalyst for the PBL design of the programme. Similarly, a resourced e-learning office was critical to provide support to staff and students. In particular, one-on-one support was needed to address the technology needs of staff, and was also necessary in providing a friendly and competent voice to students embarking on using online learning methods.
6) Resource planning: A blended PBL programme requires resources in addition to the norm. For example, extra breakout rooms are desirable on the workshop days. Dedicated support for students who are engaging

with both PBL and online learning is important, and this is required from multiple sources; the e-learning support unit, lecturers, PBL experts on faculty and course leader. Comprehensive staff induction training on online learning methods is critical also. As discussed earlier in this chapter, the workload for lecturers using blended PBL is greater than in a conventional scenario, so planning such a programme needs to address this.

7) The situation of the degree within an established research centre (RIKON) with substantial links to the tourism industry, and a flourishing postgraduate and postdoctoral community disseminating and publishing on tourism management has been a key success factor for the programme. In the design of a blended PBL degree, with relevance to the tourism entrepreneur, the programme must be at the heart of coordinated institute activity in learning pedagogy, tourism research and practice and online learning capability.

8) Collaborative approach: A collaborative and consultative approach was adopted in the design and development of the BSc in Small Enterprise Management from the beginning. Faculty who are expert in PBL joined the design team, as well as lecturers with particular knowledge of the various functional areas covered in the programme, many with tourism entrepreneurship knowledge and experience. The funding agency was a key player from the beginning, and informed the course design, and delivery mode. The e-learning support unit interventions were critical, and without a resourced e-learning unit, it would be impossible to design and develop a blended PBL programme.

9) Learner centrality: The design process illustrated in this chapter highlights the centrality of the learner and the criticality of the interaction and collaboration between major stakeholders to ensure that higher education meets not only the knowledge needs of its targeted learners but also their generic skill needs; the design process also addressed the overarching needs of an industrial sector as well as the need for a delivery that is flexible and 'local'. The programmes underlying andragogical philosophy and action learning approach corresponds to the adult education literature whereby it

> … has long established that mature learners tend to be more motivated to learn and are more effective and efficient in the process if learning involves a role they are to perform, a task they desire to accomplish, or a problem they wish to solve (Havighrust, 1952; Knowles, 1984). Learner-centered instructional models are based on this tenet concerning adult learners and their need to be an active participant in all phases of the learning process. (Boyer, Maher, & Kirkman, 2006, p. 338)

REFERENCES

Baum, T. (2006). Global tourism higher education: The British Isles experience. *Journal of Teaching in Travel & Tourism, 5*, 27–38.

Billett, S. (2001). Increasing small business participation in VET: A "hard ask". *Education + Training, 43*(8/9), 416–425.

Boyer, N. R., Maher, P. A., & Kirkman, S. (2006). Transformative learning in online settings: The use of self-direction, metacognition, and collaborative learning. *Journal of Transformative Education, 4*(4), 335–361.

Braun, P. (2002). Networking tourism SMEs: e-Commerce and e-marketing issues in regional Australia. *Information Technology and Tourism, 5*(1), 13–23.

Braun, P., & Hollick, M. (2006). Tourism skills delivery: Sharing tourism knowledge online. *Education + Training, 48*(8/9), 693–703.

Burns, G., & Chisholm, C. (2005). Graduate to professional engineer in a knowledge organisation – Does the undergraduate curriculum provide the basic skills? *Global Journal of Engineering Education, 9*(1), 89–96.

Cunningham, A. (1999). Confessions of a reflective practitioner: Meeting the challenges of marketing's destruction. *European Journal of Marketing, 33*(7/8), 685–697.

Deakins, D., & Freel, M. (1998). Entrepreneurial learning and the growth process in SMEs. *The Learning Organization, 5*(3), 144–155.

Devins, D., Gold, J., Johnson, S., & Holden, R. (2005). Conceptual model of management learning in micro businesses – Implications for research and policy. *Education + Training, 47*(8/9), 540–551.

Dewey, J. (1938). *Experience and education.* West Lafayette, IN: Kappa Delta Pi.

Duch, B., Groh, S., & Allen, D. (2001). *The power of problem-based learning.* Sterling, VA: Stylus.

Ehrich, L. C., & Billett, S. (2004). Learning new practices in small business: Engagement and localised support. *Education & Training, 46*(8), 501–509.

Fáilte Ireland. (2004). *Competing through people: A human resource development strategy for Irish tourism 2005–2010.* Dublin: The Stationery Office.

Fáilte Ireland. (2005). Competing through people: A human resource development strategy 2005 – 2010 [online]. Retrieved from http://www.failteireland.ie/Publications

Fáilte Ireland. (2007). Tourism Product Development Strategy 2007–2013. [online]. Retrieved from http://www.failteireland.ie/Publications

Failte Ireland. (2009). *Fostering an innovation culture in Irish Tourism.* Retrieved from http://www.failteireland.ie/Information-Centre/Publications/Reviews—Reports/Policy/Innovation_Paper_22-12-2009

Failte Ireland. (2011). Tourism facts [online]. Retrieved from http://www.failteireland.ie/FailteCorp/media/FailteIreland/documents/Research

Fiol, C., & Lyles, M. (1985). Organizational learning. *Academy of Management Review, 10*(4), 803–813.

Forrest, S., III., & Peterson, T. (2006). It's called andragogy. *Academy of Management Learning & Education, 5*(1), 113–122.

Fuller-Love, N. (2006). Management development in small firms. *International Journal of Management Reviews, 8*(3), 175–190.

Gomez, P., Lorente, J., & Cabrera, R. (2004). Training practices and organisational learning capability: Relationship and implications. *Journal of European Industrial Training, 28*(2/3/4), 234–256.

Government of Ireland. (2007). *National development plan 2007–2013: Transforming Ireland – A better quality of life for all.* Dublin: The Stationery Office.

Havighrust, R. J. (1952). *Developmental tasks and education* (2nd ed.). New York, NY: Longmans, Green.

Innovation Ireland. (2010). *Review of the innovation task force.* Dublin: The Stationery Office.

Inui, Y., Wheeler, D., & Lankford, S. (2006). Rethinking tourism education: What should schools teach? *Journal of Hospitality, Leisure, Sport and Tourism Education, 5*(2). Retrieved from http://www.heacademy.ac.uk/assets/hlst/documents/johlste/vol5no2/0122.pdf

ITIC. (2011). *Future challenges for tourism.* Retrieved from http://www.itic.ie/future-challenges.html

Jameson, S. (2000). Recruitment and training in small firms. *Journal of European Industrial Training, 24*(1), 43–49.

Kelliher, F., & Henderson, J. B. (2006). A learning framework for the small business environment. *Journal of European Industrial Training, 30*(7), 512–528.

Kessels, J., & Poell, R. (2004). Andragogy and social capital theory: The implications for human resource development. *Advances in Developing Human Resources, 6*(2), 146–157.

Knowles, M. (1980). *The modern practice of adult education: From pedagogy to andragogy* (2nd ed.). Englewood Cliffs, NJ: Prentice.

Knowles, M. S. (1984). *The adult learner: A neglected species* (3rd ed.). Houston, TX: Gulf Publishing.

Kolb, D. (1984). *Experiential learning: Experience as the source of learning and development.* Englewood Cliffs, NJ: Prentice.

Lambert. (2003). *Lambert review of business university collaboration* [online]. Retrieved from http://www.hm-treasury.gov.uk/lambert_review_business_university_collab.htm

Lawless, N., Allan, J., & O'Dwyer, M. (2000). Face-to-face or distance training: Two different approaches to motivate SMEs to learn. *Education + Training, 42*(4/5), 308–316.

McAlister, M. K., Rivera, J. C., & Hallan, S. F. (2001). Twelve important questions to answer before you offer a web based curriculum. *Online Journal of Distance Learning Administration, 9*(2). Retrieved from www.westga.edu/˜distance/ojdla/summer42/mcalister42.html

Moorman, C., & Miner, A. (1998). The convergence of planning and execution: Improvisation in new product development. *Journal of Marketing, 62*(3), 1–20.

Organisation for Economic Co-operation and Development. (2004). Review of national policies for education: Review of higher education in Ireland. Retrieved from http://www.hea.ie/files/files/file/archive/policy/2006/OECD%20Review%20of%20Highe%20Education%202004.pdf

Park, J., & Choi, H. (2009). Factors influencing adult learners' decision to drop out or persist in online learning. *Educational Technology & Society, 12*(4), 207–217.

Sargeant, A. (1996). Training for growth: How can education providers assist in the development of small businesses? *Industrial and Commercial Training, 28*(2). Retrieved from http://proquest.umi.com

Sherman, W. H., & Beaty, D. M. (2007). The use of distance technology in educational leadership preparation programs. *Journal of Educational Administration, 45*(5), 605–620.

Storey, D. J. (2004). Exploring the link, among small firms, between management training and firm performance: A comparison between the UK and other OECD countries. *International Journal of Human Resource Management, 15*(1), 112–130.

Tourism Ireland. (2011). Tourism Ireland welcomes growth in overseas visitors [online]. Retrieved from http://www.tourismireland.com/Home!/About-Us/Press-Releases/2011/

Tourism Policy Review Group. (2003). *New horizons for Irish tourism: An agenda for action.* Dublin: The Stationery Office.

Tourism Renewal Group. (2009). *New horizons for Irish tourism: Mid-term review.* Department of Transport, Tourism, and Sport. Retrieved from http://www.transport.ie/Publications

Walker, E., Redmond, J., Webster, B., & Le Clus, M. (2007). Small business owners: Too busy to train? *Journal of Small Business and Enterprise Development, 14*(2), 294–306.

ENGAGING DISTANCE AND BLENDED LEARNERS ONLINE

Andrew Doig and Steve Hogg

ABSTRACT

'I like the fact that it's simple; I like the fact that it's not too complicated, and I think that whoever developed it, developed it with the people in mind'. Blended learning master's student talking about Solent Online Learning.

The authors carried out an extended project aimed at making effective use of the Virtual Learning Environment (VLE) for the delivery of high-quality online distance and blended learning. This was in response to a greater demand for such courses through the emergence of a new constituency of learner, principally professional learners, *those already in employment but seeking to improve their level of qualification and employability through the study of flexibly delivered credit bearing courses. The growth of this constituency can be seen very much as a response to the changes to the funding structure in the higher education sector in the UK. To this end, the authors worked within a team that developed an approach to effective course design, the Solent Online Learning Standard, and then a new methodology for collaborating with academic staff in the development and delivery of such courses. In order to best facilitate this, the team also created a new instance of its institutional VLE, called* Solent Online Learning *and tailored more to the needs of these new professional learners.*

Increasing Student Engagement and Retention in e-Learning Environments:
Web 2.0 and Blended Learning Technologies
Cutting-edge Technologies in Higher Education, Volume 6G, 229–260
Copyright © 2013 by Emerald Group Publishing Limited
All rights of reproduction in any form reserved
ISSN: 2044-9968/doi:10.1108/S2044-9968(2013)000006G011

INTRODUCTION

The higher education (HE) landscape in the UK is currently in a state of flux. The funding model of government subsidies is going through a radical overhaul resulting in the raising of tuition fees across the sector. Undergraduates commencing studies in 2012 may end up with debts as much as £53,000 by the time they graduate. Most HE institutions in the country are starting to recognise that in these circumstances students will begin looking for alternative and more flexible ways of completing their qualifications: part-time study, distance study or work-based learning. HE institutions are looking to provide flexible courses that give the opportunity to study while working so that the student can maintain an income and offset loan debts.

It is also intuitive to suggest that with young undergraduate students leaving university with such high levels of debt, they will be less inclined to progress immediately on to postgraduate study for which they will also incur large fees. Postgraduate courses face an uncertain future with dwindling numbers of applications. The University of Oxford has stated that the HE reforms could render the provision of postgraduate master's degrees 'unviable' (quoted in Jump, 2012). If we are fortunate, students will defer postgraduate study until later in their career, rather than omitting master's programmes from their career path entirely. Once in employment, it is difficult, or less appealing to return to full-time study, giving up a regular income. This too suggests a future move towards increasing master's provision through distance learning.

What seems inevitable is that students will begin to ask themselves more often the questions of: How much money am I prepared to spend on my education? What am I prepared to spend it on? Am I getting the value I demand for the amount of money I'm spending? This then sets the challenge for HE institutions to be able to create 'added value' learning experiences, ones which engage, involve and ultimately effectively educate the students who take them, as well as improving their employability. In the distance learning market, that means making best use of the institutional Virtual Learning Environment (VLE) or other learning technologies to engage learners, support and retain them so that they leave with high levels of student satisfaction.

However, it is important to recognise that this new type of student has different needs to the traditional undergraduate. This student is time pressed, trying to study and learn alongside work and family commitments. Moreover, as the student in this new flexible model spends more of their time learning via online technology, it is vital that the learning experience is not diminished and that the e-learning experience is engaging and rewarding and every bit is as good as attending a great lecture or really excellent classroom session.

This chapter aims to further expand on the institutional context in which Southampton Solent University (SSU) finds itself in these changing times and also to describe in greater detail the needs of the emerging new learning constituency; it will also describe the needs of tutors making the transition into online teaching before going on to explain our approach to meeting these learner and tutor needs. For the purposes of this chapter, we are using *blended learning* to refer to any structured combination of face-to-face teaching with online learning (generally we will be discussing instances where the balance falls further towards online than face-to-face learning) and *distance learning* to describe teaching and learning situations in which the student remains at a distance from the facilitating institution and does not include face-to-face teaching.

CONTEXT

SSU has a mission statement for 'The pursuit of inclusive and flexible forms of HE that meet the needs of employers and prepare students to succeed in a fast-changing competitive world' (2008a). This mission leads to the University's Teaching and Learning Strategy, which says that the University aims to support students' lifelong learning as well as providing 'flexible and accessible ways of learning' (Southampton Solent University, 2008b). SSU has a tradition of working with a widening participation agenda, supporting students into HE who may not otherwise have made that choice. This strategy also states that the University aims to 'use the latest technologies, facilities and good practice in ways that are geared to the needs of students and what they must achieve' (*ibid.*).

Strategic Development

In order to advance its mission and to pursue its key strategies, SSU successfully bid for funding from the Higher Education Funding Council for England (HEFCE). The result of this has been the University's Strategic Development Programme (SDP) running from 2009 until the end of the academic year in 2012. Among the aims of the SDP is 'the development of flexible modes of delivery to new and existing learners. Accrediting small units of learning, offering new forms of e-learning and providing relevant support for learners' (Southampton Solent University, 2009). As such, the SDP has not so much been about realignment for the University, but rather about accelerating the SSU's stated aims.

Further, this strategic development is in line with the political context in the UK. Around the time of the commencement of the SDP, the then Labour Government published 'Higher Ambitions: the future of universities in a knowledge economy' (Department of Business Innovation and Skills, 2009), setting out a vision for the future of HE in the UK. This report claimed, 'We will give priority to growing a diverse range of models of HE. These include options such as part-time and workplace-based courses aimed particularly at mature students or those from non-conventional backgrounds' (*ibid.*, p. 11), and later went on to state, 'The continuing development of e-learning is a vital element in supporting improvement of teaching and the student experience and in enabling the personalisation and flexibility that students and employers expect' (*ibid.* p. 92). Despite the change of government since Higher Ambitions was published, these emphases remain, particularly given the further context of the new fees regime. Student economic needs are anticipated to lead them to seek alternate ways of achieving their academic goals: new constituencies of learners who seek flexible, part-time and distance learning opportunities that allow the participants to also remain in a paid profession and, in the case of mature students, to care for their families.

Online Distance and Blended Learning

One approach recognised by SSU in reaching these new constituencies has been in the development of a robust online provision of distance and blended learning. Our Teaching and Learning Strategy talks extensively about increased use of e-learning, and in each of their bids for SDP funding, the four faculties of the University made reference to increasing the use of e-learning or online learning to support the new students they were seeking.

At the beginning of the SDP, SSU already had experience in running predominantly online blended learning courses. MA in Business Studies, Foundation Business and MSc in Six Sigma all had blended delivery versions that involved predominantly online learning with occasional on-campus lessons. It was on this experience that the University and its faculties recognised that there was scope to expand its online provision further.

NEW CONSTITUENCIES OF STUDENTS

In 2008, Bill Rammell, then Minister of State for HE, speaking to the Open University's Student's Association Conference said, 'We're going to need to get many more mature people into higher education over the next decade ... For most of the 171 higher education institutions in this country, the consequences of all that are going to be very challenging. They're going to have to enter what is, for most, very unfamiliar territory: dealing with older, possibly more demanding and certainly more discerning students'.

Rammell was speaking two years before the Government White Paper that brought in the new fee structure for HE in England and Wales, but the resonance of what he said holds true. In the emerging HE market, particularly the postgraduate market, we should expect increased numbers of students who are mature, in work and demanding high quality from their learning experience. This is in line with the findings of a course team at SSU who have been delivering a blended learning masters for several years (in this case the blend involves a course that is predominantly delivered online with four-week on-campus sessions in the academic year) and described some recurring characteristics of the learners who take their degree programme.

Characteristics of Professional Learners

These students

- are in work
- are in a variety of industries
- have reached a 'peak' level in their profession and so require further qualification to move up or on
- have a very specific first degree
- often have young families
- have limited available time
- have not been in formal education for some time
  (Doig, 2011, p. 3).

Through these characteristics, at Solent we refer to these students in general terms as *professional* learners. The impact of recognising this constituency of learner is that it is important to also recognise that they will have needs that are different to our traditional (and still predominant) cohort of students who are typically aged 18–21, school leavers, and attending campus in full-time education.

McGivney (2003) when looking at retention in adult learners noted among 'some common elements that set them apart from younger students' the following:

- They are likely to have a range of external constraints arising from their financial, work and domestic commitments;
- They may lack confidence in their learning ability if there has been a lengthy interval since they last engaged in formal or structured learning.

She states, 'All of these factors can significantly affect an individual's ability or readiness to complete a programme of study'.

Flexible Access to Learning

The professional learner needs to be able to access their learning at times that are suitable to them, benefiting from asynchronous delivery. They also need to be able to access their learning resources quickly and easily, with little extra information to clutter the way – there is a high need for signposting of expectations, deadlines and paths through the learning process.

It is clear that full-time on-campus study is not going to meet the needs of this learner constituency. Indeed, it is our experience that even blended learning with only a small proportion of face-to-face contact is less preferable to distance learning; when SSU's MSc in Shipping Operations was first advertised with a one-week residential component, applications were too low to justify running the course; when the face-to-face component was taken out, making it fully online distance, the applications quickly met and went well beyond quorum for the course to run.

Retention Rates

However, one issue that must be kept in mind when putting forward online distance learning as a panacea for all that ails the mature professional learner is the fact that these courses commonly have very poor rates of retention. At the International Education, Technology and Development Conference 2011 in Valencia, Kristen Betts, presenting on the effectiveness of an 'Online human touch' began by quoting startling statistics, 'While online enrolments are predicted to increase, attrition still remains higher for online programs than on-campus programs. Online attrition rates are often cited within the literature as 20% to 50%' (Betts, 2009).

The fact that our professional learners are also generally mature students may also have an impact on their retention. McGivney (2003) quoting statistics from HEFCE tells us, 'Withdrawal rates of those aged over 21 were particularly high at some institutions – between 20 and 30%, or even higher. A further split between mature students with and without previous HE qualifications shows that the latter were 3% more likely to have left HE following their year of entry, with again, some particularly high rates of attrition in some institutions'.

At SSU, similar patterns have been recorded, with our initial provision of predominantly distance blended learning courses such as the MA in Business Studies and MSc in Six Sigma both showing very early dropouts within each cohort of students.

NEW ROLES FOR STAFF

With all new movements in education, there are early adopters who are eager for change and may be adept at taking on board the new skills required. In SSU's current case, these are the tutors of the courses that have been running as blended learning for a number of years; they have been pushing back boundaries for the University in what we understand as our capability to provide online learning.

However, as change becomes embedded, it is inevitable that other staff will need to catch up with these early adopters; those staff who are persuaded, coerced or obliged to take on blended or distance courses will need to become familiar with online learning, both from a technical perspective and a teaching and learning perspective.

Tutor Needs

In working with academic staff new to online teaching, the Learning Technologies team at SSU has recognised a number of needs common to tutors in this position:

- A need to learn to use the technology;
- A need to understand the appropriate uses of the available learning tools;

- A tendency to approach the online learning environment as a location for resources and links to activities, rather than a teaching space;
- A lack of anticipation for how much time and effort is required to fully develop the content of an online course;
- An unfamiliarity with the amount and spread of workload involved in online tutoring;
- A need to experience the use of the online teaching environment in a meaningful context.

(This list is derived from our experience of collaborating with academics in the development and running of their online courses.)

One teacher commented,

> It's completely different teaching online; there's so much more organisation involved that you don't see when you are teaching face-to-face. You have to get everything seriously prepared beforehand, and you have to get stuck in and be really involved.

These needs are easy to understand, and are likely to be born out of an unfamiliarity with this type of teaching. They can also be impacted by the individual academic's computer competency or *digital literacy*, both in terms of their familiarity with the online learning environment and with digital tools in general. Understandably, these academics can benefit from support from learning technologists and from more experienced colleagues.

SETTING NEW INSTITUTIONAL QUALITY STANDARDS FOR ONLINE COURSES

The new economic context for HE institutions in the UK means that universities need to be competitive in what is increasingly seen as a *market* in HE. This was emphasised in the Browne Report when it recommended that, 'HEI s actively compete for well informed, discerning students, on the basis of price and teaching quality' (Browne, 2010, p. 8), and the resultant White Paper has an entire chapter dedicated to 'Well-informed students driving teaching excellence' (Department of Business Innovation and Skills, 2011, p. 25).

This has led to a focus on student engagement and retention. The need to engage learners online is just as important, and arguably more so, as it is to engage students in on-campus classes. The attrition rates commonly experienced in online distance learning, as mentioned previously, are considerable, and effective engagement is key to retaining students on these courses. High-quality, well-produced and well-managed online learning resources may be deployed as a way to enhance this engagement. For this to become standard practice at the University, it has proven necessary, or certainly desirable, to establish institutional quality standards that suggest how online learning experiences should be developed, and how they may be benchmarked.

The Flexible Delivery Development and Support Team

When SSU was awarded funding for strategic development by HEFCE, each of its four faculties put forward bids to develop new courses that led to employer engagement and increased flexibility of delivery. In their bids, they variously made reference to some form of technology-enhanced learning such as 'e-learning', 'online learning' or 'blended learning'. In the University's Learning Technologies Department, we recognised that something lacking from these bids was a shared concept of what was meant by high-quality online learning. Logically, as the section of the University that is populated by learning technologists, e-learning support officers and online content designers, it was clear that a function of our support to the faculties could be to develop an institutional definition of the key terms and a set of agreed standards that all of us could work towards. In order to do so, we successfully bid into the Strategic Development Fund for the creation of a new team within the department that could do so, and the Flexible Delivery Development and Support Team (FDDST) was created.

Informal Survey of the Online Learning Landscape

One of the first activities of the FDDST was to carry out an informal survey of the marketplace for online distance learning within the UK and internationally in order to develop a sense of what learning experiences were being provided. This process was advantaged by the move towards open educational resources which has meant that respected institutions such as The Open University (2012) in the UK and Massachusetts Institute of Technology (2012) in the USA have made large amounts of their courseware freely available on their web pages. The FDDST members each reviewed the available courses, as well as resources put online by private providers such as the BBC, Lynda.com and Adobe TV, identifying key aspects that they felt contributed positively to the online student's learning experience. Further, the FDDST along with the wider team within Learning Technologies took time to reflect on their collected experience of supporting academics in the development of the online components of their full time, part-time, face-to-face or blended learning courses, to evaluate which aspects had the most impact. This was a collective group aimed at gathering a variety of perspectives on the online learning experience and was comprised three Learning Technologists, two e-Learning Support Officers, an Instructional Developer, a Multi-media Production Coordinator, a Web Developer, a Learning Technology Development Manager and the Head of Learning Technologies.

The Solent Online Learning Standard

The outcome of this process was the development of the Solent Online Learning (SOL) Standard. The SOL Standard currently has eight main strands which are further expanded into sub-topics or activities. These are illustrated in Fig. 1.

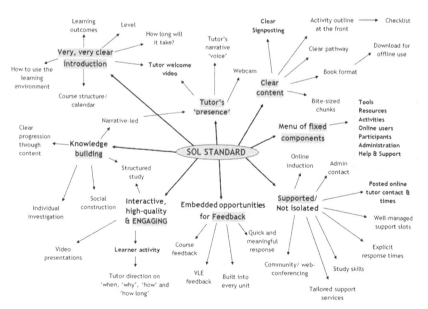

Fig. 1. Southampton Solent University 'Solent Online Learning Standard' for Online and Blended Learning VLE Design.

These standards relate to the design of the online course content, in terms of appearance and instructional design, as well as the practices and processes involved in running such courses effectively. The diagram usefully illustrates the key topics which are then expanded in both written explanations and in the verbal activity of the FDDST's collaboration with academic teaching staff. The set of standards is constantly developing and evolving as we continue to reflect on the impact of the FDDST's activities and respond to student activity and feedback as the courses run.

Strands of the SOL Standard

In brief outline, the strands of the SOL Standard are

1) Very, very clear introduction

Each student should have a clear idea of what each unit of study will help them to learn and how the learning process will be formed. This is achieved by tutor-provided content such as a welcome video and *Unit Overview* section to the page. There are also very clear resources introducing the learning environment and the tools it makes use of.

2) Tutor presence

Having a real and present tutor in a learning process helps to humanise and personalise the students' experience. This can be achieved by the tutor appearing in their pages, in name, but also in video talking directly to the students and in the narrative content of the text on page – this can be written in such a way that it feels like the tutor is in the room guiding the student. Once the course is live, it is also important that the tutor is present in online discussions and other interactions.

3) Clear content

All learning processes must be well signposted: a clear pathway through the learning materials is described; links between contents and activities are made explicit. The tutor knows how and why things join up, so it is important that this is explained to the students.

4) Menu of fixed components

A consistent experience across units within a course and across different courses eases the learner's process of adapting to each new unit of learning. To this end, a menu of fixed components is provided on screen in each unit or course page. These include *Tools, Resources, Activities, Participants, Administration* and *Help & Support.*

5) Supported, not isolated

Support lines with the unit tutor, course team, course administration and fellow learners must be clearly established from the start. Contact details for all relevant course team personnel are posted via the course home page. All students new to online learning need to be provided with an induction to the learning environment along with course-specific induction. Further, the learning activities of the unit should involve plenty of opportunities for students to communicate with their classmates and their tutor in a collaborative and supportive manner.

6) Embedded opportunities for feedback

As with face-to-face classes, feedback should be sought mid-unit and through the final student unit evaluation. Further opportunities for feedback are embedded in every unit through the provision of an anonymous feedback tool. It is important that feedback is responded to promptly, increasing the students' sense of contact and being supported, as well as taking the opportunity to improve the learning experience for all participants in the course.

7) Interactive, high quality and engaging

The goal of all online units is to best enable the students to achieve the intended learning outcomes, and there are a number of learning technologies that can help to facilitate that process. Further, attractive, well-designed, well-planned pages of content, combined with high-quality video, will help to keep the students' attention on and enjoyment of the materials.

8) Knowledge building

Units must be developed with an understanding of current principles in HE and technology-enhanced learning. Learner engagement, interaction and communication are vital so that the students are able to construct their own understanding of the subject. Learner activity must be included at every stage of the learning process to encourage both individual investigation and social construction of understanding.

The implementation of these SOL Standard elements is expanded below.

TAILORING A NEW VIRTUAL LEARNING ENVIRONMENT

The second main activity of the FDDST was to use the SOL Standard as the basis for the development of a new instance of the University's VLE.

Since 2006, SSU has built its VLE in the Moodle platform, branded as 'myCourse'. MyCourse has worked very well as the online medium to enhance the delivery of the University's face-to-face courses. However, in embarking on the project to recruit new student constituencies, the 'professional learner' as described above, we recognised that the imagery, language, news and information feeds that predominate on myCourse and are aimed at the undergraduate student in the 18–21 age group, would be less likely to suit the needs of our new learners. Further, we took into account feedback received from existing blended learning students. In the words of one of these, 'One point about myCourse is, that's effectively our university, that's our lives' (Patrick & Newell, 2009). For the distance learner, their experience of the University is exclusively (or very close to for blended learners) delivered via the online environment. Distance learners do not have the opportunities for clarification and correction that are provided by face-to-face contact with tutors in the classroom. Hence, for these students, it is vital to provide a consistently high-quality VLE in order to keep them engaged.

Solent Online Learning

This new instance of the University's VLE is called Solent Online Learning (and can be visited at http://learn.solent.ac.uk, where guests can view introduction materials and taster pages for existing courses). Graphic designers, learning technologists, instructional designers and academic teaching staff collaborated in the design of this platform and the build for the template course and unit structure that is used across all of the courses within it. Care has been put into creating a consistent and professional look and feel, using imagery and styling that better illustrate its use by mature working people. Care was also made to ensure that the way in which courses are presented within SOL includes the key components of the SOL Standard; for instance, consistent navigation blocks are used to allow students access to key information sets and communication tools. Also, the way in which tutors present their learning content is consistent, making use of the Moodle book format, which allows for sequential index-linked pages of narrative content written by the tutor.

Tutor Presence

One of the key principles of the SOL Standard, and of the support the FDDST gives, is that the online materials need to have a clear tutor presence. Having a real and present tutor in a learning process helps to humanise and personalise the students' experience. Betts (2009) highlighted Drexel University's efforts to create an 'Online Human Touch' (OHT) in order to combat the attrition rates in their online distance learning, 'The OHT concept asserts that students are more likely to persist in an online program if they are engaged in and outside of their courses and if the educational experience is personalized'. The strategies in the OHT process are geared towards effective induction, with first contact being humanised through direct telephone calls from student advisors, and robust student support, linking their online distance learners into support services and campus events to increase the students' sense of belonging to a living university.

It is part of the practice of the academic teams that the FDDST has worked with to establish direct human contact with all of their students; we have also put in place very clear signposting to all of the student services that are available to distance learners. A further key emphasis in our course development process is to bring the human presence of the tutor into the teaching materials. Jones, Naugle, and Kolloff (2008, p. 1) commented on the impact of video content on the students' sense of tutor presence in online materials,

> We evaluated student perceptions relating to the significance of producing an introductory video to introduce the instructor to students in both a fully online course and a hybrid course. From the results of this study, we concluded that introductory videos can help to establish the instructor's teaching presence with the students, regardless of the method of delivery of the course.

SOL course pages and units all include a video introduction from the course or unit leader outlining the purpose of the learning content and what the student can hope to learn by completing it. As part of the FDDST, we have a film maker (the multimedia production coordinator) who works closely with academic teaching staff to find ways of building further video teaching content into the course materials, as much as possible presented by the course tutor to increase their presence within the material. The multimedia production coordinator said, 'Video plays a key part in SOL because it actually puts the teacher in the environment. These videos are a great way for the students to meet their tutor for the first time'.

Narrative Content

The Moodle book format presents pages within which the tutor can provide links to resources and to learning activities (using the communication tools available in SOL). Around these links, we encourage the tutors to provide textual explanations, rationale for why to carry out reading or activities, and context for how these relate to their learning on the course. This narrative voice provides a further way for the tutor presence to come across to the student. As well as bringing in the tutor's knowledge and experience, this also allows for their own individual way of addressing their students, further personalising and humanising the learning experience. At SSU, we have also embedded a webcam widget into the Moodle HTML editor. This means that any tutor with a webcam attached to their computer can very easily drop in short videos in which they address the students directly and informally, further enhancing the sense of tutor-led narrative through the learning. These can be used for both the general learning content addressed to the whole class and specific content for individual students such as feedback on assignments.

INDUCTING AND SUPPORTING LEARNERS

Because you aren't on campus all the time, you have to have very clear information about what you are required to learn. You also need to have a very good environment where you can still communicate with your peers so that the on-campus environment is essentially replicated virtually. SOL does that very well.

Blended learning master's student.

McGivney (2003) from her research of the literature on the issue of retention among adult learners identifies various factors leading to non-completion within this group such as financial problems, lack of family support or personal factors which may be more out of the control of a distance learning provider. However, she also identifies factors that we can aim to have an impact on, such as 'Inadequate pre-course information and guidance', 'institutions that are not adult friendly' and 'lack of support'. She goes on to provide a useful list of steps that education institutions can take to encourage adult learners to persist:

• Provide full and detailed information and advice on course content and the required workload, as well as on sources of financial and other supports, before enrolment;

- Discuss with prospective students who are likely to have time constraints arising from work and domestic commitments, potential ways of managing a study programme and the kinds of supports that are available;
- Ensure that, where possible, the organisation of programmes takes account of people's outside commitments;
- Ensure that teaching staff deal sensitively with students and to give prompt and constructive feedback on their progress;
- Provide facilities where mature students can meet socially;
- Encourage mature students to form their own study and support groups;
- Ensure that there are effective procedures in place to identify and promptly follow up the most vulnerable students.

(McGivney, 2003)

We have addressed McGivney's concerns in a variety of ways, and also have established our own concerns and approach through dialogue with our distance and blended learners.

DESIGNING THE ONLINE LEARNING ENVIRONMENT

As mentioned above, a lot of care and consideration was put in to developing the SOL VLE. This was done to meet the expectations and needs of the cohort of professional learners that the University's expansion into online distance learning is attracting. A large part of the purpose of doing this was to ensure the engagement and retention of these learners.

The Associate Dean (Enhancement) for the Maritime and Technology Faculty at SSU who was instrumental in providing course team support on a distance learning course development project said,

> These are professional people we are working with. They are not used to online learning. The online environment needed to be professional, and it needed to be easy to navigate at the same time. SOL is both of those things.

Designing for Learning

One of our first considerations was in trying to make the platform attractive, easy to use and friendly for mature learners, people with other life commitments, people who may be time short and in need of accessing their learning activities quickly and consistently. One web developer and graphic designer on the SOL project said,

> The look and the feel of the site were mainly aimed at the professional learner. We wanted to bring them into an environment that they find really friendly and really easy to navigate through, and be able to find the information they needed right away.

We have gone for consistency right across all of the units and courses in SOL, keeping key information sets and resources in the same place, with recurrent menus and content presentation styles. This is important for the distance learner who may take a variety of units, and may take units from disparate courses and faculties.

One of our online learners commented,

> I think it's really easy to understand, and the other thing I like about the design of the units is that very much click on the link and it brings you straight into what you need. So, there's limited fuss to it. I also like the fact that there are video tutorials that go along with lots of links that you can get into, so you actually see somebody and it's not just having to read through a lot of information. There is actually someone talking it through for you.

This student has picked up on various components of the SOL Standard that are in place across all units in order to create a positive learning experience, such as providing clear content, with a clear introduction and clear signposting to the learning resources and activities. She also identifies the feature of a clear tutor presence, here provided through video instruction, as something important to her. These features can be seen in the screen grab from one of our unit home pages (Fig. 2)

The menus in the left hand column are fixed, kept consistently across all units on a course. Similarly, each unit starts with a short piece of introductory text, the expected learning outcomes for the unit and, importantly, a video of the unit leader welcoming the students and outlining the purpose, content and delivery method for the unit.

Supporting the Learners

As much as we have built our SOL pages to be user-friendly and as intuitive as possible, we are aware that it is also important to guide students into the process of online learning. Prensky (2009) may describe our students as *digital immigrants*. Certainly many of the students who come on to our courses are lacking in immediately usable IT skills, and are slow adopters with new technologies, even to the point of being resistant in the take up of

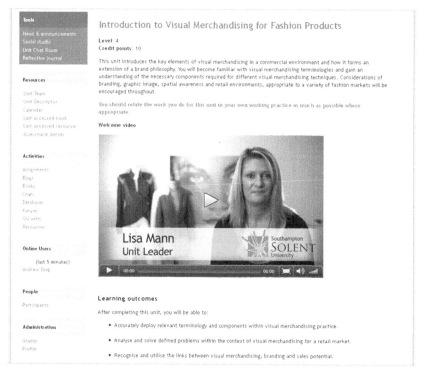

Fig. 2.   Unit Homepage of 'Introduction to Visual Merchandising for Fashion Products'.

those which are being put forward as learning tools by their tutors (see the examples in the section 'Evaluating Impact').

In order to acclimatise our students into their online learning environment, we have spent considerable effort in developing online support resources that acquaint and train the students in the basic functions of SOL and the learning and communication tools they will use to access their learning activities. These resources encourage students to engage, for instance to complete their SOL profiles and to practice sending a request for help, and they also provide video instruction on the little technical aspects that people often get stuck on. The resources are grouped into categories such as 'Welcome to Solent Online Learning' (the general guide to using SOL), the Successful Study Guide (an academic skills training resource) and a guide to using the University's library. All of these resources are accessible without the need to log in, which means that students can be directed towards them as soon as they have expressed an interest to register on the course (if you would like to view our resources use the 'Help & Support' tab at the top of http://learn.solent.ac.uk/).

For those students starting on their courses, we work closely with the course teams to make sure that these resources are embedded in the induction process. This induction is provided via the course home page. Here the students are inducted to the use of SOL along with the course content, and are also inducted into communication with their tutors and their peers through the use of online ice-breaking activities and peer-partner interviews.

Developing a Sense of Cohort

Another concern for us is that we want to provide the students with a sense of cohort, feeling they belong to a class that are prepared to share and work together, forming learning partnerships and support networks. This is done by making formal and informal methods of communication available and obvious, such as the chat room and the messaging system within SOL. Many communication tools are used for learning activities, such as forums, blogs and wikis, but we always ensure that there are open forums for less structured interactions; these are named depending on the learning context, such as 'Common room' or 'Social studio'.

Students are given peer partners to collaborate with and are encouraged to form self-managed study groups to work collaboratively on classroom tasks. We also encourage the learners to use external tools such as Skype to communicate with their partners and also to use appropriate social media to communicate in non-formal ways and, importantly for them, contexts in which they are not monitored by teaching or administrative staff.

The Course Leader for fashion professional development units in SOL said,

> There's real interaction here. We set them up with a peer partner and they can have online discussions with their peer partner, as well as with us. So, everything they are doing is effectively working through this online VLE.

Further, another blended learner in SOL commented,

> I feel there are a lot of people around me, my lecturers, my co-students; I'm able to message them, ask questions, they are able to help me with my work, I help them with their work. Everything just seems as if I'm in a classroom online.

This sense of collaborative and supportive cohort is expressed repeatedly as a strong feature of the online learning experience we provide and is generally viewed by tutors and students as a key element of keeping their students engaged and learning. One distance learner sums this up very well,

> One of the most enjoyable aspects of the course, and one which I had not accounted for prior to starting, has been the banter and plentiful discussion between the student cohort, aided by course activities. There always seems to be somebody interested in your particular topic or indeed willing to offer some encouragement and support when times get tough and deadlines loom.

Support from Staff

We are aware also that there may be communication needs that the students have which are not necessarily social. For instance, the students' pastoral issues relating to their ability to meet the workload successfully or academic fears in regard to their ability to complete. Our distance and blended learners are given opportunities from very early in their studies to have direct contact with their tutors in order to discuss these issues. In degree programmes, involving the study of a number of units, the students are given individual academic tutors who remain with them for the duration of their course. These support the students alongside the tutors specific to each unit of study. In shorter courses, such as professional development units, which are taken singly, the students are given the opportunity to have regular one-to-one meetings with the unit tutor.

We have also built in to our Help and Support pages a wide range of tailored information letting the students know about ways in which they can gain support from the student services, librarians and counsellors (these pages are viewable without login under the 'Help & Support' tab at http://learn.solent.ac.uk/). Clear signposting is imperative here; we make sure the students know where to get the information and support they need, whether it is administrative, academic or pastoral.

A NEW MODEL FOR SUPPORTING ACADEMICS

As mentioned previously, there are some considerable and usually unanticipated pressures placed on teaching staff when they start teaching online for the first time. In our paper published in the Journal of Learning Development in Higher Education (Hogg & Doig, 2012) we described how,

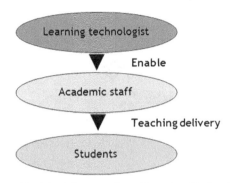

Fig. 3. Model of Support from Learning Technologists.

under the funding provided by the SDP and the creation of the FDDST, we were able to move from a more common enabling model of support for academics developing technology-enhanced learning to a collaboration model, which we have abridged here.

Traditional Support for Academic Staff

In the past, the learning technologists at SSU worked in a capacity of enabling academic staff members to deliver their VLE content independent of continuous support (Fig. 3).

This model has several advantages, but most especially it means that the expert knowledge held by the learning technologists can be shared effectively with a large number of academic staff.

A New Approach

However, with the FDDST, we have been able to create a model that works slightly differently (Fig. 4).

The huge advantage with this model is that the academic staff, individually or (more usually) as a course team, are continuously enabled and supported by a cross-disciplinary team in order to deliver their VLE content. This means that the output in terms of online course content is maintained to a more consistent standard, and the provision of online learning is enabled by a more consistent approach to delivery.

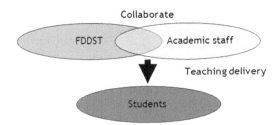

Fig. 4. Model of Support from the Flexible Delivery Development and Support
Team.

The Course Leader for the fashion Professional Development Units in
SOL said,

> I did work closely with Instructional Developers and Learning Technologists to
> understand really clearly what's needed from developing curricula that are going to be
> developed online in an e-learning environment. I'm used to delivering in the classroom,
> not online, so I needed lots of help and lots of advice on how to actually make it work as
> an interactive experience online.

The Director of the Business School at SSU said,

> The support of the Flexible Delivery Team is absolutely vital. It's really important that
> we have a professional Virtual Learning Environment. We are actually delivering
> courses to professionals and they expect a very high quality experience and without the
> team we wouldn't be able to deliver that.

Taking the Approach One Step Further

Now that we have come to the end of the period of Strategic Development
Funding and the work of the FDDST becomes integrated into the regular
activity of the University, we have come to realise that a slightly different
model is most appropriate, one that can draw not only on the expertise of
the Learning Technologies team, but also on the experience gained by
the academic teaching colleagues who have collaborated with us thus far
(Fig. 5).

The champions are academics who have already had success developing
and running online courses for distance or blended learning. It is most
likely, but not exclusively, that these champions will also previously have
collaborated with the FDDST and are familiar with the SOL Standard and
ways in which it can be applied.

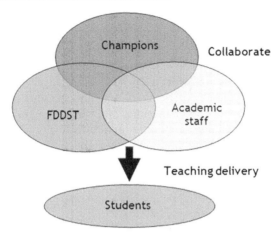

Fig. 5. New Model of Online Course Development Incorporating Academic Champions.

In an ideal situation, the expert online teachers who work as champions would be part of the course development team and part of the teaching team, delivering one or more units in the course. However, they may also be colleagues from other courses or other faculties who are brought in to share their experience and expertise with academics who are becoming online tutors for the first time. Note that the model has moved away from one about 'support' to one about 'development', emphasising the idea that the coming together of these three groups is an ongoing collaboration towards effective course development. It will also hold together through the actual running of the course, with the course team and other parties meeting regularly to discuss the way in which the course is progressing, and in the long run will lead to the generation of many more champions to collaborate in future projects.

There are two distinct advantages to bringing online teaching champions in to the support and development model:

1. It is our experience that the development of effective online courses is very resource intensive. It takes a great deal of tutor time to pick up the skills and to build the necessary online content, and it takes a great deal of the FDDST's time to directly support each individual towards meeting the SOL Standards. The introduction of the champions brings in tutors who have the experience and ability to build courses more efficiently and who can have a supporting role for those colleagues who are new to the process.

2. The second advantage is that these experienced online tutors bring authentic practice into the model. As much as the FDDST can assert their understanding of effective technology-enhanced learning, academics will be much more influenced by the knowledge gained by those who have had firsthand experience of teaching students in contexts very similar to their own. The champions know through real practice what is involved in engaging, retaining and effectively teaching students who they meet entirely or predominantly online, experience that has a positively invaluable influence on the academics who are new to all of this.

An Online Resource to Support Online Tutors

The ideal support situation involves the collaboration described above. However, in acknowledgement of the level of support necessary to create really great online learning for our students, the FDDST also built an online training resource for our academic staff titled 'How to be a Solent Online Learning Teacher' (Fig. 6).

The use of this resource sits alongside the direct collaboration with the FDDST, but by having a really robust set of training materials available online the requirement for person-to-person support can be reduced; the academics can become more self-enabling. We have to be realistic that we are a small team working with a growing number of academics. The availability of 'How to be a Solent Online Learning Teacher' (I will refer to this as 'How to...' for brevity) means that we can focus our discussions on how to effectively align learning outcomes with teaching activities, rather than on the minutiae of technical details.

We have developed 'How to ...' to be a pragmatic resource that works in a two ways:

1. It provides information, theory and training so that tutors can visit it whenever they need to learn a new component of developing or running their online units;
2. It models the use of the SOL Standards in its own design; we use the same unit format as used for teaching units; it makes use of the same clear introduction, signposting and tutor presence; it makes use of high-quality video content and also refers to appropriate and topical external resources.

Fig. 6. Unit Homepage of 'How to be a Solent Online Learning Teacher'.

One of the most powerful learning aids for teaching staff in this situation is to have the experience of being a student online, and this is something 'How to … ' provides. We have made use of 'How to … ' as part of a facilitated training programme for academic course teams. The online resource has been blended effectively with on-campus workshops and this has meant that we can engage the academics in online discussion and collaboration. Through reflection on their own experience as online learners, and their own level of engagement with the learning activities, the tutors gain real insight into how they can better facilitate online learning for their students.

Two illustrative comments from academic staff who have participated in this blended training (answering the question 'How has this training helped?') were:

- By giving hands-on interactive experiential learning of the tools available to me, thus making it more possible that I might pick the right tools for each job!
- Greater understanding of online communication tools available to me, and an idea on which forms will work best for our target audience.

EVALUATING IMPACT

We have set about evaluating the impact of the implementation of the SOL Standards and the SOL VLE in a variety of ways.

Usability Testing

We are fortunate that SSU has its own usability lab. We began making use of it with the very first prototype of the 'How to be a Solent Online Learning Teacher' resource. Since then we have run tests with each successive course to be delivered via SOL. The observation of user participation and choices made during testing and their comments following the test have been highly illuminating.

As an example, we tested 'How to ... ' with three SSU academic staff fulfilling a 1 hour observed use of the site, followed by questionnaire completion. It was observed that each of the three participants in our first test engaged with the online content in a different way. The first was very diligent at reading the content of every page, the second moved through landing on each page with a video and watching these before choosing any other activity and the third came across the first reflective journal task and spent the majority of the test writing up his thoughts.

We have continued to use small test groups, usually four to six participants, with between 1 hour and 2 hours of observed use of the test VLE sections. With taught units, we have also then asked the usability test participants to continue with a week's worth of authentic use of the unit or course materials in question. Participants are asked to keep test journals, recounting their experience of accessing and learning from the materials. We also review the frequency and duration of participant activity on the pages through activity logs.

Some of the issues raised during testing were principally technical, such as the need for signposts for how to return to the main content after navigating away to learning or communication tools; others were more instructive into the teaching and learning approach used in SOL. For instance, the fact that we can observe different users approaching the materials in very different ways has emphasised the need to ensure sufficient opportunity to work via a variety of learning processes and resources.

Test Runs

From usability testing, we go on to partial and full test runs of online units. We recruit non-fee paying students who agree to participate in the understanding that they will keep a test diary for the duration and also be responsive to feedback and other enquiries we make in regard to their use of the VLE and learning on the unit. This form of testing allows us to ensure that the methods and design we have chosen to implement the SOL Standards are effective in helping students achieve their learning outcomes. It also gives us the opportunity to test specific aspects of the online delivery, such as access to the platform and learning activities through mobile devices.

For the MSc in Shipping Operations, we choose a pilot unit, 'Post-graduate and Self-managed Study'. A group of four test participants carried out 2 hours of observed use of the site, and then went on to complete 10 days of live use of the unit, participating in learning and communication activities. The participants completed questionnaires and test journals for the duration of the test. The test participants were existing master's students studying at SSU on maritime related subjects.

In order to test a template structure for professional development units created in SSU's design school, a group of five distance learners were recruited. In this instance, they completed the full 12 weeks of the unit, carrying out the learning, communication activities and assessments, but without gaining certification. Again, these participants both completed feedback questionnaires and kept a test journal.

Feedback Activities

Part of the SOL Standard requires that we include 'Embedded opportunities for feedback', which is provided in the first instance through the use of a permanent feedback tool available on each unit home page, encouraging the students to comment anonymously on the unit and on the use of the online platform. We also actively seek out feedback from our students at various points in the duration of their studies. This is useful in that it often draws out comments that support our belief that we have developed a really effective and engaging platform, such as, 'Overall, the environment is great and we seem to have everything available that we could hope for'. Realistically though, we have to accept that such feedback will often throw up comments that are not so complimentary.

Early in the implementation of SOL, we collected feedback from a group of students studying an MA in Business Studies through blended learning. These second years had studied their first year via the University's general instance of the VLE titled 'myCourse' and were moved into SOL for their second year. In response to the question, 'What do you like about SOL?' one student responded, 'Nothing. Unlike myCourse, it is not intuitive'. Another commented, 'I used to use myCourse as a sort of list of tasks and tick off as I went. Now I have to navigate a number of different windows to find out what I need to do so think it could be easy to miss something important'.

This provided us with the opportunity to investigate further in order to recognise what elements of SOL presentation were causing these difficulties. It was surprising for us to discover that the very nature of the student profile, which we felt we had worked hard to meet, was put forward as a reason for SOL's failure:

> [MA Business Studies] is a blended learning course and in trying to combined studying, full-time work and family commitments being well organised is key so as to maximise study time. The way I managed to keep track of what was covered for each module at the study weekends and what it was expected I should undertake between the sessions last year was to print off the module page and then tick off each item as I did it. If I was not able to study for a couple of days, when I sat down to start I could see immediately what I had done and what I had left to do.

Continued discussion with the students and the course team led us to introduce further components to enhance the usability of the SOL content so that these students felt their needs were addressed. One of the students quoted above later commented:

> Yes, the page is 100 times better. I particularly liked the checklist of all the activities to be completed before the next session - clear, easy to follow and exactly what is required (at least from my perspective). I also liked the new front page for each off campus session - again clear and easy to use.

Responsiveness to Student Issues

Perhaps the most common way in which we find opportunities to evaluate the impact of our online provision is through the participation and questioning from our students when the courses are running.

Significantly, the early cohorts studying on courses in SOL demonstrated a great deal more reluctance to make use of certain online tools that the course team viewed important to their learning progress, such as an online portfolio and social networking tools. The students, fitting into our profile of *professional learners*, were mature and often lacked experience in the use of online communications. They expressed strong reservations about the security of such tools which in turn created obstruction to their willingness to put in the time and effort required to master the use of these. In fielding the issues raised by the students, and managing their expectations against those of their tutors, we were able to come to the conclusion that it was not so much the use of these tools, but rather then nature of the way in which they were introduced, contextualised and supported for the students that was at stake. We were able to resolve the issue in the live unit, and to plan for a better structured induction to these tools for future iterations of the course.

It is interesting to note that one student who was perhaps the most vocal in his reluctance and at times refusal to adapt to new online tools, progressed beyond this to the point where he would later state that all of his data and permission worries were resolved and that he found the online units to be an invaluable resource.

Impact on Retention Rates

As the SOL project is still very much in its infancy, we do not yet have extensive retention data to include here. However, we can quote the following examples:

- In the first academic year of delivery via SOL, the MA in Business Studies retained its entire cohort of 12 first-year students through the first teaching period from September 2010 to year end. In previous years, this period had proved to be the time when most student withdrawals occurred.
- The MSc in Shipping Operations began in June 2011 with 26 registered students. By June 2012, there had been only one withdrawal.
- All instances of the Design School PDUs that have run so far have retained all students across their 12-week duration.

ONGOING CONSIDERATIONS

In the main, the processes and successes described above have been the result of the FDDST project enabled through external funding to the University. As we move beyond the period of external funding, we now must look how the successes of this project can be embedded in the practice of the University. This has presented certain challenges, not least of which is the need to demonstrate the value of the pursuit of high-quality online distance and blended learning for the University.

There is a naive view often taken that online provision is a cheap option; if you remove the need for bricks and mortar and reduce the contact time between students and tutor, then it would seem logical that you reduce the expense of running the course. However, this assumption rests on the idea that courses can be put online and left to effectively run themselves. What the project of collaborating with academic teams on the development and running of online courses has shown us is that this work requires at least as much time commitment in terms of teaching hours as face-to-face teaching, and that the preparation for delivery of online courses is considerably more resource hungry because of the need to have extant at the outset all of the units of study. Over the duration of our two-year project, we have worked on several successful course developments, but we have also worked on projects which did not see it through to delivery because the teams pushing the projects forward had not given serious enough account of how much time and effort would be required to develop a course sufficiently to the point where it would be ready to run.

Thankfully, the Vice Chancellors Group of SSU have recognised that the work of the FDDST can contribute dynamically to the pursuit of the University's mission for 'the pursuit of inclusive and flexible forms of Higher Education' (Southampton Solent University, 2008a), and have acknowledged this by agreeing that the funded members of the team can be retained in post beyond the end of the SDP. This counts as a substantial commitment to the pursuit of online distance learning, especially in such times of fiscal restraint and caution in the UK HE sector.

In order for this form of course delivery to become substantive in the work of the University, it is crucial now that we are able to establish university policy and procedures for its development and quality assurance. To this end, we have begun work with SSU's Academic Services to develop guidelines for online course development that will go into the University's Academic Handbook, and to develop procedures for course teams in order to move their courses through validation and on to successful delivery. The introduction of online teaching champions from within the faculties will be extremely helpful in this process as it is very likely that part of course validation for online teaching will be the development of a minimum of one complete unit to demonstrate the course team's capacity and capability to develop these courses. Clearly, the expertise of our champions will make this initial development much more achievable.

Further, a final consideration has to be what we can do to make sure all of this good work has positive impact on our regular teaching practice. After all, our online cohorts currently present only a very small percentage of our student intake compared with our traditional on-campus students. We are now in the process of trying to ensure washback of the gains in our understanding of how to support and enhance learning with technology through the development of a suite of online self-help resources aimed at supporting our on-campus tutors with their adoption of learning technologies to support and enhance their students' learning experiences. In very much the spirit of the support we provide in collaboration with academics on SOL projects, and in the nature of the training provided via 'How to be a Solent Online Learning Teacher', these new resources will combine pedagogic advice with technical help to ensure that a wider group of teachers are able to use the online communication and learning tools provided by the VLE and also understand why they may choose to use them.

REFERENCES

Betts, K. (2009). Online human touch (OHT) training & support: A conceptual framework to increase faculty engagement, connectivity, and retention in online education, part 2. *MERLOT Journal of Online Learning and Teaching, 5*(1). Retrieved from http:// jolt.merlot.org/vol4no3/betts_0908.htm. Accessed on 25 April 2012.

Browne. (2010). *Securing a sustainable future in higher education.* London: Department of Business Innovation and Skills. Retrieved from http://www.bis.gov.uk/assets/biscore/ corporate/docs/s/10-1208-securing-sustainable-higher-education-browne-report.pdf. Accessed on 10 January 2013.

Department of Business Innovation and Skills. (2009). *Higher ambitions: The future of universities in a knowledge economy.* Retrieved from http://webarchive.nationalarchives. gov.uk/ + /http://www.bis.gov.uk/policies/higher-education/shape-and-structure/higher-ambitions. Accessed on 14 January 2013.

Department of Business Innovation and Skills. (2011). *Higher education: students at the heart of the system.* Government Paper. Retrieved from https://www.gov.uk/government/news/ putting-students-at-the-heart-of-higher-education. Accessed on 14 January 2013.

Doig, A. (2011, 8 March). *Online usability for students in employment.* Conference Paper INTED 2011: Valencia. Retrieved from http://solent.academia.edu/AndrewDoig/ Papers/1261337/ONLINE_USABILITY_FOR_STUDENTS_IN_EMPLOYMENT

Hogg, S., & Doig, A. (2012). Engaging blended learning students: An evolving approach to engaging students through the VLE. *Journal of Learning Development in Higher Education, 4.* Retrieved from http://www.aldinhe.ac.uk/ojs/index.php?journal=jldhe. Accessed on 2 May 2012.

Jones, P., Naugle, K., & Kolloff, M. (2008). *Teacher presence: Using introductory videos in online and hybrid courses. Learning Solutions Magazine,* 31 March. Retrieved from http://

www.learningsolutionsmag.com/articles/107/teacher-presence-us. Accessed on 25 April 2012.

Jump, P. (2012). Reforms may make master's degrees unviable. *Times Higher Education*. Retrieved from http://www.timeshighereducation.co.uk/story.asp?storycode=419121. Accessed on 14 January 2013.

Massachusetts Institute of Technology. (2012). *MIT open courseware*. Retrieved from http://ocw.mit.edu/index.htm. Accessed on 25 April 2012.

McGivney, V. (2003). *Understanding 'persistence' in adult education*. Conference Paper. Retention Symposium, May. Retrieved from http://kn.open.ac.uk/public/workspace.cfm?wpid=1887. Accessed on 11 April 2012.

The Open University. (2012). *Learning Space*. Retrieved from http://openlearn.open.ac.uk/. Accessed on 25 April 2012.

Patrick, S., & Newell, J. (2009). *Transition into or back into HE by Flexible Learning*. Conference presentation. Solent Event, September. Southampton Solent University.

Prensky, M. (2009). *Digital natives, digital immigrants – a new way to look at ourselves and our kids*. Retrieved from http://www.marcprensky.com/writing/. Accessed on 2 May 2012.

Southampton Solent University. (2008a). *University strategic plan 2008–13* [institutional intranet]. Southampton: Southampton Solent University.

Southampton Solent University. (2008b). *Teaching and learning strategy* [institutional intranet]. Southampton: Southampton Solent University.

Southampton Solent University. (2009). *Strategic Development Programme: The Strands* [Institutional intranet]. Southampton: Southampton Solent University.

A PEDAGOGICAL FRAMEWORK FOR COLLABORATIVE LEARNING IN A SOCIAL BLENDED E-LEARNING CONTEXT

Martina A. Doolan

ABSTRACT

The aim of this chapter is to introduce a pedagogical framework, the dialogic shamrock, for collaborative learning through technology, which is not a replacement for other learning theories rather it is a synthesis of the literature which draws upon learner centric, constructivist, and socio-cultural perspectives and is related to the concepts of online learning and collaborative technology including Web 2.0 in higher education. The examples of use focus on the learner as participator in curriculum design. The dialogic shamrock and examples of use presented test the framework and are intended to help educators across the educational sector to understand the key concepts to encourage learners to work collaboratively supported by technology within a socially blended learning framework in a social learning context.

The framework is not intended to be prescriptive rather to act as a guide for educators who seek to use a blend of technology and class-based activities to engage learners in collaborative social learning contexts.

Increasing Student Engagement and Retention in e-Learning Environments:
Web 2.0 and Blended Learning Technologies
Cutting-edge Technologies in Higher Education, Volume 6G, 261–285
Copyright © 2013 by Emerald Group Publishing Limited
All rights of reproduction in any form reserved
ISSN: 2044-9968/doi:10.1108/S2044-9968(2013)000006G012

LEARNER AS PARTNER IN CURRICULUM DESIGN

Over the years, experience has shown (Doolan, 2004, 2006, 2007a, 2007b, 2008, 2009, 2010) that learners and educators are invariably responsible for learning, that learning involves being an active participant in the learning process. These studies took place in a blended learning context. Blended learning has multiple definitions. According to Garrison and Vaughan (2007, p. 9) blended learning is *the thoughtful fusion of face-to-face and online learning experiences*. Similarly, Doolan, Thornton, and Hilliard (2006, p. 14) define blended learning where *students actively engage with the technology alongside traditional face-to-face meetings and class contact*. In this way, educators encourage learning by acting as a facilitator orchestrating the co-creation of understanding with learners and between learners. Educators build learners' into the curriculum design by giving learners control over parts of their learning environment; this includes creating learning-oriented assessment designs (Knight, 1995). This requires setting up the conditions such as the group, technology or blend, and to design learning activities which are divisible by the number of group members, and are inter-dependent (Doolan et al., 2006) which means each group member has a structured job to do and is more likely to encourage individuals to actively engage with learning (Biggs, 1990, 2003). Learners in a group must perceive that each member is responsible for the groups learning as a whole and accept the interdependency between the relationship and the overall success of the group (Lewin, 1951). This is embedded in learning designs that scaffold productive interactions and is achieved by encouraging learners to agree interaction rules that require learners themselves to monitor and regulate interactions. It is important to ensure that learners are adequately briefed and understand the role of the educator and the requirements of the learning activities. The educator role shifts from a didactic, instructive approach which sees the educator as an expert possessing and imparting knowledge; to one of a facilitator of learning. In this way, the educator and learners together engage in a dialogue and in partnership in the social construction of knowledge guided by the educator. This is illustrated in the *dialogic shamrock* presented in Fig. 2. This concept is known as social constructivism and explained later in this chapter.

The learning environment whether online, offline or a blend of both is perceived as one that is learner-centric and organic; growing and developing collectively with learners over time. The emphasis is on the development of curriculum designs that recognise the significant influence of learner-centric approaches. At best this involves a partnership approach between the educator and learner that purposely builds learners in as co-designers of curriculum with educators. At its elementary, the design of authentic learning activities by the educator provides opportunities for learners to engage in discourse, whilst working in groups, on real-world problems, relevant to practice and participate in an active learning environment situated in social contexts – class based, online or a blend of both.

The following section presents the context of changes currently taking place in higher education notably a gap between the educator and learner and between the use of technology in pre-and post-digital age generations in order to highlight the need for the *dialogic shamrock* pedagogical framework.

The Higher Education Landscape

As the sector adapts to social and technological changes in its own environment, at the same time the definition of what a learner is and what his or her needs are is changing (Cheese, 2008; Oblinger, 2005; Prensky, 2001). Each of these studies shows the perceptions of learners are changing within their own social context, as they engage with technological innovation and discover new ways to incorporate these changes into their lives. Advances in technological development have resulted in the introduction of technical infrastructure including managed learning environments (MLEs) and virtual learning environments (VLEs), now widely used in higher education. The design of these environments is developing and constantly evolving to accommodate changes in the higher education landscape. However, educational practice has been slower to respond to the pace of change, creating a gap between the educator and the learner that in turn may be failing to meet the expectations of this new generation of learners.

When referring to technology Biggs (2003, p. xi) posits

It has established a place in the normal delivery system of most universities, whether on or off campus.

Given the availability of the technological infrastructure, Sharpe, Benfield, and Francis (2006) assert that educators should now be thinking about how to use technology to support learners, particularly as it is prevalent in the lives of learners. Garrison and Anderson (2003) purport that those in higher education need to see the value technology brings to learning. They suggest it plays an increasingly important and key role in the educational experience within a higher education system. It is quite clear that technology is widely regarded and adds value to the educational experience; the technological infrastructure is in place in education, students are using it; it is a key component in higher education.

It is apparent, however, that there is a gap between how technology is used by the pre- and post-digital age generations. This is evident in the differences in actions and behaviours by the different generations whilst using technologies. For instance, digital learners frequently use electronic resources to support learning (Sharpe, Benfield, Lessner, & Decicco, 2005). It is not uncommon for the pre-digital age generation to print a document for amendment. Conversely, the post-digital age simply edits the document using the technology (Prensky, 2001). An overview of the different generational eras is shown in Table 1.

As illustrated in Table 1 'baby boomers' are described by Jones (1980) as those born in the post-war years between 1946 and 1964 and constitute the largest part of the population to fall outside of the natural technological mindset of the 'digital native' (Prensky, 2001). The digital native on the other hand has grown up with technology that is currently regarded as ubiquitous. Born since the very end of the 1980s, digital natives, generally speaking, find the use of technology such as computers, the Internet and mobile phones to be a far more natural experience. Coming from this background it has been stated, 'students today are all 'native speakers' of the digital language of computers, video games and the Internet' (Prensky, 2001, p. 1). Like digital native, the net generation (Oblinger, 2005), generation Y or the millennial generation (Cheese, 2008) are all terms for a demographic definition of people born between the mid-1970s and the early 2000s. The similarities between these are a generation familiar with the use of digital communications and technology. They see such devices as second

Table 1. Established Generational Eras.

Names	Birth Period	Reference
Baby boomers	1946–1959	Jones, 1980
Generation X	1960–1979	Coupland, 1991
Baby busters		
Generation Y	1975–2004	Cheese, 2008; Oblinger, 2005
Millennial generation		
Net generation		
Generation Z	1991–2012	Mitchell, 2008; Prensky, 2001
Digital natives		

nature as well as a natural extension of work and play. This generation see technology as an 'enabler', and are active information seekers with a need to undertake activities with immediacy, from anywhere, anyplace and at any time. However, although familiar with technology, the true concept of a naturalised digital native falls into the generation now beginning to enter higher education, those born since the Internet became widely available, the 1991 to 2012 born 'Generation Z' (Mitchell, 2008). As learners, generation Z are connected and personally equipped with the latest technologies such as mobile phones, personal digital assistants and wireless laptops and use these as a tool to support learning. 'They use the computer, the internet, and books simultaneously' (Canole, DeLaat, Dillon, & Darby, 2006, p. 6).

To contrast this, digital immigrants are 'those of us who were not born into the digital world but have, at some later point in our lives, become fascinated by and adopted many or most aspects of the new technology are, and always will be compared to them' (Prensky, 2001, p. 2). Thus, the digital immigrants like the baby boomers have witnessed the introduction of technologies such as the Internet. These have a far broader set of responses towards technology, from strong resistance to being as technologically immersive as a digital native, but they will always in some way retain their link to their own past in their engagement with technology. The digital immigrant and baby boomers can be seen as the opposite of the digital native, generation Y and the millennium generation. The gap between the educator and learner and the use of technology in pre- and post-digital age generations presents challenges as well as opportunities for educators whilst designing curriculum.

The Dialogic Shamrock Theoretical Literature

The key theoretical concepts from the literature underpinning the *dialogic shamrock* are presented and drawn from learner-centric, constructivist and sociocultural perspectives and related to the concepts of online learning and collaborative technology including Web 2.0 in higher education. The *dialogic shamrock* is then presented followed by examples of use.

Learning as a Sociocultural Dialogic Activity

Educator-centric traditional learning models are superseded by learner centric, and sociocultural models as they take their rightful place in the underpinning of collaborative learning (Doolan, 2006; Garrison, 2003; Garrison & Kanuka, 2004). Learner-centric models tend to have specific traits that focus on learning rather than teaching, with an emphasis on authentic context-specific learning such as solving 'real-world' problems, providing opportunities for learners to build their own understandings and skills. The learner-centric model in higher education places emphasis on the educator supporting learners as they socially construct knowledge (Vygotsky, 1978), collaboratively (Dillenbourg, 1999), in groups (Brown, 1998; Lewin, 1951; Thorley & Gregory, 1994); where learning is socially situated (Lave & Wenger, 1991) within a community of practice (Wenger, 1998). In this way, learning is not simply carried out by individuals but is socially constructed and situated, as, for instance, in a classroom. Participation is a key component in the acquisition of knowledge and takes place between educator and learner and learner and learner. Hence, the sociocultural model places emphasis on the fundamental role that social interaction plays in the process of learning and on the fact that social learning precedes development of higher order thinking, given that this takes place internally following the social interaction. According to Vygotsky (1978), people use mechanisms that develop from a culture, such as discourse, to mediate their social environments and to communicate, after which this development is internally build on.

Social Contructivism

Social constructivists (Vygotsky, 1978) argue that learners learn by constructing their own knowledge through active engagement and interactions with others. It is argued this is mediated by language in social discourse within a socialcultural context. Thus, knowledge acquisition is context dependent rather than abstract and general. Vygotskian theory stresses the role of social interaction in the development of cognition. In this way, learners construct their own personal meanings and develop knowledge through their engagements with other learners. Thus, the social constructivist argument makes clear that there is no one 'truth' since 'reality' and 'meaning' are dependent on the social context and this may be constructed, understood and interpreted differently given there are multiple 'truths' and 'realities' which are context dependent for the learner. A key component in Vygotskian theory is a tenet of the pedagogical framework in the *learning domain* shown in Fig. 1 comprising the collaborative, social and participative nature of learning, where the process of learning is situated in

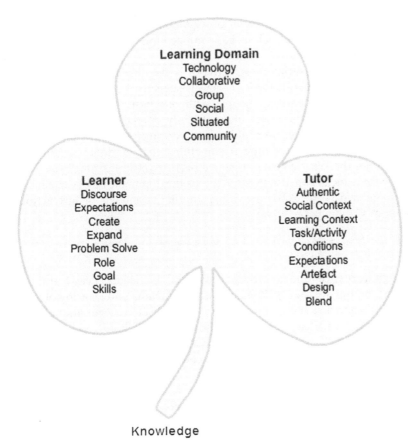

Knowledge

Fig. 1. The Dialogic Shamrock – Components of an Active Learning Environment.

social interactional contexts. Thus, learning activities should be designed specifically to stimulate active participation between and within groups, where dialogue and practical activity converge (Vygotsky, 1978, p. 24).

The Zone of Proximal Development Vygotsky (1978, p. 86) is defined as

> the distance between the actual developmental level as determined by independent problem solving and the level of potential development as determined through problem solving under adult guidance or in collaboration with more capable peers.

This concept was derived from the study of children; it was observed that children learnt more whilst engaged with other children, thus knowledge creation was found to be a social process and occurred within the zone of proximal development. This has implications for learners learning collaboratively.

The antithesis of social constructivism is the objectivist theoretical view (Jonassen, 1992; Lackoff, 1987). This view suggests there is only 'one' reality that exists independently of people with one basis of realism. Thus, the meaning of the world exists independently of the human mind and is external to the knower. An objectivist educator believes in driving the learning process as if teaching is something that is 'done' to the learner rather than the learner being an active participant in learning.

However, social constructivism remains the dominant theory in education (Beetham & Sharpe, 2007) providing alternative models of instruction by (Bonk & Cunningham, 1998)

> placing the emphasis on guiding and supporting learners to understand the communities of which they are a part (1998, p. 27)

through learner centred and sociocultural activity. Hence, deep learning and understandings are the result of a culture in teaching and learning of a social context comprising social interactions, and collective negotiations through participations with learners and educator whilst collaboratively constructing knowledge which is reinforced internally when an individual learner is learning alone, such as when studying course materials.

Authentic Learning

Whilst shifting the emphasis from educator-centric to learner-centric models of teaching and learning, there is a need for the educator to anchor such learning practice in authentic 'real-world' learning contexts (Cohen & Ellis, 2002; Gupta, 2004). For learning to occur, activities need to be set in a meaningful context which is plausible to the student and presented to engage the student (Biggs, 1999, 2003; Canole, 2002) and the activities need to be highly authentic, interactive and collaborative (Doolan et al., 2006) and designed to involve learners in problem solving, seeking integration between components, between learning activities and playing with ideas as illustrated in the *tutor* leaf in Fig. 1. The educator creates these conditions through the learning design which embeds learning activities where learners are required to actively participate in meaningful contexts. In this way, in social learning contexts authentic learning places emphasis on learners working in groups on real-world problems relevant to practice to help learners make sense and make meaning of their learning (Duffy & Cunningham, 1996). Dewey (1916) posits that learners learn through engagement with real activities. Thus, learners engage in learning when learning activities involve active participation and have meaning.

Race (1994) reinforces this theory through *the wanting, doing, feedback, digesting* model. These aspects interrelate and suggest that learners are not passive receivers of information and that there is a need for practical application in terms of wanting to engage in learning, doing 'something', receiving feedback on what has been done to 'the something' and digesting and assimilating the feedback in order for learning to occur. Piaget (1970) emphasises that conceptual development is achieved in learners through intellectual activity and found that children construct knowledge through activity and practice as opposed to simply absorbing information; thus, learners develop knowledge through doing. Attention must be paid to the learners' activity' seeing learning as a process of guided construction of knowledge and cognitive processing (Goodyear, Asensio, Jones, Hodgson, & Steeples, 2000). By this Goodyear means the acquisition of new concepts, ways of thinking, the development of skills and knowledge resulting in a changed behaviour and new ways of thinking. This view is supported by Vygotsky (1978) for whom cognitive processes are developed through active engagement and interactions with others; this maybe an educator and/or a learner.

Collaborative Learning

Collaborative learning is defined as a *situation in which two or more' people learn or attempt to learn something together* Dillenbourg (1999, p. 1). Each key component of the definition is described by Dillenbourg (1999, p. 1) as

> two or more may be interpreted as a pair, a small group (3–5 subjects), a class (20–30 subjects), a community (a few hundreds or thousands of people), a society (several thousands or millions of people) ... and all intermediate levels.

What is clear in Dillenbourgs' work is that collaborative learning provides the opportunity for students to work together in groups, share ideas and to engage in discussing problem solving and critical thinking (Dillenbourg, 1999). Thus, collaborative learning is distinctive in creating opportunities for learners to work together in groups. Collaborative learning in online collaborative learning communities has been shown to engage learners in knowledge sharing, to provide support, provide an environment where learners can depend on another, negotiate and manage their own learning needs (Doolan, 2006, 2011a). Similarly Hiltz and Wellman (1997) argue that collaborative learning involves learners who are active and interactive. The argument is made that, through these actions and interactions, learners learn effectively through collective intellectual debate and discussion. Hiltz and Wellman's work used an asynchronous conferencing system where students were engaged in postings and responding to postings. In this work, they argue that learners learnt by understanding each other's point of view whilst articulating their own.

Given the preceding discussion, it seems reasonable, therefore, to suggest that collaborative learning be used as a means to learn in classrooms and beyond, given its application to social practices which are widely applicable, for example, in small group discussions, whole class discussions, then between the class and the educator in the classroom and beyond. Situated in these contexts collaborative learning supports a common action, mutual intellectual negotiation, the potential for collective decision making and that, through these, learners acquire knowledge and skills. Yet, in higher education, dominant theories of learning in the 21st century retain the notion of educator as transmitter and mediator of information (Biggs, 1989, 1997, 2003).

Additionally, collaborative learning is discouraged due to concerns relating to plagiarism (Bruffee, 1973; Bower & Richards, 2006), unfair distribution of work and difficulties in attributing marks to individuals within groups (Bower & Richards, 2006). Peer assessment (Brown & Knight, 1994) can play a significant part in collaborative learning such as a group presentation of shared artefact. At times academics perceive group work as a means to deal with growing student numbers and reduced resources (Thorley & Gregory, 1994). That said, it is clear that collaborative learning provides the opportunity for learners to work together in groups, share ideas and to engage in discussing problem solving and critical thinking (Dillenbourg, 1999), and therefore socially construct knowledge (Vygotsky, 1978). Collaborative learning over the decades has been shown to enable individuals to participate actively and meaningfully in group learning (Bruffee, 1973; Dillenbourg, 1999; Lewin, 1951), deep and meaningful learning through active engagement with learning (Biggs, 1990, 2003; Cohen & Ellis, 2002). Collaborative learning (Dillenbourg, 1991, p. 5)

is not one single mechanism; if one talks about **learning from collaboration** one should also talk **about learning from being alone** (emphasis through bold added).

Community Learning

Synonymous with collaborative learning is community of practice theory which is built on Vygotsky (1978) social learning theory that supports the notion that knowledge acquisition is through participation with others. The community of practice theory further builds on situated learning theory (Lave & Wenger, 1991) which views learning as embedded within social activity, social context and a social culture. Thus, communities of practice essentially practice social learning in social experiences where meaning is constructed and formed through dialogic negotiations with others through these social experiences within the community of practice. These negotiated meanings are formed through participation where participators actually take part and relate to others in the community of practice. The practice exists where

> people are engaged in actions whose meanings they negotiate with one another. (Wenger, 1998, p. 73)

Wenger (1998) suggests communities of practice are a part of peoples' everyday lives from the home, family to the workplace including educational settings. *Communities of practice are everywhere* (Wenger 1998, p. 6) and the communities we belong to throughout life will change over time. These communities can be small, for example, a group, or large such as a university. Thus, the community in the community of practice implies learning is social, involves mutual engagement and respect and a willingness to share; interaction is a necessity to keep the community alive, one that is open in nature and open to questioning. According to Wenger (1998) within communities of practice there is a sense of belonging amongst participants where trust and goodwill are shared in the community. Wenger (1998) argues that communities develop over time a developed culture, characteristics, beliefs, shared practice, assumptions, rituals, behaviours and roles that define the community.

In the community of practice concept, Wenger's work talks of practice within the community as developed over time, shared and maintained by engagement in knowledge and in the sharing of ideas and artefact such as rules, technology, products, documents, ideas, stories and crucially knowledge. Hence, Wenger (1998) argues that through the community of practice knowledge development is promoted through sharing and as a result helps community members to develop skills such as problem solving. The community of practice is defined by Wenger, McDermott, and Snyder (2002, p. 4) as a group of people

who share a concern, a set of problems, or a passion about a topic, and who deepen their
knowledge and expertise in this area by interacting on an on-going basis.

Importantly the purpose of community of practice is to share, create,
expand and exchange knowledge through participation with others who
may help to advance individual knowledge and skills (Lave & Wenger, 1991;
Vygostky, 1978; Wenger, McDermott, & Synder, 2002).
  Additionally, a community of practice may comprise

project teams, to accomplish a specified task, belonging to people who have direct role in
accomplishing the task, the boundary is defined as clear, what holds the community of
practice together is the project goals and milestones. Such a community of practice has a
predetermined ending related to the project completion. (Wenger, 1998, p. 42)

Thus, the community of practice concept is supported by group learning
(Lewin, 1951) and collaborative learning (Dillenbourg, 1999) theory. The
concept of collaborative teams as communities of practice to solve authentic
problems is reported by Wick (2000). A study was conducted which related
to groups of professionals who completed similar tasks and shared the tasks
through communicating within and across groups to cross-fertilise expertise
in order to promote learning. In this way, this makes concrete Wenger's
(1998) notion of groups as communities of practice.
  To summarise the argument thus far, the use of learning as a sociocultural
activity is seen as the interrelationship between the theories critiqued thus
far, that of knowledge acquisition, social, group, collaborative, situated,
cultural and authentic learning and through active engagement in learning
that knowledge is socially constructed as shown in Fig. 2. This view is
supported by Lave and Wenger (1991), Wenger (1998), Wenger et al. (2002),
Vygotsky (1978), Dillenbourg (1999), Lewin (1951), Brown (1998) and
Thorley and Gregory (1994). The social paradigm built on in the *dialogic
shamrock* presented in Fig. 2 views the social and cultural context of
learning as crucial and a central tenet of learning itself. It is argued that
learning occurs through participation, negotiation and a dialogue with
others whilst situated in the context of learning in groups through learning
activities using technology. The learning supports learners taking part in
authentic learning activities to develop knowledge and skills facilitated by
the educator in class and by each other out of class. Learning takes place
using technology such as a discussion forum, blog, wiki and/or podcast,
although not limited to these; and class-based setting which is purposely
built to support learners in undertaking learning activities and may be
driven by assessment designs (Biggs, 1989, 1997, 2003, Doolan, 2011a) to
bring authenticity to learning (Gupta, 2004). Dillenbourg (1999) cautions

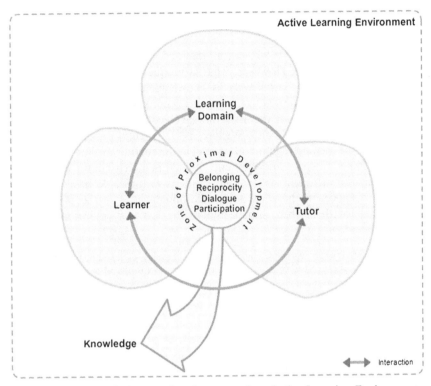

Fig. 2. The Dialogic Shamrock – Outcome of an Active Learning Environment.

that in collaborative learning learners are expected to interact, and that this may not occur without guidance. Thus, the role of the educator shifts to one of a facilitator of learning; this is a key to guide the learning process off line and online as explained earlier in this chapter.

Situated Learning

Based on Vygotsky's (1978) argument that knowledge is socially constructed, situated learning theory by Lave and Wenger (1991) posits that learning is situated in context and occurs as a result of participation or engagement in social relationships and activity with others. The authors ask the question what kinds of social engagement provide the proper context for learning to take place. (1991, p. 14)

Similar to Vygoktsy's work, social interaction is a key component of situated learning theory. However, what is uniquely different is that, rather than looking at learning cognitively as knowledge construction, it is argued that co-participation is the key to the acquisition of knowledge – a view shared by the collaborative learning theorists. Similar to collaborative learning theory, situated learning theory (Lave & Wenger, 1991) is based on the premise that learning is in the coming together of people, in the conditions that bring people together, situated in space and time and situated in activity in the context and learning environment and in the conversations that people have with each other, for instance, in the classroom. Additionally it is in the observations people make of themselves, others and in the learning environment. They further purport that a

persons' intentions to learn are engaged and the meaning of learning is configured through the process of becoming a full participant in a socio cultural practice. (Lave & Wenger, p. 29)

The argument in Lave and Wenger's work sees learners engaged through participations with others in a community of practice. This view is supported by Wenger (1998), and Wenger et al. (2002) and (Vygotsky, 1978) who argue that learning is socially construed through a sociocultural activity where learning occurs through participations with others and where knowledge is embedded in the situated context. This is supported by collaborative learning theory which views learners working together socially in the context of groups, sharing ideas, and engaging in intellectual negotiations, discussions, problem solving and critical thinking skills (Dillenbourg, 1999).

Lave and Wenger (1991) further offer that learning in addition to being social is continuously evolving and renewed dependent on one's view of the world and actions engaged in within the sociocultural environment. Thus, learning community theory is not only situated in a social practice, rather learning occurs through meaningful engagement with other participants in the social context.

Lave and Wenger (1991) and Wenger (1998) present an analytical view. They shift the focus on learning from the individual such as in one's head to the participation in and with the social world. In this way it can be perceived as the zone of proximal development (Vygotsky, 1978). As it applies to Lave and Wenger's (1991) work, facilitation by peers promotes knowledge development through collaborations, participation and peer interaction.

This aligns with the community of practice concept (Wenger, 1998) where the argument is made that peer interaction, mutual engagement, negotiation, co-participation and co-construction are key to the development of community knowledge and at the same time the development of individual members' knowledge. With this in mind, community knowledge develops through mutual engagement or collaborations (Dillenbourg, 1991) as individual knowledge develops (Bielaczyc & Collins, 1999).

Collaborative learning and situated learning theory is synonymous. The *dialogic shamrock* in Figs. 1 and 2 views learning through the relationships and conditions that bring learners together, in and out of the classroom, through collaboratively engaging in groups to complete learning activities, situated in authentic contexts simulating 'real-world' experience, which encourage learners to practically apply taught material to develop the required knowledge and skills. Additionally, learning is encouraged through social interaction and collaboration in and beyond the classroom such as whilst engaging with peers using a wiki provided to support the collaborative experience. Social interaction and collaboration are both essential components of situated learning theory (Lave & Wenger, 1991).

The Dialogic Shamrock

The pedagogical framework for collaborative learning through technology in Fig. 1 is a synthesis of the literature critiqued earlier in this chapter based on the learner centric, constructivist and sociocultural perspectives. The pedagogical framework was developed and tested and evidenced in the educator practice of using a blend of Web 2.0 technology (comprising a wiki, blog, podcast and the university MLE) and face to face learning experiences to support collaborative learning. Evidence of the impact on student engagement and learning is presented alongside examples of use. The resultant co-construction of knowledge is illustrated in Fig. 2.

The pedagogical framework in Fig. 1 illustrates *the dialogic shamrock* bearing three leaves *learning domain*, *learner* and *tutor* which are interconnected. In this framework the tutor is the *educator*.

Fig. 1 details the components of curriculum design and pedagogical practice to engage learners in collaborative and community learning and learners as participators in curriculum design whilst learning is situated in a blended and social context. The pedagogical framework presented is not prescriptive rather intended to act as a guide for educators to use a blend of technology and class based activities to engage learners in collaborative social learning contexts.

The *learning domain* encompasses a learning environment that comprises collaborative, group, social, situated, community learning and technology. The technology is used to supplement, not replace, class based learning; thus, learning is in a blended mode. The *learner* engages in shared learning in and out of class through the development of a repertoire of shared and mutually agreed artefacts between learners and educator, such as co-produced and co-authored documents and media such as audio and video. The learning activities are set by the educator to promote interaction, participation, and collaboration with the learning domain, learners and the educator. The *tutor domain* represented in the *dialogic shamrock* in Fig. 1; view the educator as one who initially designs the conditions for learning and evolves based on learner participations and interactions with the learning domain. In this way reciprocity is between the educator, learner and the learning domain in a collaborative blended learning context.

The context provides a learning resource for learners that is progressively and continually added to and reviewed with peers and educators as learning progresses. Learners are perceived as a valuable resource as co-producers of content. Learning in this way is supported by technology in a blended learning mode. This is achieved by designing curriculum and engagement in pedagogical practices comprising some of the key components outlined in Fig. 1. It is argued that designs for learning that encourage participation, reciprocity and mutual engagements whilst learners are engaged in an active learning experience, knowledge is co-constructed as shown in Fig. 2.

The Dialogic Shamrock–Examples in Practice

An in-house built, university wide MLE was introduced at the University of Hertfordshire in the UK in 2001. This introduction was in response to the changes in the higher education landscape as alluded to earlier in this chapter. The potential of the MLE to set up and manage group working online was investigated and a comparison was made between the group based experiences online and face-to-face traditional group working (Doolan, 2004; Doolan & Barker, 2005). These two studies highlighted the need for a more learner-centred technology; one that enabled learners and educators alike to develop content rather than the MLE that was predominately used as 'shovel ware' to post notes, news items, and learning materials. The discussion facilities did support out-of-class dialogue;

however, this was limited to 'post and respond'; hence, the move to the exploration of a wiki, offering the ability to co-author and co-construct dynamic learning environments to support collaborative learning and a sense of belonging to a community (Doolan, 2006, 2007a, 2007c, 2010, Wenger, 1998). The wiki concept was born in 1995 by Bo Leuf and Ward Cunningham (Leuf & Cunningham, 2001). A wiki is an example of one of a group of social networking technologies known as Web 2.0.

As a result of this work the 'Collaborative Learning Through Assessment and Technology' (CLAT) pedagogical model (Doolan, 2011b) was developed. This model clarifies the role of the educator in enabling collaborative learning through assessment designs using Web 2.0 technologies. CLAT supports a blended learning framework; that combines learning activities online with traditional practices supplemented by class-based learning activities what was found to be a key role for the educator was facilitating student ownership, empowerment and engagement in fostering a learning community. A natural progression from this work was the study of the effectiveness of the wiki for creating a sense of community (Wenger, 1998) amongst ninety-six learners studying the second year of a BSc combined modular degree programme whilst engaged in group-based assessed activities (Doolan, 2006, 2011a, 2011b). Results showed that learners valued the experience of using a wiki in fostering a learning community and highlighted that both people and task aspects of learning design are important when considering the design of a blended online and face-to-face group based experience. From those who were people-focused there was a concern expressed relating to the lack of visual cues.

In response to these concerns in 2006 a multi-mode collaborative student learning environment was developed incorporating wiki, blogs, podcasts and video (Doolan, 2006, 2007a, 2007b, 2008, 2009, 2010, 2011a). In this way, blogs have been used to support constructivist and social learning with second-year students studying Information Systems. Essentially, a blog is authored solely by one person; however, it allows for others to make comments on the author's posts. Blogs can be useful to capture reflections on learner's experiences of using social media. Doolan (2004) and Doolan and Barker (2005) undertook content analysis on 111 blogs and related themes specifically to theoretical and practical concepts relating to the student experience and collaborative learning supported by technology. In later work, Doolan (2009, 2010, 2011a, 2011b) undertook content analysis on 96 and 60 student blogs respectively. Blogs are predominately texted based. In contrast, podcasts are audio files and has been shown to engage learners in constructive learning on a multimedia module in Computer Science at the University of Hertfordshire (Barker, 2007).

Additionally podcasting has been used at the University of Hertfordshire as part of a large UK JISC funded project (Stewart & Doolan, 2008) with law students engaged in collaborative experiences to support authenticity in professional learning by using audio to simulate real-world scenarios. Recordings were produced in class by learners following their study of an audio recording provided by the educator to prepare for the in-class learning activities. Results from this study showed that, as staff became more proficient and confident, they were keen to explore new ways of supporting learners in the practice of collaborative learning and shifting more emphasis onto the learner to become more of a facilitator of learning. This study showed that the educator role progressively changed from didactic to a facilitator of learning following the appropriate and timely support from a student mentor. The study also found the need to provide one-to-one support for educators to use the technology and to adapt the technology to suit the learning and teaching context.

Doolan and Simpson (2010) investigated the use of audio in the Business school at the University of Hertfordshire. In the first instance students were required to record a group discussion based on their reading of a peer-reviewed journal article. Learners were then required to edit their audio recording to submit as part of the assessment. The stipulation by the educator on time was six to eight minutes. This was intended to help with managing marking the assessment. In collaborating to create this audio file, the educator reflected that the students seemed to put more work into preparing this presentation than in previous years when audio was not used. The educator reported that the use of audio as a learning tool to support the assessment was more effective than in previous years when audio was not used.

However, the second use of audio with 280 students to provide feedback on assessment was problematic. The educator managed to record feedback for 50 students. Problems were encountered in getting assessment feedback to students. Using the institutional MLE and the Business school's feedback forms in conjunction with recording feedback was time consuming and awkward. Using MP3 recorders to record the assessment feedback meant that educators could not easily identify which student the recording related to, and in the end they had to stop between each recording, upload and name the audio file provided by the learner to the educators' personal computers. Therefore, it was deemed important when using audio in this way, to be provided with the appropriate resources to help educators to choose the most appropriate recording device and to find a fast and efficient way of identifying and sending the assessment feedback to students.

Stewart and Doolan (2008) examined the use of audio to record and transmit speech, to support, enhance and personalise the learner experience at two UK universities, namely the University of Bradford and the University of Hertfordshire. The project explored and evaluated the use of audio in three key areas of teaching and learning: self-reflection and self-assessment, formative and summative feedback, and collaborative learning and within some of the new and emerging technologies such as wikis and social networking spaces to support teaching and learning. The project studied a diverse range of learners: undergraduate and postgraduate, campus learners and distance learners across different disciplines including Health Studies, Management, Optometry, Computing, Accountancy and Law. The project led to modification and refinement of learning and teaching practices in the six disciplines across both institutions. The studies showed that audio as part of a blend with face-to-face learning was a powerful tool, providing opportunities for personalising learning, promoting greater student engagement, and encouraging creativity.

In introducing audio into their practice, lecturers reported that they had the opportunity to reflect on their pedagogical approaches and learning design, which helped whilst adopting new and innovative ways to enable their students to be more actively involved in the learning process. Using audio for assessment feedback, lecturers reported a more personal and richer feedback experience to students and audio use was found to increase the level of interaction and dialogue amongst students and between students and lecturers. Audio was found to encourage wider and deeper self-reflection in students, and was shown to improve learners' communication skills.

However, the impact of audio to support student self-assessment was not clearly identified from the findings of the study. It was reported that most students found the process of self-assessment difficult and audio did not make this any easier.

The preceding works influenced and tested the pedagogical framework presented in Fig. 1 and led to the designs of curriculum which enable both learners and educators to jointly co-develop content. This practice tapped into the potential of learners as a 'valuable learning resource' rather than relying solely on the expertise of the educator. In this way, learners and educators can engage in the co-creation of learning resources such as audio, video, documents and presentations. To this end, the sharing of content enables a shared repertoire (Wenger, 1998) and a repository of socially constructed knowledge to be developed. In so doing, these may be used as a learning repository to share and receive feedback on assessment or any aspect of the curriculum whilst engaged in collaborative learning. From these a learning resource can be collectively created to revisit year on year (Doolan, 2006, 2007a, 2009, 2010).

CONCLUSION

The *dialogic* shamrock places emphasis on learner-centric models in higher education which supports the notion of learner as participant in curriculum design. This places the focus on the educator and the learner together to socially construct knowledge. It is argued that learning requires active participation, in a social participatory context, is not an isolated activity rather is encouraged through active engagement with others learner and educator in collaborative, situated contexts which take place in and out of the class room. This may be supported by technology. Although learning resides with the learner, the educator has a role to play in designing for learning that is authentic, situated in context and social in nature.

The social paradigm built on in the *dialogic shamrock* presented in Figs. 1 and 2 views the social and cultural context of learning as crucial and a central tenet of learning itself. It is argued that learning occurs through participation, negotiation and a dialogue with others (learner and educator) whilst situated in the context of learning in groups through learning activities in and out of class. The learning supports learners taking part in authentic learning activities to develop knowledge and skills facilitated by the educator in class and by learners out of class. The examples presented in this chapter illustrated learning in a blended context using technology such as a discussion forum, blog, wiki and podcast, although not limited to these; and class based setting which were purposely built to support learners in undertaking learning activities to bring authenticity to learning. This required a shift in the educator role to a facilitator of learning; this is a key to guide the learning process off line and online as explained in this chapter.

What is shared between the learning theories discussed and related to the *dialogic shamrock* is the agreement that learning resides with the learner, not the educator and that learning is promoted by curriculum design that recognises the significance of learner-centric approaches. At best – a partnership approach that purposely builds learners in as co-designers of learning with educators. At its elementary the design of authentic learning activities providing opportunities for learners to engage in discourse in active learning environments situated in social contexts which may involve Web 2.0 technologies such as wiki, blogs and podcasts.

The pedagogical framework has been shown through the examples of use presented; to encourage contact between educator and learners and between learners, to develop reciprocity and co-operation and a sense of belonging amongst learners and between learners and educators. The emphasis of the *dialogic shamrock* presented is on a partnership approach which involves engagement in a dialogue between all parties in the practice of teaching and learning. It was shown though the examples of use that the outcome of student engagement in an active learning environment is co-constructed knowledge as illustrated in Fig. 2.

Indeed, it is argued by creating an active learning environment that the proximal zone between the learner, learning domain and educator as shown in Fig. 2 leads to the zone of proximal development. This is evidenced through the discourse needed to complete the learning activities designed by the educator; social in nature and situated in the practices outlined in the learning domain as shown in Fig. 1. The educator has a role to play in making explicit their learning and teaching approach to encourage a reciprocal relationship between the educator and learners. In this way, learners are encouraged through the learning design to practice social learning situated in collaborative contexts. The *dialogic shamrock* is built on the premise that the underlying teaching philosophy used by the tutor that of social learning highlights that learning is not static; rather involves engagement, participation and a dialogue with others.

REFERENCES

Barker, T. (2007). Podcasting in an advanced computer science module: Supporting constructive learning. *Proceedings of the 6th European Conference on e-learning*, 4–5 October. Copenhagen, Denmark: Copenhagen Business School.

Beetham, H., & Sharpe, R. (2007). *Rethinking pedagogy for a digital age: Designing and delivering e-learning*. New York, NY: Routledge.

Bielaczyc, K., & Collins, A. (1999). Learning communities in classrooms: A reconceptualization of educational practice. In C. M. Reigeluth (Ed.), *Instructional-design theories and models: A new paradigm of instructional theory* (Vol. 2, pp. 269–292). Mahwah, NJ: Erlbaum.

Biggs, J. B. (1989). Approaches to the enhancement of tertiary teaching. *Higher Education Research and Development, 8*, 7–25.

Biggs, J. B. (1990). *Asian students approaches to learning: Implications for teaching overseas students*. Paper presented at the 8th Australasian tertiary learning skills and language conference, July. Australia: Queensland University of. Technology, pp. 11–13.

Biggs, J. (1997). Teaching across and within cultures: The issue of international students. In R. Murray-Harvey & H. C. Silins (Eds.), *Learning and teaching in higher education: Advancing international perspectives–Proceedings of the Higher Education Research and Development Society of Australasia Conference* (pp. 1–22), 8–11 July, Flinders University Press, Adelaide.

Biggs, J. (1999). What the student does: Teaching for enhanced learning. *Higher Education Research & Development*, *18*(1), 57–75.

Biggs, J. B. (2003). *Aligning teaching for constructive learning*. York: The Higher Education Academy Press.

Bonk, C. J., & Cunningham, D. J. (1998). Searching for learner-centered, constructivist, and sociocultural components of collaborative educational learning tools. In C. J. Bonk & K. S. King (Eds.), *Electronic collaborators: Learner-centered technologies for literacy, apprenticeship, and discourse* (pp. 25–50). Mahwah, NJ: Erlbaum.

Bower, M., & Richards, D. (2006). Collaborative learning: Some possibilities and limitations for students and educators. In *Proceedings of the conference for the Australasian Society for Computers in Learning in Tertiary Education (ASCILITE'06)* (pp. 79–89), December, Sydney University Press, Sydney.

Brown, S. (1998). Re-inventing the university. *ALT-J*, *6*(3), 30–37.

Brown, S., & Knight, P. (1994). *Assessing learners in higher education*. London: Kogan Page.

Bruffee, K. A. (1973). Collaborative learning: Some practical models. *College English*, *34*(5), 634–643.

Canole, G. (2002). The evolving landscape of learning technology. *Association for Learning Technology Journal (ALT-J)*, *10*(3), 4–18.

Canole, G., DeLaat, M., Dillon, T., & Darby, J. (2006). *JISC student experiences of technologies*. Final Report. OpenBusiness. London: JISC

Cheese, P. (2008, March 13). *Netting the net generation* [Online]. *Bloomberg Businessweek: Companies & Industries*. Retrieved from http://www.businessweek.com/managing/content/mar2008/ca20080313_241443.htm?

Cohen, M. S., & Ellis, T. J. (2002). Developing a criteria set for an online learning environment. In *Proceedings frontiers in education, annual 2002* (pp. T3E-8–T3E-13). 6-9 November, Boston, IEEE, Piscataway, NJ.

Coupland, D. (1991). *Generation X: Tales for an accelerated culture*. New York, NY: St. Martin's Press.

Dewey, J. (1916). *Democracy and education: An introduction to the philosophy of education*. New York, NY: Macmillan.

Dillenbourg, P. (1991). Human-computer collaborative learning. Doctoral dissertation. Department of Computing, University of Lancaster, Lancaster, UK.

Dillenbourg, P. (1999). What do you mean by collaborative learning? In P. Dillenbourg (Ed.), *Collaborative learning: Cognitive and computational approaches. Advances in learning and instruction series* (pp. 1–19). Oxford: Elsevier.

Doolan, M. A. (2004). An empirical study evaluating the use of a managed learning environment to support group work: A comparative study. *Computer Aided Assessment*, September 2004. Loughborough: Loughborough University.

Doolan, M. A. (2006). Effective strategies for building a learning community online using wiki. *Proceedings of the 1st annual blended learning conference 2006* (pp. 51–63), 15 June.

Hatfield, Hertfordshire: University of Hertfordshire [Online]. Retrieved from http://homepages.stca.herts.ac.uk/~ct07abf/comqmad/publications/download/2006/Doolan-2006-Effective_strategies_for_building_a_learning_community_online_using_a_wiki.pdf

Doolan, M. A. (2007a). Collaborative working: Wiki and the creation of a sense of community. *Proceeding of the 2nd international blended learning conference 2007*, 14 June (pp. 72–85), University of Hertfordshire, Hatfield, Hertfordshire[Online]. Retrieved from http://homepages.stca.herts.ac.uk/~ct07abf/comqmad/publications/download/2007/Doolan-2007-Collaborative%20working_Wiki_and_the_creation_of_a_sense_of_community.pdf

Doolan, M. A. (2007b). Our learners are the net generation growing up in a digital world. How then do we engage with and support this type of learner? In D. Remenyi (Ed.), *Proceedings of the 6th European conference on e-learning, 4–5 October* (pp. 159–172), Copenhagen Business School, Copenhagen, Denmark. Retrieved from http://homepages.stca.herts.ac.uk/~ct07abf/comqmad/publications/download/2007/Doolan-2007-Our_Learners_are_the_Net_Generation_Growing_up_in_a_Digital_World.pdf

Doolan, M. A. (2007c). Setting up online collaborative learning groups using wiki technology – a educators' guide. *SEDA Staff Development Magazine*, 8.2. Retrieved from http://homepages.stca.herts.ac.uk/~ct07abf/comqmad/publications/download/2007/Doolan-2007-Setting_up_online_collaborative_learning_groups_using_Wiki_technology_-_a_tutors_guide.pdf

Doolan, M. A. (2008). Bridging the gap: Adapting curriculum design and teaching practice to engage the net generation learner in an online learning community *Proceedings of the 3rd annual blended learning conference 2008*, 18–19 June. University of Hertfordshire, Hatfield.

Doolan, M. A. (2009). Making the tacit explicit: Developing a pedagogy using Web 2.0 to engage the net generation learner. In *ICERI 2009*, November, ICERI, Madrid.

Doolan, M. A. (2010). Developing a Web 2.0 pedagogy to engage the net generation learner in a community for learning in higher education. In *The fifth international blended learning conference: "Developing Blended Learning Communities"*, 16-17 June, University of Hertfordshire, Hatfield, Hertfordshire.

Doolan, M. A. (2011a). The role of the tutor: Preparing learners to engage in collaborative learning using a wiki as part of a blend. *Proceedings of the Ed-Media World conference on education, mulitimedia, hypermedia and telecommunications*, Ed-Media, Lisbon, Portugal.

Doolan, M. A. (2011b). Developing a pedagogy: The role of the tutor in enabling student learning through the use of a wiki. In C. Wankel (Ed.), *Educating educators with social media* (pp. 189–206). Bingley, UK: Emerald Group.

Doolan, M. A., & Barker, T. (2005). Evaluation of computing students performance using group based learning online and offline. In *Proceedings of the 9th CAA international computer assisted assessment conference 2005*, 5-6 July. Loughborough University, Leicestershire [Online]. Retrieved from http://homepages.stca.herts.ac.uk/~ct07abf/comqmad/publications/download/2005/Doolan-Barker-2005-Evaluation_of_computing_students_performance_using_group_based_learning_online_and_offline.pdf

Doolan, M. A., & Simpson, M. (2010). Engaging tutors and learners through audio supported pedagogy. In: *Proceedings of the 5th annual blended learning conference 2010*, 16-17 June, University of Hertfordshire, Hatfield, Hertfordshire. Retrieved from http://homepages.stca.herts.ac.uk/~ct07abf/comqmad/publications/download/2010/Doolan-Simpson-2010-Engaging_tutors_and_learners_through_audio_supported_pedagogy.pdf

Doolan, M. A., Thornton, H. A., & Hilliard, A. (2006). Collaborative learning: Using technology for fostering those valued practices inherent in constructive environments in traditional education. *Journal for the Enhancement of Learning and Teaching, 3*(2), Retrieved from http://homepages.stca.herts.ac.uk/~ct07abf/comqmad/publications/download/2006/Doolan-Hilliard-Thornton-2006-Collaborative_learning_using_technology_for_fostering_those_valued_practices_inherent_in_constructive_environments_in_traditional_education.pdf

Duffy, T. M., & Cunningham, D. J. (1996). Constructivism: Implications for the design and delivery of instruction. In D. H. Jonassen (Ed.), *Educational communications and technology* (pp. 170–199). New York, NY: Simon & Schuster Macmillan.

Garrison, D. R. (2003). Cognitive presence for effective asynchronous online learning: The role of reflective inquiry, self-direction and metacognition. *Elements of Quality Online Education: Practice and Direction, 4*, 47–58.

Garrison, D. R., & Anderson, T. (2003). *E-learning in the 21st century: A framework for research and practice*. London: Routledge Falmer.

Garrison, D. R., & Kanuka, H. (2004). Blended learning: Uncovering its transformative potential in Higher Education. *The Internet and Higher Education, 7*(2), 95–105.

Garrison, D. R., & Vaughan, N. D. (2007). *Blended learning in higher education: Framework, principles, and guidelines*. San Francisco, CA: Jossey-Bass.

Goodyear, P., Asensio, M., Jones, C., Hodgson, V., & Steeples, C. (2000). Relationships between conceptions of learning, approaches to study and students' judgements about the value of their experiences of networked learning. *Association for Learning Technology Journal, 11*(1), 17–27.

Gupta, M. L. (2004). Enhancing student performance through collaborative learning in physical sciences. *Assessment and Evaluation in Higher Education, 29*(1), 63–73.

Hiltz, S. R., & Wellman, B. (1997). Asynchronous learning networks as a learning classroom. *Communications of the ACM, 40*(9), 44–49.

Jonassen, D. H. (1992). Objectivism versus constructivism: Do we need a new philosophical paradigm? *Educational Technology Research and Development, 39*(3), 5–14.

Jones, L. (1980). *Great expectations: America and the baby boom generation*. New York, NY: Coward, McCann and Geoghegan.

Knight, P. (1995). *Assessment for learning*. Oxfordshire, UK: RoutledgeFalmer.

Lackoff, G. (1987). *Women fire, and dangerous things*. Chicago, IL: University of Chicago Press.

Lave, J., & Wenger, E. (1991). *Situated learning legitimate peripheral participation*. Cambridge: Cambridge University Press.

Leuf, B., & Cunningham, W. (2001). *The wiki way quick collaboration on the web*. Boston, MA: Addison-Wesley.

Lewin, K. (1951). *Field theory in social science*. New York, NY: Harper and Row.

Mitchell, D. A. (2008). Generation Z–striking the balance: Healthy doctors for a healthy community. *Australian Family Physician, 37*(8), 665–667. Retrieved from http://www.ncbi.nlm.nih.gov/pubmed/18704218

Oblinger, D. (2005). Learners learning and technology: The Educause learning initiative. *Educause Review, 40*(5), 66–75.

Piaget, J. (1970). Piaget's theory. In P. H. Mussen (Ed.), *Carmichael's manual of child psychology* (pp. 703–772). New York, NY: Wiley.

Prensky, M. (2001). Digital natives, digital immigrants. *On the Horizon, 9*(5), 1–6.

Race, P. (1994). *The open learning handbook: Promoting quality in designing and delivering flexible learning.* London: Kogan Page.

Sharpe, R., Benfield, G., & Francis, R. (2006). Implementing a university e-learning strategy: Levers for change within academic schools'. *ALT-J, 14*(2), 135–151.

Sharpe, R., Benfield, G., Lessner, E., & Decicco, E. (2005). *Study for the pedagogy strand of the JISC e-learning programme.* Retrieved from http://www.jisc.ac.uk/uploaded_documents/scoping%20study%20final%20report%20v4.1.doc

Stewart, W., & Doolan, M. A. (2008). Listen to this: Enhancing the learner experience through the use of audio within next generation technologies. *Proceedings of HEA annual conference,* 1–3 July, HEA, Harrogate.

Thorley, L., & Gregory, R. (1994). *Using group based learning in higher education.* London: Kogan Page.

Vygotsky, L. S. (1978). *Mind in Society: The development of higher physiological processes.* Cambridge, MA: Harvard University Press.

Wenger, E. (1998). *Communities of practice: Learning, meaning and identity.* Cambridge: Cambridge University Press.

Wenger, E., McDermott, R., & Snyder, W. M. (2002). *Cultivating communities of practice: A guide to managing knowledge.* Boston, MA: Harvard Business School Press.

Wick, C. (2000). Knowledge management and leadership opportunities for technical communicators. *Technical Communication, 47*(4), 515–529.

DEVELOPING TECHNOLOGY AND COLLABORATIVE GROUP WORK SKILLS: SUPPORTING STUDENT AND GROUP SUCCESS IN ONLINE AND BLENDED COURSES

Julia L. Parra

ABSTRACT

The use of collaborative group work is an important teaching and learning strategy for online and blended courses. However, the challenges of collaborative group work, such as the lack of online technology skills, time conflicts, differences in team member participation, and logistics of online and blended teamwork, often leave students dissatisfied by the process. To maximize the benefits and minimize the challenges, students should be supported in the development of skills with the use of relevant (often emerging or Web 2.0) online technologies and the development of skills related to online and blended collaborative group work. The Phases and Scaffolds for Technology Use and Collaborative Group Work course design process was developed to address this need and is shared in this chapter along with an action research-based case study designed from an

Increasing Student Engagement and Retention in e-Learning Environments:
Web 2.0 and Blended Learning Technologies
Cutting-edge Technologies in Higher Education, Volume 6G, 287–337
Copyright © 2013 by Emerald Group Publishing Limited
All rights of reproduction in any form reserved
ISSN: 2044-9968/doi:10.1108/S2044-9968(2013)000006G013

action research approach. The purpose of this study was to find out what students thought about the aforementioned course design process, as well as to find out which online tools were most beneficial for online collaborative group work. Based on the results of the survey, the Phases and Scaffolds for Technology Use and Collaborative Group Work course design process had a positive impact on student satisfaction, student learning, and student success and the most beneficial and valued online collaborative group work tools included Skype, Google Docs, and Adobe Connect.

INSTRUCTOR AS COURSE DESIGNER AND ACTION RESEARCHER

Social Constructivism, Connectivism, and Transformative Learning theories frame my beliefs about teaching and learning and culminate in my approach to research as that of an action researcher. According to Lewin and Stringer, "Action research is focused on solving specific problems that local practitioners face in their schools and communities" (as cited in Johnson & Christensen, 2012, p. 11). Johnson and Christensen further note:

> To carry out an action research project, you would need to diagnose the specific problem you are facing and conduct a thorough literature review to see if a useful answer already exists. If the literature doesn't suffice, then you will need to carry out your own research study (i.e., collect data to help answer your question) in your environment with your students or clients. When you finish interpreting your results, you can implement the changes needed to help solve your local problem. (p. 11)

Thus, taking the role of an action researcher, I filled a missing gap in the literature – the lack of a comprehensive course design process to support students in both areas of technology use and collaboration toward the goal of successful group work – and designed the Phases and Scaffolds for Technology Use and Collaborative Group Work process discussed in this chapter. I applied this course design process to my online and blended courses, and conducted a case study to understand what students in one of my online courses thought and to share the background and results with others.

This rest of this chapter includes the following sections – Background, Collaborative Group Work in Online and Blended Courses, Online and Blended Courses, Online and Emerging Technologies, Building on Existing Strategies, Phases and Scaffolds for Technology Use and Collaborative

Group Work, Research Method, Data Analysis, and Implications for Online and Blended Course Design. Additionally, added to this chapter, as appendices, are key resources, that I share with the educators that I teach about online teaching and learning, to use as needed.

BACKGROUND

In the Online Teaching and Learning (OTL) Graduate Certificate program at New Mexico State University's (NMSU) College of Extended Learning, educators are taught the fundamentals of teaching online. This program has used the Quality Matters Rubric (Quality Matters, 2011) since the original came out in 2004 as the standard for program and course design and as a guide for content development. Additionally, key texts have provided foundational support for program, course, and content design and development. These texts include, but are not limited to, Garrison and Anderson's (2003) E-Learning in the 21st Century: A Framework for Research and Practice, Theory and Practice of Online Learning (Anderson & Elloumi, 2004), Gilly Salmon's (2000) E-moderating: The Key to Teaching and Learning Online, Conrad and Donaldson's (2004) Engaging the Online Learner; and Palloff and Pratt's (2003) Virtual Student: A Profile and Guide to Working with Online Learners.

Of course, these texts and authors have more current works, some of which are cited in this chapter. However, their key concepts such as interaction, presence, collaborative learning, and community building, have been tested by time and remain important for online teaching and learning. These concepts all have a role in online collaborative group work, a fundamental teaching strategy in the NMSU OTL program.

COLLABORATIVE GROUP WORK IN ONLINE AND BLENDED COURSES

Conrad and Donaldson (2004, p. 4), note that historically, "Bruner, Vygotsky, and Piaget all embraced the philosophy that humans do not learn in a vacuum but rather through interaction." It is through interactions that collaboration can take place. Palloff and Pratt (2005a, p. 6) describe collaboration as "the 'heart and soul' of an online course or, for that matter a course that bases its theoretical foundation in constructivism."

Students in online learning programs and courses often report feelings of isolation, lack of social interaction, lack of self-direction and management, lack of technical skills, and eventual decreases in motivation levels (Abrami & Bures, 1996; Carr, 2000; Ludwig-Hardman & Dunlap, 2003; Muilenburg & Berge, 2007). When designing for online and blended learning, it is important to incorporate strategies such as collaborative group work that decreases the aforementioned negative elements and increases positive elements. Collaborative group work in online and blended courses is a strategy that can increase student success, satisfaction, and learning by increasing social presence and student–student interaction; and by promoting student engagement, critical skill development, and the opportunity for real-life teamwork activities (Anderson, 2009; Palloff & Pratt, 2005a; Swan, 2001; Tu, 2004).

Palloff and Pratt (2005b) take the concept of collaboration to a deeper level and discuss the importance of learning groups in a learning community wherein "students have the opportunity to extend and deepen their learning experience, test out new ideas by sharing them with a supportive group, and receive critical and constructive feedback" (p. 1). They further note that student success in the "achievement of learning objectives and achieving course competencies increases through collaborative engagement" (p. 1). Collison, Elbaum, Haavind, and Tinker (2000) concur and note the importance of collaborative and collective inquiry:

> A process that involves inquiry confronts the unknown and relies on personal or collective resources to resolve questions. The online environment in which inquiry can flourish is gradually built by collaborative and collective contributions. Such collaboration efforts are likely to result in better outcomes, designs, practices, or products. (p. 30)

Palloff and Pratt (2005a) note the specific pedagogic benefits of collaborative learning to include the development of critical thinking skills, co-creation of knowledge and meaning, reflection, and transformative learning. These skills are in demand with a national and global work force that is constantly changing due to economic stresses and rapidly changing technological landscapes. The NMC Horizon Report 2012 (Johnson, Adams, & Cummins) identifies a key trend about workplace dynamics – "The world of work is increasingly collaborative, driving changes in the way student projects are structured (p. 4)." This trend is further described as follows:

> As more and more employers are valuing collaboration as a critical skill, silos both in the workplace and at school are being abandoned in favor of collective intelligence.

To facilitate more teamwork and group communication, projects rely on tools like wikis, Google Docs, Skype, and online forums. Projects are increasingly evaluated by educators not just on the overall outcome, but also on the success of the group dynamic. In many cases, the online collaboration tool itself is an equally important outcome as it stores – and even immortalizes – the process and multiple perspectives that led to the end results. (Johnson, Adams, & Cummins, 2012, p. 4)

Online and blended courses are well suited to support students with collaborative group work opportunities and the development of such skills, fostering a move from silo, individual contribution, into genuine real-time collaboration of group members.

The term collaborative group work is important because group work can be completed without collaboration and simply by designating individual tasks to group members without much real collaboration or purpose. A better goal for group work is to be as collaborative as possible. With collaborative group work, students working together, move toward, and hopefully become, an "extraordinary group" (Bellman & Ryan, 2009) or a team, "with complementary skills who are committed to a common purpose, performance goals, and approach for which they are mutually accountable" (Katzenbach & Smith, 1993, p. 45).

With the benefits of collaborative group work, there are of course, challenges, which become even more challenging when collaborative group work is taken into online or blended courses. Lack of online technology skills, time conflicts, differences in team member participation, and logistics of teamwork, are just a few, and because of these challenges, students are often left dissatisfied by the process (Kim, Liu, & Bonk, 2005; Koh & Hill, 2009). To maximize the benefits and minimize the challenges, students should be supported in the development of skills with the use of relevant (often emerging) technologies and the development of skills related to collaboration and group work. This is applicable for all courses and learning environments but especially important for online and blended courses.

ONLINE AND BLENDED COURSES

For the purposes of this chapter and the embedded case study, online courses are courses that are taught completely online, and blended courses "combine face-to-face instruction with online learning and reduced classroom contact hours (reduced seat time)" (Dzubian, Hartman, & Moskal, 2004, p. 2). Though this chapter could just focus on online courses, there is value in including blended courses. The strategies for designing blended courses can be adopted from the strategies for designing online courses.

Blended courses have the potential to combine the best of face-to-face teaching and the best of online teaching. In fact, the U.S. Department of Education published a study titled, Evaluation of Evidence-Based Practices in Online Learning: A Meta-Analysis and Review of Online Learning Studies (Means, Toyama, Murphy, Bakia, & Jones, 2010), and noted two things, (1) "Students in online conditions performed modestly better, on average, than those learning the same material through traditional face-to-face instruction" (p. xiv), and (2) "Instruction combining online and face-to-face elements had a larger advantage relative to purely face-to-face instruction than did purely online instruction" (p. xv).

ONLINE AND EMERGING TECHNOLOGIES

Teaching and learning in online and blended courses requires the use of online and often emerging technologies. To understand these technologies, it is helpful to briefly review the concepts of asynchronous, synchronous, and nearly synchronous tools.

Asynchronous, Synchronous, and Nearly Synchronous Tools

Asynchronous, synchronous, and nearly synchronous as terms are important in relation to online and blended course design. Examples of traditional asynchronous components include e-mail, list servs, discussion boards and forums, reading texts, and tutorials. Other asynchronous tools gaining popularity for use in online and blended courses include blogs, microblogs, wikis, site creation, and social networks.

Examples of synchronous tools include chats, video or web-conferencing, and even teleconferencing. Common tools used for synchronous online learning and communication include, 1-1 or small group chat tools or video conferencing tools as well as class web conferencing tools. When these web conferencing tools have recording capability, the recordings can be used as asynchronous resources.

Additionally, nearly synchronous communication can play a big role in online learning and communication. An example of nearly synchronous communication is with e-mail where e-mail messages are going back and forth very quickly. Text messaging can work this way as well. A term similar to synchronous is real-time. Google Docs is a popular collaborative document tool that is noted to work in real-time, where up to 50 document participants can add content to the same document at the same time and immediately see the results of each others' work.

Emerging Technologies for Collaborative Group Work

The early days of online learning were very focused on mostly asynchronous communications and tools. However, the rapidly developing landscape of emerging synchronous, nearly synchronous, and real-time technologies bring a wealth of opportunity for online and blended learning (McBrien, Jones, & Cheng, 2009).

Emerging technologies often blur the lines between asynchronous and synchronous giving us degrees of communication and interaction (Hrastinski, 2008). There is currently an engaging tool being used on smart phones called Voxer, which supports audio communication by allowing people to send audio snippets back and forth. This tool is used asynchronously, nearly synchronously, and synchronously for a dynamic communication experience.

Many currently used online technologies can be considered emerging technologies or Web 2.0 tools (Diaz, 2010). Google and Facebook are commonly known examples that may not be new but are continually changing and incorporating the newest or emerging technologies into their interfaces. Some learning management systems (LMSs), like Canvas, that host online course content, can also be considered emerging as they evolve similarly to Google and Facebook.

Emerging technologies can be used to support students who engage in collaborative group work in online and blended courses. For this chapter, some key emerging technologies were built into the Phases and Scaffolds for Technology Use and Collaborative Group Work process and specific tools were included in the end of course survey used to collect data in this case study. These tools include the learning management system (LMS), specifically Blackboard; a small group web conferencing tool, specifically Skype; a class web-conferencing tool, specifically Adobe Connect; Google tools including Forms and Docs; and fun, engaging new tools like Twitter. For the process and the course designer, the type of tool is what is important. For the survey and for actual implementation of the process, the specific tools are important.

BUILDING ON EXISTING STRATEGIES

A personal motto of mine is, "Don't recreate! Investigate, Collaborate, and Co-create!" In other words, find out what already exists and build upon it. If possible do this with like-minded colleagues. This is a key reason that I have provided the resources and appendices at the end of this chapter, for readers to easily access, use, and personalize if desired. Additionally, the foundation for the Phases and Scaffolds for Technology Use and Collaborative Group Work course design process is built upon three existing key concepts that I learned from being a part of the NMSU OTL program's co-design process – (1) the use of content and metacognitive scaffolding, (2) supporting student use of technology as described by Gilly Salmon's (2000) 5-Stage Model, and (3) Conrad and Donaldson's (2004) Phases of Engagement framework.

Content and Metacognitive Scaffolding

One way to support student development of technology and collaboration/group work skills is to provide scaffolding throughout the process of group work. Two types of scaffolds, content scaffolds and metacognitive scaffolds (Su & Klein, 2010) can support students in the processes related to successfully collaborate and complete group work. Examples of content scaffolds include warm up sheets, note-taking sheets, and project templates (Su & Klein, 2010). Metacognitive scaffolds include project planning sheets, information collection logs, and project reflection sheet (Su & Klein, 2010).

Both content and metacognitive scaffolds were used in the Phases and Scaffolds for Technology Use and Collaborative Group Work course design process. Content scaffolds included mini technology tutorials, a group work guide, and an activity guide/worksheet (see the Appendix A for examples). Metacognitive scaffolds included a class communications spreadsheet derived from a class communications survey, a group work form, and the activity guide/worksheet that can also be considered a content scaffold (see the Appendix A for examples).

Gilly Salmon's 5-Stage Model

Another way to support student development of technology and collaboration/group work skills is provided by Gilly Salmon's (2000) 5-Stage Model for student use of technology in an online course and provides the steps and stages for how an online course instructor can moderate, facilitate, and/or support student technology use. Gilly Salmon updates her book and website related to this model and I highly recommend this model as a resource for anyone designing online and blended courses.

Conrad and Donaldson's Phases of Engagement

Conrad and Donaldson (2004) provide the Phases of Engagement framework that incorporates ideas for phasing in levels of student engagement including collaboration and group work activities. The Phases of Engagement include the Co-Exist phase for the first 1–2 weeks of a 16-week course, Communicate for the next 3–4 weeks, Cooperate for weeks 5–6, and Collaborate for weeks 7–16. Conrad and Donaldson (2004) identify different instructor roles throughout the Phases of Engagement including social negotiator, structural engineer, facilitator, community member, and challenger.

PHASES AND SCAFFOLDS FOR TECHNOLOGY USE AND COLLABORATIVE GROUP WORK

In 2010, I decided to start sharing some of the strategies and scaffolds that we used in the OTL program and I also started teaching for NMSU's College of Education in the Curriculum and Instruction Department's Educational Learning Technologies (EDLT) graduate programs. With complete autonomy in EDLT course design, I fully implemented my favorite strategies and scaffolds for technology use and collaborative group work, as previously described, into the online and blended EDLT courses I was assigned. However, I never found a model, framework, or process that comprehensively provided support for students in both areas of technology use and collaboration toward the goal of successful group work. For the purposes of consistent implementation and sharing with others, I developed the Phases and Scaffolds for Technology Use and Collaborative Group Work (Appendix A) that provided the comprehensive support I was looking for. This process has proven to be a valuable tool for both online and blended course design and is meant for proactive rather than reactive support for students as they engage in collaborative group work. My newest motto then is, "Build for it and they will collaborate."

Process Development and Implementation

Content and metacognitive scaffolding, the 5-Stage model (Salmon, 2004), and the Phases of Engagement framework (Conrad & Donaldson, 2004) were instrumental in the development of a course design process wherein students developed the skills for both collaborative technology tool use and collaborative group work. In fact, I liked the Phases of Engagement so much for its clarity in implementation, that it was a model for me in designing the Phases and Scaffolds for Technology Use and Collaborative Group Work. In Spring 2011, I fully implemented the Phases and Scaffolds for Technology Use and Collaborative Group Work into an online course (see Appendix A for a two-page handout of this process). The course was divided into six units. This process was integrated into the units and included four phases: (1) Getting Started with Group Work, (2) Practicing Group Work Phase, (3) Conducting Group Work, and (4) Celebrating Group Work.

Getting Started with Group Work

In the Getting Started With Group Work phase, students participated in a Blackboard discussion for an introduction activity, also known as an ice-breaker activity; they were provided with a set of mini-tutorials (content scaffolding) to support the development of their technology tool kits; and they took part in activities that prepared them for group work (metacognitive scaffolding).

The technology tool kit included the 1-1 and small group chat and videoconferencing tool, Skype; the collaborative document tool, Google Docs; the wiki tool, PBWorks; and the organizational microblogging tool, Yammer. Over time, these tool kits have changed and will continue to change to reflect changes in tool preference and the emergence of new tools. An example is that Twitter, another microblogging tool, replaced Yammer in following semesters. In the future, I'm considering a Pinterest activity. Additionally, students might expand their tool kits as they encounter tools that they prefer to use for collaboration and creation of group projects (Appendix B).

To prepare for group work, students answered a small survey created using a Google Form. They were then provided access to the accompanying Google Spreadsheet (metacognitive scaffold) to view each other's posted data of information including technology access, Skype ID, Google account, and day/time availability. When viewing the Google Spreadsheet and in conjunction with the introduction activity, students were able to start to make decisions about group formation. The day/time availability supports the possibility of having synchronous group meetings. The use of synchronous group meetings is encouraged, if possible as the use of collaboration tools like Skype and Google Docs can be highly efficient and save students a lot of time. The survey has evolved, per students' request, to include student skills and strengths. For example, one class wanted to know who were the students skilled in website development (Appendix C for an example survey).

In this phase, students were also prompted to use the grouping tool in the learning management system (LMS), in this case, Blackboard, to sign up for and create their own groups. They were provided a content scaffold, the Group Work Guide (Appendix D) and were prompted to start with practice communications using the LMS mail and discussion tools; the 1-1 and small group chat and videoconferencing tool, Skype; and/or any other tools chosen by the group.

Depending on the course content, the instructor's own teaching philosophies, and student demographics (undergraduate vs. graduate students, overall technology skill levels for the school, etc.), this phase can take anywhere from one week up to a quarter of the course. For the course in this case study, the duration was two and a half weeks for a regular semester of approximately 16 weeks. The instructor's perceived roles in this phase included everything from leader, role model, coordinator, motivator, and my favorite, master learner. The instructor felt active and busy in this phase, leading the online learning community, modeling technology use, coordinating group activities, motivating groups to become teams, and ultimately motivating students to become master learners themselves.

Practicing Group Work

In the Practicing Group Work phase, students continued to practice collaboration technology use and group work skills by completing in their groups and sharing with instructor, their Group Work Forms (metacognitive scaffold). Group Work Forms were provided as a class template in Google Docs (Appendix E). The term "class template" is used here because Google also has its own type of formal template system.

In one class, a student recommended a practice exercise for group development. With this class, an optional, extra credit activity about

Twitter, titled The Twitter Top 5, was used. A class template guide (content and metacognitive scaffold) was provided this activity (Appendix F). Over time, this strategy is no longer optional and has been formally integrated. Of course, the activity may change over time.

The duration of this phase could be brief or go halfway through the course. In this case, the duration was 2 out of an approximately 16-week semester. The instructor still felt busy and active in this phase with perceived roles of leader, role model, coordinator, and master learner.

Conducting Group Work

In the Conducting Group Work phase, students worked on their group projects, submitted group progress reports, and attended optional online class meetings in Adobe. Students in this class were educational technology students and the group project was to design a technology enhanced and technology integrated learning plan (Appendix G). During this phase, students were required to submit progress reports to the instructor, about every 2 weeks. Submitting progress reports was important to help groups stay on track and feel a sense of accountability.

The instructor used a class web conferencing tool, Adobe Connect, for optional class meetings including a course orientation; one meeting for each new unit to discuss relevant topics, group work, and their questions; and end of course group presentations. During this phase, the class meetings served as an opportunity for students and groups to touch base with the instructor and get feedback or advice. This class web conferencing tool is an example of a technology that has the capacity for both synchronous and asynchronous communication. The meetings were available for live, synchronous attendance but were also recorded so that students could view the recordings as needed.

This phase takes the class up to near the end of the course. In this case, the Conducting Group Work phase continued until the last two weeks of class. The instructor did not feel nearly as busy in this phase with perceived roles of counselor and mediator for individuals and teams during this time of what was termed high-risk group work, a group project worth a lot of points. When high-risk group work was in process some groups needed advice about group issues. Additionally, about 10–12 weeks into a course, everyone seems to lose steam, experiencing, as we like to say, "the late semester blues." Thus, during this phase the instructor also took the role of motivator, posting and sending positive messages to students and groups.

Celebrating Group Work

In the Celebrating Group Work phase the students turned in final products, practiced presenting their group projects, and presented their group projects. As a culminating and celebratory activity, students presented their group projects in the class web conferencing system. The use of PowerPoint slides is helpful in the web conferencing environment so the groups submitted their slides to the LMS assignment tool and the instructor added the slides to the web conferencing tool. This phase occurs during the last week or two of class. With the tension of everything due during this phase, the instructor felt busy again with the perceived roles of counselor and mediator and due to the presentation process, the instructor also took the role of coordinator.

RESEARCH METHOD

In the role of instructor as action researcher, I wanted to explore the impact of the Phases and Scaffolds for Technology Use and Collaboration course design process on students. Additionally, I wanted to know which online tools were most beneficial to the students for completing online collaborative group work. I used a framework of impact on student satisfaction, student learning, and student success. This framework was partially derived from the SLOAN Consortium's Quality Framework – The Five Pillars, specifically the pillars for Learning Effectiveness and Student Satisfaction (Moore, 2005).

Audience and Data Collection

To research the effectiveness of the Phases and Scaffolds for Technology Use and Collaboration course design process, I designed an end of course survey (Appendix H) in Survey Monkey. About one month after the last day of classes, all students from the graduate level college class were sent the necessary consent e-mail that included a link to the end of course survey (Appendix H).

DATA ANALYSIS

Seventeen of the 25 students in the class (68%) completed the survey. The end of course survey was mostly quantitative in nature but provided the option for comments, allowing for qualitative response. There were only a few qualitative responses. Note that the percentages in the data analysis are rounded to the nearest numbers.

Student Feelings About Group Work and Online Tools for Collaboration

Students were first asked to consider group work prior to the course that included the online course design process of Phases and Scaffolds for Technology Use and Collaborative Group Work. The majority of students had positive feelings about group work (64% somewhat positive and positive) and online tools for collaboration (71% somewhat positive and positive).

Student Use of Tools – Prior Use and Helpfulness of Tool

A particular set of tools were used in this course and the survey included questions about these tools. They included: Adobe Connect, Skype, Blackboard Discussion, Blackboard Chat, Blackboard Mail, Gmail, Google Docs or other collaborative document, PBWorks or other wiki tool, Yammer, and Twitter.

Students were asked if they had used a particular tool prior to taking this online course and then asked to rate the helpfulness of that tool. Three tools stood out – Adobe Connect, Skype, and Google Docs (see Appendix I for the complete table). Adobe Connect, our class web conferencing tool was at 65% never used but ended up being helpful or very helpful at almost the same percentage at 64%. Skype was never used at 18% and was noted at 100% as helpful or very helpful, and Google Docs was never used at 41% and was noted at 94% as helpful or very helpful (Table 1).

Student Use of Tools – Student Satisfaction, Impact on Overall Learning, and Impact on Student Success

The next set of data about the set of tools used in this online course was about student satisfaction, impact on overall student learning, and impact on student success.

For student satisfaction, the three tools that stood out were, again – Adobe Connect, Skype, and Google Docs (see Appendix J for the complete table). Adobe Connect, our class web conferencing tool had a positive impact rate of 71%. Skype was at 94% and Google Docs was at 82% (Table 2).

Table 1. Top Three Percentages for Tool Use Prior versus Helpfulness of Tool for Group Work.

Tool	Percentage of Student Use Prior to This Course	Percentage Found Helpful
Adobe Connect	Never used – 65% Moderate use – 24% Frequent use – 12%	Didn't use or not helpful – 18% Somewhat helpful – 18% Helpful or very helpful – 64%
Skype	Never used – 18% Moderate use – 35% Frequent use – 47%	Didn't use or not helpful – 0% Somewhat helpful – 0% Helpful or very helpful – 100%
Google Docs or other collaborative document	Never used – 41% Moderate use – 29% Frequent use – 29%	Didn't use or not helpful – 0% Somewhat helpful – 6% Helpful or very helpful – 94%

Table 2. Top Three Percentages for Student Satisfaction of Tools Used to Complete Group Project.

Tool	Tool Satisfaction
Adobe Connect	Didn't use, unsatisfied, or somewhat unsatisfied – 18% Somewhat satisfied – 12% Satisfied – 71%
Skype	Didn't use, unsatisfied, or somewhat unsatisfied – 0% Somewhat satisfied – 6% Satisfied – 94%
Google Docs or other collaborative document	Didn't use, unsatisfied, or somewhat unsatisfied – 6% Somewhat satisfied – 12% Satisfied – 82%

For impact on overall student learning along with the helpfulness of tools and student satisfaction data, the three tools that stood out were, again – Adobe Connect, Skype, and Google Docs (see Appendix K for the complete table). Adobe Connect, our class web conferencing tool had a satisfaction rate of 71%. Skype was at 100% and Google Docs was at 94% (Table 3).

For impact on learner success, the three tools that stood out were, again – Adobe Connect, Skype, and Google Docs (see Appendix L for the complete table). Adobe Connect, our class web conferencing tool had a positive impact rate of 65%. Skype was at 100% and Google Docs was at 94% (Table 4).

Table 3. Top Three Percentages for Impact of Tool Use on Student
Overall Learning.

Tool	Impact of Tool on Overall Learning
Adobe Connect	Negative impact – 0% Neutral or no impact – 29% Positive impact – 71%
Skype	Negative impact – 0% Neutral or no impact – 0% Positive impact – 100%
Google Docs or other collaborative document	Negative impact – 0% Neutral or no impact – 6% Positive impact – 94%

Table 4. Top Three Percentages for Impact of Tool Use on Student
Success.

Tool	Impact of Tool on Overall Learning
Adobe Connect	Negative impact – 0% Neutral or no impact – 35% Positive impact – 65%
Skype	Negative impact – 0% Neutral or no impact – 0% Positive impact – 100%
Google Docs or other collaborative document	Negative impact – 0% Neutral or no impact – 6% Positive impact – 94%

Related to the data about student use of tools, one student added a
comment about Google Docs, saying that, "having access to the shared docs
in Google Docs was a great benefit as we could all edit and change things as
suggestions were made."

Group Work Process Data

Finally, the students were asked about the impact of the course design
process discussed in this chapter. Students were asked about their

Table 5. Impact of Group Process on Student Satisfaction, Overall Learning, and Success.

Impact of Group Process on Student Satisfaction	Impact of Group Process on Student Overall Learning	Impact of Group Work Process on Student Success
Unsatisfied or somewhat satisfied – 0%	Negative impact – 0%	Negative impact – 0%
Somewhat satisfied 29%	Neutral or no impact – 6%	Neutral or no impact – 6%
Satisfied – 71%	Positive impact – 94%	Positive impact – 94%

satisfaction with the group work process for completing the group project. Responses for unsatisfied or satisfied were 0%, somewhat satisfied was at 29%, and satisfied was at 71%. Students were asked about the impact of the group work process on their overall learning. Responses for negative were 0%, neutral or no impact was at 6%, and positive impact was at 94%. The students were asked about the impact of the group work process on their success. Responses for negative impact were at 0%, neutral or no impact was at 6%, and positive impact was at 94% (Table 5).

Finally, as the course instructor, one of my favorite parts of an online course is the presentation and sharing at the end. In the online course used for this case study, each group presented about their group work projects. Everyone was represented and all projects were completed. This was evidence for me, that the Phases and Scaffolds for Technology Use and Group Work course design process and the tools used had a positive impact on student learning and student success.

IMPLICATIONS FOR ONLINE AND BLENDED COURSE DESIGN

Anecdotally, I knew that Adobe Connect, Skype, and Google Docs were key emerging technologies that supported students in the successful completion of group work in online and blended courses. The data gathered and analyzed about student use of tools in this case study verified that the tools most beneficial and valued by students for collaborative group in an online class were, in fact, Adobe Connect, Skype, and Google Docs. These tools are important for the categories they represent of class web conferencing tools; 1-1 and small group web conferencing tools; and collaborative document creation tools. Thus, for the near future in online course design and development, these are the recommended tools and categories of tools for anyone when designing for collaborative group work in online or blended courses.

Anecdotally, I knew that providing students in online and blended courses with comprehensive support for successful completion of collaborative group work was important. Based on the survey results and the student presentations provided by every group at the end of the course, the design process discussed in this chapter, Phases and Scaffolds for Technology Use and Group Work, supports student satisfaction, student learning, and student success. This process is summarized in a two-page handout in Appendix A for easy access, personalization, use, and sharing. The Phases and Scaffolds for Technology Use and Group Work is, of course, a process that should continue to be evaluated and revised in order to maintain relevance in our rapidly changing educational technology landscape.

ACKNOWLEDGMENTS

Thank you to the NMSU Fall 2011 EDLT 528/628 Class! And a special thank you to my friends in online teaching and learning, Bethany Bovard and Holly Rae Bemis-Schurtz; this chapter would not be possible without you!

REFERENCES

Abrami, P. C., & Bures, E. M. (1996). Computer-supported collaborative learning and distance education. *American Journal of Distance Education, 10*(2), 37–42.
Anderson, T. (2009). Teaching in an online learning context. In T. Anderson & F. Elloumi (Eds.), *Theory and practice of online learning* (2nd ed., pp. 343–472). Athabasca, AB: Athabasca University.
Anderson, T., & Elloumi, F. (2004). *Theory and practice of online learning.* Athabasca, AB: Athabasca University. Retrieved from http://cde.athabascau.ca/online_book/
Bellman, G. M., & Ryan, K. D. (2009). *Extraordinary groups: How ordinary teams achieve amazing results.* San Francisco, CA: Jossey-Bass.
Carr, S. (2000). As distance education comes of age, the challenge is keeping the students. *The Chronicle of Higher Education, 46*(23), A39–A41.
Collison, G., Elbaum, B., Haavind, S., & Tinker, R. (2000). *Facilitating online learning: Effective strategies for moderators.* Madison, WI: Atwood Publishing.

Conrad, R. M., & Donaldson, A. (2004). *Engaging the online learner: Activities and resources for creative instruction.* San Francisco, CA: Jossey-Bass.

Diaz, V. (2010). Web 2.0 and emerging technologies in online learning. *New Directions for Community Colleges, 150,* 57–66. doi: 10.1002/cc.405

Dzubian, C. D., Hartman, J. L., & Moskal, P. D. (2004). Blended learning. *EDUCAUSE Center for Applied Research (ECAR).* Retrieved from http://www.educause.edu/library/resources/blended-learning

Garrison, D. R., & Anderson, T. (2003). *E-learning in the 21st century.* New York, NY: RoutledgeFalmer.

Hrastinski, S. (2008). Asynchronous and synchronous e-learning. *Educause Quarterly, 31*(4), 51–55.

Johnson, L., Adams, S., & Cummins, M. (2012). *The NMC horizon report: 2012 higher education edition.* Austin, TX: The New Media Consortium. Retrieved from http://www.nmc.org/publications/horizon-report-2012-higher-ed-edition

Johnson, B., & Christensen, L. (2012). *Educational research: Quantitative, qualitative, and mixed approaches.* Thousand Oaks, CA: Sage.

Katzenbach, J. R., & Smith, D. K. (1993). *The wisdom of teams: Creating the high-performance organization.* Boston, MA: Harvard Business School.

Kim, K.-J., Liu, S., & Bonk, C. J. (2005). Online MBA students' perceptions of online learning: Benefits, challenges and suggestions. *Internet and Higher Education, 8*(4), 335–344.

Koh, M. H., & Hill, J. R. (2009). Student perceptions of group work in an online course: Benefits and challenges. *Journal of Distance Education, 23*(2), 69–92.

Ludwig-Hardman, S., & Dunlap, J. (2003). Learner support services for on-line students: Scaffolding for success. *International Review of Research in Open and Distance Learning, 4.* Retrieved from http://www.irrodl.org/index.php/irrodl/article/view/131/602

McBrien, J. L., Jones, P., & Cheng, R. (2009). Virtual spaces: Employing a synchronous online classroom to facilitate student engagement in online learning. *International Review of Research in Open and Distance Learning, 10*(3), 1–18.

Means, B., Toyama, Y., Murphy, R., Bakia, M., & Jones, K. (2010). *Evaluation of evidence-based practices in online learning: A meta-analysis and review of online learning studies.* Retrieved from http://www2.ed.gov/about/offices/list/opepd/ppss/reports.html#edtech

Moore, J. (2005). *The SLOAN Consortium quality framework and the five pillars.* Newburyport, MA: SLOAN-C. Retrieved from http://sloanconsortium.org/publications/books/qualityframework.pdf

Muilenburg, L. Y., & Berge, Z. L. (2005). Student barriers to online learning: A factor analytic study. *Distance Education, 26*(1), 29–48.

Palloff, R., & Pratt, K. (2003). *The virtual student: A profile and guide to working with online learners.* San Francisco, CA: Jossey-Bass.

Palloff, R., & Pratt, K. (2005a). *Collaborating online: Learning together in community.* San Francisco, CA: Jossey-Bass.

Palloff, R., & Pratt, K. (2005b). Learning together in community: Collaboration online. *Proceedings of the 20th annual conference on distance and teaching and learning.* University of Wisconsin, Madison, WI, August. Retrieved from http://www.uwex.edu/disted/conference/Resource_library/proceedings/04_1127.pdf

Quality Matters. (2011). *Quality matters rubric standards 2011–2013 edition with assigned point values.* Retrieved from http://www.qmprogram.org/rubric

Salmon, G. (2000). *E-moderating: The key to teaching and learning online.* London: Kogan Page.

Salmon, G. (2004). *E-moderating: The key to teaching and learning online.* RoutledgeFalmer.

Su, Y., & Klein, J. D. (2010). Using scaffolds in problem-based hypermedia. *Journal of Educational Multimedia and Hypermedia, 19*(3), 327–347.

Swan, K. (2001). Building learning communities in online courses: The importance of interaction. *Distance Education, 22*(2), 306–331.

Tu, C. (2004). *Online collaborative learning communities.* Westport, CT: Libraries Unlimited.

APPENDIX A: PHASES AND SCAFFOLDS FOR TECHNOLOGY USE AND GROUP WORK PROCESS TWO-PAGE HANDOUT

Synopsis

This process phases and scaffolds both technology use and collaborative group work skill development. This synopsis and table provides an easy to follow view of the course design process for a full semester online course wherein the students were provided support with specific phases and scaffolds for technology use and collaborative group work skill development.

The course was divided into six units. The phases and scaffolds were integrated into the units and included:

- A Getting Started with Group Work phase, where students engaged in introduction activities, developed their beginning technology tool kit, and prepared for group work. The beginning collaborative technology tool kit included Skype, Google (start with Gmail, model and scaffold the use of GDocs), PBWorks, and Yammer. To prepare for group work, students filled out a class communications and group work survey created in Google Docs/Form. They were provided access to the accompanying spreadsheet to view each others' contact information and day/time availability. They were prompted to use the LMS sign up tool to create their groups. They were provided group work resources and prompted to start with practice communications.
- A Practicing Group Work phase during which, students completed and shared with instructor their Group Work Forms completed in Google Docs. With this class, a fun, low-risk activity about Twitter was used (a student from a previous semester recommended the use of a practice activity).
- A Conducting Group Work phase during which students worked on their Group Projects, submitted group progress reports, and attended online class meetings in Adobe Connect to discuss relevant topics, group work, Q&A, etc.
- A Celebrating Group Work phase during which students turned in final products, practiced presenting, and presented their group projects.

PHASES AND SCAFFOLDS FOR TECHNOLOGY USE
AND COLLABORATIVE GROUP WORK

Phases based on 16-week Schedule	Instructor Roles	Recommended Student Activities	Technology and Scaffold Examples for Collaboration and Group Work
Phase 1 Getting Started with Group Work For example: Unit 1, Weeks 1–2	Leader Role Model Coordinator Motivator Master Learner	1. Engage in course introduction activities 2. Develop basic student technology tool kits 3. Prepare students for group work 4. Form groups 5. Review group work resources 6. Practice group work communications and tool use	1. Learning Management System (LMS) discussion tool 2. Mini Technology Tutorials[a] 3. Technology/ Collaboration Survey and Spreadsheet[b] 4. LMS Group Sign-Up process and tools 5. Group Work Guide[a] 6. Small group collaboration tools such as Skype and Google Docs
Phase 2 Practicing Group Work For Example: Unit 2, Weeks 3–5	Leader Role Model Coordinator Master Learner	1. Practice group work communications and tool use 2. Complete a group work form/contract 3. Complete a fun low-risk collaborative group activity to practice collaboration technology skills as well as the skills needed to successfully complete group work	1. Small group collaboration tools 2. Group Work Form[b] 3. Activity that uses a fun emerging technology tool like Twitter, Pinterest, etc.

Appendix A. (*Continued*)

Phases based on 16-week Schedule	Instructor Roles	Recommended Student Activities	Technology and Scaffold Examples for Collaboration and Group Work
Phase 3 Conducting Group Work For example: Units 3–5, Weeks 6–12	Motivator Counselor Mediator	1. Work on the Group Projects 2. Submit group artifacts or progress reports 3. Attend online class meetings or review recordings to discuss relevant topics, group work, Q&A, etc.	1. Small group collaboration tools 2. LMS assignment tool 3. Class web conferencing tool
Phase 4 Celebrating Group Work For example: Units 5–6, Weeks 13–16	Counselor Mediator Coordinator	1. Turn in final products (slides, site, documents, etc.) 2. Practice group presentations 3. Present group projects in online class meeting	1. LMS assignment tool 2. Small group collaboration tool or class web conferencing tool 3. Class web conferencing tool

[a]Content Scaffold.
[b]Metacognitive Scaffold.

APPENDIX B: GETTING STARTED EXAMPLE

Unit 1: Getting Started

Overview

It is a best practice in an online course (and in any course) to make sure that everyone is familiar with the course room, that communications are established, that everyone has a chance to get acquainted, and that everyone is familiar with the course requirements. This aids in community building, reduces stress, and increases learner satisfaction – especially for those new to the online environment. Therefore, in Unit 1, we will engage in class introductions, a synchronous orientation, and provide you a course navigation video to get you started. There is, of course, some reading for you to do.

Additionally, for this class, there are a few tools that you should become familiar with right away. These tools are some of my favorites for communication, collaboration, and personal learning network (PLN) development.

If you have any problems with any of the technology, you can get assistance by posting a message to Discussions Topic Course Help – I encourage everyone to help each other! Yammer is another option for help.

Unit 1 lasts about 2.5 weeks and I have provided about 14–16 hours of work. Many activities can take much less than the time recommended depending on you comfort level with computers and the Internet. However, if you find you are spending more than I've recommended, PLEASE meet with me about this.

The course competencies addressed in this course are fully noted in the syllabus and the ones specifically addressed in this unit are at the bottom of the page.

Orientation. Time: 1 hour. Value: Priceless!
Attend the Course Orientation if possible. If you miss the Orientation session, it's a good idea that you watch the recording. I will post the link to the recording in the Schedule as soon as there is one.

If you have any course-related questions, post a message in Course Help discussion topic. The Course Help is a place we all need to check on and work as a learning community to make sure every question is answered and everyone feels supported.

Course Navigation. Time: 1/2 hr. Value: Priceless!
Watch the Course Navigation Video (under 15 minutes long) that is posted on the Course Home Page. Seriously, you should watch it:)

Make sure to fully understand the layout and navigation of your course. If you have ANY questions, bring them to Orientation or post in the Course Help discussion topic.

Reading. Time: 2 hours. Value: Priceless.

- Major Course Documents
- Online Identity
- Scan your textbooks

Introductions. Time: 2 hours. Value: 20 points.
Note: Contribute to Discussion activities by going to the relevant topic in the Discussions tool. Points for Discussions are built into the Discussions tool.

Introductions are an important part of any course because they help people get comfortable with each other and with some of the course technology.

1. In Discussions Topic Introductions, start a new thread (use the Compose Message button) and tell us a little about yourself. Here are some guiding topics:
   a. Share a few personal facts that you wish to share (married? kids? hometown? home country? hobbies? etc.).
   b. Share a few professional facts such as educational background, what you teach, what you hope to teach, where you've worked, etc.
   c. Share what you hope to learn in this class. (PLEASE do this for sure!)
2. Reply to other learners' posts by hitting the Reply button while viewing their post to respond to what they have written. I really want to see you all visiting and chatting with each other over the entire duration of Unit 1. Make an appointment on with yourself, on your calendar, however that works best for you to make sure you are checking into this course at least 3 times a week. This is an important habit to form early!
3. Full points for simply doing this assignment. :)

Starter EdTech Tool Kit. Time: 6 hrs. Value: 20 pts.
Make sure you have read the Online Identity document. There are four (4) tools for you to get started with. AFTER you get started in the 4 tools, complete the survey noted at the end of this section.

Tool #1: Create a Skype Account & Chat w/ Instructor. Time: 2 hrs. Value: 5pts.
What is it?
Skype is an instant messenger, audio conferencing and much more technology.

Why use it?
To communicate with me and your small groups, a must have tool in every Tech Tool Kit!

Directions:

1. Go to Skype to download the software. See the Help for Windows users or Help for Mac users if you need help. During the installation process, you'll be asked to create a Skype user name and to add contacts to your contact list. Add students you know to your contact list – their Skype IDs are listed on the class communications survey spreadsheet.
2. If you need help, post a message in Course Help discussion topic.
3. Before January 30, begin a text chat with me when you see me online so I will know that you were successful in installing and using Skype. My Skype contact is in the class communications survey spreadsheet.

Tool #2: Create Gmail Account & send a Gmail message. Time: 1 hr. Value: 5pts.
What is it?
It's The Google and includes Gmail, Gdocs, Calendar, Sites, Scholar, and MUCH MORE.

Why use it?
It's THE GOOGLE for heaven's sake! Need I say more?

Directions:

1. If you already have an account, skip to #3
2. Go to http://gmail.com and click Create an account on the right, follow the directions.
3. Send me a gmail message, my gmail address is [instructor gmail here].

Tool #3: Join the NMSU EDLT Wiki. Time: 1 hr. Value: 5pts.
What is it?
It's a wiki and wikis are important tools for teachers to know about. Watch the video, Wikis in Plain English, to learn more about wikis.

Why use it?
Wikis allow for instant publishing on the web. It's a place for you and I to post information related to our class.

Directions:

1. Go to [class wiki link here] and request access on the right.

Tool #4: Join NMSU Yammer and create an update. Time: 2 hrs. Value: 5pts.
Directions:

1. Join NMSU Yammer at http://yammer.com
2. Join the EDLT 528/628 group.
3. Create a post/update in Yammer.
4. Consider using the Desktop application and/or cell phone applications.

Take the Survey. Time: 1 hr. Value: The total points available for this Starter EdTech Toolkit activity!
AFTER completing all previous tasks, complete the class communications survey (google form). This is how I will be able to update your points! NOTE: THE SURVEY AND THE SPREADSHEET ARE TWO DIFFERENT DOCUMENTS!!!

Group Work Setup. Time: 2 hrs over Units 1 & 2. Value: 10 pts in Unit 2.
By Unit 3, you will be working in groups. Use the class communications survey spreadsheet (NOTE: THE SURVEY AND THE SPREADSHEET ARE TWO DIFFERENT DOCUMENTS!!!) and the Blackboard Group Manager linked on the course Home Page to create your groups and begin practice communications with your group. I recommend using Skype with voice and Google Docs for group communications and collaboration. Include a conversation about group roles and good meeting times.

For more about group work, see the Group Work resource. By the end of Unit 2, make sure to complete the Group Work Form. Share it with me and send me a Blackboard Mail message that you have completed this.

Next Step: See Unit 2 Guide

APPENDIX C: COMMUNICATIONS AND GROUP WORK SURVEY EXAMPLE

Survey Note: This survey is to support my understanding of the technology access in this class; it will help me give you the points for your EdTech Toolkit; and it will help you all develop your groups.

First Name & Last Initial

```
[                              ]
```

What is your Skype ID?

```
[                              ]
```

What is your Gmail/Google Account?

```
[                              ]
```

What is the link to our class wiki?

```
[                              ]
```

What is the link to your Twitter account?
Mine is http://twitter.com/desertjul

```
[                          ]
```

What mobile technology do you have? Select all that apply

- Mac laptop w/wireless capacity
- Windows laptop w/wireless capacity
- iOS Device (iPad, iPhone, iPod Touch)
- Android Device
- None
- Other

What A/V media creation technology do you have? A/V stands for Audio/ Video. Select all that apply.

- Video camera
- Video camera on laptop or other mobile device such as iPad, Xoom, HTC Flyer, etc.
- Video on phone and the video can be sent to the web

- Mobile recording device and the audio can be sent to your computer or the web
- None
- Other

What are some skills that you have? Select at least one and all that apply.

- I am often the leader in a group
- I an often the document editor in a group
- I am often a researcher in a group
- I'm good at creating multimedia (audio, video, etc.)
- I'm good at creating web-based materials (websites, wikis, google docs)

What are some good times for you to meet with a group online? Be comprehensive.

APPENDIX D: GROUP WORK AND ROLES GUIDE

Overview

Group work or teamwork is an important strategy for teachers and students to know about.

Here are just a couple of reasons:

- Collaborating with others provides us with other perspectives besides our own, increasing the potential for knowledge gained and products created. Thus, increasing learning.
- For some students, teamwork provides the social presence needed to be successful, especially in an online course.
- Living and working in today's "flat world" means we have to know about working online with others.

Of course, there are challenges to address and potential roadblocks to avoid. As we are finding out, there are many ways to arm ourselves with knowledge and solutions so that the challenges and roadblocks disappear.

So get the challenges out of the way first. This guide provides resources and examples to help you and your group address the challenges and start out on the right track in the development of your collaborative product.

Please note that in my classes, the most important part is the process. It is through the process that learning, collaboration, knowledge sharing, etc. occurs. Treat each other with kindness and do your best to include everyone. Oh yeah, and HAVE FUN!

Further Information

Establishing Group Policies and Procedures
As a group you will need to consider:

- How you plan to get the work done
- Communication/meeting plans
- Timelines/Deadlines
- Goals/Milestones
- Individual roles Problem/Conflict resolution

If you establish organizational strategies and roles in the beginning, then it's much easier to get your group organized and headed in the right direction. I suggest a synchronous group meeting using your LCMS chat tool or Skype to discuss the Group Work Form. To get work done I recommend continued use of Skype if possible and using your LMS Group Tool for asynchronous discussion. For actual product development, tools I find helpful are wiki tools such as the Google Docs and Spreadsheets tool or a PbWiki page. A fun new tool to try out is the Google Hangout, but you need to be in Google +. I recommend that we work together to get you in so you can try it out. You can request an invite at https://plus.google.com/welcome and I'll put you all in a Circle.

Collaborative Tools

There are so many collaboration tools available that the biggest problem for groups really ends up being agreeing on which tools to use. Here are my recommendations.

LMS Group Discussion

You have a group area in our LMS for your content area. You can use this discussion area to discuss your group projects in private. The Group area also allows you to store and share files and send group e-mail.

SKYPE – http://www.skype.com
Skype is great for FREE synchronous collaboration allowing text, audio, and video chat. Sharing files and large chunks of text are excellent features of Skype.

Google Docs – http://docs.google.com
Google Docs is a great tool for online collaborative writing. It's just like using MS Word and everyone in your group can edit the same document online at anytime. If you have a gmail account, you may already have Google Docs as a feature when you log in to your gmail account.

PbWorks – http://pbworks.com *(create your own) or use the class wiki*
PbWorks is a great tool for collaboration. It's different from Google Docs in that only one person can edit a page at a time.

Group Norms (aka policies & procedures but I like the term "norms")
As you think about how your group will work together and accomplish your tasks, discuss and fill out the Group Work Form.

Further Information Resource Links

Use the following resources to learn more about online collaborative group work. If you find any other great resources, let us know so we can add them to the list.

Online Resources

- Group Projects: Organizing and working with groups in projects – http:// www.studygs.net/groupprojects.htm
- Working in Groups: http://bokcenter.harvard.edu/docs/wigintro.html
- A Definition of Collaborative vs. Cooperative Learning http://www. londonmet.ac.uk/deliberations/collaborative-learning/panitz-paper.cfm

APPENDIX E: GROUP WORK FORM CLASS TEMPLATE

Directions for this *Template:*

1. Go to your Google Docs, create a new doc, and do a copy of the template here and paste to your doc there. Then:
2. Close this document.
3. Name your document by clicking on the name area in the upper left.
4. In the upper right of each of your evaluations, use the Share > select Sharing Settings > add me to the contacts area as an editor.

Group Name	Fun Group Name
Group Members & Roles	List the Names of your group members and their roles. Roles are helpful to build on the strengths of the team/group members. There are many models for teams and roles. One model includes: leader – strength in organizing, may organize the Skype meeting, create an agenda, facilitate the conversation, etc.; recorder – strength in typing and summarizing, takes notes about what is discussed, makes sure notes are added to group space, keeps on top of group's shared knowledge, etc.; editor – strength in grammatical areas and how documents/presentations work, makes sure that group's product is grammatically correct, follows the guidelines, etc.; connector – strength in networking people, ideas, etc., helps leader keep track of team, keeps track of time, submits assignments to the instructor, etc. You are not bound to this model. It's just an example.
Participation	Members must share information, resources, and their unique ideas and perspective. Every member is responsible to participate in any weekly meetings or complete postings by a specific deadline for threaded discussions. How will you handle situations where a member is not participating?

Appendix E. (*Continued*)

Group Name	Fun Group Name
Communication	What tools will your group be using to collaborate? How often will you be getting together virtually? It's a REALLY good idea to compare schedules and set up meeting times right away.
Document Protocols	How will you handle subject line descriptors? File names? File revisions? E-mail courtesies?
Decisions	How will the group make decisions? Will the group be polled and differences explored? When is a high level of agreement needed and appropriate? When should the group ask for instructor input or help?
Conflicts	How will the group handle differences of opinion and conflicts?

APPENDIX F: TWITTER TOP 5 CLASS TEMPLATE GUIDE

How to use this document:

- *Copy the below information into your own Google doc*
- *Share your group document with all members of your group*
- *Share your group document with your instructor using gmail account*

Twitter Top 5 Group Work Guide

Group Member Names:

Group/Team Name:

Everyone take this pre-assessment quiz [link to pre-assessment quiz]

Social Media Resources

- What is Social Media in Plain English? http://www.youtube.com/watch?v = MpIOClX1jPE
- Other timely and relevant resources selected by the instructor

Twitter Resources You Should Explore Prior to Group Work

- What is Twitter? http://www.youtube.com/watch?v = ddO9idmax0o
- Other timely and relevant resources selected by the instructor

Part 1 Instructions. Value = 2 pts.

1. Create a Group Name: Your group name should be short (3–5 characters) and hashtagged
2. As a group, do some research about Twitter and add five new resources that you find here:
3. As a group, choose the one resource you would recommend the most here and explain what makes it your recommendation:
4. Create your Twitter accounts and list them here:

Part 2 Instructions. Value = 2 pts.

1. As a group search for the best people you can find to follow in the area of educational technology. List the Top 5 people to follow in the area of educational technology here:
2. As a group, identify the one person, you think is the best of the 5, create and tweet it with a very brief explanation of why that person is the best

and add your group's hashtag and the tag for the class you are taking. Copy your tweet here:

3. Optional: Identify other areas of interest to develop Top 5 lists for. (Meta Note: these lists make this type of activity friendly for any content area.)

Part 3 Instructions. Value = 1 pt.

Individually, throughout this activity, create a minimum of 2 tweets about what you learned. Make sure to use the class hashtag. Add a copy of each of your tweets here:

Everyone take this post-assessment quiz [link to post-assessment quiz]

APPENDIX G: GROUP PROJECT GUIDE

Project #2: Create a Group Learning Plan. Time: 2 hrs per week. Value: 100 pts by end of semester.

Overview

In order to support your school's teachers, you should know how to design technology enhanced and integrated learning experiences. Having something you've designed supports your credibility. With this Project, you will:

- Work in groups of 2–4 for this project.
- Review resources for developing a technology-enhanced and technology-integrated learning plan.
- Design a Learning Plan (for teachers or students) using the provided Learning Plan Template.
- In Units 3, 4, and 5 (at the end of the unit time frame) send me a progress report via Blackboard Mail. As part of your report, you can share chat logs, a link to your project, and reflections on the group work process. Create it together, but one person sends one progress report for the group. You can create a Google Doc where you add your reports and share it with your instructor at [instructor gmail here] and one person just notify me via LMS Mail when your report is ready.
- Present your Learning Plan to the class during Unit 6.

You will start this project now but it is not due until your presentation date/time near the end of the semester.

Project Instructions

Design a Learning Plan for your chosen audience. Make sure to review the rubric. Some key instructions include:

1. Use the Learning Plan Template provided and complete all elements of the Learning Plan
   a. See examples:
      1. https://c21cl.pbworks.com/NETS-S + 2 + Matrix + What + is + the + Internet + Lesson + Plan
      2. https://c21cl.pbworks.com/NETS-S + 4 + GPS + Lesson + Plan

2. Host your learning plan at class wiki or host your learning plan with your own online resource such as a wiki or a Google site. If you need to embed in the class wiki, pick someone from your group to ask to be an administrator in our class wiki.
3. Integrate media/multimedia in some way. You can create something or you can use something that already exists.
4. Integrate student use of technology.
5. Design options into your learning plan for individual and group work.
6. Post a link or upload your presentation slides in the Assignment tool > Project #2.
7. Present your Learning Plan via class presentation. Presentations will take place in the class Adobe Connect room which is linked in the Course Tools menu. HOWEVER, 10 extra credit points are available for groups who present via a livestreaming tool such as Livestream or Ustream or some other innovative means.
8. For criteria, see the Project #2 Rubric.

APPENDIX H: SURVEY

This survey asks questions about the group work (Project #2), including your perceptions about the group work collaboration process and online tools you used for group work collaboration in EDLT 528/628.

How did you feel about group work prior to taking EDLT 528/628?

Negative feelings | Somewhat negative feelings | Neutral or no feelings | Somewhat postive feeling | Positive feelings

Comments:

How did you feel about online tools for collaboration prior to EDLT 528/628?

Negative feelings | Somewhat negative feelings | Neutral or no feelings | Somewhat postive feeling | Positive feelings

Comments:

Did you participate in the class group work project in EDLT 528/628? This was the learning plan with presentation project that you did for Project #2.

Yes
No

If no, please explain why not? (if no, participant is done with survey)

There was a process for the use of tools in the course and the group work project, Project #2, that included the development of a Tech Toolkit and the use of online tools to complete a group work form. The following questions are about the online tools available for collaboration in EDLT 528/628.

Of the following online tools, which have you used before EDLT 528/628?

Never used | moderate use | frequent use

Adobe Connect
Skype
Blackboard Discussion
Blackboard Chat
Blackboard Mail
Gmail
Google Docs or other collaborative document
PBWorks or other wiki tool
Yammer
Twitter
Other

Comments:

Of the following tools, which tools were were most helpful to you in conducting your group work in EDLT 528/628?

Didn't use | Not helpful | somewhat helpful | helpful | very helpful

Adobe Connect
Skype
Blackboard Discussion
Blackboard Chat
Blackboard Mail
Gmail
Google Docs or other collaborative document
PBWorks or other wiki tool
Yammer
Twitter
Other

Comments:

How satisfied were you with the tools you used to complete Project #2 in EDLT 528/628?

Didn't use | unsatisfied | somewhat unsatisfied | somewhat satisfied | satisfied

Adobe Connect
Skype
Blackboard Discussion
Blackboard Chat
Blackboard Mail
Gmail
Google Docs or other collaborative document
PBWorks or other wiki tool
Yammer
Twitter
Other

Comments:

How did the tools you used to complete Project #2 impact your overall learning in EDLT 528/628?

negative impact | neutral or no impact | positive impact

Adobe Connect
Skype
Blackboard Discussion
Blackboard Chat
Blackboard Mail
Gmail
Google Docs or other collaborative document
PBWorks or other wiki tool
Yammer
Twitter
Other

Comments:

How did the tools you used to complete Project #2 impact your success in EDLT 528/628?

negative impact | neutral or no impact | positive impact

Adobe Connect
Skype
Blackboard Discussion
Blackboard Chat
Blackboard Mail
Gmail
Google Docs or other collaborative document
PBWorks or other wiki tool
Yammer
Twitter
Other

Comments:

There was a process for the group work including a group work and communication survey, group sign-up, group work form, learning plan template, group reporting, group presentations. The following questions are about this process.

How satisfied were you with the group work process for completing Project #2 in EDLT 528/628?

unsatisfied | somewhat unsatisfied | somewhat satisfied | satisfied |

Comments:

How did the group work process for Project #2 impact your overall learning in EDLT 528/628?

negative impact | neutral or no impact | positive impact

Comments:

How did the group work process for Project #2 impact your success in EDLT 528/628?

negative impact | neutral or no impact | positive impact

Comments:

Final Comments:

APPENDIX I: PERCENTAGES FOR TOOL USE PRIOR VS. HELPFULNESS OF TOOL FOR GROUP WORK

Tool	Percentage of student use prior to this course	Percentage found helpful
Adobe Connect	Never used – 65%	Didn't use or Not helpful – 18%
	Moderate use – 24%	Somewhat helpful – 18%
	Frequent use – 12%	Helpful or Very helpful – 64%
Skype	Never used – 18%	Didn't use or Not helpful – 0%
	Moderate use – 35%	Somewhat helpful – 0%
	Frequent use – 47%	Helpful or Very helpful – 100%
Blackboard Discussion	Never used – 6%	Didn't use or Not helpful – 30%
	Moderate use – 18%	Somewhat helpful – 6%
	Frequent use – 76%	Helpful or Very helpful – 65%
Blackboard Chat	Never used – 18%	Didn't use or Not helpful – 71%
	Moderate use – 65%	Somewhat helpful – 12%
	Frequent use – 18%	Helpful or Very helpful – 0%
Blackboard Mail	Never used – 0%	Didn't use or Not helpful – 12%
	Moderate use – 18%	Somewhat helpful – 12%
	Frequent use – 82%	Helpful or Very helpful – 76%
Gmail	Never used – 35%	Didn't use or Not helpful – 6%
	Moderate use – 24%	Somewhat helpful – 24%
	Frequent use – 41%	Helpful or Very helpful – 70%
Google Docs or other collaborative document	Never used – 41%	Didn't use or Not helpful – 0%
	Moderate use – 29%	Somewhat helpful – 6%
	Frequent use – 29%	Helpful or Very helpful – 94%
	Never used – 65%	Didn't use or Not helpful – 36%
	Moderate use – 24%	Somewhat helpful – 18%

Appendix I. (*Continued*)

Tool	Percentage of student use prior to this course	Percentage found helpful
PBWorks or other wiki tool	Frequent use – 12%	Helpful or Very helpful – 47%
Yammer	Never used – 76%	Didn't use or Not helpful – 47%
	Moderate use – 18%	Somewhat helpful – 6%
	Frequent use – 6%	Helpful or Very helpful – 47%
Twitter	Never used – 65%	Didn't use or Not helpful – 53%
	Moderate use – 29%	Somewhat helpful – 18%
	Frequent use – 6%	Helpful or Very helpful – 30%

APPENDIX J: PERCENTAGES FOR STUDENT SATISFACTION OF TOOLS USED TO COMPLETE GROUP PROJECT

Tool	Tool satisfaction
Adobe Connect	Didn't use, Unsatisfied, or Somewhat unsatisfied – 18%
	Somewhat satisfied – 12%
	Satisfied – 71%
Skype	Didn't use, Unsatisfied, or Somewhat unsatisfied – 0%
	Somewhat satisfied – 6%
	Satisfied – 94%
Blackboard Discussion	Didn't use, Unsatisfied, or Somewhat unsatisfied – 18%
	Somewhat satisfied – 24%
	Satisfied – 59%
Blackboard Chat	Didn't use, Unsatisfied, or Somewhat unsatisfied – 59%
	Somewhat satisfied – 18%
	Satisfied – 24%
Blackboard Mail	Didn't use, Unsatisfied, or Somewhat unsatisfied – 18%
	Somewhat satisfied – 18%
	Satisfied – 65%
Gmail	Didn't use, Unsatisfied, or Somewhat unsatisfied – 6%
	Somewhat satisfied – 29%
	Satisfied – 65%

Appendix J. (*Continued*)

Tool	Tool satisfaction
Google Docs or other collaborative document	Didn't use, Unsatisfied, or Somewhat unsatisfied – 6%
	Somewhat satisfied – 12%
	Satisfied – 82%
PBWorks or other wiki tool	Didn't use, Unsatisfied, or Somewhat unsatisfied – 24%
	Somewhat satisfied – 18%
	Satisfied – 59%
Yammer	Didn't use, Unsatisfied, or Somewhat unsatisfied – 42%
	Somewhat satisfied – 35%
	Satisfied –24%
Twitter	Didn't use, Unsatisfied, or Somewhat unsatisfied – 48%
	Somewhat satisfied – 35%
	Satisfied – 18%

APPENDIX K: PERCENTAGES FOR IMPACT OF TOOL USE ON STUDENT OVERALL LEARNING

Tool	Impact of tool on overall learning
Adobe Connect	Negative impact – 0%
	Neutral or no impact – 29%
	Positive impact – 71%
Skype	Negative impact – 0%
	Neutral or no impact – 0%
	Positive impact – 100%
Blackboard Discussion	Negative impact – 0%
	Neutral or no impact – 35%
	Positive impact – 65%
Blackboard Chat	Negative impact – 6%
	Neutral or no impact – 71%
	Positive impact – 24%
Blackboard Mail	Negative impact – 0%
	Neutral or no impact – 47%
	Positive impact – 53%
Gmail	Negative impact – 0%
	Neutral or no impact – 18%
	Positive impact – 82%
Google Docs or other collaborative document	Negative impact – 0%
	Neutral or no impact – 6%
	Positive impact – 94%

Appendix K. (*Continued*)

Tool	Impact of tool on overall learning
PBWorks or other wiki tool	Negative impact – 0%
	Neutral or no impact – 41%
	Positive impact – 59%
Yammer	Negative impact – 0%
	Neutral or no impact – 65%
	Positive impact – 35%
Twitter	Negative impact – 0%
	Neutral or no impact – 71%
	Positive impact – 29%

APPENDIX L: PERCENTAGES FOR IMPACT OF TOOL USE ON OVERALL STUDENT SUCCESS IN ONLINE COURSE

Tool	Impact of tool on overall learning
Adobe Connect	Negative impact – 0%
	Neutral or no impact – 35%
	Positive impact – 65%
Skype	Negative impact – 0%
	Neutral or no impact – 0%
	Positive impact – 100%
Blackboard Discussion	Negative impact – 0%
	Neutral or no impact – 24%
	Positive impact – 76%
Blackboard Chat	Negative impact – 0%
	Neutral or no impact – 76%
	Positive impact – 24%
Blackboard Mail	Negative impact – 0%
	Neutral or no impact – 29%
	Positive impact – 71%
Gmail	Negative impact – 0%
	Neutral or no impact – 12%
	Positive impact – 88%
Google Docs or other collaborative document	Negative impact – 0%
	Neutral or no impact – 6%
	Positive impact – 94%

Appendix L. (*Continued*)

Tool	Impact of tool on overall learning
PBWorks or other wiki tool	Negative impact – 0%
	Neutral or no impact – 47%
	Positive impact – 53%
Yammer	Negative impact – 0%
	Neutral or no impact – 65%
	Positive impact – 35%
Twitter	Negative impact – 0%
	Neutral or no impact – 65%
	Positive impact – 35%

BALANCING STUDENTS' PRIVACY CONCERNS WHILE INCREASING STUDENT ENGAGEMENT IN E-LEARNING ENVIRONMENTS

Lynne Siemens, Catherine Althaus and Charlotte Stange

ABSTRACT

The ultimate objective of any learning platform is student engagement with the material, instructor, and classmates. Little is currently known about students' concerns regarding privacy, confidentiality, and information safety and the potential impact these may have on engagement within an online learning environment. Existing literature and practice must be supplemented with awareness of the importance of student perceptions concerning privacy and confidentiality if online learning engagement is to be maximized. Our exploratory research shows that students do experience concerns, that these concerns can be impacted by the professional school status of the students in question, and that students take steps to create safety accordingly. As a result, student engagement within an online learning environment is different than its physical counterpart. Our

Increasing Student Engagement and Retention in e-Learning Environments:
Web 2.0 and Blended Learning Technologies
Cutting-edge Technologies in Higher Education, Volume 6G, 339–357
Copyright © 2013 by Emerald Group Publishing Limited
All rights of reproduction in any form reserved
ISSN: 2044-9968/doi:10.1108/S2044-9968(2013)000006G014

findings and subsequent recommendations suggest more can be done to maximize the notion of learning safety and student online learning engagement.

INTRODUCTION

Advances in many emerging technologies have provided new opportunities within e-learning environments to extend students' engagement with course material, each other, and their instructors (Chen, Gonyea, & Kuh, 2008). In response, many postsecondary institutions are using these online technologies as the primary medium of instruction and interaction in distance education courses and as supplements to the instructional techniques pursued in the more traditional on-campus classroom. Examples of these learning platforms include Moodle, Blackboard, WebCT, and many others.

The physical and virtual classrooms are in many respects similar in that students often draw upon their experiences to engage with course material. At the same time, the online medium allows for information to be communicated quickly and affords learners convenience and flexibility with regard to completing coursework on their own time and in their own place. However, unlike the physical classroom, information shared in an e-learning environment may be stored longer and copied more easily into other formats and distributed beyond the course than is typically the case with the traditional class. As a result, students may see the online environment as less private and may be less inclined to share information and be engaged in their learning; admittedly, a position that may be at odds with their use of social media in their personal lives (Lewis, Kaufman, & Christakis, 2008; Tu & McIsaac, 2002). This situation may be especially a risk in professional schools where learning encourages practitioner- and client-focused perspectives; information and experience exchange forms a crucial part of the learning process and due respect and confidentiality protection must be incorporated.

However, at this point, little is known about students' concerns regarding privacy and the corresponding confidentiality and safety of their information and the potential impact these may have on engagement within an online learning environment. Given the clear link between students' perceptions about the learning context and their engagement with course material, each other, and the instructor, it becomes important to clearly understand the student perspective on privacy, confidentiality, and safety within the online course context (Frey, Faul, & Yankelov, 2003; Huang, 2002; Yang, Tsai, Kim, Cho, & Laffey, 2006). With this information, instructors can then design online courses that balance students' understandings and requirements for privacy while developing and supporting student engagement.

This chapter explores students' perceptions of privacy and the manner in which these may impact engagement within e-learning environments and makes recommendations for both students and instructors alike to maximize student learning. First, the context for online learning and definitions for privacy and associated factors surrounding confidentiality and safety of that information are outlined, followed by discussion of the research methodology. Next, the research findings from interviews with students who have taken at least one online course within a Canadian professional graduate program are discussed. The chapter concludes with recommendations as well as arguing for more research in this important advancing area of learning and teaching.

DISCUSSION OF THE ONLINE LEARNING ENVIRONMENT

Information technology is now commonplace on most postsecondary campuses and pervades all aspects of instructor and student life from communication to course delivery (Earp & Payton, 2001). An online course provides many advantages to students, including the ability to study while working and remaining in one's home community (Chen et al., 2008; Frey et al., 2003). While benefits to the use of these platforms and technologies exist, little is understood about the challenges that these learning platforms and technologies present to students' privacy and the subsequent impact on student engagement (Culnan & Carlin, 2009; Yang et al., 2006).

Use of Online Learning Technologies

In addition to being a supplement within a traditional on-campus course, postsecondary institutions are using online technologies to deliver distance education (Conaway, Easton, & Schmidt, 2005). As a result, universities are able to attract students who may not otherwise have been able to pursue further education, including older learners and those wishing to study on a part-time basis (Chen et al., 2008). This trend is likely to continue both from advances in technology which facilitate distance education and increased demand from students (Bell, 2010).

As a form of distance education, online learning can be defined as "any class that offers its entire curriculum in the online course delivery mode, thereby allowing students to participate regardless of geographic location, independent of time and place" (Richardson & Swan, 2003, p. 69). Most, if not all, aspects of a course, including discussions, assignment submission, and communication with the instructor, tend to be facilitated through online course management platforms such as Moodle, Blackboard, Webboard, and supplemental communication technology such as Elluminate, Skype, and others. Given this context, online courses are different from their on-campus counterparts in several aspects (Blair & Hoy, 2006; Muilenburg & Berge, 2005; Powers & Mitchell, 1997). One difference focuses on the delivery of the course material, shifting from oral to predominately written format. Unlike a traditional classroom which tends to be based around a lecture, online students often take a more active role in their learning by reading assigned material and instructor notes and then participating in facilitated interactive written discussions. They may also never meet their classmates in person. Further, students tend to conduct most communication with the instructor and each other through discussion postings, messaging systems, and e-mails, which often occur asynchronously. Learners post at their convenience, which often occurs after time for thought and contemplation on the course material (Richardson & Swan, 2003). Further, the time commitment for participation and response tends to be high and perhaps less dynamic and interactive within real time and place as compared to the physical classroom (Powers & Mitchell, 1997). Students also encounter a technological and pedagogical learning curve in their first online course which must be mastered before they feel fully comfortable (Arbaugh, 2004; Muilenburg & Berge, 2005). Instructors themselves also face pedagogical challenges as they move from traditional lectures to facilitation through targeted discussion forums.

As online learning grows in application, universities, instructors, and students alike need to ensure that the quality of learning experience through these courses is not impacted or lessened when compared to more traditional learning models. Initial research has demonstrated that online learning outcomes are at the very least equal to those of traditional courses, despite perceptions to the contrary (Arbaugh, 2004; Muilenburg & Berge, 2005). Having said this, continual steps must be taken by both instructors and students to mitigate any challenges that might lessen student learning and engagement, including a lack of familiarity with the technology, differing comfort levels with communicating almost exclusively in writing and conducting online group work, and concerns about privacy and confidentiality within a school context (Kuh, 2001; Sheehan, 2002).

Understanding of Privacy Within the Online Learning Environment

Research on privacy and the willingness to share information online, especially as it relates to students' personal lives as opposed to their school ones, is becoming robust (Culnan & Carlin, 2009). However, privacy can have multiple meanings and must be clearly defined and clarified for application within an online learning environment.

At the heart of online privacy is the concept that people are and should be in control of who sees their personal information and when this occurs (Culnan & Carlin, 2009; Tang, Hu, & Smith, 2008). This understanding encompasses both real and perceived conditions, where the latter refers to conditions that people believe something to be private even when it is not and vice versa (Monfils, 1993). Further, one's sense of what is private is shaped by context and personal factors, such as age, education, and other characteristics, making the concept very individualistic (Sheehan, 2002; Tu, 2002). Tied closely to privacy is the safety and confidentiality of that private information. While students may feel comfortable sharing some types of information, they want to ensure that only those for whom the information is intended actually see it. This means that individuals also want to ensure that this is safely stored and limits are in place to prevent access and use for purposes other than intended (Culnan & Carlin, 2009). Within this context, confidentiality means that one's data is only seen by those who need it (Connolly, 1994). It should be noted that in the university environment a student's personal information includes not only their names and grades but also their assignments, personal views, and opinions (University of Victoria, 2011).

Privacy in the online learning environment can be protected through a variety of means. First, the learning service provider, either the university or the owner of the technology used by the university, must ensure that appropriate policies and privacy protection mechanisms are in place. Privacy risks may be posed when instructors use nonuniversity based learning platforms where the privacy protection measures of the learning tool may be beyond the scope and legislative framework in which the university must operate (Blazic & Klobucar, 2004). Second, while recognizing that learning is inherently a social act, the instructor and students themselves have the responsibility to ensure that appropriate information is shared within the course and stays within its boundaries (Edmondson, 1999; Lowyck & Poysa, 2001).

Consequently, the ability to secure privacy and the corresponding safety and confidentiality of the data within an online course may take different concerns than those found in its physical counterpart (Sheehan, 2002; Tu, 2002). First, since most interactions within an online course are written, a more permanent record of a discussion is created, stored, and retrievable over the course of a term. Conceivably, and with some justifiable concern, these written interactions can be more easily copied and distributed to individuals outside the class than the oral discussions in the traditional classroom, meaning that extra steps may be needed to ensure that these written records are kept private, safe, and confidential. It is typically more inconvenient to share conversations verbatim outside the physical class. (Of course, this may be changing with the ubiquity of smart phones and tablet computers with voice recorder capability.) A student may also be able to deny any comments attributed to them because a verifiable record from the physical classroom often does not exist. Given that online students seldom meet each other face-to-face, it may be more difficult to develop a level of trust with each other that might preclude the sharing of personal information without the permission of the individual, as is the case with the traditional classroom.

Given this context, distance education students may be more concerned with their ability (or lack thereof) to control with whom and how their information is shared and will change their behavior accordingly. At the same time, students may not be aware that they should be familiar with privacy issues within the online environment and read privacy notices (Milne & Culnan, 2004; Tu, 2002). It is also possible that students may realize that some degree of privacy must be given up to participate in online learning activities (Gerjets & Hesse, 2004; Sheehan, 2002; Tu, 2002; Tu & McIsaac, 2002). However, before they do so, students need to educate themselves about the nature of trade-offs between advantages and risks of sharing personal information in an online course, a step that they often do not take (Johns & Lawson, 2005; Milne & Culnan, 2004; Sheehan, 2002; Tu, 2002). It is important to note that students may evaluate their privacy and willingness to share their information differently depending on whether they are considering their school lives or private ones. For example, they may share some information available on Facebook, Twitter, and other social media outlets that they might not feel comfortable sharing with their classmates (Lewis et al., 2008).

Link Between Privacy and Student Engagement

Regardless of the manner in which a course is delivered, the ultimate objective is student engagement with the material, instructor, and classmates. Within this context, higher student engagement, as evidenced by an individual student's mind-set and overall approach toward learning, translates into learning, high grades, and satisfaction with the course (Chen et al., 2008; Conaway et al., 2005; Kuh, 2001). By working together, students and instructors can take active steps to develop and sustain the required mind-set that ensures that learners have the ability to use and feel comfort with the technology and course material and that they see themselves as a member of a learning community, albeit one that never meets in person (Conaway et al., 2005; Tu & McIsaac, 2002; Yang et al., 2006). In describing effective teams, Edmondson (1999, p. 354) describes this as the creation of psychological safety where individuals will have the "sense of confidence that the team will not embarrass or reject someone for speaking up" and mutual trust and respect, allowing for learning and accomplishment. Applying these ideas to the classroom, Xu and Yi (2010) suggest that instructors and students have developed psychological safety when they are open to different perspectives. This idea can be extended further to consideration of privacy and a trust that other members of the course will not share personal information with outsiders.

Given the differences between virtual and physical courses, student engagement may occur and develop differently in an e-learning environment. However, it is not known how, if at all, students' concerns regarding privacy impacts their engagement within the online course by potentially limiting participation and sharing information and connecting with their classmates and instructor (Tu, 2002; Tu & McIsaac, 2002; Yang et al., 2006). This means that there may be different and even decreased student engagement in online courses as compared to physical ones (Chen et al., 2008; Kuh, 2001). By understanding this relationship and the nature of the privacy concerns, students and instructors alike can take steps to mitigate the privacy concerns and encourage engagement.

METHODOLOGY

This chapter examines students' perceptions of privacy and potential impact on engagement within an online learning environment through the use of exploratory in-depth interviews with students. This qualitative approach was considered appropriate given that the relationship between privacy perceptions and student engagement is not yet well understood. Through the interviews, the participants could develop a rapport with the interviewer, allowing for more open discussions shaped by their own perceptions and contexts (Marshall & Rossman, 1999; Rubin & Rubin, 1995).

This study's population are students in the School of Public Administration's Masters of Public Administration (MPA) program at the University of Victoria, British Columbia. Offered both in full-time on-campus and part-time online program formats, the MPA is designed to prepare students for work in the public sector (School of Public Administration, n.d.-b, n.d.-c). The online program uses Moodle as the learning platform to manage course notes, discussions forums, assignment submission, and correspondence with the instructor (School of Public Administration, n.d.-a). While part-time students take all their courses online, some full-time students also participate in these courses and use Moodle technology for supplemental instructional delivery in their on-campus classes.

A recruitment notice was circulated through the school's e-mail distribution list, inviting students who had taken at least one online course in the MPA program to voluntarily participate in the research. An interview guide was developed following a review of the relevant literature (Montgomery, 1999). This review allows the researcher to develop a clear understanding of the research question and facilitates the data analysis during the interview and the formation of follow-up questions (Strauss & Corbin, 1998).

Interviewed individually, these participants were asked questions in the following areas: the extent and nature of their concern for privacy in the context of their online courses, knowledge of privacy policies, the privacy characteristics of the online learning environment, students' engagement in online courses, factors that affect their online engagement, and recommendations for improving student online engagement (see Stange, 2011 for a list of specific questions). The participants were only given a general idea of the research purpose in advance of the interviews. The rationale behind this approach was that the researcher wanted to understand the interviewee's prior knowledge and concern with privacy issues without the potential influence created by receiving the questions in advance.

Data analysis involved a grounded theory approach to focus on the themes that emerged from the data. This analysis was broken into several steps. First, the data was organized, read, and coded to determine categories, themes, and patterns. These were tested for emergent and alternative understandings, both within a single case and across all the cases. This was an iterative process, involving movement between data, codes, and concepts, constantly comparing the data to itself and the developing theory. Data analysis and interpretation was further supported through a review of theoretical literature (Glaser & Strauss, 1967; Marshall & Rossman, 1999).

FINDINGS

A total of 20 students, 11 from the online program and 9 from the on-campus version, were interviewed. These students ranged in age from 24 to 60 years, with the average age of 34. The part-time students were on average older than the on-campus ones. Some students had extensive experience learning online while others had only taken one or two courses in this manner. The participant characteristics are outlined in Table 1. Overall, the findings indicate that despite statements to the contrary, students have privacy concerns and undertake several strategies to mitigate these concerns and engage in the course material.

Privacy Concerns

When initially asked, the participants stated that they felt safe within the online learning environment. Often, these positive feelings stemmed from the fact that they had not had any negative experiences that might create feelings of a lack of safety, that they felt universities, instructors, and classmates would treat their personal information with the care it was due, and they could not think of potential risks.

However, as more questions were asked, the students began to reveal their concerns, especially as they related to the safety of information related to their workplaces. Instructors often ask students to provide workplace

Table 1. Participant Characteristics.

$N = 20$	All Students	Online Students	On-Campus Students
Students interviewed	20	11	9
Courses taken online (average)	5.5	9	2
Courses taken online (range)	1–16	3–16	1–3
Age in years (average)	34.1	37.8	34.1
Age in years (range)	24–60	27–52	24–60

information in introduction activities and discussion and assignment questions. While students did not mind sharing job titles and descriptions, they indicated they were hesitant to go beyond that and share more specific data with their classmates. Because they often had not met them, they did not feel that they could trust their classmates to not share this information outside class, where it might be misinterpreted, taken out of context, or viewed as unfavorable criticism of an employer, program, or policy. They were also concerned that their opinions may be misinterpreted as representing official ones of their employer or as partisan, a characteristic not desirable within a public servant. Some students indicated that they were legally bound not to share workplace information outside their offices, further complicating their ability to fully engage in online discussions and other learning activities. Ultimately, the participants were aware that the written nature of online course interactions made their participation potentially more permanent than those in the physical classroom.

At the same time, the participants also expressed some reservation about sharing certain forms of personal information. They tended to use official university e-mail accounts, rather than personal ones, for correspondence and were not always comfortable posting pictures of themselves as part of their online course profiles.

Despite these concerns, the participants admitted that their knowledge of privacy was limited and they had not really thought about the issue within the online course context. They did not know the university's specific policies and legal obligations regarding the privacy, confidentiality, and security of students' personal data, but admitted that they were unlikely to read these policies even if they were made more clearly available. In particular, students noted that these policies tended to be lengthy and not easily understandable and lacked direct relevance. Some felt that they did not need to be informed because they trusted that the university would not abuse their personal data. Further, the students often made assumptions about what happens to course material, including assignments, discussions, and correspondence after term, ranging from the possibility that it "imploded" to indefinitely archived. (In reality, courses with student participation are kept for one year, corresponding to the period for the grade appeal process. At that time, all student data is stripped out and the course shell is backed up and used again (E. Price-Edney, personal communication, November 9, 2010)). It should be noted that in contrast to the above knowledge (or lack thereof) of university policies on these issues, many students were very aware of privacy policies and regulations in the context of their professional lives. Some had participated in mandatory privacy training and were cognizant of the types of information that they were permitted to share.

Strategies to Address Privacy Concerns and Create a Feeling of Safety Within the Course

While students suggested that they were relatively unconcerned about privacy and the safety and confidentiality of their information within their online course, they did take active steps to create feelings of learning safety. Many felt that they had a responsibility themselves to behave in such a way as to avoid potential risks to their privacy by limiting the information that they shared. These participants tended to alter details about some workplace examples or chose not to share certain kinds of private and workplace information. For example, in their introductory statements, participants outlined generalities that met the instructor's requirements without revealing specific workplace information. A student might list a government department as their employer, rather than a specific unit. They might also discuss their general work duties rather than provide specific job title.

These students also created a distinction between their personal and school lives. Some students used their less private university e-mail account, rather than a Hotmail or Google one, for course work. They often shared less important e-mail addresses that could be easily closed after a course if necessary. For those students who attached photographs to their profiles, they used ones from a professional setting or where they were unrecognizable, shaping the way in which they would be viewed. As an example, one student posted a picture of themselves in a winter parka and toque that was taken from afar.

Finally, given their concern that their postings might be distributed beyond the classroom, the participants often carefully edited them to remove potentially sensitive information or opinions and to ensure that they could not be easily misinterpreted. A majority of students held back on content in their discussion because they were not sure how particular information, including workplace examples, opinions, and others, might be received and understood by classmates, especially since they could not read verbal and nonverbal cues. One student stated, "I was still expressing my opinions but maybe not as forcefully as I would necessarily if I was in a face to face discussion with someone who could read my body language." The fact that they did not know their classmates further served to make them hesitant to share certain types of information in the online discussion forums. One student stated that "you don't always realize who knows who with respect to your online classmates."

At the same time, students indicated that instructors also play an important role in creating a safe learning environment. For example, instructors should acknowledge and take actions to minimize students' privacy concerns by providing information and policies about privacy in course outlines and/or as brief statements on Moodle course sites. This information would be at both the official policy level but also as a "code of conduct" for students and instructors to ensure the private and confidential nature of students' contributions. The interview participants indicated that they preferred to get information about privacy policies in this forum, rather than having to seek it out from the general university website. However, several indicated that they realized that an instructor's guidelines could not be easily enforced, and as such, had little value to actually ensuring privacy.

Students also felt more comfortable sharing their own private information when instructors led by example by sharing their own personal and background information. Instructors' comfort and technological proficiency with the particular learning platform was necessary to ensure that a student's private information was not accidently released. A perception existed among some participants that "... in a few cases the faculty members have had absolutely no training in how to deal with a class in an online setting whatsoever." In one case, a student had an assignment returned, with instructor comments, via a public posting on Moodle for all to see.

By taking these above-mentioned steps, students created a feeling of safety and trust which influenced their course participation in learning activities and discussion forums. With this trust in place, they felt comfortable to share information, knowing it would stay within the course "walls."

Relationship between Privacy Concerns and Student Engagement

Ultimately, the interviewed students engaged differently in their online courses, as compared to on campus class participation. These differences are more a function of the online medium's characteristics, rather than the perceived privacy concerns; they may simply be the expected difference between more informal oral communication within the traditional class-room and the formal written communication in a virtual course.

Given that most class participation took place in the form of written postings, these students felt that more time and effort was needed to ensure that content was coherent, well-written, and did not potentially reveal certain kinds of workplace information than they might have otherwise. They were also cognizant of the fact that these postings were visible all term and may be revisited and subject to further discussion. Further, the participants perceived that online instructors had higher expectations for the quality and length of their postings, thus creating a burden that could not be avoided due to participation marks. For example, "I was very mindful of wanting to post regularly because that's an easy mark to get." Another student echoed this sentiment by stating "if there's two minimum postings a week, then I'll post three or four times, but not really because I'm into it, just because I want to make sure that I hit those marks on their [the instructors] spreadsheets." While they may have been more hesitant to share certain types of information online, they still posted regularly due to course requirements.

The interviews suggest the relationship between privacy concerns and student engagement is more nuanced than initially envisioned. Students do have privacy concerns for which they take active steps to mitigate and create a safe learning environment. They also look to their instructors as role models and important participants in this process. And in the end, students engage differently by often being more formal and less candid than they might be in a traditional classroom.

DISCUSSION

This research shows that students do experience privacy, safety, and confidentiality concerns and take steps to manage these within the e-learning environment. While this research confirms the generally accepted definitions of privacy, it also provides a more nuanced understanding of the type of information that students are interested in protecting within the context of online courses. For this particular group of students, the concerns were more professional in nature, rather than personal, meaning that they did not feel comfortable reporting workplace-related information or experiences. Further, this concern was expressed in the context of the discussion forums, which tend to be the least private parts of an online course. Assignments which only the instructor sees and evaluates were less of a concern (Blair & Hoy, 2006; Tu & McIsaac, 2002). This finding is perhaps not surprising given the professional nature of the graduate program and the privacy concerns may be different for undergraduate students or even different types of graduate programs. Regardless, trust between students and instructors needs to be cultivated for students to feel comfortable sharing information, an inherent part of learning (Lowyck & Poysa, 2001; Milne & Culnan, 2004).

Further, while they are not necessarily cognizant of privacy policies, students employed a variety of coping strategies to protect their privacy and control who can see what aspects of their information, including comments, postings, and identities, and create a feeling of safety in the class (Culnan & Carlin, 2009; Tang et al., 2008). At the same time, they ceded some responsibility for that protection of their personal data to the university by not searching out, reading, and understanding the relevant institutional policies (Johns & Lawson, 2005; Milne & Culnan, 2004; Proctor, Athar Ali, & Vu, 2008). Within the University of Victoria context, six policies address issues of privacy, confidentiality, and security of data, including protection of privacy policy, responsible use of information technology services, records management policy, information security policy, policy regarding access to student records, and archives: freedom of information guidelines (see Stange, 2011 for a fuller discussion). Perhaps, given that this array of policies is not necessarily directly related to the online classroom, it is not surprising that many students (and instructors) have not read these (Milne & Culnan, 2004). In many cases, the interview participants placed trust in the university that it would not do anything contrary with their data, a trust that they did not necessarily grant other organizations (Sheehan, 2002). This lack of awareness of the issues and policies for protection may be because the policies are long, abstract, and are not necessarily applied to the specific context of an online course and the particular perspective of the user (Culnan & Carlin, 2009; Proctor et al., 2008). However, as recent events surrounding an info breach at the University of Victoria show (University of Victoria, 2012), even the most trusted of organizations can make mistakes with personal data, despite the appropriate policies being in place (Culnan & Carlin, 2009).

Finally, the nature of the online medium becomes tied into students' engagement with the course material. Contrary to earlier studies which suggest that students in online courses are less engaged (Tu, 2002), these findings suggest that students engage differently, rather than more or less. While they participated as required, these students shaped (or in some cases, censored) their contributions in terms of content, format, and tone. They did not feel that they could be candid and had to be cautious to ensure that comments were not misinterpreted and/or taken out of context, particularly if their postings were distributed beyond the class. As suggested in the literature, part of this hesitation demonstrates the difficulty of building the necessary trust between classmates and instructor which can be an important foundation for the sharing of any kind (Milne & Culnan, 2004). This speaks to the important role that instructors play in creating a safe learning environment by protecting student privacy within appropriate guidelines, sharing information about themselves, and understanding the technology to prevent accidental disclosure (Edmondson, 1999; Nembhard & Edmondson, 2006; Xu & Yi, 2010).

RECOMMENDATIONS AND CONCLUSIONS

Several recommendations to address privacy concerns and create a safe learning environment can be made (Culnan & Carlin, 2009; Milne & Culnan, 2004). Within the larger university context, both the instructor and student have responsibilities for the creation of this environment and encouragement of student learning (Conaway et al., 2005).

First, while students tend not to seek out and read relevant university privacy and confidentiality policies, they are more likely to read course outlines and course platform forums. As a result, these become a more logical place to incorporate a learner-centered privacy notice with information about privacy risks, the privacy capacity of the online learning platform, and the long-term storage policy as they specifically relate to online courses, and steps to manage the risks. This wording should also acknowledge the fact that there are other individuals, beyond the students and instructors, who have access to the course site. These can include program administrative staff and online help desk staff (Distance Education Services, 2012). These statements would be the first step to ensure that students have correct information about the privacy, security, and confidentiality protection that already exists. Further, these notices can outline norms of appropriate online classroom behavior and remind students that information should not be shared outside the course (e.g., see Distance Education Services, 2012; Stange, 2011). While this may not fully guarantee privacy and safety, these statements do ensure that students understand their responsibilities to each other, thus building trust that is necessary for learning (Culnan & Carlin, 2009; Milne & Culnan, 2004; Xu & Yi, 2010). Instructors can also share additional resources that can educate students on their responsibilities toward their own information, such as University of British Columbia's Digital Tattoo Program (n.d.). Further, opportunities may also exist to ensure specialized training on privacy and confidentiality when these students and instructors begin university, similar to that provided on library and other university resources.

With this knowledge about relevant policies and expectations, students' comfort interacting in their online courses will likely be positively affected. An increase in trust in the university's privacy and confidentiality policies could provide a counterbalance to the lack of trust that students have in each other due to unfamiliarity. An additional outcome of these course notices is the education of instructors, particularly those on contract, in their own responsibilities with regards to relevant university policies on personal information.

Second, instructors should provide students with a set of clear expectations for participation in online courses, including the level of formality required in course postings, and the level of detail needed when using workplace examples. Students would then be aware that sharing workplace information and examples in classes is not compulsory, and that it is acceptable to alter or combine workplace examples to make them more anonymous. This clarification of required level of formality in online discussion postings would reduce the perceived burden of extra work and allow students to focus on the content of their contributions. Further to this, instructors can model the type of behavior that balances privacy and confidentiality with engagement and sharing that they expect of their students within the online course. By providing alternatives and informing students of ways in which relevant examples can be shared with the class while at the same time respecting the employer's and student's privacy, students' comfort and engagement in online classes could be positively affected (Edmondson, 1999).

Third, instructors should ensure that they receive the necessary technological and pedagogical training to effectively use these emerging technologies to facilitate and create a safe e-learning environment that leads to increased student engagement; recognizing that such training will need to accommodate professional school concerns. This training can cover topics like how to facilitate an online course, differences between on-campus and online teaching and student engagement, and their role and leadership in creating a safe learning environment (Distance Education Services, n.d.; Edmondson, 1999; Nembhard & Edmondson, 2006). Ideally, with appropriate training, instructors will be less likely to inadvertently share private information.

Lastly, more research is needed to expand this exploratory research into other groups of students, such as undergraduates and graduate students in traditional programs vis-à-vis professional schools. It would also be useful to understand these issues from the instructor point of view with regards to their awareness of their responsibilities, students' perceptions, and ways to create a safe online learning environment (Siemens & Althaus, 2011). The results from this research will create a better understanding of student privacy concerns and ways to encourage engagement in online classes, thereby enhancing the learning objective that rests at the heart of all post-secondary education.

This chapter has shown that literature and practice concerning emerging learning technologies must be supplemented with awareness of the importance of student perceptions concerning privacy and confidentiality if learning engagement is to be maximized in the online environment. Our exploratory research shows that students do experience concerns, that these concerns can be impacted by the professional school status of the students in question, and that students take steps to create safety accordingly. As a result, student engagement is different in online learning in comparison to its physical classroom counterpart. From student information alone, we suggest that more can be done to maximize the notion of learning safety and student engagement. Instructors and learning institutions can take proactive steps such as developing specialized course notices, making clear statements of expectations and modeling behavior to further empower students in their privacy and confidentiality awareness. These recommendations are aimed at improving training and awareness for all contributors to the learning process so that online learning can advance in its contribution to the education endeavor.

REFERENCES

Arbaugh, J. B. (2004). Learning to learn online: A study of perceptual changes between multiple online course experiences. *Internet and Higher Education, 7*(3), 169–182.

Bell, N. (2010). *Graduate enrollment and degrees: 1999–2009*. Washington, DC: Council of Graduate Schools.

Blair, K., & Hoy, C. (2006). Paying attention to adult learners online: The pedagogy and politics of community. *Distance Learning: Evolving Perspectives, 23*(1), 32–48.

Blazic, K., & Klobucar, T. (2004). Privacy provision in e-learning standardized systems: Status and improvements. *Computer Standards & Interfaces, 27,* 561–578.

Chen, P.-S. D., Gonyea, R., & Kuh, G. D. (2008). Learning at a distance: Engaged or not? *Journal of Online Education, 4*(3). Available at http://www.innovateonline.info/pdf/vol4_issue3/Learning_at_a_Distance-_Engaged_or_Not_.pdf

Conaway, R. N., Easton, S. S., & Schmidt, W. V. (2005). Strategies for enhancing student interaction and imediacy in online courses. *Business Communications Quarterly, 68*(1), 23–35.

Connolly, F. W. (1994). Who are the electronic learners? Why should we worry about them? Introducing a bill of rights and responsibilities for electronic learners. *Change, 26,* 39–41.

Culnan, M. J., & Carlin, T. J. (2009). Online privacy practices in higher education: Making the grade? *Communications of the ACM, 52,* 126–130.

Distance Education Services. (2012). *Privacy considerations in moodle.* Retrieved from http://distance.uvic.ca/onlinehelp/tutorials/moodle/privacy.htm

Distance Education Services. (n.d.). *Your online presence/role.* Retrieved from http://distance.uvic.ca/instructors/presence.htm

Earp, J. B., & Payton, F. C. (2001). Data protection in the university setting: Employee perceptions of student privacy. Paper presented at the 34th Hawaii international conference on system sciences, Hawaii.

Edmondson, A. (1999). Psychological safety and learning behavior in work teams. *Administrative Science Quarterly, 44*(2), 350–383.

Frey, A., Faul, A., & Yankelov, P. (2003). Student perceptions of web-assisted teaching strategies. *Journal of Social Work Education, 39*(3), 443–457.

Gerjets, P. H., & Hesse, F. W. (2004). When are powerful learning environments effective? The role of learner activities and of students' conceptions of educational technology. *International Journal of Educational Research, 41*(6), 445–465.

Glaser, B. G., & Strauss, A. L. (1967). *The discovery of grounded theory: Strategies for qualitative research.* New York, NY: Aldine de Gruyter.

Huang, H.-M. (2002). Student perceptions in an online mediated environment. *International Journal of Instructional Media, 29*(4), 405–422.

Johns, S., & Lawson, K. (2005). University undergraduate students and library-related privacy issues. *Library & Information Science Research, 27,* 485–495.

Kuh, G. D. (2001). Assessing what really matters to student learning: Inside the national survey of student engagement. *Change, 33*(3), 10–17.

Lewis, K., Kaufman, J., & Christakis, N. (2008). The taste for privacy: An analysis of college student privacy settings in an online social network. *Journal of Computer-Mediated Communication, 14*(1), 79–100.

Lowyck, J., & Poysa, J. (2001). Design of collaborative learning environments. *Computers in Human Behavior, 17*(5–6), 507–516.

Marshall, C., & Rossman, G. B. (1999). *Designing qualitative research* (3rd ed.). Thousand Oaks, CA: Sage.

Milne, G. R., & Culnan, M. J. (2004). Strategies for reducing online privacy risks: Why consumers read (or don't read) online privacy notices. *Journal of Interactive Marketing, 18*(3), 15–29.

Monfils, B. (1993). Privacy in the computer age: Perceptions and realities. Paper presented at the 3rd international symposium of the international visual literacy association. Verbovisual literacy: Understanding and application of new educational communication media technologies. Delphi, Greece, June 26–29.

Montgomery, J. C. (1999). *An investigation into the issues shared by professionals living and working in rural communities in British Columbia.* PhD thesis, James Cook University, Townsville, Queensland, Australia.

Muilenburg, L. Y., & Berge, Z. L. (2005). Student barriers to online learning: A factor analytic study. *Distance Education, 26*(1), 29–48.

Nembhard, I. M., & Edmondson, A. C. (2006). Making it safe: The effects of leader inclusiveness and professional status on psychological safety and improvement efforts in health care teams. *Journal of Organizational Behavior, 27*(7), 941–966.

Powers, S. M., & Mitchell, J. (1997). Student perceptions and performance in a virtual classroom environment. Paper presented at the annual meeting of the American Educational Research Association, Chicago, IL.

Proctor, R. W., Athar Ali, M., & Vu, K.-P. L. (2008). Examining usability of web privacy policies. *International Journal of Human-Computer Interaction, 24*(3), 307–328.

Richardson, J. C., & Swan, K. (2003). Examining social presence in online courses in relation to students' perceived learning and satisfaction. *Journal of Asynchrous Learning Networks, 7*(1), 68–88.

Rubin, H. J., & Rubin, I. S. (1995). *Qualitative interviewing: The art of hearing data.* Thousand Oaks, CA: Sage.

School of Public Administration. (n.d.-a). *Delivery method.* Retrieved from http://www.uvic.ca/hsd/publicadmin/programs/graduate/mpaOnline/deliverymethod/index.php

School of Public Administration. (n.d.-b). *MPA on campus.* Retrieved from http://www.uvic.ca/hsd/publicadmin/programs/graduate/mpaOncampus/index.php

School of Public Administration. (n.d.-c). *MPA online.* Retrieved from http://www.uvic.ca/hsd/publicadmin/programs/graduate/mpaOnline/index.php

Sheehan, K. B. (2002). Toward a typology of internet users and online privacy concerns. *The Information Society, 18*(1), 21–32.

Siemens, L., & Althaus, C. (2011). *Impact of instructors' understanding of privacy and confidentiality within an online classroom.* Victoria, BC: Learning and Teaching Centre.

Stange, C. (2011). *Privacy concern and student engagement in the virtual classroom.* Master of Public Administration, University of Victoria, Victoria, BC.

Strauss, A. L., & Corbin, J. (1998). *Basic qualitative research: Techniques and procedures for developing grounded theory* (2nd ed.). Thousand Oaks, CA: Sage.

Tang, Z., Hu, Y. J., & Smith, M. D. (2008). Gaining trust through online privacy protection: Self-regulation, mandatory standards, or caveat emptor. *Journal of Management Information Systems, 24*(4), 153–173.

The Digital Tattoo Project. (n.d.). *Digitaltattoo.Ubc.Ca.* Retrieved from http://digitaltattoo.ubc.ca/

Tu, C.-H. (2002). The relationship between social presence and online privacy. *Internet and Higher Education, 5*(4), 293–318.

Tu, C.-H., & McIsaac, M. (2002). The relationship of social presence and interaction in online classes. *American Journal of Distance Education, 16*(3), 131–150.

University of Victoria. (2011). *Freedom of information guidelines, No.2.* Retrieved from http://library.uvic.ca/archives/records_management/info_bulletins/foi_bulletin_02.html

University of Victoria. (2012). *Privacy breach at Uvic.* Retrieved from http://www.uvic.ca/infobreach/

Xu, Y., & Yi, Y. (2010). Student learning in business simulation: An empirical investigation. *Journal of Education for Business, 85*(4), 223–228.

Yang, C.-C., Tsai, I. C., Kim, B., Cho, M.-H., & Laffey, J. M. (2006). Exploring the relationships between students' academic motivation and social ability in online learning environments. *The Internet and Higher Education, 9*(4), 277–286.

PROBLEM-BASED LEARNING IN HYBRID, BLENDED, OR ONLINE COURSES: INSTRUCTIONAL AND CHANGE MANAGEMENT IMPLICATIONS FOR SUPPORTING LEARNER ENGAGEMENT

Katerina Bohle Carbonell, Amber Dailey-Hebert, Maike Gerken and Therese Grohnert

ABSTRACT

Problem-based learning (PBL) is an instructional format which emphasizes collaborative and contextual learning and hence has favored face-to-face course design. However, with the plentitude of online tools which technology offers nowadays, PBL courses can also be effectively offered to students who cannot physically be present at the campus. The change process from offline to hybrid, blended, or online PBL courses need to be carefully managed and the right combination of technology and learning activities selected from the ever increasing available set. Hybrid, blended, or online courses differ in the amount of integration between

Increasing Student Engagement and Retention in e-Learning Environments:
Web 2.0 and Blended Learning Technologies
Cutting-edge Technologies in Higher Education, Volume 6G, 359–386
Copyright © 2013 by Emerald Group Publishing Limited
All rights of reproduction in any form reserved
ISSN: 2044-9968/doi:10.1108/S2044-9968(2013)000006G015

offline and online activities. A mixed-method design was used to elaborate on how the different (hybrid, blended, or online) PBL courses can be effectively build and taught to create learner engagement. Twelve people (change agent, instructor, and participants) were interviewed and 82 students filled out a course evaluation form. The data was used to describe how a hybrid, blended, or online course was created and how the instructor and students perceived it. Instructional and change management implications for implementation are presented. Instructional implications deal with the needs of the learner, the role of the instructor, and the importance of sound technology integration in the course. Change management implication highlights the need to foster intra-institutional collaboration.

INTRODUCTION

If I had an hour to save the world, I would spend 59 minutes defining the problem and one minute finding solutions.
                                                                    – Albert Einstein

Problem-based learning (PBL) has been an effective educational approach to support learner engagement and collaboration since its introduction by Barrows and Tamblyn (1980). Yet, its relevance and importance in our learning process today becomes even more crucial. Solving today's problem requires learners to engage in self-directed, nonlinear learning under dynamic and evolving contexts (DiPadova-Stocks, 2008; Friedman, 2005). PBL, through its focus on contextualized problems, prepares graduates for this world. Given PBL's emphasis on collaborative knowledge building and team-based learning, new collaborative tools (e.g., wikis, blogs, virtual worlds, simulations, gaming, discussion forums, video chats, and much more) pose a specific opportunity to connect various learner populations, and to expand the reach, scope, and function of the PBL learning process. "It thus enables students to explore and create new modes of discourse suited to the ways of reading, writing and collaborating that are increasingly used in a digital age" (Savin-Baden & Wilkie, 2006, p. 18). As a result, exploration of new possibilities in the "next generation" of PBL is growing, particularly through innovations with online PBL (Savin-Baden & Wilkie, 2006). These areas tend to hold the greatest promise for combining the benefits of the PBL model, with competencies developed through learning in multiple modalities. The benefits in creating this combination include: promoting and enhancing collaborative learning beyond the classroom experience, engaging students through learning tasks that fit their social networking practices, offering students more flexibility and choice in how/when they learn, and offering innovative resources and support during the learning experience (Savin-Baden, 2008). Online PBL highlights a burgeoning area for educational innovation, and consequently, a field in need of further study and investigation. The different phases in PBL allows for a rich mixture of online and offline activities, yielding different "blends" of PBL. As with any instructional format, integrating technologies into existing course formats requires careful consideration on how tools and instructional design can best be combined to create a higher level of learning. The aim of this chapter is *to elaborate on how you can effectively build, and teach hybrid, blended, or online PBL courses to create learner engagement.*

To answer this research question, the chapter first conceptualizes and differentiates between offline PBL, hybrid PBL, blended PBL, or online PBL. Upon introducing this learning environment continuum (with varying levels of technology integration), working definitions of each will be explained. Subsequently, the authors will share considerations needed when moving to a hybrid, blended, or online PBL model. This section will elaborate on the advantages of hybrid, blended, or online PBL, and will describe important elements in the change process to consider when transitioning from a traditional PBL course to another modality or instructional format. Following the theoretical framework, the authors will describe the process of data collection using both quantitative and qualitative data. The results section will share three case studies (one which transitioned into a hybrid PBL, one which transitioned into a blended PBL course, and one which transitioned into an online PBL course). These case studies will explicate the pilot leader, instructor, and learner experience through this process and will conclude with a discussion of the conclusions that can be drawn from each. This will provide the reader with a picture of how change implementation is experienced by the learner, instructor, and course designer. The chapter offers recommendations for those who wish to implement hybrid, blended, or online PBL courses successfully to create learn engagement.

INSTRUCTIONAL AND CHANGE MANAGEMENT CONSIDERATIONS IN CREATING HYBRID, BLENDED, OR ONLINE PBL COURSES

To investigate the posed research question, the following three sections will create a framework for analyzing instructional and change management considerations in creating hybrid, blended, or online PBL courses. First of all, offline, hybrid, blended, and online PBL are defined. Second, instructional considerations are collected from literature, focusing on the translation of traditional PBL characteristics to a (partly) online setting in a meaningful way. Third, considerations for change management processes within universities are considered that accompany the design of new (partly) online PBL courses.

Defining Offline, Hybrid, Blended, or Online PBL

The concept of PBL (Barrows, 1996) has become increasingly prominent over the past years, being implemented by various disciplinary programs worldwide. Classic PBL is an instructional approach that uses authentic tasks, conceptualized as problem statements representing realistic, wicked challenges, to be addressed independently by a group of learners, supported by an instructor (Tynjälä, 2008). It was first used for medical education by MacMaster University in Canada, but has also been used in different fields such as business, psychology, or political sciences. Barrows (1996) defines the concept of PBL through six core characteristics, which stimulate self-regulated, contextual, collaborative, and constructive learning (Dolmans, De Grave, Wolfhagen, & van der Vleuten, 2005): First, learning is student-centered where students must take responsibility for their learning and identify what they need to know to solve the problem at hand (self-regulated learning). The second characteristic states that students are randomly assigned to small groups with 10 students on average (collaborative learning). Third, teachers act as facilitators or guides (constructive learning). Fourth, ill-structured problems form the basis for organized focus and serve as a stimulus for learning (contextual learning). These problems can be presented in different formats, such as written cases or video casts, and provide the relevance and motivation for learning. Fifth, problems are presented in a way that stimulates the development and use of (collaborative) problem-solving skills. Finally, new knowledge is obtained through means of self-directed learning (Barrows, 1996). These characteristics of PBL make it clear that this instructional approach can be used for disciplines which (a) have a specific context on which learning problems can be based and (b) offer greater levels of learning through student interaction. This being said, the level of interactive learning will differ between fields. Disciplines which rely on a given set of true answers, for example, mathematics or finance, can result in lower levels of interaction than fields which accept numerous perspectives to yield a correct answer.

PBL as described above traditionally takes place in a face-to-face setting, engaging the traditional student population of full-time tertiary learners, having successfully graduated from high school and pursuing a degree to prepare for a profession. However, institutes of higher education need to consider how to adapt their methodologies to include professional and distance learners in their existing curricula, particularly given the increasing proportion of nontraditional learners, such as learners returning to education after or while working full- or part-time, seeking additional knowledge or qualification (Thorpe, 2002). Moreover, the manner in which people collaborate has changed and will continue to evolve as the result of emergent technologies. In an effort to include diverse learners and their unique needs, many institutes of higher education have enriched their educational offerings with online components or courses held fully online, which allow students (for some part of the course), to work independently and flexibly, spending reduced face-to-face time in class. This form of education has been named, for example, hybrid learning, blended learning, flexible learning, and mixed mode learning (Moore, Perlow, Judge, & Koh, 2006). These terms have sometimes been used interchangeably, or were treated as separate concepts (Garrison & Kanuka, 2004). The complexity lies in the many different combinations of face-to-face and online learning activities (Garrison & Kanuka, 2004). Moreover, defining the different forms of learning between the two poles of the continuum is a challenging task due to the numerous understandings of the mentioned terms used in existing literature. Within the PBL framework, a continuum emerges (Garrison & Kanuka, 2004), with offline PBL in its traditional form on the one side, and fully online PBL on the other. Between these two end points, offline and online components can be combined in various ways. However, clarification is needed on how terms such as hybrid, blended, or online apply to the middle section of the continuum. Fig. 1 provides a visualization of how offline, hybrid, blended, or online PBL are conceptualized in this study.

According to the proposed framework, a course can be classified as offline, hybrid, blended, or online along two dimensions. First, the ratio of collaborative online to offline tasks (x-axis), and second the extent to which the two types of activities are integrated (y-axis). Starting with offline PBL, in which all collaborative learning activities are carried out in a face-to-face setting, the degree of online tool integration increases until all course components are offered fully online.

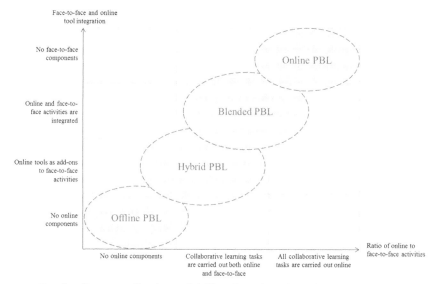

Fig. 1.   Conceptualizations of Offline, Hybrid, Blended, or Online PBL.

Hybrid courses aim at offering the same learning experiences as a traditional face-to-face class, by replacing existing face-to-face learning activities with online activities. Garrison and Kanuka (2004) name this "enhanced eLearning" as a hybrid course design which aims to increase flexibility and limit face-to-face class time. This conception is confirmed by Thorpe (2002), who defines hybrid courses as "courses where students have electronic access to resources and where they are expected to be in regular contact online with their peers and instructor(s)" (p. 105). Translating this conception to the PBL context, we define hybrid PBL as *the meaningful use of online learning activities to replace some face-to-face interaction, offering learners the same educational value at a distance as the traditional face-to-face class.*

In contrast to this definition of hybrid learning, blended learning has been defined as combining "online and face-to-face activities in order to offer a more effective education. Blended learning is structured around the strengths of the face-to-face instructions and e-learning and attempts on harmonizing the two approaches with the intent of maximizing the advantages of the two pure educational models" (Singer & Stoicescu, 2011, p. 1528). This definition emphasizes that blended learning enables learner engagement beyond what is possible in a face-to-face course. Both kinds of activities – offline and online – are integrated into a coherent pedagogical framework and are complementary. Applying this definition to the PBL context, we define blended PBL as *the meaningful integration of online and face-to-face learning activities to create superior constructive, self-directed, collaborative, and contextual learning experiences to what can be achieved in an offline or hybrid PBL course*. Naturally, the two concepts of hybrid and blended PBL as conceptualized here can include a variety of course designs and combinations of various activities. No two hybrid or blended course designs need structurally be the same (Garrison & Kanuka, 2004), but will aim for a different level of integration between the two components.

Finally, reaching the other end of the continuum, online PBL is defined as "students working in teams numbering 8 to 10 on a series of problem scenarios that combine to make up a module" (Savin-Baden & Wilkie, 2006, p. 7), *in which all collaborative learning activities take place in an online environment, aiming to create effective constructive, self-directed, collaborative, and contextual learning experiences.*

Advantages of hybrid, blended, or online PBL classes include the flexibility for both students and faculty in learning, enabling the coordination of multiple demands from work and family (Hiltz & Turoff, 2005), as well as the increased access to education (Owston, Wideman, Murphy, & Lupshenyuk, 2008). A wider audience can be reached by offering courses (partly) online (Mansour & Mupinga, 2007). Instructors can monitor the learning progress in a variety of ways, providing multiple opportunities for feedback (Cornelius & Gordon, 2009). Finally, for organizations, hybrid courses allow effective competition for nontraditional learner populations not on location (Hiltz & Turoff, 2005) in a cost-effective manner (Mansour & Mupinga, 2007; Owston et al., 2008), in terms of offering customizable, flexible and active learning experiences.

However, also a series of disadvantages of hybrid, blended, or online courses have been identified. First, the different study opportunities might create a lack of direction for students, who need to possess self-directed learning skills to benefit from the set-up (Mansour & Mupinga, 2007). Moreover, elements that need to be completed individually and outside contact hours can slow down the learning process, since they cannot be well controlled by the instructor (Wang & Newlin, 2001). Finally, on the organizational level, hybrid, blended, and especially online courses have been associated with high degrees of drop-out in the past (Bernard, de Rubalcava, & St-Pierre, 2000).

Given these advantages and disadvantages, previous research offers mixed results on the effectiveness of such courses in facilitating student learning. DeNeui and Dodge (2006) found that in a group of college students taking part in a hybrid class, those that had engaged more in the online activities also received higher exam scores, indicating a better learning outcome. However, in their review study, Bernard et al. (2000) summarize studies yielding a poorer quality of learning attainment of students in hybrid conditions compared to learners in face-to-face courses (e.g., Bullen, 1998; Dede, 1996). As possible causes for these findings, Bernard et al. (2000) list feelings of isolation, lack of communication, and difficulties in self-regulating learning activities. These findings suggest that in practice, the implementation of hybrid, blended, or online PBL courses hinges on the degree to which instructors manage to engage participants in constructive, self-directed, collaborative, and contextual learning activities, forming the core of the PBL approach.

Instructional Considerations in Designing Hybrid, Blended, or Online PBL Courses in Higher Education

To foster learner engagement in hybrid, blended, or online PBL, several considerations need to be taken into account. First, previous research highlights the importance of creating the optimal group size to ensure participation by all learners. Depending on the task set for participants and collaboration in project settings, a group size of three to five is recommended (Fisher, Thompson, & Silverberg, 2005), while for group discussion and general interaction, a size of seven is recommended (Mennecke & Valacich, 1998). However, when combining face-to-face PBL sessions, where the average number of group members is 10 (Barrows, 1996), with online components, it is advisable to make use of sub-groups in order to maintain a suitable communication climate, giving all participants the opportunity to share.

Second, to make sure participants can engage in their learning activities through multiple channels and in a flexible manner (Martyn, 2003), both synchronous or asynchronous strategies are needed to ensure high-quality hybrid, blended, or online PBL courses. Such synchronous activities may include classical face-to-face meetings, in combination with the use of synchronous tools (such as chat, video-conferencing, and online meeting environments) which allow students to communicate at the same time (Hiltz & Turoff, 2005; Martyn, 2003). Furthermore, it is also crucial to include asynchronous tools (such as e-mail, discussion boards, wikis, and blogs) which allow flexible communication by participants at independent points in time (Hiltz & Turoff, 2005; Martyn, 2003).

Third, previous research has identified the need for instructors to be trained in using and explaining the different tools integrated in a course (Martyn, 2003). Without being able to make effective use of a course's opportunities, instructors will find it difficult to guide their learners, provide feedback, and customize the course's offerings to the participants' needs.

Consequently, instructors face three key tasks in hybrid, blended, or online PBL courses when fostering learner engagement: managing tool use to enable active student–student collaboration, offering different channels of communication to individualize the learning experience by participant preference, and finally, providing prompt feedback to the learner on a content and process level.

Change Management Considerations in Implementing Hybrid, Blended, or Online PBL Courses in Higher Education

A second perspective to consider when implementing hybrid, blended, or online PBL courses, is the aspect of change itself. This change process acts on two aspects of university's routines: First, the instructor has to change his or her teaching routines. Second, the resulting change may contradict the university's established teaching philosophy. This gap needs to be prevented or managed to avoid conflict within the university between the groups of instructors who adopt a new teaching philosophy and those who continue teaching according to the established tradition.

The shift toward a course with varying degrees of online components requires faculty to be more than merely knowledgeable about the possibilities different technologies offer. They need to know how the course content, pedagogy, and technology interact with each other (Koehler & Mishra, 2010). This can be problematic as not everybody has knowledge on those three areas. To fulfill the need of diverse expertise in order to integrate technology in a course, a project team should be established (Edmondson & Nembhard, 2009).

The exchange of ideas and opinions creates a shared mental model of the project's goal and tasks and thus helps team members create a common understanding of what they want to achieve (Cronin & Weingart, 2007; Decuyper, Dochy, & Van Den Bossche, 2010). This common understanding is important for teams working on innovative projects as it makes the outcome of the change process more explicit. To create this shared mental model, project members need to collaborate closely with each other. However, exchanging information is not sufficient, project members also need to spend time on integrating their different points of view (Decuyper et al., 2010). Through this, the project team is able to build a shared mental model and increases their performance. The team members need to feel comfortable to share their opinions, knowledge, and experiences with each other. As they are working together on an innovative project, the learning experiences are especially important in order for the team to gain knowledge regarding the effectiveness of the innovation.

The sharing of learning experiences is aided by the level of psychological safety in the team (Van Den Bossche, Gijselaers, Segers, & Kirschner, 2006). Psychological safety is the level of inter-personal trust to be exposed to risky situation, such as sharing failures (Edmondson, 1999). It is expressed in a team through high levels of collaboration and feedback.

The move from offline to hybrid, blended, or online PBL can be organized in two manners: First, instructors can be required by management decisions to redesign offline courses or to create hybrid, blended, or online courses. Second, staff members can initiate the change themselves by redesigning their courses. In the first scenario, change is managed top-down, resulting in high standardization of hybrid, blended, or online course design. The second scenario yields a high diversity of course design and thus knowledge, however, can run the danger of not reaching all corners of a university. In both situations it is important to sustain instructor involvement in the change process to reduce resistance to change (Edmondson, 2008). Another important point for both change scenarios is that instructors are supported in their experimentation with new course designs (Fullan, 2008). Lastly, regardless what change scenario has been chosen, the new teaching routines need to suit the mission and values of the university (Bland et al., 2000).

Having outlined the instructional and change management consideration for fostering learner engagement in hybrid, blended, or online PBL courses, the next section will introduce three case studies illustrating how these considerations impact the success of courses within a PBL curriculum by creating learner engagement. Creating a successful hybrid, blended, or online PBL course is dependent on processes on several levels. At the core, the participants decide whether the course is successful. Participants are in contact with the course instructor who manages the course. He or she also has an impact on the success of the course. At the highest level, the person initiating the change influences the outcome of the change process through his or her visions and actions. Therefore, all three levels need to be considered to investigate how you can effectively build, and teach hybrid, blended, or online PBL courses to create learner engagement.

METHOD

Setting

One university, with an institutional curriculum centered on PBL, set off on new frontiers to investigate online PBL applications. The primary goal of this project was to explore and innovate online learning strategies to support PBL, to develop new educational formats and modes of delivery to engage learners; all while suiting the university's overarching teaching philosophy of PBL. Each faculty was represented by a staff member who will be referred to as "pilot leader." The responsibility of the pilot leader was (1) to create pilots (i.e., hybrid, blended, or PBL) courses within their faculty together with colleagues from their faculty and (2) to share the experiences made within their faculty with the other pilot leaders of the project team. Pilot leaders participated in the project based on their commitment to integrating technology into courses. Thus, they all felt a sense of urgency for change. Based on this selection method, the expertise of the pilot leaders differed. The team consisted of instructional designers, educational scientists, organizational psychologists, economists, and technology experts. The project was led by a project leader who was not responsible for day-to-day activities of implementing a pilot. The task of the project leader was to bring together the pilot leaders, to disseminate the project's success to other people, to report to the management board, and to communicate solutions for institution-wide roadblocks to the management board.

Each pilot leader planned to implement at least one pilot. These pilots ranged from a single course to the introduction of a whole new degree. The pilot leaders met every six to eight weeks to exchange ideas and discuss the progress of their pilots and the overall project goal. However, they were dependent on the support of staff members and managers at their respective faculty for the implementation of their individual pilot. Thus, while they could count on feedback from project members, they had to organize the execution of their pilot themselves. The project began in 2009 and, in the first year, required the different faculties/schools to search for commitment, expertise, and support within the organization for the development and implementation of online courses for professionals/part-time learners. Ideas were explored, discussed, and researched during this timeframe and core members of the project team were established. In the second and third year of the project, several pilots were created, offered, and subsequently, were analyzed and reshaped before completing a second and/or third run. Opportunities to collect rich data through case study analyses, participant focus groups, and core survey questions also informed the project team's work. Such insights led to the scaling up in the number of pilots for professionals and the didactical adjustments, functionalities, and conditions needed to create an effective online learning environment for professionals. As a result of this project, 13 pilots were created, resulting in 25 course offerings, reaching 391 learners. This chapter will share experiences gathered during a three-year project across *all disciplines* of a mid-sized European university. The findings will focus on three pilots in various disciplines (Law, Political Sciences, and Psychology) as examples of how (partly) online PBL courses can enhance learner engagement.

Sample

The participants in this study are part of three groups: Pilot leaders, instructors, and students. Three pilot leaders were interviewed, three course instructors, and six course participants, covering the three levels for each of the three case studies. In addition, 82 students filled out a course evaluation form. Pilot leaders were educational scientists, psychologists, economists, or technology experts. Pilot leaders had a mean tenure of 10 years. Instructors taught courses in the areas of law, policy design, and social psychology. On average, they had 12 years of teaching experience. Two instructors had experience with teaching hybrid, blended, or online PBL courses. The course participants were bachelor students (mean age 21.5) and professionals (mean age 38).

Data Collection

In order to answer the research questions on how you can build and teach hybrid, blended, or online PBL courses to create learner engagement, we used a mixed-method approach with both qualitative and quantitative data collection. The use of course evaluation forms, focus groups, formal interviews, and informal communication allow for insights into the experiences of the instructor and participants.

Quantitative data was collected about the participants' perceptions. Participants of all courses were given a survey at the end of the course. This survey contained the following categories: instructor feedback (7 items from Lizzio & Wilson, 2008), course design (4 items from Lee, 2008 and 2 from Selim, 2007), task design (integration scale from Frick, Chadha, Watson,

Wang, & Green, 2007), communication climate (based on 3 items from Swan, Richardson, & Ice, 2008 and 4 from Gibson & Gibbs, 2006), knowledge sharing (7 items from Hooff & Ridder, 2004), and satisfaction and learning (3 and 5 items from Frick et al., 2009). All questions used a Likert-type scale ranging from 1 (totally disagree) to 5 (totally agree).

Qualitative data was collected from all groups (pilot leaders, instructors, and participants). The interviews for the pilot leaders contained questions about the aim and processes in the project (e.g., what is the goal of the project, what are the main challenges) and in their individual pilots (e.g., what is the goal, how did you implement the pilot, with whom could you discuss it). Instructors were asked about their positive and negative experiences, best practices, and challenges in their role as course builder and instructor. Participants were asked about their experience with the course regarding the collaboration, the instructor, and the course format. Unfortunately, not all instructors and participants could be interviewed due to time limit and reachability.

Analysis

All interviews were recorded, transcribed, and coded using Atlastt. i. qualitative data analysis software. For all interviews, comments were chosen as a basic unit of analysis, ranging from individual sentences to whole paragraphs (Minichiello, Aroni, Timewell, & Alexander, 1990). Direct content analysis as specified by Hsieh and Shannon (2005) was then conducted, structuring messages according to findings from literature. For pilot leaders the following aspects were analyzed: Expertise diversity, team processes, and change process. For instructors, messages were grouped according to the three main challenges facing instructors: collaborative course design, teaching support, and technical support. For participants, the answers were grouped according to student–student collaboration, teacher support, and student learning motivation. A descriptive analysis was done with the evaluation form and mean scores are reported in the event that qualitative data could not be collected.

RESULTS

Three cases are presented in the results section, each from the pilot leader, instructor, and participant perspective. These cases present three

Table 1.   Instructional and Change Management Considerations in Creating Learner Engagement.

	Case 1: A Hybrid Course	Case 2: A Blended Course	Case 3: An Online PBL
PBL Characteristics of the pilots			
PBL format	Hybrid	Blended	Online
Main form of interaction	Student–instructor	Student–student	Student–student
Instructor role	Lecturer	Tutor	Tutor
Stimulating self-directed, contextualized learning	Using ethical dilemmas to trigger thinking of self-explanatory power of laws	Providing information to be used as a basis for interactive, international discussions	Presenting complex problems based on realistic tasks of a psychologist, leaving manner to address the problem to the learners

different courses in which either hybrid, blended, or online PBL was implemented. Each case represents a different way in which tools can be integrated in a course to support learner engagement. Case 1 illustrates an unusual path to implementing a hybrid course, meeting many challenges. Case 2 on the other hand illustrates the successful implementation of a blended course connecting learners from two countries. Case 3 then illustrates how a classical PBL approach to teaching can be transported into an online environment. Table 1 summarizes the characteristics of the three courses.

Case 1: Creating a Hybrid Course

In PBL courses lectures are used to provide some basic knowledge before letting learners attempt to solve realistic problems. This is especially used in introductory courses. This practice is frequently used in, for example, statistics and law. This pilot addresses the learning during lectures of an introductory law course. A plug-in for Microsoft PowerPoint was used to enhance the interaction between student and lecturer. The lecturer provided multiple choice questions which the students answered by sending a text message via their phone. The answers were directly displayed in the presentation. Two to three times in a lecture, the instructor would post a question, for example, to give an estimate, pick one of a series of options, answer a yes/no question around a controversial or already dealt-with topic. Students were given a short break to think about the question and send their answer from their phones.

The Pilot Leader Perspective

Case 1 describes the process of a failed course design attempt which experienced a turn-around in the last year of the project. The pilot began with the vision of the program director, and the faculty member charged with implementing the pilot had no technical or instructional design knowledge. In addition to this, the potential pool of participants could not be made enthusiastic for the blended course, and the pilot was stopped due to little progress. After this initial attempt, a new pilot leader was hired from outside the faculty. This person spent considerable time on updating his technical knowledge. While he had expertise in instructional design and the necessary technical knowledge, his situation was complicated by not being a member of the academic field of this faculty and placed in a support group. This made it difficult for him to connect with the content experts and to create a successful pilot. Nevertheless, he was able to set-up a small-scale pilot. However the success of this pilot is limited, as the instructor did not follow the advice of the pilot leader when implementing the tool: *The teacher who used this tool, he said: "I just want to try something new, I want to try something nice for students to experience something that they've never experienced before" [...] I wasn't that happy with [the outcome]. I would have liked to have more discussion with him about the goals and purposes of the tool. But on the other hand now it confirmed what I already thought, and it confirmed that you really have to think about these topics, these issues, before using a tool.*

The Instructor's Perspective

The instructor defined the main goal of the pilot as *it was some kind of personal interest, I simply wanted to know how students would react.* Moreover, he described the collaboration with the pilot leader in very clear terms: *I didn't really need him on a day to day basis except for getting me the login codes, so that was fine I would say.* The SMS voting tool was used in a lecture series, *simply to see how a large group of students, what their opinion is when don't know anything yet.* However, he observed a drop in interest on the student side after the first round of voting: *in the first lecture we had three voting questions, and the first two had a response rate of about 80 to 90 of 200 students present, the third one had about 60 people participating, which is more than sufficient I think.* Due to the nature of the tool used, interaction between students was limited to discussing a predefined option with your immediate neighbors in the lecture hall, allowing only for one way of submitting information. Moreover, feedback is necessarily of a factual nature only, giving the response "correct/incorrect."

The Participants' Perspective
Student feedback of this pilot is derived from a standardized course evaluation. Results show that the problems at the course coordinator level trickle down to the lower levels as the tool did not increase students learning. On a technical level, students *were totally familiar with SMS voting*, and they evaluated the use of the tool positively in talks with the instructor. Students also indicated that the tool made the lectures more interactive. Overall, students liked that the tool was used (mean score of 4.1/5, SD = 1.1). However, using the tool did not help them to understand the material better (mean score 2.7/5, SD = 1.1). One drawback they mentioned was the cost of the SMS the students had to pay in order to participate, which not all were willing to do, and the decreased effect of the tool to stimulate reflection on the content.

Case 1 demonstrates the importance of course development team membership and their collaboration based on a shared mental model of the course. This shared mental model needs to consist of an integrated picture of content, pedagogy, and technology. If this view is not shared across the course team, implementation will not lead to the desired results, as illustrated by this first case. To conclude, this case demonstrates the need for collaboration to arrive at a successful hybrid course.

Case 2: Creating a Blended Course

The aim of this blended course in political sciences was to enrich learner perspectives on the topic of EU enlargement by connecting learners from two countries, Turkey and the Netherlands, through blended PBL. Participants in both countries took part in an 8-week module, during which they engaged in a series of synchronous and asynchronous learning activities, online and offline. All participants watched a series of web lectures, engaged in self-study, shared their knowledge on a discussion board, and participated in four online tutorial meetings, next to face-to-face meetings at their home institutes.

The Pilot Leader Perspective

The creation of this blended course began several years with a test of the technology, Polycom, to establish if two classrooms can be connected. Some time passed, before the program directory contacted the pilot leader, an e-learning expert with an extensive technological knowledge base, to discuss opportunities to create a joint course. Together with the partnering university in Turkey, a course was created which suited both curriculums and technological possibilities. In hindsight this proved to be more problematic, due to different curriculum structures and work habits. In addition, while the pilot leader was supported by the program director to go ahead and design this blended course, the tutor did not seem to be too enthusiastic to have to work with a different course set-up. As the pilot leader remarked: *a large part of our staff is well they're not really thinking in an innovative way when it comes to implementing technology into their education […] And another reason is the lack of time.* These factors, collaboration with foreign university, and enthusiasm of the home university instructor, made it difficult for the pilot leader to develop the course. His traditional approach of giving the tutor *as much freedom as possible to design the course in a way that it was also to his satisfaction and that not only technology was dominating the way the course should be taught* did not work in this context. In order to finish the course in time, he had to press ahead and work less collaborative than what he was used to.

The Instructor Perspective

To enable student–student collaboration in multiple ways, a combination of synchronous and asynchronous tools was used. Synchronous communication was conducted through Polycom with the partnering university for joint discussion rounds and with only students from the home university for PBL discussions. While the technology did not prove to be a problem, students from the home university remarked on the different learning culture from the partner university which did not expose students to the same amount of collaboration and group discussion than at the home university.

While the tutor did not respond to any request for an interview, information she has provided prior to her leaving the faculty suggested that she felt overwhelmed by the technological changes and in some regard left to fend by herself. For example, she remarked on the lack of support from her home faculty with regard to technological hardware to conduct the synchronous PBL sessions.

The Participants' Perspective
Students were satisfied with the course, though a high standard deviation was registered (mean score 3.53/5, SD = 2.78). They also perceived that the course had significantly added to their knowledge (mean score 3.53/5, SD = 0.52). Particularly, participants appreciated the support and feedback of the instructor (mean score 3.75/5, SD = 0.46), and believe that it made the course a valuable experience. The online material, including the video lecture and the synchronous activities, were positively evaluated: *You can view it [the video lectures] at any time that suits you (...) video lectures give participants the chance to constantly review and understand major issues.* Students agreed that the collaboration with students from another country was the most enriching experience during the module, which would not have been possible without the blended learning component. No technical difficulties were reported, and accessibility of the tools used was rated rather high (mean score 3.83/5, SD = 0.408).

Case 3: Creating an Online PBL Course

Case 3 describes the development of a PBL course held fully online, focusing on facilitating student–student collaboration and self-directed learning. The course made use of an online collaboration tool that allows the participants to share documents, links, and their home screens, to draw on a virtual whiteboard, to use audio-, written-, and video-chat to communicate with each other, take small polls, and to record all online sessions for later review. In addition, to stimulate reflection, a web-based mind mapping tool was chosen to help students create their own study and revision guides in a collaborative manner.

The Pilot Leader Perspective
In one department, resistance to technological integration did not inhibit one innovative faculty member from exploring new ways to reach his learners. On his own he thought about how to structure the video conferences and how to support the students in an attempt to create a PBL experience fully online. The pilot leader noticed that students bridged the physical distance by enriching their discussion with graphics and other visual aspects. *They had no problems just transporting the entire PBL routine from a face to face setting to a virtual setting. And even enriching it.* He concluded that synchronous activities seemed to be necessary to engage students in asynchronous activities. This could be because synchronous

activities can create a group feeling more easily than asynchronous activities, due to the instant reaction participants get from each other. While the pilot leader had minimal support from his colleagues, his technical and content knowledge allowed him to go ahead with the pilot. In addition, he was aware of instructional design aspects and had – through his personal network – access to central technical support. But it was his commitment and sense of urgency which made him persist. He traces the lack of support from colleagues to a lack of entrepreneurial spirit and no sense of urgency.

The Instructor Perspective
To facilitate learner engagement, the course coordinator, who also acted as the instructor, emphasized the importance of accessing information asynchronously and preparing the synchronous sessions well, for example, by engaging in the provided reading, videos, and working on assignments individually. The synchronous sessions were organized as literature discussions, giving the students opportunities to contribute in all the different formats the online environment offers (see above). The instructor found that *discussions become far more efficient because you have a clear idea of what everyone is talking about (...) you gain time when it comes to checking whether everyone understood.* Moreover, he found that students used the software very effectively with little help: *one student made great use of his graphical skills, creating and posting images, and you could tell that that the other students were quick to post graphs and tables on the whiteboard, too, which is something you wouldn't normally do.* He also found that *some students you may not have noticed in a face-to-face group were now less inhibited (...) You notice this especially with the chat, that some students would use more than the audio and (...) sometimes a comment came in via chat that otherwise would not have been heard (...) or they would put something on the whiteboard secretly.*

Looking at the provision of feedback to students, the instructor mostly used the synchronous sessions to review his students' progress and provide feedback using probing questions. He also used the sessions to initiate group evaluation processes after the first half, and toward the end, of the course. Generally he found that students were very enthusiastic, needing little extra feedback to stimulate active learning. Thus, feedback given pertained mostly to the content, not the process.

The Participants' Perspective
Students taking part in this course reported that they were really satisfied with the group because everyone was highly motivated and enthusiastic. As

one student put it *this was a group where you could really trust each other that everyone had read the material and prepared for the discussions.* In the beginning students had to get used to the system and the fact that you do not see each other face-to-face: *for me it was really a learning experience on how you could share information efficiently (…) and at first I thought that it might be difficult because you do not see each other and are talking to the computer screen (…) I actually missed the visual cues because you do not know if you need to talk slower or explain anything.* However, students indicated that they could focus on the content instead and did not get distracted by visual aspects. They also quickly familiarized themselves with the online tools: *sometimes there were 3 discussions, through the chat, whiteboard and the microphone (…) and the mind mapping program I found very convenient to use actually (…) that makes it easier to do a little recap on what we discussed that day.* However, some students indicated that dividing attention across chat, audio, whiteboard, and the mind mapping web tool was exhausting. In addition, they suggested that new groups get a training to become familiar with the system. Feedback was given by the instructor at the end of each session: *He always said at the end of the meeting whether we had discussed reasonably well or if we missed some things.* According to the students the instructor had a more passive role during the discussion and only gave feedback when the discussion went into the wrong direction. The passive role was highly appreciated by students as it stimulated them to search for answers themselves thereby having a more pro-active role.

The fully online PBL course described in Case 3 proved to be successful. Although the pilot leader was not able to set up a formal project team, he used his networking skills to gain the right support needed to pursue his idea. The instructor noted that discussions were very effective even though nonverbal cues were lacking. Additionally, the students enjoyed this course set up, yet noted that some discussions were difficult to follow based on multiple communication channels used simultaneously. To conclude, offering PBL sessions via video conference is a viable alternative to face-to-face discussions.

DISCUSSION

The three case studies highlight instructional implications for using hybrid, blended, or online PBL to engage learners. These implications include (1) the importance of understanding your learners, (2) understanding the role of the instructor as a facilitator, and (3) the importance of course design

Table 2. Instructional and Change Management Implications.

	Case 1: A Hybrid Course	Case 2: A Blended Course	Case 3: Online PBL
Instructional Implications for fostering learner engagement			
Understanding your learner	Increasing interest and attention through varying methods	Geographical flexibility Availability of tools; combining learning with other demands	Geographical flexibility; different preferences for how to collaborate
Role as facilitator	Guiding the meaningful use of the tool	Structure group discussions	Passive support on demand for group; provider of collaborative tools
Intentional course design	No connection between pedagogy and tool choice	Tool use created learning experience not possible otherwise	Enabling collaboration online in a full PBL setting
Change management implications for implementing hybrid, blended, or online PBL courses			
Focus on collaboration	Limited collaboration with (external) course designers and technical experts	Enthusiastic team designing content, format, and tool use with support from central project team	One change agent manages to create an informal network strong enough to support his course development

with intentionality. The research also highlights the change management implications for using hybrid, blended, or online PBL to engage learners, which include (1) strategies to align change with institutional philosophy and mission, (2) the importance of intra-institutional collaboration, and (3) creating an environment to support change toward scaling up success. Insights from all three cases are summarized in Table 2.

Instructional Implications for Supporting Learner Engagement in Hybrid, Blended, or Online PBL Courses

Understanding Your Learners

The introduction and exploration of hybrid, blended, or online PBL was prompted in an effort to better accommodate learners and to attract professional learner populations. Hybrid, blended, or online PBL made it possible to create a personalized study experience (Cornelius & Gordon, 2009), while also providing convenience and flexibility for working professionals managing multiple priorities (Hiltz & Turoff, 2005; Mansour & Mupinga, 2007). Students appreciated multiple channels for communication and found benefits through the use of visualizing tools (such as mind mapping, whiteboards, etc.), yet some found it confusing to utilize too many interactions if they occur simultaneously. Results from this study confirm the need to provide explicit direction, resources, and training (in advance of the course start) to support the technological learning curve. Some students may be novice or expert users of technological tools, and can become irritated or stressed if technology causes problems (Mansour & Mupinga, 2007). Therefore, it is essential to prepare for all levels of technological aptitude to help students gain comfort using new tools. Consequently, it becomes equally important for the instructor and course designer to identify support resources in advance (content experts, technological experts, etc.) who can help support their efforts as well. Research participants were curious regarding the profile for learners drawn to hybrid, blended, or online PBL and were interested in learning more about how their motivation could influence their learning in this unique environment.

Role as Facilitator
Results in this chapter also revealed the importance of instructor conduct in the course. As in the model of PBL, the instructor assumes the role of facilitator and guide, who empowers the learners and promotes engagement and ownership in their learning (Barrows, 1996; Dolmans et al., 2005; Hmelo-Silver, 2004). In this study, students appreciated the more passive role for the instructor, who let the students have room to learn together. They were stimulated by online collaborations and activities which transferred to the workplace and which were made possible through hybrid, blended, or online PBL. Furthermore, students found it helpful for instructors to summarize key points, send friendly reminders electronically, and were attracted to the opportunity to share information online with their entire learning community. While some students were overwhelmed by the technology, others enjoyed using new tools for conceptual mind mapping and collaborative knowledge building, which gave more flexibility to their schedules and which gave a visual representation to the formation of their collective ideas. They came to rely on the instructor as guide for navigating the content of the course but also for navigating the use of new tools.

Intentional Course Design

While results from the study indicated a positive reaction to hybrid, blended, or online PBL learning overall, lessons were learned and failures were made related to the intentionality of course design. In Case 1, for example, an emergent technology was integrated into the course, but this was done with little connection to the learning goals, nor with consideration for the advantage it would offer over face-to-face strategies. Consequently, the tool did not promote increased student engagement, it was not linked to the institutional PBL philosophy, and the pilot failed. Hence, the experience reiterates the importance of integrating learning tools with intentionality and toward an improved learning experience. Rather than selecting a tool to begin course redesign, course designers must first consider the learning goals and determine how to reach those learning goals more effectively, or with more flexibility, through technology. Such intentionality is essential in course design that matches emergent technologies and learning goals to achieve student engagement. Aligning with other research, collaboration is a crucial element for course design as well. In PBL, students are encouraged to apply their existing knowledge and to identify their further learning needs in collaboration with other students (Dolmans et al., 2005). The pilots also discovered the importance of creating opportunities to collaborate in virtual ways. Students reported seeing value and relevance in their collaborative exchanges online and were able to establish an environment of trust, respect, and accountability with one another. Such course design elements can promote engagement and build learning networks outside the classroom.

Change Management Implications for Implementing Hybrid, Blended, or Online PBL Courses in Higher Education Institutes

Although learner engagement has typically been considered a domain addressed in the classroom, this study also highlights the importance of institutional support in scaling up innovation to promote learner engagement through hybrid, blended, or online PBL. It began when the university recognized a need to pursue creative alternatives toward technology integration, but was unsure how to do it within the foundation and philosophy of PBL. Therefore, the university funded an innovation project to explore how emergent technologies could be used within the university-wide PBL philosophy (across all disciplines), and how it could be used to attract new learner populations. The conclusion which can be drawn from the cases is the importance of collaboration for the successful creation of hybrid, blended, or online courses.

The university gave time, autonomy, and funding to base-level faculty who wanted to explore the possibilities of technologies for PBL instruction. They worked within a project team to learn from one another and to pool their resources and ideas. This team was cross-functional and intra-institutional, tapping into the expertise from various sources throughout all departments and functions of the university. A climate of psychological safety was also established, with mutual respect, trust, and collaborative knowledge sharing (Bohle Carbonell, Dailey-Hebert, & Segers, 2011; Edmondson, 2003). There was an expectation that failure would occur and that it would be viewed as something to learn from moving forward. This type of cross collaboration allowed the team to discover areas of institution-wide bottlenecks in processes and policies, and allowed the university to consider widespread changes needed prior to scaling up such innovations.

CONCLUSION

All universities and faculties strive to achieve optimal levels of student engagement and learner satisfaction/learning effect, yet new research and emergent technologies challenge us to reframe our traditional views and strategies about how to engage learners. One mid-sized European university discovered the benefits of using PBL and integrated it as the foundation of their practice. In this constructivist philosophy, students are considered to be active agents who engage in social knowledge building to become constructive, self-directed, collaborative, and contextual learners (Dolmans et al., 2005). There is evidence that students taking part in the PBL learning format also outperform those that follow conventional learning formats (Van den Bossche, Segers, Gijbels, & Dochy, 2004). Such evidence outlines the value in PBL and justifies the rationale for one university's philosophical approach; an approach that defines the institution and its strategy for engaging learners. However, we are experiencing four major forces affecting higher education institutions and their faculty members: (1) fiscal con-straints and increased competition, (2) calls for accountability, (3) growing enrollment and increasing diversity of students, and (4) the continuous evolution of new technologies in the Information Age (Gappa, Austin, & Trice, 2007). Each of these areas requires innovative solutions that promote a complimentary blend of relevant, intentional course design with low-cost collaborative tools for connected learning. As higher education continues to experience significant volatility in the educational needs of learners today (DiPadova-Stocks, 2008; Friedman, 2005), it is also uniquely positioned to respond to such needs and engage learners in extraordinary ways. Learners are no longer confined to the conversations that occur within the walls of a classroom, but are now able to connect and explore ideas with fellow learners across oceans, instantaneously, toward a shared learning goal, and for fairly little cost (Allen & Seaman, 2010). And while universities are seeking cost-conscious solutions to grow enrollments and expand into new markets (while maintaining their rigor, reputation, and integrity), faculty and instructors are seeking meaningful ways to engage learners through new collaborative learning strategies and tools. Furthermore, students are seeking ways to connect content with real world application, to develop a transferable skillset that will be needed in the workplace today, using multiple modalities for learning (Allen & Seaman, 2010; Oblinger & Oblinger, 2005; Pink, 2006). Needless to say, all of these stakeholder groups should consider new approaches to achieve learner engagement, which align with their institutional philosophy and framework (in this case, PBL) and which incorporate improved collaborative learning tools and technology.

One university invested in exploring ways to use emergent technologies to support their traditional PBL philosophy. This venture resulted in an innovation project with accompanying research informed by the learner, instructor, and pilot leader perspectives on the change process. The innovation project and pilot results shared in this chapter identify several areas to consider in planning and implementing hybrid, blended, or online PBL to promote student engagement. Furthermore, it offers strategies and recommendations to consider when exploring new horizons in learning and discusses the challenges and successes of such endeavors. As we enter a new era in student engagement and strategies to implore it, we should always remember the importance of intentional course design and the value of collaboration in achieving learning innovations that are grounded in our organizational philosophy.

ACKNOWLEDGMENTS

The authors would like to thank the pilot leaders and all former members of the project for taking their time to participate in the research and their commitment and enthusiasm for developing a new course format suitable for PBL. We also want to thank the course instructors for their time in the research and the valuable feedback they have provided. Lastly, our thanks also go out to the participants of the various courses for participating in the interviews and filling out the survey.

REFERENCES

Allen, E., & Seaman, J. (2010). *Learning on demand: Online education in the United States 2009.* Needham, MA: Sloan-Center for Online Education.

Barrows, H. S. (1996). Problem-based learning in medicine and beyond: A brief overview. In L. Wilkerson & W. H. Gijselaers (Eds.), *New directions for teaching and learning* (pp. 3–11). San Francisco, CA: Jossey-Bass. doi: 10.1002/tl.37219966804

Barrows, H. S., & Tamblyn, R. (1980). *Problem-based learning: An approach to medical education.* New York, NY: Springer.

Bernard, R. M., de Rubalcava, B. R., & St-Pierre, D. (2000). Collaborative online distance learning: Issues for future practice and research. *Distance Education, 21*(2), 260–277. doi: 10.1080/0158791000210205

Bland, C. J., Starnaman, S., Wersal, L., Moorhead-Rosenberg, L., Zonia, S., & Henry, R. (2000). Curricular change in medical schools: How to succeed. *Academic Medicine, 75*(6), 575–594.

Bohle Carbonell, K., Dailey-Hebert, A., & Segers, M. (2011). Sharing knowledge with the help of a safe communication climate. In B. Rienties, P. Daly, S. Reeb-Gruber & P. Van den Bossche (Eds.), *Proceedings of the 18th EDINEB conference: From innovation to Crème de la Crème Education!*, FEBA ERD Press, Lyon, France.

Bullen, M. (1998). Participation and critical thinking in online university distance education. *Journal of Distance Education, 13*(2), 1–32.

Cornelius, S., & Gordon, C. (2009). Adult learners' use of flexible online resources in a blended programme. *Educational Media International, 46*(3), 239–253. doi: 10.1080/095239 80903135392

Cronin, M. A., & Weingart, L. R. (2007). Representational gaps, information processing, and conflict in functionally diverse teams. *Academy of Management Review, 32*(3), 761–773.

Decuyper, S., Dochy, F., & Van Den Bossche, P. (2010). Grasping the dynamic complexity of team learning: An integrative model for effective team learning in organisations. *Educational Research Review, 5*(2), 111–133. doi: 10.1016/j.edurev.2010.02.002

Dede, C. (1996). The evolution of distance education: Emerging technologies and distributed learning. *American Journal of Distance Education, 10*(2), 4–36. doi: 10.1080/089236 49609526919

DeNeui, D. L., & Dodge, T. L. (2006). Asynchronous learning networks and student outcomes: The utility of online learning components in hybrid courses. *Journal of Instructional Psychology, 33*(4), 256.

DiPadova-Stocks, L. N. (2008). Fostering social and civic responsibility by organizations and their people. In C. Wankel (Ed.), *Handbook of 21st century management.* Thousand Oaks, CA: Sage.

Dolmans, D. H. J. M., De Grave, W., Wolfhagen, I. H. A. P., & van der Vleuten, C. P. M. (2005). Problem-based learning: Future challenges for educational practice and research. *Medical education, 39*, 732–741. doi: 10.1111/j.1365-2929.2005.02205.x

Edmondson, A. C. (1999). Psychological safety and learning behavior in work teams. *Administrative Science Quarterly, 44*, 350–383.

Edmondson, A. C. (2003). Managing the risk of learning: Psychological safety in work teams. In M. A. West, D. Tjosvold & K. G. Smith (Eds.), *International handbook of organizational teamwork and cooperative working* (Vol. 48, pp. 255–276). West Sussex: Wiley-Blackwell.

Edmondson, A. C. (2008). The competitive imperative of learning. *Harvard Business Review, 86*(7–8), 60–68.

Edmondson, A. C., & Nembhard, I. M. (2009). Product development and learning in project teams: The challenges are the benefits. *Journal of Product Innovation Management, 26*(2), 123–138. doi: 10.1111/j.1540-5885.2009.00341.x

Fisher, M., Thompson, G., & Silverberg, D. (2005). Effective group dynamics in e-learning: case study. *Journal of Educational Technology Systems, 33*(3), 205–222.

Frick, T. W., Chadha, R., Watson, C., Wang, Y., & Green, P. (2007). College student perceptions of teaching and learning quality. *Educational Technology Research and Development, 57*(5), 705–720. doi: 10.1007/s11423-007-9079-9

Friedman, T. L. (2005). *The world is flat: A brief history of the twenty-first century.* New York, NY: Farrar, Straus, and Giroux.

Fullan, M. (2008). *The six secrets of change: What the best leaders do to help their organizations survive and thrive.* San Francisco, CA: Jossey-Bass.

Gappa, J. M., Austin, A. E., & Trice, A. G. (2007). *Rethinking faculty work: Higher education's strategic imperative.* San Francisco, CA: Jossey-Bass.

Garrison, D. R., & Kanuka, H. (2004). Blended learning: Uncovering its transformative potential in higher education. *The Internet and Higher Education, 7*(2), 95–105. doi: 10.1016/j.iheduc.2004.02.001

Gibson, C. B., & Gibbs, J. L. (2006). Unpacking the concept of virtuality: The effects of geographic dispersion, electronic dependence, dynamic structure, and national diversity on team innovation. *Administrative Science Quarterly, 51*(3), 451–495.

Hiltz, S. R., & Turoff, M. (2005). The evolution of online learning and the revolution in higher education. *Communications of the ACM, 48*(10), 59–64.

Hmelo-Silver, C. (2004). Problem-based learning: What and how do students learn? *Educational Psychology Review, 16*(3), 235–266. doi: 10.1023/B:EDPR.0000034022.16470.f3

Hooff, B. V. D., & Ridder, J. A. D. (2004). Knowledge sharing in context: The influence of organizational commitment, communication climate and CMC use on knowledge sharing. *Journal of Knowledge Management, 8*(6), 117–130. doi: 10.1108/1367327 0410567675

Hsieh, H. F., & Shannon, S. E. (2005). Three approaches to qualitative content analysis. *Qualitative Health Research, 15*, 1277–1288. doi: 10.1177/1049732305276687

Koehler, M. J., & Mishra, P. (2010). Technological pedagogical content knowledge: A framework for teacher knowledge. *Teachers College Record, 108*(6), 1017–1054.

Lee, Y.-C. (2008). The role of perceived resources in online learning adoption. *Computers & Education, 50*, 1423–1438. doi: 10.1016/j.compedu.2007.01.001

Lizzio, A., & Wilson, K. (2008). Feedback on assessment: Students' perceptions of quality and effectiveness. *Assessment & Evaluation in Higher Education, 33*(3), 263–275.

Mansour, B. E., & Mupinga, D. M. (2007). Students' positive and negative experiences in hybrid and online classes. *College Student Journal, 41*(1), 242–248.

Martyn, M. (2003). The hybrid online model: Good practice. *Educause Quarterly, 26*(1), 18–23.

Mennecke, B., & Valacich, J. (1998). Information is what you make of it: The influence of group history and computer support on information sharing decision quality and member perceptions. *Journal of Management Information System, 15*(2), 173–197.

Minichiello, V., Aroni, R., Timewell, E., & Alexander, L. (1990). *In-depth interviewing: Researching people.* Hong Kong: Longman Cheshire.

Moore, G., Perlow, A., Judge, C., & Koh, H. (2006). Using blended learning in training the public health workforce in emergency preparedness. *ASPH, From the Schools of Public Health, 121,* 217–221.

Oblinger, D., & Oblinger, J. L. (2005). *Educating the net generation* (Vol. 264). Washington, DC: EDUCAUSE.

Owston, R., Wideman, H., Murphy, J., & Lupshenyuk, D. (2008). Blended teacher professional development: A synthesis of three program evaluations. *Internet and Higher Education, 11*(3–4), 201–210.

Pink, D. H. (2006). *A whole new mind: Why right-brainers will rule the future.* New York, NY: Riverhead Trade.

Savin-Baden, M. (2008). *A practical guide to problem-based learning online.* New York, NY: Routledge.

Savin-Baden, M., & Wilkie, K. (2006). *Problem-based learning online.* London: Open University Press.

Selim, H. (2007). Critical success factors for e-learning acceptance: Confirmatory factor models. *Computers and Education, 49*(2), 396–413. doi: 10.1016/j.compedu.2005.09.004

Singer, F., & Stoicescu, D. (2011). Using blended learning as a tool to strengthen teaching competences. *Procedia Computer Science, 3,* 1527–1531.

Swan, K., Richardson, J., & Ice, P. (2008). Validating a measurement tool of presence in online communities of inquiry. *E-Mentor, 2*(24), 1–12.

Thorpe, M. (2002). Rethinking learner support: The challenge of collaborative online learning. *Open learning, 17*(2), 105–119. doi: 10.1080/0268051022014688

Tynjälä, P. (2008). Perspectives into learning at the workplace. *Educational Research Review, 3*(2), 130–154. doi: 10.1016/j.edurev.2007.12.001

Van Den Bossche, P., Gijselaers, W. H., Segers, M., & Kirschner, P. A. (2006). Social and cognitive factors driving teamwork in collaborative learning environments. Team learning beliefs and behaviors. *Small Group Research, 37,* 490–521.

Van den Bossche, P., Segers, M., Gijbels, D., & Dochy, F. (2004). Effects of problem-based learning in business education: A comparison between a PBL and a conventional educational approach. In R. Ottewill, L. Borredon, L. Falque, B. Macfarlane & A. Wall (Eds.), *Educational innovation in economics and business VIII: Pedagogy, technology and innovation* (pp. 205–228). Dordrecht: Kluwer Academic Publishers.

Wang, A. Y., & Newlin, M. H. (2001). Online lectures: Benefits for the virtual classroom. *T. H. E. Journal, 29*(1), 17–18. Retrieved from http://www.thejournal.com/articles/15513

ABOUT THE AUTHORS

Catherine Althaus, Ph.D., is an Assistant Professor at the University of Victoria in Canada. Her present research interests focus on public policy and public administration as well as bioethics, leadership in the public service, and the interface between politics and religion. She teaches online courses in the Master of Public Administration and Master of Arts in Community Development programs.

Marcia L. Ashbaugh, Ph.D., has over 25 years of experience in technology, implementation, and training for a wide range of industries and currently serves as mentor/academic advisor with the University of the People, a tuition-free online university reaching learners from over 130 countries. Leadership in business as well as nonprofit organizations, particularly in education and instruction, has uniquely positioned her to conceptualize aspects of leadership for instructional design (ID) – her current research interest – for moving the online education initiative forward. Always on the cutting edge of technology, Dr. Ashbaugh has led in systems development, built and managed local area networks (LANs), trained staff on integrated information systems, instituted enterprise-wide e-mail, web access, and security protocols. More recently, as principal consultant and researcher for MLA Instructional Designers, Dr. Ashbaugh has designed courses for university and high school computing education, EPS (Employee Performance Support) systems, novel online education plans, drug awareness training courses, and others. Her recent research projects include evaluation of innovations in educational technologies, online pedagogical quality, designer leadership competencies, alignment of instructional strategies to learning environments, and contextual relevance. Dr. Ashbaugh's education includes: Ph.D., Instructional Design for Online Learning, Capella University; M.Ed., E-Learning Technology & Design, Jones International University; and B.S., Computer Science: Management of Information Systems, Colorado Christian University.

Tara S. Behrend, Ph.D., is an Assistant Professor of Industrial/Organizational Psychology at the George Washington University. She received her Ph.D. in Industrial/Organizational Psychology at North Carolina State

University. Her research is focused on understanding and resolving barriers to technology use in the areas of selection, training, and recruitment. She also conducts research regarding the nature of STEM careers and career choice. Her work has been featured in the *Wall Street Journal, Fast Company*, and the *Chronicle of Higher Education*. She is a member of the society for Industrial and Organizational Psychology and the Academy of Management. Her current work is funded by the National Science Foundation.

Patrick Blessinger is the founder and Executive Director of the International Higher Education Teaching and Learning Association and a Research Fellow at the School of Education at St. John's University in Queens, New York, USA. He has taught over 150 college and university courses and he has served as a program chair at colleges and universities in the United States and the European Union. He consults with HE institutions in the areas of technology innovation and internationalization and he serves as an academic and accreditation advisor for HE institutions. He is the cofounder and codirector of the Institute for Meaning-Centered Education. He is the founder and editor of the *International HETL Review* and coeditor of the *Journal of Applied Research in Higher Education*. He is coeditor of several volumes within the Cutting-edge Technologies in Higher Education book series (Emerald) and coeditor of the book, *Meaning-Centered Education: International Perspectives and Explorations in Higher Education* (Routledge). He attended Auburn University, Georgia Tech, and the University of Georgia. He is a peer-recognized expert and thought leader in the field of teaching and learning and he has received several academic awards including a Fulbright Scholarship from the U.S. Department of State and a Governor's Teaching Fellowship from the State of Georgia, USA.

Katerina Bohle Carbonell obtained her Master's degree in Management of Learning in 2009 from Maastricht University in the Netherlands. Currently she is working on her Ph.D. in Educational Sciences investigating the development of adaptive expertise through divergent thinking and critical thinking in multidisciplinary teams. She also researches team performance from a transactive memory perspective by using social network analysis. She has taught several courses in Bachelor's and Master's degree programs. In the past, she has investigated the quality of support and infrastructure offered to Ph.D. candidates at Maastricht University and set-up a list of recommendations which have been implemented. In addition, she has developed and evaluated online courses for professionals. Katerina is working on a university-wide project on innovative learning approaches for part-time students and professionals. In this project she is leading the research team and focuses on organizational learning through innovation. She is currently setting up an online self-study course for Ph.D. students. Her research interests include professional development and team learning.

Amber Dailey-Hebert, Ph.D., is a Professor of Adult Education and Professional Studies, Department of Adult Education, Park University, United States; and Project Leader in the Department of Educational Research and Development, Maastricht University, the Netherlands. She has worked in the United States and abroad for continuing higher education programs focused on adult learners, distance education and training, and grant-funded projects that serve working professionals. She earned her Ph.D. in Adult Education from Cornell University, and completed her undergraduate and Master's studies in Leadership Development and Distance Education at Texas A&M University. As a tenured Full Professor, she has taught traditional, accelerated, and online courses in the Graduate School of Professional Studies at Park University, focusing on critical teaching for social change. Her administrative academic experience includes Department Chair, Program Coordinator, Associate Dean, and Founding & Executive Director of the Center for Excellence in Teaching & Learning (CETL), which provides faculty development for over 1,600 full- and part-time faculty located around the globe.

Andrew Doig is an Instructional Developer at Southampton Solent University in the United Kingdom, working as part of the Learning Technologies team, holding the title of Associate Professor. His role is to collaborate with academic faculty in the development and delivery of online distance and blended learning courses. His research interests are into ways to effectively create and support positive learning experiences for those studying entirely or predominantly online. Andrew's career background is in teaching English as a foreign language and in educational development. In these capacities, he has lived and worked in a variety of countries, including Hong Kong, Australia, and Turkey. Andrew is also a creative writer of fiction and published his first novel, *Wee Davy*, in 2012.

Martina A. Doolan, Ph.D., is a UK National Teaching Fellow, an institutional-wide senior Blended Learning/Teaching Fellow, and a Principal Lecturer in Computer Science at the University of Hertfordshire in the United Kingdom. Martina is a fellow of the UK Higher Education Academy (HEA), and a member of the British Computer Society and an Associate of the Chartered Management Institute (CMI). Martina was one of the first recipients of the Vice Chancellor award (2004). Martina was awarded a UK National Teaching Fellowship (personally) from the minister of Higher Education in 2007. Martina has been awarded national funding and managed national projects, that is, JISC, HEA, SEDA. Martina sits on a number of national and international advisory and editorial boards and other groups and committees, the majority by invitation. Martina also undertakes key note, consultancy, and publishes widely nationally and internationally. Her research interests are varied, including learner-centric and socio-cultural models in learning, collaborative and social learning in blended e-learning contexts (including web 2.0) and learning-oriented assessment designs. Martina focuses on the pedagogy, not the technology per se.

Anthony Foley, Ph.D., is a member of the European Marketing Academy, Irish Marketing Institute, and Irish Institute of Training and Development. His research interests revolve around marketing strategy and in particular the development of superior marketing management capability. Anthony has over 15 years' experience in retail and tourism and has continued these sectoral interests, particularly tourism-related, into academic activity in a number of industry-focused initiatives funded by the European Regional Development Fund (ERDF) and Fáilte Ireland. He is active in research and taught postgraduate thesis supervision and also teaches on the MBS (Marketing) program at Waterford Institute of Technology (WIT), as well as on the South East Enterprise Platform Programme (SEEPP). Anthony is a course leader for the B.Sc. in Small Enterprise Management, which is a new tourism program developed with Fáilte Ireland. He has published in a number of journals including the *Journal of Strategic Marketing*, *European Journal of Marketing*, and *Tourism and Hospitality Research*, as well as wrote cases, book chapters, and practitioner publications. Anthony has presented at a number of national and international conferences, including the Academy of Marketing, and Academy of Marketing Science. He is also a guest reviewer for the *European Journal of Marketing*, *Services industries Journal*, and *Irish Journal of Management*, and was Co-Chair of the Global and Cross-cultural Marketing track at the AMA Summer Conference 2009.

Maike Gerken obtained her Master's degree in Work and Organizational Psychology in 2009 from Maastricht University in the Netherlands. She is researcher in e-learning at the Department of Educational Research and

Development at Maastricht University. Maike has led several projects that offered blended learning solutions for students and professionals. These projects included different pilot studies that were aimed at supporting learning in the workplace through e-learning tools. She has developed and evaluated online courses for students and professionals in several disciplines. Maike also served as online tutor teaching economics to prospective Bachelor's degree students using the problem-based learning method. Her main research interests are the effectiveness of blended learning programs thereby including the design of instruction and supporting individual and informal learning in the workplace.

Therese Grohnert graduated from the M.Sc. Management of Learning from Maastricht University in 2011. She is currently working as a researcher in educational development, focusing on the evaluation of online and blended learning courses for part-time students and professionals. In addition, she is in the planning group for M.Sc. and a B.Sc. degree programs, working on course structure and design. Her research interests include professional development, expertise development, and intuitive decision-making.

Cathy Gunn, Ph.D., has played key roles in Australasia's tertiary e-learning sector during 17 years at the University of Auckland. She works collaboratively across disciplines in New Zealand's leading research university to design and deliver a range of technology-enhanced courses for students, school and university teacher education and faculty development. She developed strategies to build e-learning capacity across the university and to promote sustainable innovations. Cathy's research investigates contemporary issues in e-learning, including impact evaluation, educational leadership, and sustainable innovation. She has more than 20 years' experience working in tertiary institutions in Scotland, New Zealand, Hong Kong, and Australia.

Cathy currently leads a multi-skilled e-learning research and development team promoting strategic objectives for excellence in teaching and learning. She contributed to the international research community as Executive Member (1999–2001), Vice President (2002–2003), and President (2004–2008) of Ascilite, Australasia's leading professional society for e-learning researchers and practitioners. In the past few years, she has contributed to six Australian Teaching and Learning Council (ALTC) initiatives on learning innovation and educational leadership capacity development.

Before moving to New Zealand in 1995, Cathy was a Research Associate at Heriot-Watt University in Edinburgh, where she gained a Masters in Human Computer Interaction and a Ph.D. in Computer-Based Learning Research. Prior employment as an Economics Researcher/Writer for Lloyds of London Press provided complementary experience from the commercial sector. A portfolio of more than 100 scholarly publications reflects her broadly based portfolio of interests and experience.

Denis Harrington, Ph.D., is Head of Graduate Business at Waterford Institute of Technology in Waterford, Ireland. He has extensive research and consultancy experience, having worked on research programs with the European Commission in Eastern Europe and within the Russian Federation. He is a Council member of the MBA Association of Ireland and the Irish Academy of Management. His work has been published in the *International Journal of Tourism Research* (*Surrey Quarterly Review*), *European Journal of Management*, *International Journal of Hospitality Management*, *Services Industries Journal*, and the *Thunderbird International Business Review* among others. He serves on the Editorial Board of the *Services Industries Journal*, the *Irish Business Journal* and the *Irish Journal of Management*. Denis is coauthor of *Managing Quality in Tourism* and also coeditor (with Dr. James Cunningham, NUIG) of *Irish Management 2.0 – New Priorities for Changing Economy* in association with the MBA Association of Ireland.

Steve Hogg is Head of Learning Technologies at Southampton Solent University in the United Kingdom, holding the title of Associate Professor. In this post, Steve is responsible for one of the University's most innovative departments, a team of around 18 highly skilled staff including web designers, programmers, and learning technologists. This team is responsible for the University's student and staff facing online provisions. He is interested in investigating ways of improving the student experience through a variety of technology-enhanced means. In addition to running this busy department, Steve teaches Online Media to undergraduate students and Digital Streaming to professional blended learning students for the Faculty of Media, Arts and Society. Steve is a successful web designer and music video director with broadcast credits on music channels in the United Kingdom, Canada, and the United States.

Mary T. Holden graduated with distinction in a B.Sc. from the University of Michigan in 1991, completed an M.B.S. by Research at Waterford Institute of Technology, Ireland, in 1999, and received a Diploma in Statistics (distinction) from Trinity College Dublin in 2001. She completed her Ph.D. in 2006 at Waterford Institute of Technology focusing on interpersonal communication in interorganizational relationships. Her specialism involves interorganizational relationships, networks, and interpersonal communication. Specific interests include the role of communication in the governance of business network relationships; communication; and customer relationship management. She has published in numerous peer-reviewed journals and conferences and is a founding member and senior researcher in the RIKON research group. Dr. Holden's industrial experience spans over 20 years, working with firms in Ireland and the United States. Her consultancy role in the School of Business based on her expertise in the design and analysis of quantitative methodologies involving surveys, most particularly in the design and analysis of causal models developed for assessment/diagnostic purposes. Currently, Mary is assisting in the testing and analysis of a causal model in the IT sector for assessing the success of user interaction with organizational websites. She is also currently assisting in a segmentation study in the health and recreation sphere.

Peter Hubber, Ph.D., is an Associate Professor in the Faculty of Arts and Education, Deakin University, Australia. Peter spent 27 years in the classroom as a science and mathematics teacher before coming to Deakin University in 2000. He has a strong record in professional development, working with teachers and schools in local, state, and federal initiatives. His research has been in the fields of students' learning in science and pedagogies that support engagement with learning. Within these fields there has been an added interest in ICT integration in science classrooms and preservice science education. Peter's doctoral research, as a teacher researcher, involved a longitudinal study of secondary students' understanding of optics within a conceptual change and mental models theoretical framework. Peter teaches in both the undergraduate and post-graduate science education areas. He has had considerable success in several of Deakin's overseas partnership programs (Malaysia, UAE, Indonesia) in terms of the construction and delivery of units of study. From a service perspective, as coordinator of the B.Sc. BTeach course, Peter has successfully led the course through two accreditation periods. His current Australian Government funded research projects include: *ICT Innovation Fund project: Teaching to the Future (TTF) – Embedding ICT into pre-service teaching courses; ICT Innovation Fund Project: ICT in Everyday Learning: Teacher Online Toolkit - Provision of online professional development and teaching and learning* *resources to enhance P-10 teachers' capacity to embed ICT into their teaching of science, mathematics, history and English; Enhancing the quality of science learning through a representation-intensive pedagogy; Exploring quality primary education in different cultures: A cross-national study of teaching and learning in primary science classrooms.*

Jennifer Hussey worked in a variety of Irish and international hotel companies before deciding to pursue her Master's by Research on *The Evaluation of Fáilte Irelands Tourism Learning Network (TLN) Initiative: Modeling of Best Practice* (http://www.rikon.ie/Research/ResearchGroups-Centres/Groups/RIKON/Projects/JennifferHussey). Jennifer is currently pursuing her Ph.D. in the area of tourism enterprise manager development, with specific regard to the professionalization of the SME owner/manager through the use of a problem-based and blended learning approach. Jennifer's current Ph.D. research project is entitled *Developing Profession-alism in the Tourism Industry: Evaluating the Effect of a Purposely Built BSc in Small Enterprise Management.* Her study seeks to examine a new B.Sc. program in Small Enterprise Management, with a view to informing theory and future education/development practice, which culminated in the best paper award at the European Council on Hotel, Restaurant & Institutional Education (EUROCHRIE) Conference in 2011 and a best postgraduate paper at the Irish Academy of Management Conference in 2010. Jennifer's research interests include: andragogy, educational evaluation, professional-ism and professional development, innovation, and tourism networks.

Michael N. Karim holds a B.Sc. in Psychology from The Ohio State University and is currently a doctoral student in Industrial/Organizational Psychology at The George Washington University. Michael worked with two research teams while at Ohio State University: one focusing on individual decision-making processes, the other focusing on uncertainty and social cognition. By combining psychological and learning theories, his research focus is on the psychological processes that underlie individuals' interactions with technology. Current projects focus on learner control, the determinants and effects of perceived control, intelligent agents, and the use of electronic proctoring for tests.

Esther Loong, Ph.D., is a lecturer in mathematics and information technology education at Deakin University. For a period of time, she was seconded as Information and Communications Technology (ICT) Pedagogy Officer to the $8 million nationally funded Teaching Teachers for the Future

(TTF) project at Deakin University. In this role, Esther worked with teacher educators and preservice teachers to share exemplary uses of ICT in educational curriculum and pedagogy, and contributed to leadership in the use of ICT in Science and History education within Deakin University. Due to her avid interest in the use of ICT in education, her research agendas inexorably revolve around exploring the effective use of ICT in mathematics and science education. Her Ph.D. researched web-based teaching strategies for secondary school mathematics and her current research interest is in the use of ICT in primary school mathematics. In addition to teaching preservice teachers, Esther also has a long history of providing professional development to in-service teachers in the area of technology, mathematics, and science education. This included conducting in-service professional development courses for mathematics teachers from South East Asia and Africa under the auspices of the South East Asian Ministers of Education Organisation – Regional Education Centre for Science and Mathematics (SEAMEO-RECSAM). Esther has presented at several national and international mathematics and technology-related conferences and published in national and international scholarly and research journals.

Patrick Lynch, Ph.D., is the Director of RIKON research group at Waterford Institute of Technology (WIT) in Ireland, where he obtained his Ph.D. in Innovation. Patrick has extensive research expertise, having published a range of articles in national and international conferences and journals and his book *Managerial Challenges in Irish Organisations: A Case Study Collection* has recently been published by Blackhall (2010). His research specialism is service innovation within interorganizational and network relationships, in particular, close relationships. Current research interests include strategic innovation, knowledge transfer, interorganizational conflict, and regional tourism destination networks. Patrick also teaches Technology Commercialization and Knowledge Management at WIT's School of Business. Patrick's extensive business experience includes the creation and growth of early stage companies and this experience has allowed him to understand the realities involved in running and sustaining a successful business. Since 2008, Patrick has worked on over 180 service innovation projects with small- and medium-sized companies across Ireland, creating and developing strategic innovative solutions to their business problems. He is also a guest reviewer for the AMA Winter Conference, *Services industries Journal*, and *Irish Journal of Management*, and was Chair of the Relationship Network track at the 9th Relationship Marketing Conference 2009.

Kamna Malik, Ph.D., is an educator and consultant in the field of IT management. Her teaching and research focus lie in enabling better use of information technology for improved business value. Her works have been published as books, edited books, research articles, and edited journal issues in the area of software quality, strategic information systems, e-business, and e-learning. Dr. Malik has a wide range of industry and academic experience spanning practice, teaching, research, and administration. She has handled key roles in IT management and software projects across different stages of life cycle and worked very closely with end-users. She has also conducted management development programs for middle- and senior-level management in the area of strategic information systems, software quality and testing, knowledge management, and contemporary technologies. She has successfully headed many academic program offices such as Research, MBA, and IT Infrastructure among others and is an active conference organizer. Currently Associate Dean for Research at GlobalNxt University, Malaysia, Dr. Malik has been the recipient of faculty excellence award in online teaching for five consecutive years since 2008.

Julia L. Parra, Ed.D., teaches and conducts research in the areas of professional and faculty development, online teaching and learning, educational learning technologies, emerging technologies, and social media. Julia is an Assistant Professor at New Mexico State University with a role in both the College of Extended Learning and College of Education. She helped to design, and is an instructor for the College of Extended Learning's Graduate Certificate in Online Teaching and Learning program and is an instructor for the College of Education's Educational Learning Technologies program. As a new faculty member in the College of Education, Julia has taken on faculty development responsibility and develops training such as the NMSU Going Mobile with iPad summer workshops. She also teaches for the SLOAN-C Online Teaching Certificate Program and is a certified Quality Matters Peer Reviewer. In 2006, Julia coauthored a book chapter titled *Transitioning to E-Learning: Teaching the Teachers* that was first published in *Cases on Global E-Learning: Successes and Pitfalls* (IGI Global, 2006), and later republished in *Web-Based Education: Concepts, Methodologies, Tools, and Applications* (Information Science Reference, 2010). In 2011, her article *Online Course Design for Individuals With and Without Disabilities: Pedagogy, Tools, and Universal Design for Learning* was published in *Learning Technology publication of IEEE Computer Society's Technical Committee on Learning Technology*. Julia has conducted presentations, workshops, and webinars at local, state, regional, and national conferences on a variety of topics. Dr. Parra is always up for a challenge or adventure, evidenced recently by her foray into geography education when she agreed to be the co-coordinator for the New Mexico Geographic Alliance, a member of the National Geographic Network of Alliances for Geographic Education. For more about Julia, see her website at www.juliaparra.com.

Lynne Siemens, Ph.D., is an Assistant Professor at the University of Victoria in Canada. Her interests include entrepreneurship, small business, government policy, rural economic development, academic entrepreneurship, and team development. She teaches online courses in the Master of Public Administration and Master of Arts in Community Development programs.

Charlotte Stange is a recent graduate of the Master of Public Administration Program in the School of Public Administration at the University of Victoria in Canada. She currently works with the Canadian Federal Government. She took several online courses as part of her graduate degree.

David Starr-Glass is a senior mentor in Business Administration with the International Programs (Prague, Czech Republic) of Empire State College (SUNY). He is also an adjunct faculty member of the European Division of the University of Maryland University College (UMUC). In these positions, he has gained experience and insight into the creation of effective online learning environments. He has earned Master's degrees in Business Administration, Organizational Psychology, and Online Instruction.

Charles Wankel, Professor of Management at St. John's University, New York, earned his doctorate from New York University. Charles is on the Rotterdam School of Management Dissertation Committee and is Honorary Vice Rector of the Poznań University of Business. He has authored and edited 46 books including the bestselling *Management*, 3rd ed. (Prentice-Hall, 1986), 11 volumes in the IAP series Research in Management Education and Development, the *Handbook of 21st Century Management* (Sage, 2008), and the *Encyclopedia of Business in Today's World* (Sage, 2009), which received the American Library Association's Outstanding Business Reference Source Award. He is the leading founder and director of scholarly virtual communities for management professors, currently directing eight with thousands of participants in more than 90 nations. He has been a visiting professor in Lithuania at the Kaunas University of Technology (Fulbright Fellowship) and the University of Vilnius (United

Nations Development Program and Soros Open Society Foundation funding). Fortune 50 consulting clients include McDonald's Corporation's Hamburger University and IBM Learning Services. International consulting includes TNK-Nizhnevartovsk (former ChernogorNeft) Oil Company, Siberia.

AUTHOR INDEX

SUBJECT INDEX